Handy Guide to
Virginia Wineries

—— 10th Anniversary Edition ——

DONNA R. GOUGH

Copyright © 2021 Donna R. Gough

All rights reserved.

ISBN-10: 0985585457

ISBN-13: 978-0-985585457

DEDICATION

To Edward, my loyal and unfailingly patient wine research companion.

CONTENTS

Maps i

Wine Basics iv

Acknowledgments v

1. Introduction to Virginia Wineries 1

2. The History of Winemaking in Virginia 7

3. Northern Virginia Region & Middleburg AVA 17

   Inside the Beltway: *Lost Boy Cider* 21

   Leesburg North: *Bleu Frog, Eagletree, Fabbioli, Hidden Brook, Lost Creek, Winery 32* 23

   Northwest Loudoun: *8 Chains North, 868 Estate, Bozzo, Breaux, Carriage House, Corcoran, Creek's Edge, Crushed Cellars, Doukénie, Hiddencroft, Hillsborough, Maggie Malick, Notaviva, Sunset Hills, Terra Nebulo, Two Twisted Posts, Walsh Family, Wine Reserve* 31

   Leesburg West: *Barns at Hamilton Station, Casanel, Dry Mill, Firefly Cellars, Forever Farm, Otium, Stone Tower, Three Creeks, Williams Gap, Willowcroft, Zephaniah* 53

   Bluemont: *Bluemont, Bogati, Henway Cider, Twin Oaks Tavern, Veramar* 67

   Middleburg-Fairfax: *50 West, Boxwood, Cana, Chrysalis, Effingham Manor, Fleetwood Farm, Greenhill, Mt. Defiance Cider, Paradise Springs, Pearmund, Quattro Goomba's, Vint Hill, Winery at Bull Run, Winery at La Grange, Winery at Sunshine Ridge* 75

Delaplane: *Arterra, Barrel Oak, Blue Valley, Delaplane Cellars, Fox Meadow, Naked Mountain, Slater Run, Three Fox* 95

Northern Blue Ridge: *Aspen Dale, Chapelle Charlemagne, Chateau O'Brien, Chester Gap, Cobbler Mountain, Linden, Philip Carter, Rappahannock* 107

Warrenton: *Gadino, Granite Heights, Gray Ghost, Little Washington, Magnolia, Mediterranean, Molon Lave, Morais, Narmada, Quièvremont* 119

Fredericksburg: *Chateau MerrillAnne, Coyote Hole, Hammerstone, Lake Anna, Mattaponi, Potomac Point, Rogers Ford Farm, Wilderness Run* 133

4. Shenandoah Valley Region & AVA 143

Northern Shenandoah: *Briedé, Cave Ridge, Glen Manor, James Charles, Muse, North Mountain, Old Hill Cider, Shenandoah, Star in the Valley, Third Hill at DeMello, Valerie Hill, Winchester Ciderworks, Winery at Kindred Pointe, Wisteria Farm, Wolf Gap* 147

Southern Shenandoah: *12 Ridges, Above Ground, Barren Ridge, Bluestone, Brix & Columns, CrossKeys, Ecco Adesso, Halcyon Days, Lexington Valley, Marceline, Ox-Eye, Purple Wolf, Rockbridge* 167

5. Eastern Virginia Region & Eastern Shore AVA 185

Eastern Virginia: *Chatham* 189

6. Chesapeake Bay Region & Northern Neck-George Washington Birthplace AVA 191

Northern Neck: *Backporch, Caret, Ditchley, Dog and Oyster, Estate at White Hall, General's Ridge, Good Luck, Hague, Ingleside, Monroe Bay, Rivah Vineyards, Triple V, Vault Field* 195

7. Central Virginia Region & Monticello AVA 213

Richmond: *Ashton Creek, Black Heath Mead, Blue Bee, Bodie, Buskey, Castle Glen, Courthouse Creek, Garden Grove, James River, Sassafras Shade, Skippers Creek, Spring Run* 217

Louisa: *Byrd, Elk Island, Fifty-Third, Grayhaven, Weston Farm* 231

Madison: *Blue Quartz, DuCard, Early Mountain, Mountain Run, Old House, Old Trade, Prince Michel, Revalation, Sharp Rock* 239

Upper Monticello: *Barboursville, Burnley, Castle Hill, Chestnut Oak, Chisholm, Five Oaks, Glass House, Grace Estate, Hark, Honah Lee, Horton, Keswick, Kilaurwen, Knight's Gambit, Montifalco, Moss, Reynard Florence, Stinson, Stone Mountain, White Hall* 253

Afton-Crozet: *Afton, Cardinal Point, Flying Fox, Hazy Mountain, King Family, Pollak, Septenary, Valley Road, Veritas* 279

Lower Monticello: *Albemarle Cider, Blenheim, Blue Toad, Bold Rock, Brent Manor, Cunningham Creek, Delfosse, Eastwood Farm, Gabriele Rausse, Hardware Hills, Hill Top Berry, Jefferson, Loving Cup, Lovingston, Michael Shaps, Mount Ida, Mountain Cove, Pippin Hill, Potter's Craft, Thatch, Trump, Wisdom Oak* 293

Lynchburg: *Ankida Ridge, DeVault, Lazy Days, Rebec* 323

8. Hampton Roads Region 329

Hampton Roads: *Gauthier, Haley's Honey, Hampton Roads, Jolene Family, Mermaid, New Kent, Saudé Creek, Silver Hand Meadery, Sly Clyde Cider, SummerWind, Upper Shirley, Williamsburg* 333

9. Southern Virginia Region 353

Halifax: *Bright Meadows, Hunting Creek, Rosemont, Three Sisters of Shiney Rock* 355

Danville: *2 Witches, Altillo, Hamlet, Homeplace, Preston Ridge, Stanburn* 361

10. Virginia Mountains Region 369

Bedford: *Brooks Mill, Feathers & Fables, Hickory Hill, LeoGrande, Peaks of Otter, Ramulose Ridge* 371

Roanoke: *AmRhein, Blue Ridge, Valhalla, Virginia Mountain* 379

Alleghany Highlands: *Big Fish Cider, Rock Roadhouse* 385

11. Blue Ridge Region & Rocky Knob AVA 389

Blue Ridge Parkway: *Blacksnake Meadery, Chateau Morrisette, Villa Appalaccia* 393

Blue Ridge/I-81: *Abingdon, Beliveau Farm, Davis Valley, Iron Heart, New River, Rural Retreat, Spinning Jenny, Tumbling Creek Cider, West Wind Farm, Whitebarrel* 399

12. Heart of Appalachia Region 413

Heart of Appalachia: *MountainRose, Vincent's Vineyard* 415

Appendix 1: Virginia Wine Trails 419

Bibliography 423

Glossary of Wine Terms 427

Alphabetical Index of Wineries 441

Wineries with Breweries 447

Wineries with Lodgings 449

General Index 451

About the Author 455

MAPS

Map 1.0. Virginia Wine Regions & American Viticultural Areas (AVAs) vi

Map 3.0. Northern Virginia Region & Middleburg AVA 16
    Map 3.1. Inside the Beltway 20
    Map 3.2. Leesburg North 22
    Map 3.3. Northwest Loudoun 30
    Map 3.4. Leesburg West 52
    Map 3.5. Bluemont 66
    Map 3.6. Middleburg-Fairfax 74
    Map 3.7. Delaplane 94
    Map 3.8. Northern Blue Ridge 106
    Map 3.9. Warrenton 118
    Map 3.10. Fredericksburg 132

Map 4.0. Shenandoah Valley Region & Shenandoah AVA 142
    Map 4.1. Winchester 146
    Map 4.2. Edinburg-Mt. Jackson 148
    Map 4.3. Harrisonburg-Staunton 166
    Map 4.4. Lexington 175

Map 5.0. Eastern Virginia Region & Eastern Shore AVA 184
    Map 5.1. Eastern Virginia 188

Map 6.0. Chesapeake Bay Region & Northern Neck-George Washington Birthplace AVA 190
    Map 6.1. Northern Neck (southern section) 194
    Map 6.2. Northern Neck (northern section) 197

Map 7.0. Central Virginia Region & Monticello AVA 212
    Map 7.1. Richmond 216
    Map 7.2. Louisa 230
    Map 7.3 Madison 238
    Map 7.4. Free Union-White Hall 252

Map 7.5. Stony Point 255
Map 7.6. Afton-Crozet 278
Map 7.7. North Garden 292
Map 7.8. Scottsville 295
Map 7.9. Lovingston 297
Map 7.10. Lynchburg 322

Map 8.0. Hampton Roads Region 328
Map 8.1. New Kent 332
Map 8.2. South of the James 332
Map 8.3. Hopewell-Upper Shirley 334
Map 8.4. Virginia Beach-Hampton Roads 338
Map 8.5. Silver Hand 342
Map 8.6. Williamsburg Winery 348

Map 9.0. Southern Virginia Region 352
Map 9.1. Halifax 354
Map 9.2. Rosemont 357
Map 9.3. Altavista 360
Map 9.4. Danville City 360
Map 9.5. Martinsville 365

Map 10.0. Virginia Mountains Region 368
Map 10.1. Bedford 370
Map 10.2. Roanoke (northern section) 378
Map 10.3. Roanoke (southern section) 378
Map 10.4. Big Fish Cider 384
Map 10.5. Rock Roadhouse 384

Map 11.0. Blue Ridge Region & Rocky Knob AVA 388
Map 11.1. Floyd 392
Map 11.2. Mabry Mill 392
Map 11.3. Abingdon 398
Map 11.4. Beliveau 398
Map 11.5. Rural Retreat 402

>   Map 11.6. Max Meadows/Pulaski 405
>   Map 11.7. Radford 406
>
> Map 12.0. Heart of Appalachia Region 412
>   Map 12.1. Heart of Appalachia 414

WINE BASICS

Wine Origins 29

Phylloxera 73

Reading a Virginia Wine Label 93

Wine Closures 105

Sparkling Wines 117

White, Red, and Pink Wines 165

Red Bordeaux-Style Blends 183

Sweet Wines 211

Fortified Wines 229

Norton 251

Fruit Wines, Ciders, and Meads 321

Wine Aromas 351

Serving Temperatures 377

Tasting Tips 387

Tasting Room Etiquette 397

ACKNOWLEDGMENTS

For this 2021 edition, my thanks and appreciation, as before, go out to all the winery owners, winemakers, and tasting room staff who have so graciously shared their time and information with me. It has been a real pleasure and an honor getting to know you and see how dedicated you all are to making Virginia wine great.

I also want to thank my fellow Virginia wine enthusiasts and friends I've come to know for their cheerful friendship, mutual support, and dedication to promoting Virginia wineries and wine.

In addition, I'd like to thank Kelly Brown for the lovely cover re-design that she created for this edition.

Finally, none of this would have been possible without the warm and continuous support of my family, who have all continued to join in exploring Virginia wineries with me, both revisiting familiar places and discovering new ones. Thank you!

All errors and inadvertent omissions in this book are mine alone.

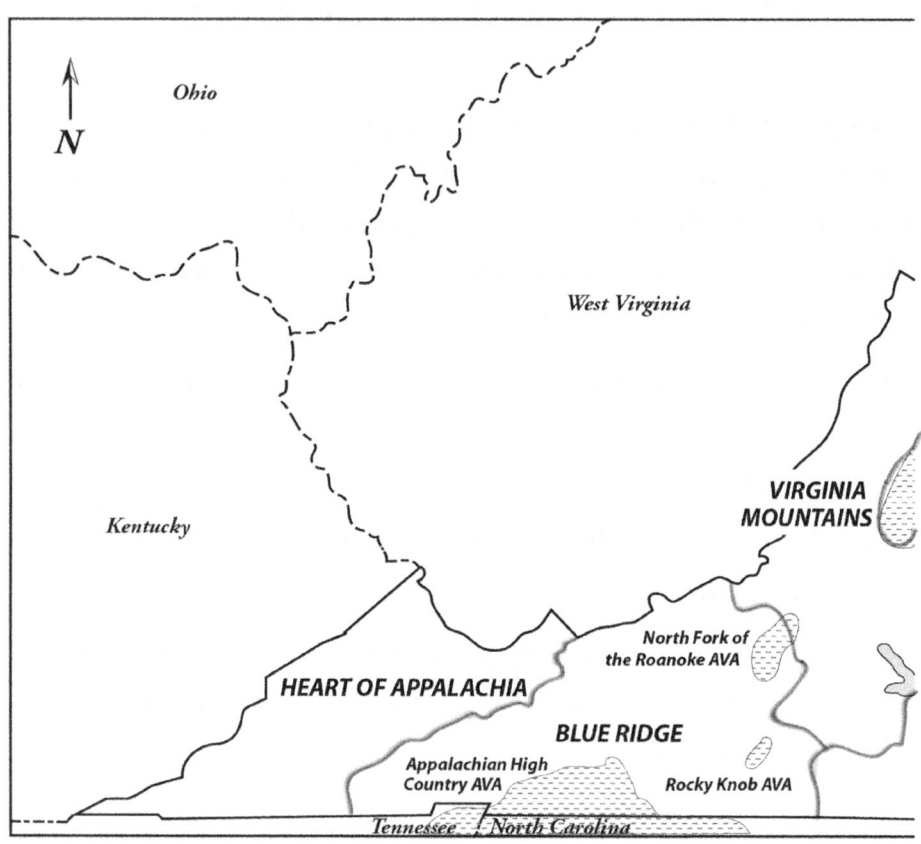

Map 1.0. Virginia Wine Regions & American Viticultural Areas (AVAs)

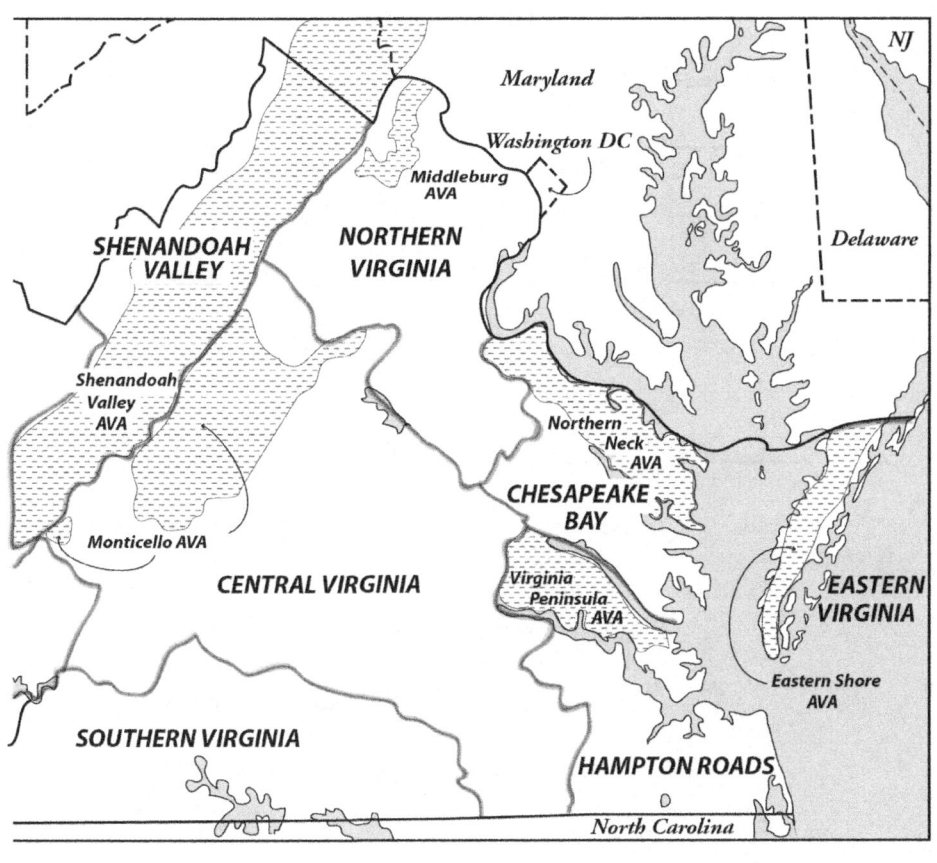

Map Legend

Roads and Road Symbols

═══════	Interstate Highway	🛡81	Interstate Highway
───────	U.S. Highway	(11)	U.S. Highway
───────	State or Local Route	(39)	State or Local Route
··········	Ferry Crossing	⌘	Interstate Exit

Administrative Divisions

─ ─ ─ ─	State Lines	◯ ◯	City or Town
··········	County Lines	··········	Military Base

Wineries & Points of Interest

☆	Winery	⬡	Points of Interest
◯	American Viticultural Area	◯	Bodies of Water
◯	National or State Park or Forest	△	Mountains

1. INTRODUCTION TO VIRGINIA WINERIES

Thank you for reading this tenth anniversary edition of the *Handy Guide to Virginia Wineries*! Virginia was the first place in America to cultivate grapes with the intent of making wine and is currently the seventh largest wine producer in the country, as measured by the number of wineries. Its diverse topography, geologic complexity, and numerous mesoclimates give rise to distinct differences in its wines, from dry to sweet, light to full-bodied.

Temperatures and precipitation vary not only from region to region but also from year to year, resulting in wide variations in vintages in a way that resembles France far more than California. Summers in Virginia can alternate between cool and rainy or very hot and dry, seasonal differences that produce very different expressions of a wine's character and personality.

While Virginia's winemaking roots are deep, its modern wine industry is young, having blossomed only within the past forty years. The reputation of Virginia wines continues to expand beyond state lines, however. For instance, the Wine Enthusiast magazine's current online buying guide lists 77 wines from around the state with scores of "excellent" (90 or higher), while over 450 earn scores of "good" (87 to 89).

The size of Virginia's wine industry continues to grow steadily. This edition includes 260 wineries, cideries, and meaderies with regular business hours, a net rise of nearly 60 percent over the past ten years when the very first Handy Guide was published. Since the 2018 edition (the most recent update), 19 wineries have closed (including the iconic Tarara Winery) while 51 new businesses opened during that period. A number of wineries have also changed ownership, with quite a few being purchased by new owners with backgrounds in the hospitality industry.

In addition, several trends have emerged that are worth mentioning:

Tastings: The pandemic changed how tastings are conducted at many wineries. Most offer tastings by pre-poured self-serve flights, though some are now beginning to resume traditional tastings as they hire and train new staff. A few continue to operate by glass or bottle sales only. And some with regular hours are now requiring reservations for visits.

Shipping: The pandemic also led to a significant increase in the number of wineries that now sell their wines to multiple states, most through Vinoshipper. This will give more customers, particularly those out of state, additional options for acquiring their favorite Virginia wines.

Wineries with breweries: Since the Virginia legislature passed the farm brewery act, the number of craft breweries in the state has soared, and two dozen wineries now house a craft brewery on their premises, with more reportedly in the planning phases. For visitors whose friends and families prefer a brew over a glass of wine, check the list on page 447 for wineries that offer craft beers to find a place that will leave everyone happy.

Wineries with rental lodgings: Over the past four years, the number of wineries that offer some kind of rental lodging has risen to three dozen, with options ranging from apartments to complete guest houses, including some on the winery grounds next to the vineyards. The list on page 449 includes all wineries with rentals available to help you plan a destination vacation to Virginia wine country.

Introduction

This book starts with a review of the history of winemaking in Virginia. Each of Virginia's ten wine regions has an introductory chapter with a very brief snapshot of things to see and do. For the larger wine regions, wineries are further sorted into geographic clusters for ease of trip planning. **Only those wineries with regular tasting room hours are included in this guide.** All information is current as of mid-July 2021.

For each winery, the address and contact information is provided, as well as current business hours and seasonal closings. However, always check the website or call ahead as hours may change, particularly if the winery can be rented for weddings or special events. A quick description of the facilities and features is offered, including a sampling of special events and festivals, whether the winery may be rented for special occasions, and, if known, whether children or pets may accompany visitors.

Wines: Each winery's wines are sorted by type, from sparkling wines to sweet wines as well as fortified styles. While the specific wines offered will change from year to year, this list will give you a window into the types of wines and styles to help tailor your visit according to your own interests and preferences. Please be aware that even wines labeled as varietals may be a blend that includes up to 25 percent of another grape variety, including grapes from another state. It is always acceptable to ask about the blend in a specific wine.

If you spot a specific varietal or blend that intrigues you, always call ahead to confirm if it is still available if that is one of the main goals of your visit. Many of Virginia's wineries are small producers and can quickly run out of a given vintage. Advance research will help prevent disappointment.

Tastings: Nearly all wineries charge a tasting fee that may vary depending on the number of wines being sampled. In some cases, souvenir glasses convey with the tasting, particularly for groups. If no tasting fee is specified, the tasting is complimentary. At small wineries, tastings are often handled informally, with guests paying for their tasting at the very end, but high-volume wineries may ask that a tasting ticket be purchased first.

Groups: Most wineries require advance reservations for groups, especially of six or more. Please note that more wineries now limit the size of groups they will accept, and some do not permit van, bus, or limo tours at all. Check the winery listings for more details. If you are planning to tour wineries with friends or family, call at least one day in advance to confirm that they can accommodate your group. This is especially helpful for smaller wineries with limited indoor space in their facilities. Weekends have become very popular times for group tours, particularly in the northern Virginia and Charlottesville areas. Early reservations can make all the difference.

Hours: Call ahead to confirm closing times and last pours if you are planning to arrive late in the day. Hours can quickly change, and many wineries rent out their spaces for private parties, dinners, or weddings and can close earlier than the posted hours to accommodate those special events.

Food: Cheese, crackers, bread, dips, and/or cold cuts are available for purchase at many wineries, while several wineries have bistro-style menus to choose from. Some wineries also allow guests to bring their own food for a picnic on the grounds. Always call or e-mail first to determine a particular winery's restrictions if you are planning to bring food.

Alcoholic Beverages: Nealy all wineries sell their wine by the glass or bottle to have on-site after a tasting. Please note, however, that Virginia state law prohibits the consumption of any alcoholic beverage on winery property that was not produced by that winery itself. If you are planning to snack or picnic at a winery, be prepared either to bring water or soft drinks (if the winery allows this) or to purchase drinks on-site to have with your food.

Pets: A number of wineries are pet-friendly and allow leashed, well-behaved dogs on the winery grounds, though Virginia law prohibits dogs in the tasting rooms. A few, such as Breaux and Magnolia Vineyards, even host Dog Days that are very popular with two- and four-legged visitors alike. Even pet-friendly wineries may not allow pets during special events and festivals. Check the winery events calendar for any restrictions, or call ahead to confirm that your pet will be able to join you on the grounds.

Children: Rules on children vary from winery to winery. Many welcome children and families while others restrict access to adults twenty-one and older. Wineries can be boring places for children, and bored children often are eager to let adults know just how unhappy they are. If you are planning a family excursion to Virginia's wine country, it is easy to map out an itinerary that focuses on wineries offering adequate outdoor or indoor spaces for children to amuse themselves. And never hurts to call ahead to confirm.

Purchasing: All Virginia wineries offer their products for sale in the tasting room, but not all offer telephone or online ordering, and their ability to ship to out-of-state customers can vary significantly. If nothing is listed in the Purchasing section, the winery does not ship at this time but always check with the tasting room as options can quickly change.

Directions: Basic driving directions to each winery are given from the closest major highway, either an interstate highway, U.S. highway, or major roadway, and reflect the recommendations of the winery when possible. Please keep in mind that some winery addresses are not easily recognized by mapping apps or GPS devices, particularly if they are off the beaten track.

Two good atlases to consider are the *Virginia State Road Atlas* (American Map) and the *Virginia Atlas and Gazetteer* (DeLorme). The *Virginia State Road Atlas* is easier to read and has more wineries marked; the *Gazetteer* is a topographic map that provides more detail but is a bit harder to decipher. While both are now out of print, used editions can still be found online.

A Final Note: Wine tastings and tasting tours can be a fun and enjoyable way to spend a weekend afternoon. However, even small pours can add up to a considerable amount of alcohol when multiplied over numerous samplings. It is also worth remembering that under Virginia law, all wineries have the right to refuse service to patrons who are noticeably intoxicated. Please be responsible and choose either a designated driver or use one of the many wine country tour groups now operating in the state.

As mentioned earlier, please keep in mind that Virginia's Department of Alcoholic Beverage Control (ABC) has ruled that the only alcoholic beverages permitted on winery grounds are those produced by that winery or cidery itself. Please leave any other alcoholic beverages, including wines from other wineries, in your car, limo, or tour bus.

The Handy Guide also includes a bibliography, information on Virginia wine trails, a glossary of wine terms (including the grapes used in Virginia wines), an alphabetical index of Virginia's wineries, lists of wineries with breweries and rental lodgings, and a general index at the very end.

For readers already familiar with Virginia wines, this guide may introduce you to wineries and wines you might not otherwise have tried. For visitors or those just starting out, it provides a broad overview of the vibrancy and diversity of all that Virginia has to offer. For everyone, may this guide help you discover something new about Virginia and its wines.

Cheers!

2. THE HISTORY OF WINEMAKING IN VIRGINIA

Virginia is credited with a number of firsts in American history: the first permanent English settlement in North America; the first representative assembly in the American colonies; the first Africans brought to English North America; the birthplace of our first President. What is less well known is that Virginia can also be called the birthplace of winemaking in the United States, although its rise as a wine-producing state was long in coming and, until recent decades, marked more often by failure than success.

But why would English colonists in early Virginia even try to cultivate grapes, much less to make wine from them? After all, England was never one of the great wine-producing countries in Europe. It has no long history of grape cultivation and no deeply rooted wine culture. In the seventeenth century, as now, England's alcoholic production and consumption centered around beer, ale, and hard cider, not wines—and certainly not fine wines.

The answer lies both in the natural resources the colonists found in Virginia when they arrived and in the governing structures and aims of the Jamestown colony in its early years.

A COLONY IN SEARCH OF A PRODUCT

In the late sixteenth century, England lagged far behind other European countries—especially its archrival, Spain—in wealth, power, and prestige, and English leaders were determined to catch up. Trade offered the best prospect for doing just that, and English merchants and investors launched numerous ventures aimed at breaking into trade relationships in Africa and the East, and exploring new opportunities in lands across the Atlantic. Nearly all these initiatives were set up as joint stock companies, a structure that allowed investors to pool their resources and finance projects in the expectation of sharing in the profits.

In 1606, the London Virginia Company was established to finance and direct an exploratory venture in the general Chesapeake Bay area. Its goal was to establish a small colony to develop a marketable commodity—gold, spices, or dyes, for instance—that would serve as a foundation for trade between the native peoples and England, much as the French had successfully done in establishing a lucrative fur trade with native tribes in Quebec some years earlier. One result of their efforts was the English colony at Jamestown, founded the year after the Virginia Company was launched.

As Jamestown passed its tenth anniversary, however, the colony was still struggling as it searched for products to help it become self-sufficient and profitable. Colonists shipped a range of goods to England—sassafras, clapboard, and pitch, among others—but their marketability was limited because of distance and cost. Officers in the London Virginia Company offered ideas as well, sending to the colony silkworms and silk experts, ironworkers and refiners, and glassblowers from Italy, but none of these projects panned out. Tobacco was growing in popularity and importance as colonists became more skilled at its cultivation and processing, but it had not yet become the breakthrough crop that would fuel Virginia's future growth.

From the colony's earliest days, Jamestown settlers also explored the production of another commodity: wine. The region was rich in native grapevines, and the colonists soon turned to producing a quickly made and highly alcoholic wine. The fact that wine was being produced was noted by several of Jamestown's early leaders—as was the fact that this wine was not high in quality. Upon being appointed Governor of Virginia in 1610, for instance, Lord Delaware sent a cask of Virginia wine to London, "sour as it is." About the same time, Colony Secretary William Strachey wrote that he had tasted wine in Jamestown made by a Doctor Bohoune, Virginia's first named winemaker, describing it as "strong and heady."

By 1619, Sir Edwin Sandys had assumed the leadership of the Virginia Company. That year was known for three pivotal events: the first Africans who arrived in an English-speaking colony; the granting of land to male settlers; and the creation of the Virginia Assembly, the first representative governmental body in America. During the Assembly's initial session, delegates enacted measures on land distribution, tobacco prices, mulberry cultivation for silkworms, and hemp production intended to help improve the colony's economic health.

Delegates also passed Acte 12, a measure that required every householder to "yearly plante and maintaine ten vines, untill they have attained to the arte and experience of dressing a Vineyard, either by their owne industry, or by the Instruction of some Vigneron." The Virginia Company also arranged for eight French vignerons, or vineyardists, to go to Jamestown to help kick-start the effort. In 1621, King James I gave an extra push to the fledgling industry by ordering that translations of a French manual on cultivating vines be sent to the colonists.

All these efforts ultimately fizzled out, as the colonists increasingly turned to the much more lucrative tobacco as their cash crop of choice.

For roughly the next fifty years, Virginia's leaders continued to gently prod colonists toward vine cultivation, including dispatching more vineyard experts, importing European grape stock, even establishing a prize for anyone who could produce "two tunne of wine out of a vineyard made in this colony." Ultimately all their efforts proved unsuccessful. Some colonists dutifully planted vines and cultivated vineyards, but fungus and mildew—as well as the still unknown phylloxera louse—took their toll on the imported vines, while the profitability of the tobacco leaf lured others away.

Despite the frustrations and ultimate failures, however, the seeds of Virginia's future wine industry had been planted.

'GENTLEMEN FARMERS' AND THEIR VINES

In the decades that followed, records both public and private are largely silent about grape cultivation and wine production in Virginia. Judging from the occasional references to Virginia wine, some vineyards of native rootstock did exist and some wine was indeed produced. But ordinary small farmers would not have been engaged in winemaking, since cultivating and tending to tobacco, the main cash crop of the colony, was a labor-intensive endeavor that demanded constant attention and time in the fields. They simply had no time to spare to indulge in an effort that had little to do with the hard business of eking out a living for their families.

Instead, what winemaking occurred in Virginia during this period was done by the well-to-do, particularly members of Virginia's "First Families," a network of wealthy landowners often related by intermarriage. Only they had the time and financial resources to invest in planting a vineyard and in attempting to make wine. As large landowners whose fortunes rose and fell with the value of tobacco, these self-described "gentlemen farmers" would also have had an economic interest in developing an alternative crop for export, such as wine.

One such individual was Robert Beverley, author of the first history of Virginia. In 1709, Beverly had a three-acre vineyard of native grapes planted in King and Queen County to the north of what is now the city of Richmond. Six years later, the Irish diarist John Fontaine visited Beverley's home and reported that his vineyard had produced about four hundred gallons of wine, adding that they "were verry merry with the wine of his own making and drunk prosperity to his vineyard."

By 1722, Beverley was producing roughly 750 gallons a year of wine, which was described by a local pastor as being similar in taste to claret and as strong as port, suggesting it had been fortified with additional alcohol. Beverley died that same year, however, and his heirs proved less interested in viticulture than he had been.

About that same time, Beverley's brother-in-law, William Byrd, became intrigued with the idea of grape cultivation. In the 1720s, he had planted a vineyard of about twenty native grape varieties at his Westover Plantation on the James River. Byrd was an astute businessman, and his initial successes helped persuade some of his neighbors to consider planting their own vines as well. Within ten years, however, his vineyards fell victim to harsh frosts and insect infestations, and his efforts at grape cultivation ended.

In the late 1750s, Charles Carter—another First Family member—also began cultivating grapes at his Cleve plantation in King George County. By 1762, Carter had planted around 1,800 vines and sent twelve bottles of wines made from a native American grape and from what he described as a "white Portugal summer grape" to the London Society for the Encouragement of the Arts to demonstrate the quality of his product.

Grape cultivation and wine production was not solely the purview of wealthy landowners, however. In 1769 Frenchman André Estave persuaded the Virginia House of Burgesses to provide him with land, money, and labor to establish a vineyard of both native and European grapes near Williamsburg. The endeavor ultimately collapsed when the European vines failed due to disease and pests, and Estave himself proved to be a failure at managing an estate.

By contrast, Colonel Robert Bolling from Buckingham County believed Virginia's wine potential lay with European, not native American, varieties. Bolling wrote an unpublished treatise on grape cultivation in the mid-Atlantic colonies, one of the earliest studies on the subject written by an American. Unfortunately, his efforts to promote the cultivation of southern European grapes in Virginia were cut short by his sudden death in 1775.

THOMAS JEFFERSON

Perhaps the most well-known "gentleman farmer" involved in early Virginia viticulture was Thomas Jefferson, who has become emblematic of Virginia wine even though he met with no success during his lifetime. In 1773, Jefferson met Philip Mazzei, a Florentine exporter who arrived in America in the hope of establishing commercial vineyards and olive farms in Virginia's back country. Captivated by the idea, Jefferson gave Mazzei two thousand acres near Monticello to build a house and establish a vineyard.

Mazzei brought in workers and rootstock from Italy and planted the vineyard with both European and native grape varieties. The European vines successfully fruited and produced flavorful grapes, but they soon withered on the vine. The vineyard fell into near-total neglect after Mazzei left for Europe in 1779 to raise funds for the American government during the Revolutionary War. He returned only once—briefly—and then spent the remainder of his days in Europe.

After leaving the White House in 1809, Jefferson revived his efforts to cultivate vines, corresponding frequently with John Adlum, often called the Father of American Viticulture. Adlum had succeeded in producing wine from both European and native grapes from his Georgetown vineyard in what is now the District of Columbia and provided Jefferson cuttings of various vines on several occasions. Jefferson's efforts invariably ended in frustration and failure, however, although he never lost interest and faith in the ultimate success of American viticulture.

POST-CIVIL WAR RISE AND DEMISE

In the nineteenth century, the American wine industry as a whole took root and expanded significantly, including in Virginia. The first commercially successful American winemaker was Nicholas Longworth, a wealthy Cincinnati businessman. Longworth's sparkling pink Catawba became wildly popular in the United States, and by the 1850s his winery was producing 100,000 bottles a year.

Although Longworth's vineyards had fallen victim to disease and withered by the time of his death in 1863, his success inspired potential American winemakers across the country, who began to try their hand at growing grapes and producing wine. In Virginia as well, farmers began considering their options for diversifying away from the labor-intensive tobacco. The most notable successes came from German immigrants who moved to Virginia after the Civil War.

The first of these vineyards was planted by William Hotopp, a Hanover native who had come to America around 1852. After establishing a successful business in New Jersey, Hotopp moved to Charlottesville in 1866 and purchased the Pen Park estate (the modern-day Pen Park and Meadow Creek Golf Course). Four years later, he began producing both red and white wines from his own vineyard in a winery he built to process his grapes.

In 1873, several other German grape growers led by Oscar Reierson founded the Monticello Wine Company, Virginia's first large-scale commercial winery. Their four-story winery, located in the middle of what is now the intersection of Perry Drive and McIntire Road in Charlottesville, could process up to 200,000 gallons of wine from native American vines, including Virginia's own Norton grape, first cultivated in 1822.

Their success spurred others to follow suit in planting grapes, and by 1888, there were at least three thousand acres of vineyards in Albemarle County alone. By 1890, Virginia's wine industry ranked fifth in the United States, with a total production that year of 461,000 gallons.

Within two decades, however, wine production in the Commonwealth had all but disappeared. The Panic of 1893—second only to the Great Depression in its severity—struck Virginia hard, particularly its agricultural sector. Plant diseases also took their toll on the vineyards.

But it was the emerging temperance movement that ultimately played the greatest role in extinguishing Virginia's wine industry. The Anti-Saloon League was formed in Virginia in 1901 with the express purpose of banning the sale of alcoholic beverages. The League made rapid progress: by 1905, only thirty of the state's one hundred counties still allowed alcohol to be sold. And in September 1914, the Virginia legislature passed a state-wide prohibition law that made Virginia one of the earliest states to go "dry."

Five years later, the entire country followed suit with the ratification of the 19th Amendment, known as Prohibition. Although Prohibition did not ban all commercial wine production—some wine could still be produced commercially for sacramental and medicinal purposes—the net effect was the closure of most small wineries. States with mostly small wineries, such as Virginia, were particularly hard hit.

The ratification of the Twenty-First Amendment in December 1933 finally brought an end to Prohibition. Former wine-producing states throughout the country had to start almost from scratch to rebuild their wine industries. In Virginia, this rebuilding process was long in coming. From the end of Prohibition to the 1960s, Virginia regulators issued a grand total of twenty-two winery licenses, and all but four of these twenty-two wineries had closed their doors by 1970.

VIRGINIA VITICULTURE REBORN

In the early 1970s, Virginia's wine industry began to stir again. In 1973, Treville Lawrence helped found the Vinifera Wine Growers Association, which actively promoted the cultivation of European *Vitis vinifera* vines in Virginia and elsewhere on the East Coast. By 1980, half a dozen new wineries had opened, including several that are still in operation: Barboursville, Ingleside, Mountain Cove, Shenandoah, and Willowcroft.

The government of Virginia began to take an active interest in promoting the development of the state's wine industry. In 1980 the Virginia legislature passed a farm winery bill that required such wineries to have a producing vineyard in Virginia with facilities for bottling wine on the premises. The bill allowed sales at both the wholesale and retail levels, including on-site tasting rooms. Farm wineries were also permitted to buy grapes from other vineyards, as long as 75 percent of the grapes used in their wines were grown in Virginia.

This legislation allowed Virginia's wine industry to blossom. In 1980, Virginia had 286 acres under vine; by contrast, there are now over 4,000 acres of vineyards. There are now nine American Viticultural Areas, or AVAs, either entirely or partially within state lines. Virginia vineyardists cultivate over sixty different grape varieties, led especially by the late Dennis Horton, founder of Horton Winery and a pioneer in bringing Viognier to the United States, a varietal that is one of Virginia's signature wines. Horton and Jennifer McCloud of Chrysalis Vineyards also have actively cultivated the Norton grape, restoring it to greater prominence in its state of origin.

Virginia winemakers themselves come from across the country and the world. Whether from France, Germany, Greece, Italy, Portugal, South Africa, Lebanon, or Turkey, all are drawn to a winemaking community that is characterized by the same energy, determination, and vision that marked the state's earliest efforts. This wide variety in background, training, and experience is contributing additional vitality to a vibrant wine industry that is highly collaborative and ever-growing.

From fine wines that can compete on an equal basis with Europe's classic varieties to more homegrown wines that have long been part of America's wine production, there is truly something for all wine tastes and preferences in Virginia.

Handy Guide to Virginia Wineries

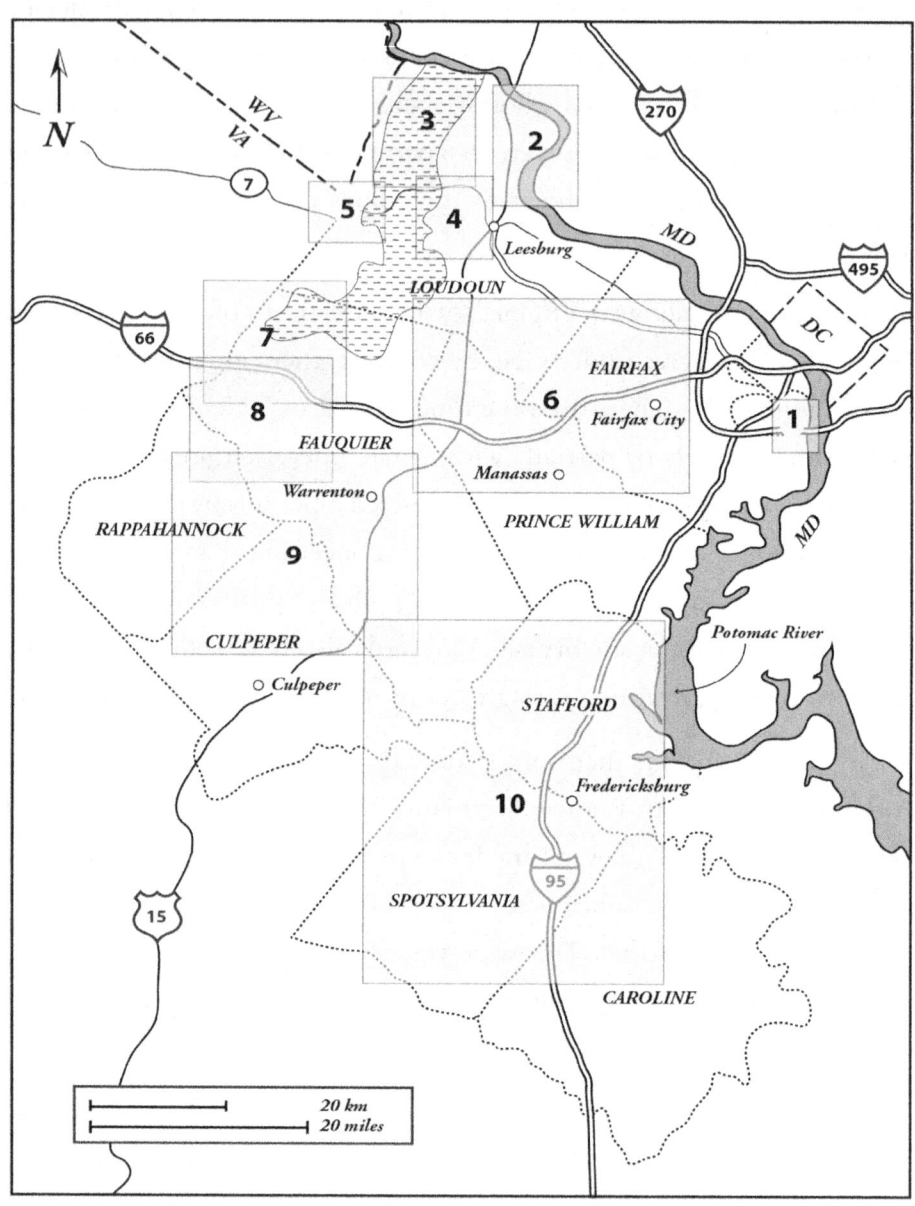

Map 3.0. Northern Virginia Region & Middleburg AVA:
(1) Inside the Beltway; (2) Leesburg North; (3) Northwest Loudoun;
(4) Leesburg West; (5) Bluemont; (6) Middleburg-Fairfax; (7) Delaplane;
(8) Northern Blue Ridge; (9) Warrenton; (10) Fredericksburg

3. NORTHERN VIRGINIA REGION & MIDDLEBURG AVA

The Northern Virginia wine region stretches from busy suburbs to small towns much calmer in pace and personality. Less than an hour's drive from our nation's capital are historic villages with deep colonial roots, working farms owned by the same families for generations, and winding country lanes that quickly go from paved to gravel.

Northern Virginia is home to 86 wineries and cideries that have regular tasting room hours, from small boutique operations that produce only a few hundred cases per year to larger wineries whose annual production is in the thousands. Given the region's proximity to Washington, D.C., and its suburbs, wineries in this region can be crowded places on weekends, especially in summer months, with peak visiting hours from noon to 3:00 p.m.

The region's topography, soils, and climate are quite diverse. The crest of the northern Blue Ridge tops out at over 3,000 feet in elevation, sloping rapidly to the east in a sequence of rolling hills and broad basins. This pattern of mountains, hills, and valleys gives rise to numerous mesoclimates which help produce a rich variety of wines.

The Northern Virginia is also home to the one American Viticultural Area, the Middleburg AVA, approved in 2012 and which stretches from Loudoun County's border with Maryland down into Fauquier County at Little Cobbler Mountain.

__Things to See and Do__: There are numerous activities and sites for visitors in the Northern Virginia region. Historic town centers, such as Old Town Alexandria and downtown Fredericksburg, are filled with Colonial- and Civil War-era homes along with numerous restaurants and cafes. George Washington's Mount Vernon, just south of Alexandria, gives visitors a thorough introduction to our nation's first president and his home.

Northern Virginia also is dotted with many small villages that allow visitors a glimpse of life in early rural Virginia. Among others, these include Waterford, founded in 1733 by abolitionist Quakers; Hillsborough, the birthplace of Susan Koehner Wright, mother of aviation pioneers Orville and Wilbur Wright; and "little" Washington, whose town grid was surveyed by a teenaged George Washington in 1749.

The region includes several Heritage Trails that take visitors through sites of historic significance. The Journey Through Hallowed Ground (www.hallowedground.org), for instance, is a scenic 180-mile driving route from Charlottesville, Virginia to Gettysburg, Pennsylvania, featuring over 10,000 sites, including African American and Native American historical sites, and battlefields from the French and Indian War, Revolutionary War, War of 1812, and the Civil War.

The Trail to Freedom (http://www.trailtofreedomva.com) begins in Fredericksburg and is a combination walking-driving tour that retraces the steps of over 10,000 enslaved people who crossed the Rappahannock River beginning in May 1862 to seek freedom by putting themselves under the protection of the Union Army that occupied the northern bank opposite that city.

Those interested in the Civil War can choose from a number of driving trails to explore the military history of that four-year war which touched Virginia more than any other state. Key battlefields in the Northern

Virginia Region include Bull Run near Manassas, where two major battles were fought; Brandy Station, the war's largest cavalry battle; and the Fredericksburg area, including battlefields at Spotsylvania, Chancellorsville, and the Wilderness, where General Ulysses Grant began his tireless pursuit of General Robert E. Lee that finally brought the war to an end. Self-guided tour maps and guides can be downloaded from Virginia's Civil War Trails website (www.civilwartraveler.com/EAST/VA/).

Nature lovers can choose from among several state parks and nature preserves that offer hiking, horseback riding, camping, and boating. These include Lake Anna, Mason Neck, and Sky Meadows State Parks; more information about these can be accessed at http://www.dcr.virginia.gov/state-parks/find-a-park. Hikers can follow the Appalachian Trail which crosses into Virginia at Clarke County and meanders south and west along the crest of the Blue Ridge Mountains. And the Shenandoah River is a popular rafting site, with several outfitters that will arrange a complete rafting trip for visitors.

Wine Trails: Over a dozen Virginia wine trails include at least one winery in the Northern Virginia region. Trails that focus primarily on Northern Virginia wineries include the Blue Ridge Whiskey Wine Loop, the Blue Ridge Wine Way, Fauquier County Wine Trail, Loudoun Wine Country, and Vintage Piedmont. See Appendix 1 for more details on these and other wine trails.

Handy Guide to Virginia Wineries

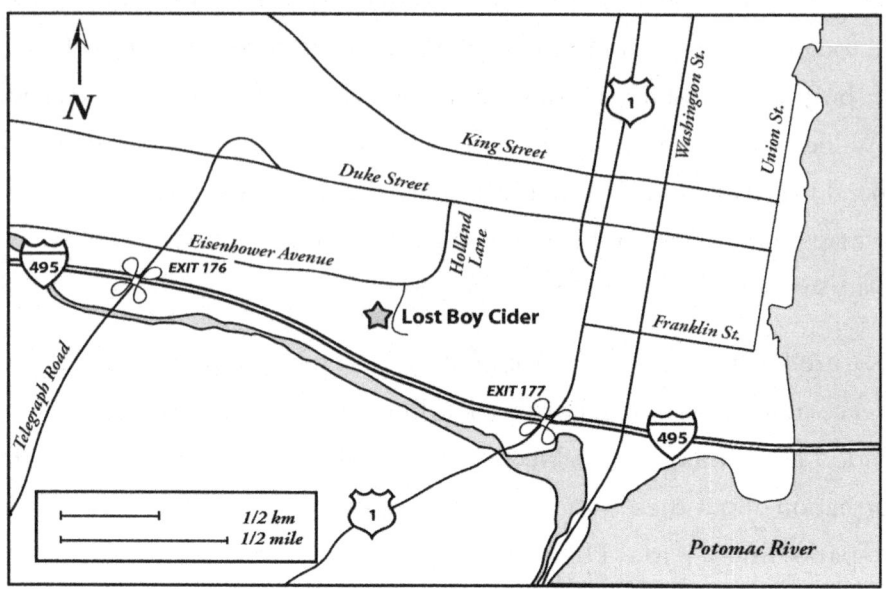

Map 3.1. Inside the Beltway

Northern Virginia Region & Middleburg AVA

INSIDE THE BELTWAY

Lost Boy Cider
317 Hooffs Run Drive
Alexandria VA 22314

Hours: W 3:00–9:00, Th–F 3:00–10:00
Sa 12:00–10:00, Su 12:00–7:00, holiday M 12:00–6:00
Closed New Year's, Thanksgiving, Christmas

703-566-5737
www.lostboycider.com
E-mail: info@lostboycider.com

Tristan Wright's cider journey began after being diagnosed with a gluten allergy in 2015; he opened his cidery five years later in a 6,000-square foot facility in Old Town Alexandria. Working with cidermakers David and Tigen Buin, he produces a wide range of dry ciders from Virginia apples and all-natural ingredients, including seasonal ciders and daily stovepipe specials. Guests can choose seating indoors or outside in a well-ventilated tent. Well-behaved children and leashed pets are welcome.

Hard Ciders: Comeback Kid, En Fuego, Hazy Hopped, Little Prince, Mud Puddle, Oaksmith, Plum Wild, Seltzer, Spring Toddy, Stardust, Wingman.

Non-Alcoholic Drinks: Prohibition, Gin & Tonic Soda.

Price Range: $10–$64 (varies, single serving to case available).

Purchasing: Online to AK, AZ, CO, DC, FL, GA, HI, IA, ID, IL, IN, KS, LA, MA, MD, ME, MN, MO, NC, ND, NE, NH, NM, NV, NY, OH, OK, OR, PA, SC, TN, TX, VA, VT, WA, WI, WV and WY.

Directions: From the Capital Beltway (I-395), take Exit 176B and turn east onto Eisenhower Avenue. Drive 0.6 mile and turn right onto Hooffs Run and the cider parking area on the right. From Old Town Alexandria, drive west on Duke Street for 1/3 mile; turn left onto Holland Lane. Drive through the traffic circle onto Eisenhower and then left onto Hooffs Run.

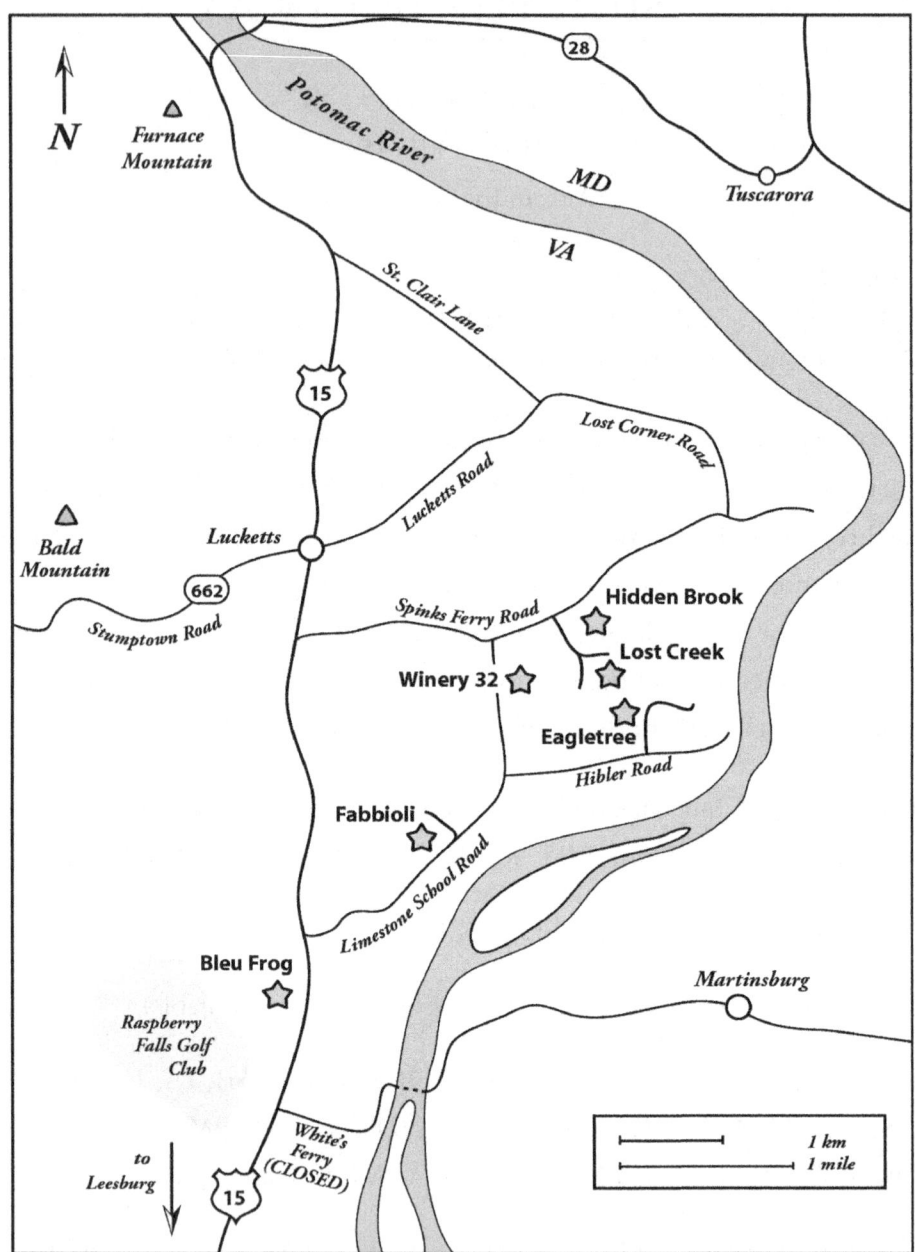

Map 3.2. Leesburg North

LEESBURG NORTH

Bleu Frog Vineyards
16413 James Monroe Highway
Leesburg VA 20176

Hours: F 2:00–5:00, Sa–Su 11:00–5:00 (winter);
F 2:00–7:00, Sa 11:00–7:00, Su 11:00–5:00 (summer)
Closed New Year's, Christmas

703-297-2617
www.bleufrogvineyards.com
E-mail: contact@bleufrogvineyards.com

Joe and Jan Kernan established Bleu Frog in 2017, a year after deciding to purchase the historic White Stone Farm north of Leesburg when Joe retired from a 30-plus year career in the Navy. Named for Joe's service as a SEAL frogman, the winery's first harvest was in 2019; their current production includes wines from their own vineyards. The winery features outdoor seating with fire pits for cooler weather, as well as a tasting room and outdoor pavilion that may be rented for special events and weddings. Children and leashed pets are welcome.

Sparkling Wines: Sparkling Chambourcin.

White Wines: Bleu Blanc *(Vidal Blanc)*.

Red Wines: Cabernet Franc, Chambourcin, Meritage, Merlot, The Red.

Price Range: $25–$36.

Directions: From Leesburg, drive north on U.S. Route 15 for two miles and turn left onto the winery drive .

Eagletree Farm Vineyards
15100 Harrison Hill Lane
Leesburg VA 20176

Hours: F 2:00–8:00, Sa 12:00–8:00, Su 12:00–6:00   703-777-5208
Closed New Year's, Christmas   www.eagletreevineyards.com

Eagletree Farm was launched by Lori McKeever after she decided to step down from running her long-time namesake Irish tavern in McLean, Virginia. Along with Jeff Judge, she oversees Eagletree's operations, which include wood-fired pizzas and other dishes made onsite by Jeff, who trained at L'Académie de Cuisine. The facilities are open for weddings, private parties, and other events. Eagletree also offers pick-your-own blueberry fields every year in June and now offers craft beers on-site. Children are welcome but must be accompanied at all times.

White Wines: Chardonnay.

Red Wines: Cabernet Franc, Talon *(red blend)*, Tannat.

Price Range: $20–$30

Tastings: $9.

Groups: Reservations required for groups of 6 or more.

Directions: From U.S. Route 15, turn east onto Limestone School Road (Route 661) (portions unpaved). Drive 2.1 miles, then turn right onto Hibler Road. Continue ½ mile. Turn left onto Harrison Hill Lane. The winery will be ½ mile further, on the right.

Fabbioli Cellars
15669 Limestone School Road
Leesburg VA 20176

Hours: Th–M 11:00–5:00
Closed New Year's, Thanksgiving, Christmas

703-771-1197
www.fabbioliwines.com
E-mail: info@fabbioliwines.com

Doug Fabbioli and his wife, Colleen Berg, founded Fabbioli Cellars in 2000 after returning to the East Coast from California where Doug had studied at the University of California/Davis and worked with various winemakers. Respected for his mentoring for many of Northern Virginia's winemakers, Doug launched the New Ag School to provide a more formal mentoring system for Loudoun County's wine growers and farmers.

The winery's tasting room offers several tasting stations for visitors, including an adults-only section upstairs. Pre-packaged light fare is available to have indoors or on the outdoor patio area that overlooks some of the vineyards. Leashed pets are welcome; a special children's section is available outdoors. Adults only after 2:00 p.m.

Ciders: Attitude Adjuster, Berry Good Friends, Ladies Man, Perry.

Fruit Wines: Una Pera *(pear)*.

White Wines: Chardonnay, Petit Manseng, Something White, Viognier.

Rosé Wines: Rosa Luna *(Sangiovese)*.

Red Wines: Barbera, Cabernet Franc, Chambourcin, Fratelli, Meritage, Paco Rojo, Padrino, Petit Verdot, Sangiovese, Tannat, Tre Sorelle *(Bordeaux-style blend)*, Zinfandel.

Sweet/Dessert Wines: Raspberry Merlot.

Fortified Wines: Pear Wine, Rosa Nera (raspberry), Royalty *(port-style)*.

Price Range: $16–$45

Tastings: $15 per person (with food pairing bites).

Groups: Reservations required for groups of 6 or more and for groups arriving by limo or bus. No groups over 10 people.

Purchasing: Online ordering to most states available through the website.

Directions: From U.S. Route 15, turn onto Limestone School Road (Route 661) (portions unpaved) to the winery, 1.3 miles on the left.

Hidden Brook Winery
43301 Spinks Ferry Road
Leesburg VA 20176

Hours: F 12:00–7:00, Sa 12:00–8:00, Su 12:00–6:00 703-737-3935
Closed New Year's, Christmas www.hiddenbrookwinery.com
E-mail: info@hiddenbrookwinery.com

Eric and Deborah Hauck established Hidden Brook in 1999, literally next door to Eric's parents, Bob and Carol Hauck, who founded Lost Creek Winery. The rustic tasting room seats 48 and provides a calm atmosphere for visitors, both indoors next to the fireplace or out on the covered porch and deck under the trees. Hidden Brook sponsors events such as live music on summer weekends, special brunches, and charity fundraisers, including the Toast for Hope in support of the Susan G. Komen Race for the Cure. The winery's gift shop offers light fare for purchase, as well as gifts and works by local artists. Children and pets are welcome.

White Wines: Chardonnay, Reserve White, Vidal Blanc.

Rosé Wines: Rosé *(Chambourcin, Vidal Blanc)*.

Red Wines: Cabernet Sauvignon, Chambourcin, Merlot, Reserve Red.

Price Range: $22–$33

Tastings: $8 per person for a flight.

Groups: Reservations required for groups of 10 or more.

Directions: From Leesburg, drive north on U.S. Route 15 for about 7 miles. Turn right onto Spinks Ferry Road (Route 657) (portions unpaved). Continue 2 miles to the winery entrance on right.

Lost Creek Vineyards & Winery
43285 Spinks Ferry Road
Leesburg VA 20176

Hours: M, Th–F, 12:00–5:00, Sa–Su 11:00–5:00
(Sa to 6:00, Apr–Nov)
Closed New Year's, Thanksgiving,
Christmas Eve & Day

703-443-9836
www.lostcreekwinery.com
E-mail: winery@lostcreekwinery.com

Originally founded in 1995, Lost Creek has been owned by Todd and Aimee Henkle since early 2012. The tasting room features a number of tables and a large stone fireplace next to the tasting bar. After a tasting, visitors can opt for a glass or bottle of Lost Creek's all Virginia-grown wines and tapas-style snacks to enjoy either indoors or outside on the patios or pavilion. Lost Creek sponsors special wine-focused events and dinners throughout the year. The winery can be rented for private events and weddings, with a caterer's kitchen that can be used. Reservations are recommended on weekends. Adults only, please.

White Wines: Chardonnay, Serenity, Vidal Blanc.

Rosé Wines: Rosé.

Red Wines: Cabernet Franc, Rouge d'Ete, Serenity, Syrah, Trinity.

Price Range: $25–$48

Tastings: $12 per person.

Groups: Reservations required for groups of 5 or more.

Purchasing: Phone and online ordering for DC, FL, MD, and VA residents.

Directions: From Leesburg, drive north on U.S. Route 15 for about 7 miles. Turn right onto Spinks Ferry Road (Route 657) (portions unpaved). Continue 2 miles to the winery road on the right, at Hidden Brook Winery; continue another ½ mile past the brewery to the winery parking lot.

Winery 32
15066 Limestone School Road
Leesburg VA 20176

Hours: Currently closed to visitors   240-687-1989

Opened in 2014 by Michael and Roxanne Moosher, Winery 32 sits on 32 acres at the end of a drive lined with 32 peach trees. The Mooshers used all Virginia-grown grapes for their production, both their own and fruit from other vineyards. In 2021, Winery 32 was sold to a new owner and had not yet announced new hours or its new name by the time this book was being finalized.

WINE ORIGINS

The *Oxford Companion to Wine* defines wine as the fermented juice of fruits or berries, a broad category that excludes ales, beers, and distilled liquors but includes fermented products flavored from flowers or herbs. Most frequently, wine refers specifically to the fermented beverage made from the juice of grapes.

The earliest archeological evidence of grape cultivation for the express purpose of winemaking was found in the southern Caucasus, the region between the Black Sea and the Caspian Sea in the areas of modern-day Georgia, Armenia, and Azerbaijan, according to Hugh Johnson in *Vintage: The Story of Wine*. It was here that wine was traditionally fermented and aged in kvevris, terracotta vessels that are buried in the soil with only their tops showing.

By 500 BC, vines were being cultivated and wine made throughout the eastern Mediterranean region. Tomb paintings from ancient Egypt include depictions of grape cultivation and winemaking, and ancient Greek historians such as Herodotus and Thucydides have left references to viticulture in their writings.

With the rise of the Roman Empire, winemaking began to expand to the areas of modern-day France, Spain, and Germany. Even in areas with limited evidence of grape cultivation, such as modern-day England, wine was a much-prized commodity.

These wines would have been made from the *Vitis vinifera* species of grapevine (sometimes abbreviated as *V. vinifera* or simply *vinifera*). Widely adaptable to a broad range of climates and regions, *V. vinifera* includes over five thousand different varieties and accounts for the vast majority of wines made around the world today.

Handy Guide to Virginia Wineries

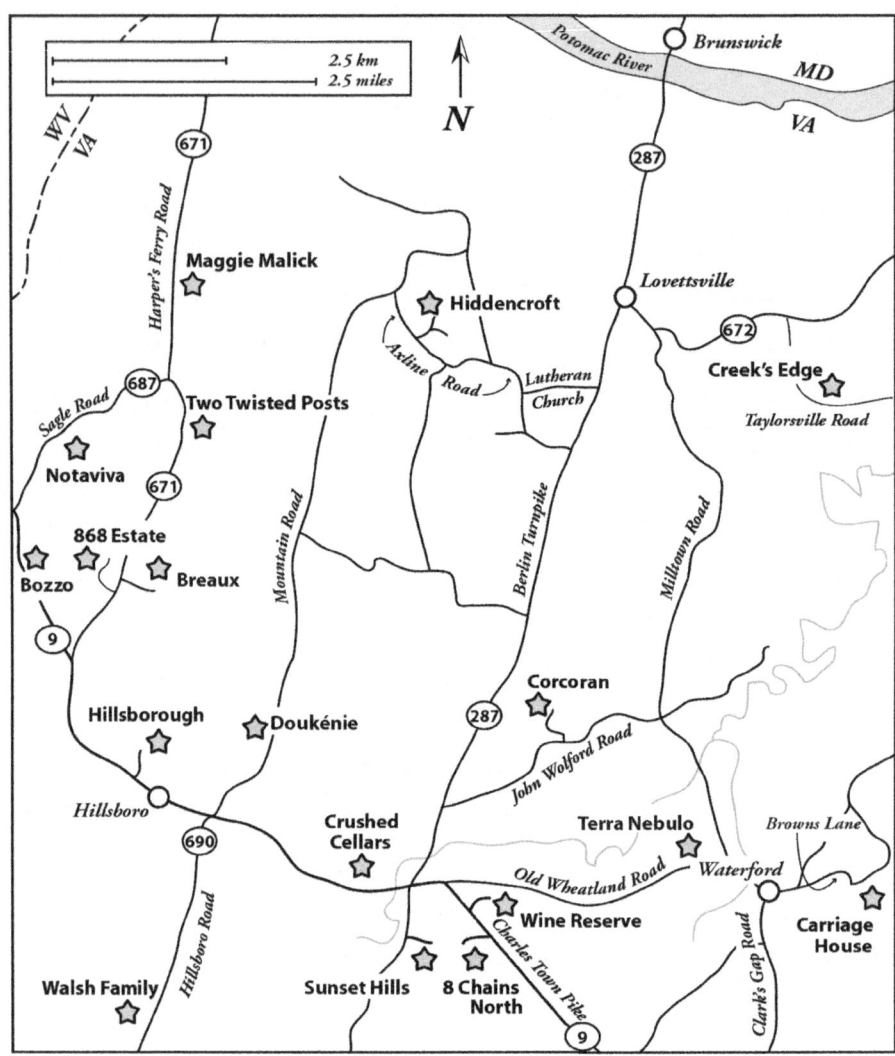

Map 3.3. Northwest Loudoun

Northern Virginia Region & Middleburg AVA

NORTHWEST LOUDOUN

8 Chains North
38593 Daymont Lane
Waterford VA 20197

Hours: Th, F 12:00–6:00, Sa–Su 11:00–6:00
Closed New Year's, Thanksgiving, Christmas

571-439-2255
www.8chainsnorth.com
E-mail: info@8chainsnorth.com

Ben and Connie Renshaw opened 8 Chains North Winery to the public in 2010, housing their tasting room in a restored barn with seating indoors and out. Now owned by Edz Sturans and Cissi DeMarco, 8 Chains sources its wines from Loudoun County as well as from the Pacific Northwest. Visitors may enjoy wines either inside (limited seating) or on the patio overlooking the vineyards. The winery features live music on some summer evenings and features a small fenced dog park area for four-legged guests. Children are welcome but must be accompanied at all times. Reservations recommended for weekends.

White Wines: Chardonnay, LoCo Vino, Sauvignon Blanc.

Rosé Wines: Pink Link.

Red Wines: Cabernet Franc, Cabernet Sauvignon, Furnace Mountain Red *(Bordeaux-style blend)*, Malbec, Mourvèdre, Off The Mountain Red, Petit Verdot, Syrah, Tempranillo.

Price Range: $22–$38

Tastings: $12 per person for flight, $17 for chocolate pairing.

Groups: Reservations required for groups of 8 or more, $15 per person.

ADA accessible.

Purchasing: Available through the website for select states.

Directions: From Leesburg, take Route 7 West and drive 2 miles. Merge onto Route 9 West (Charles Town Pike). Drive 4 miles and turn left onto Daymont Lane (portions unpaved). The winery is on the left after ¼ mile.

868 Estate Vineyards
14001 Harpers Ferry Road
Purcellville VA 20132

Hours: W, Th, Su 11:00–5:00, F–Sa 11:00–6:00 (fall to spring)
(W, Th, Su to 6:00, F–Sa to 8:30 in summer)
Closed New Year's, Thanksgiving, Christmas

540-668-7008
www.868estatevineyards.com
E-mail: info@868estatevineyards.com

Carl DiManno, Peter Deliso, and Wendy Charron opened 868 Estate Vineyards in May 2012 after working in the Maryland wine industry. The winery's name comes from the elevation of the property's highest point. Guests can sample 868's wines from the tasting room and spacious outdoor patio. During the week, a light fare menu is offered, while in summer (May–Oct) burgers and hotdogs are available from The Grill. The winery often features live music on weekends. The Grandale Restaurant, located on the property, is temporarily closed; call to confirm when it will reopen for indoor dining. Children and leashed dogs are welcome outside.

White Wines: Canvas White, Chardonel, Chardonnay.

Rosé Wines: Canvas Rosé, Rosé.

Red Wines: Cabernet Sauvignon, Merlot, Petit Verdot.

Price Range: $24–$32

Tastings: $12 per person, $18 with truffle pairing, $24 with food pairing.

Groups: Reservations required for groups of 8 or more, $18 per person.

ADA accessible.

Purchasing: Online to AK, AZ, CA, CO, DC, FL, FA, HI, IA, ID, IN, KS, LA, MA, MD, ME, MN, MO, NC, ND, NE, NH, NM, NV, NY, OH, OR, PA, SC, TN, TX, VA, WA, WI, WV, and WY.

Directions: From Route 7, merge onto Route 9 West (Charles Town Pike). Drive 9.8 miles and turn right onto Harper's Ferry Road (Route 671). Continue 0.8 mile to the winery entrance on left.

Bozzo Family Vineyards
35226 Charles Town Pike
Purcellville VA 20132

Hours: Th–F 3:00–6:00, Sa 12:00–6:00, Su 1:00–5:00 (summer) 571-918-9001
F 3:00–6:00, Sa 1:00–6:00, Su 1:00–5:00 (spring, late fall) www.bozwines.com
Closed Christmas, Jan–Mar E-mail: info@bozwines.com

Former lawyer Stephen Bozzo opened his winery in 2018 after honing his skills for many years as a home winemaker. He uses all Virginia-grown grapes for Bozzo's wines, the majority from Loudoun County, including his own vineyard. Bozzo offers crackers and cheese to have indoors or on the outdoor deck overlooking the neighboring hills. Indoor seating is limited to a maximum of four per table.

White Wines: Maureen *(Sauvignon Blanc)*, Stephanie *(Petit Manseng)*, Teresa *(Chardonnay)*.

Rosé Wines: Harle Rosé.

Red Wines: 2nd Act *(Bordeaux-style blend)*, Duke *(Cabernet Franc)*, Keith *(Merlot)*, La Famiglia *(Bordeaux-style blend)*.

Price Range: $15–$25

Tastings: $10 per person for four wines.

Groups: Reservations recommended for groups of 7 to 14 (maximum size).

Directions: From Route 7, merge onto Route 9 West (Charles Town Pike). Drive 11.4 miles to the winery entrance on right.

Breaux Estate Vineyards
36888 Breaux Vineyards Lane
Purcellville VA 20132

Hours: Daily 11:00–6:00 (Apr–mid-Oct);
M–F 11:00–5:00, Sa–Su 11:00–6:00 (mid-Oct–Mar)
Closed New Year's, Easter, Thanksgiving, Christmas

540-668-6299
www.breauxvineyards.com
E-mail: info@BreauxVineyards.com

Breaux [pronounced *bro*] Vineyards is a 404-acre estate founded in 1984 and that now has over 115 acres of vineyards. All their wines are made from estate-grown grapes. The winery's patios offer panoramic views of the vines, the valley, and nearby mountains. Gourmet snacks and breads are available for purchase. Breaux sponsors a range of festivals, including Samedi Gras Festival, Cajun Festival, and Dog Days. The winery can be rented for private events and weddings. Children and pets are welcome (pets outdoors only). Reservations required for all visitors. Last call is thirty minutes before closing.

Sparkling Wines: Breauxmance *(rosé)*.

White Wines: Chère Marie *(Vidal Blanc)*, Jennifer's Jambalaya, Jolie Blonde, Madeleine's Chardonnay, Sauvignon Blanc, Viognier.

Rosé Wines: Equation Rosé, Rosé.

Red Wines: Cabernet Franc, Cabernet Sauvignon, Equation, Marquis de Lafayette *(Cabernet Franc)*, Meritage, Merlot, Nebbiolo.

Fortified Wines: Lineage *(port-style)*.

Price Range: $18–$48

Tastings: $15 per person.

Groups: Reservations required for groups of 8 or more.

ADA accessible.

Restrictions: Dogs are not permitted on the grounds during special events or festivals with the exception of Dog Day, when dogs are the stars.

Purchasing: Online or phone for CA, DC, FL, LA, MD, NC, TX, and VA.

Directions: From Route 7, merge onto Route 9 West (Charles Town Pike). Drive 9.8 miles and turn right onto Harper's Ferry Road (Route 671). Continue 1 mile to the winery entrance on right.

Carriage House Wineworks
40817 Browns Lane
Waterford VA 20197

Hours: Sa, Su 12:00–5:30 617-957-0958
Closed Dec–Mar www.chwwinery.com
E-mail: gfritze@chwwinery.com, mfritze@chwwinery.com

Bruce Beddow and Mike Fritze's decision to open Carriage House in late 2020 sprang from Bruce's experience in growing grapes for Bluemont

Vineyards for over 14 years and Mike's training as a certified wine judge. They source their wines from all-Loudoun County fruit, as well as their own vineyards near the town of Waterford. The Windhorn tasting room is open for visitors on Saturdays (15424 Windhorn Lane), while Quartz Creek (40817 Browns Lane) hosts guests on Sundays, with outdoor patio seating overlooking the vines. Leashed dogs are welcome; children must be accompanied at all times.

White Wines: Chardonnay, Petit Manseng, Vidal Blanc.

Rosé Wines: Rosé.

Red Wines: Cabernet Franc, Cabernet Sauvignon, Chambourcin, Merlot, Petit Verdot, Red Barouche, Tannat.

Sweet/Dessert Wines: Late Harvest Vidal.

Price Range: $20–$31

Tastings: $10 per person.

Groups: Reservations recommended for groups over 6.

Purchasing: Online to VA only.

Directions: From Route 7, merge onto Route 9 West (Charles Town Pike). Turn right after ½ mile onto Clarks Gap Road. Continue 3 miles through Waterford and bear right onto Loyalty Road. Take the second right onto Browns Land and continue 1 more mile to the Windhorn entrance on the left or the Quartz Creek entrance a little further on the right.

❖ ❖ ❖

Corcoran Vineyards & Cider
14635 Corkys Farm Lane
Waterford VA 20197

Hours: Sa–Su 12:00–5:00
Closed New Year's, Easter, Christmas

540-882-9073
www.corcorancider.com
E-mail: info@corcorancider.com

Jim and Lori Corcoran opened their winery just outside Waterford in 2002. Winemaker Lori focuses on producing high-quality wine using both her own estate-grown grapes and fruit from two neighboring vineyards. She has now added ciders to her lineup, made from Virginia apples. The tasting room includes limited indoors seating as well as first-come, first-served outdoor spaces with views of the surrounding hills and pond. Corcoran offers free Wi-Fi. Corcoran also features a Cigarden for those who wish a cigar with their wines. Leashed pets are welcome.

Ciders: Hard Cider, Hop'n'Pop, Knot Head, Popo Peach, Sinful.

White Wines: Chardonnay, Seyval Blanc, Traminette, Vidal Blanc.

Rosé Wines: Rosé.

Red Wines: Cabernet Franc, Chambourcin, Petit Verdot, Pinot Noir, Tannat.

Sweet/Dessert Wines: BlackJack, RAZ.

Fortified Wines: USB *(port-style)*, Waterford *(white port-style)*.

Price Range: $16–$25

Tastings: $5 per person.

Groups: Reservations required for picnic tables; $75 (includes $40 of wine).

ADA accessible.

Handy Guide to Virginia Wineries

Directions: From Leesburg, drive west on Route 7 and merge onto Route 9 West (Charles Town Pike). Drive 5.7 miles and turn north onto Berlin Turnpike (Route 287). After 1 mile, turn right onto John Wolford Road (portions unpaved). Continue 1.5 miles. Turn left onto Corkys Farm Lane (portions unpaved); the winery's gravel driveway will be ⅓ mile on the left.

Creek's Edge
41255 Anna's Lane
Lovettsville VA 20180

Hours: Sa–Su 12:00–6:30
Closed New Year's, Christmas

540-822-3825
www.creeksedgewinery.com
E-mail: info@creeksedgewinery.com

Opened by Tedd Durden in 2014, Creek's Edge is located on the banks of Catoctin Creek in the hamlet of Taylorstown. The winery offers indoor seating in its spacious tasting room as well as on the decks overlooking the lawn and 11-acre vineyard. The tasting bar was carved from hickory trees cleared from the property. Light food is available for purchase. The winery can be rented for special events and weddings, with a private room upstairs. Children are welcome. Reservations recommended.

White Wines: Chardonnay, Vidal Blanc, Viognier, Water's Edge White.

Rosé Wines: Rosé.

Red Wines: Cabernet Franc, Cabernet Sauvignon, Family Blend, Foothills Red, Merlot, Vintner's Blend.

Sweet/Dessert Wines: Hunting Hill *(port-style)*, Sweet Caroline *(Vidal Blanc)*.

Price Range: $29–$50

Restrictions: No groups over 6.

Purchasing: Online to CA and VA only.

Directions: From Route 7, merge onto Route 9 West (Charles Town Pike). Drive 5.8 miles to the winery's gravel driveway on the right.

Crushed Cellars
37938 Charles Town Pike
Purcellville VA 20132

Hours: Sa–Su 12:00–5:00
Closed New Year's, Christmas

571-374-9463 (WINE)
www.crushedcellars.com
E-mail: info@crushedcellars.com

Bob Kalok opened Crushed Cellars in 2011 on the grounds of his family farm, and visitors may well spot a chicken or two strolling about the grounds as well as one of the winery cats sunning itself on the porch. The family currently uses grapes from other Virginia vineyards as well as from their own vines. The winery offers cheese, spreads, and bread for purchase on the front porch or grounds. The two-story tasting room may be rented for small parties. Children and dogs are welcome.

Fruit Wines: Blackberry.

White Wines: Chardonnay, Traminette, Vidal Blanc.

Red Wines: Cabernet Franc, Meritage, Petit Verdot.

Price Range: $19–$25

Tastings: $5 per person.

Restrictions: No groups over 6.

Directions: From Route 7, merge onto Route 9 West (Charles Town Pike). Drive 5.8 miles to the winery's gravel driveway on the right.

Doukénie Winery
14727 Mountain Road
Purcellville VA 20132

Hours: Th–F 12:00–5:00 (F to 9:00 on Bistro Nights), Sa–Su 11:00–6:00
Closed Easter, Thanksgiving, Christmas

540-668-6464
www.doukeniewinery.com
E-mail: busmgr@doukeniewinery.com

Doukénie Winery was founded by George and Nicki Bazaco and is named in honor of George's grandmother, Doukénie Bacos, who arrived in the United States from Greece in 1920. Located on 500 acres near the Blue Ridge Mountains, Doukénie offers scenic views of the surrounding hills, the vineyards, and winery pond from its tasting room and veranda. Adults 21 and over only, please. Pets are welcome on the winery patio and grounds. Reservations required.

White Wines: Chardonnay, Mandolin, Pinot Gris, Sauvignon Blanc.

Red Wines: Cabernet Franc, Cabernet Sauvignon, Dionysus, Merlot, NYX, Petit Verdot, Vintner's Reserve, Zeus.

Sweet/Dessert Wines: Hope's Legacy Raspberry Wine.

Price Range: $25–$64

Tastings: $12 per person for flights.

Groups: Reservations required for groups of 8 (maximum size).

Restrictions: Limos by appointment only; no buses.

Purchasing: Shipping to AK, AZ, CA, CO, DC, FL, GA, IL, LA, MD, MI, MN, NC, NH, NM, NV, NY, OH, OR, PA, TN, TX, VA, WA and WI.

Directions: From Route 7, merge onto Route 9 West (Charles Town Pike). Drive 7.3 miles and turn right onto Mountain Road (Route 690 North). Continue 1 mile to the winery entrance on the left.

Hiddencroft Vineyards
12202 Axline Road
Lovettsville VA 20180

Hours: Th–Su 12:00–6:00   540-535-5367
Closed New Year's, Thanksgiving, Christmas   www.hiddencroftvineyards.com
                                                                   E-mail: winery@hiddencroftvineyards.com

The northernmost winery in Virginia, Hiddencroft is a family-run operation owned by Terry and Clyde Housel; Clyde also serves as winemaker. The tasting room is a restored 1830s-era farmhouse with an expansive deck featuring tables, umbrellas, and a firepit. The farmhouse's original laundry and smokehouse provide a scenic backdrop for photos. While no outside food is permitted, Hiddencroft offers snacks for purchase and enjoyment over a glass of wine on its patio. Children and leashed pets are welcome.

Fruit Wines: Blackberry, Grandma's Love Potion *(blueberry)*, Persephone's Punch *(pomegranate)*, Sweet Cherry, Vitis Rubus *(raspberry, Chambourcin)*.

White Wines: Petit Manseng, Traminette.

Rosé Wines: Cabernet Franc Rosé, Chambourcin Rosé.

Red Wines: Cabernet Franc, Cabernet Sauvignon, Chambourcin, Dutchman's Creek, Petit Verdot, Tranquility.

Fortified Wines: Cackling Crow *(with blackberry)*, Grandpa's Fantasy *(with blueberry)*, Royale *(Petit Verdot)*, Vision Noir *(Chambourcin)*.

Price Range: $18–$40

Tastings: $8 per person.

Groups: Reservations required for groups of 9 or more; $10 per person fee.

Restrictions: No groups over 25.

Purchasing: Online to AK, AL, AZ, CA, CO, DC, FL, GA, HI, IA, ID, IL, IN, KS, LA, MA, MD, ME, MN, MO, NC, ND, NE, NH, NM, NV, NY, OH, OR, PA, SC, TN, TX, VA, WA, WI, WV, and WY.

Directions: From Route 7, merge onto Route 9 West (Charles Town Pike). After 5.7 miles, turn right onto Berlin Turnpike (Route 287) toward Lovettsville. Continue 5 miles. Turn left at Lutheran Church Road (unpaved). At the end of the road, turn right onto Axline Road (Route 680) (portions unpaved). Drive 1.6 miles and turn right into the winery drive. Bear left at the large red barn to the winery parking lot entrance on the right.

Hillsborough Vineyards
36716 Charles Town Pike
Purcellville VA 20132

Hours: Daily 11:00–6:00 (Apr–Dec),
F-M 11:00–5:00 (Jan–Mar)
Closed Easter, Thanksgiving,
Christmas Eve & Day

540-668-6216
www.hillsboroughwine.com
E-mail: tastingroom@hillsboroughwine.com

Bora and Zeynep Baki founded Hillsborough Vineyards after moving to the Washington, D.C., area from their native Turkey in 1979. Their son Kerem serves as winemaker. The tasting room is in a restored pre-Civil War barn, with two stone patios that offer a splendid view of the mountains and adjoining valley. Hillsborough has pre-packaged tasting plates and cheeses for sale, as well as an on-site farm brewery with a wide range of products. Outdoor and limited indoor seating available. Adults only on weekends.

White Wines: Carnelian *(Roussanne)*, Opal *(Petit Manseng)*, Petit Manseng.

Rosé Wines: Serefina *(Viognier, Tannat)*, Ruby's Blush.

Red Wines: Bloodstone *(Fer Servadou)*, Cabernet Sauvignon, Onyx *(Tannat)*, Petit Verdot, Ruby.

Sweet/Dessert Wines: Moonstone *(late-harvest Viognier)*.

Price Range: $22–$38

Tastings: $12–$16 per person for a flight.

Groups: Reservations required for groups of 8 or more.

ADA accessible.

Purchasing: Phone orders for all states *except* AL, DE, KY, MS, and UT.

Directions: From Route 7, merge onto Route 9 West (Charles Town Pike) and drive 8 miles. The winery entrance is on the right about ½ mile past the town of Hillsboro.

Maggie Malick Wine Caves
12138 Harpers Ferry Road
Purcellville VA 20132

Hours: F–Su, 11:00–5:00 (winter, spring)
Th–M 11:00–6:00 (summer, fall)
Closed New Year's, Thanksgiving, Christmas

540-905-2921
www.maggiemalickwinecaves.com
E-mail: info@maggiemalickwinecaves.com

Maggie Malick opened her winery in 2013, twelve years after she and husband Mark planted their first vineyard on their 215-acre property. The tasting room is a concrete cave, dug into a hillside and built by the Malicks themselves. Seating is available both indoors or out on the deck; additional tables and chairs are scattered across the grounds around the winery pond. Baguettes, cheeses, cold cuts, and small plate dishes can be purchased on site. Children and leashed dogs are welcome.

White Wines: Chardonnay, Duet, Sauvignon Blanc, Petit Manseng, Viognier.

Rosé Wines: Rosé, Sunset Sonata.

Red Wines: Cabernet Franc, Cabernet Sauvignon, Captain's Cuvée, Fortissimo, Kaleidoscope, Merlot, Mourvèdre, Petit Verdot, Rhapsody in Red, Tannat.

Fortified Wines: Tango *(port-style Petit Verdot)*.

Price Range: $22–$42

Tastings: $10 per person for a flight.

Groups: Reservations required for groups of 8 or more, $15 per person fee.

Purchasing: Online to AK, AL, AZ, CA, CO, DC, FL, GA, HI, IA, ID, IL, IN, KS, LA, MA, MD, ME, MN, MO, NC, ND, NE, NH, NM, NV, NY, OH, OR, PA, SC, TN, TX, VA, WA, WI, WV, and WY.

Directions: From Route 7, merge onto Route 9 West (Charles Town Pike). Drive 9.8 miles and turn right onto Harper's Ferry Road (Route 671). Continue 4.6 miles to the winery entrance on right.

Notaviva Vineyards & Craft Fermentations
13274 Sagle Drive
Purcellville VA 20132

Hours: F 4:00–7:00, Sa–Su 12:00–5:00 (to 7:00 in summer)   540-668-6756
Closed New Year's, Easter, Christmas   www.notavivavineyards.com
                                            E-mail: info@notavivavineyards.com

Stephen and Shannon Mackey established Notaviva Vineyards in 2004 in the secluded northwest corner of Loudoun County. The winery's two-story tasting room offers a scenic view of the winery pond and nearby hills; the grounds also include a number of benches and picnic tables for use. The winery frequently sponsors live musical performances on weekends. Notaviva also now produces ciders and craft beers on-site, which can be tried in flights or pint pours. Adults only, please.

Ciders: Django Pear Cider, Five & Dime Spiced Cider.

White Wines: Calor Chardonnay, Sabado, Viognier, Vidal Blanc.

Rosé Wines: Every Rosé Has Its Thorn *(Seyval Blanc, Chambourcin)*.

Red Wines: Blaufränkisch, Cabernet Franc, Chambourcin, Petit Verdot, Meritage.

Dessert Wines: Gitano Chambourcin.

Price Range: $17–$28

Handy Guide to Virginia Wineries

Tastings: $8 per person.

Groups: Reservations required for groups of 8–16; $12 per person fee.

Restrictions: Adults (21 and older) only; no pets; no groups over 16.

Purchasing: Online ordering is available for VA and FL.

Directions: From Route 7, take Route 9 West (Charles Town Pike) for 11.6 miles. Turn right onto Sagle Road (Route 687) (portions unpaved). The winery will be on the right after 1 mile.

Sunset Hills Vineyard
38295 Fremont Overlook Lane
Purcellville VA 20132

Hours: M–Th 12:00–5:00, F 12:00–6:00, Sa–Su 11:00–6:00   540-882-4560
Closed New Year's, Thanksgiving, Christmas   www.sunsethillsvineyard.com
E-mail: tastingroom@sunsethillsvineyard.com

Located on a rise overlooking the Loudoun Valley and Blue Ridge Mountains, Sunset Hills Vineyard was established by Mike and Diane Canney who now have over 160 acres of vines in the Northern Virginia and Shenandoah regions. The two-story tasting room is housed in a 130-year-old barn carefully restored by Amish carpenters and powered by solar energy. Seating is available both indoors or outside, including an open-sided Amish-built pavilion. The winery offers breads, artisanal cheeses, and spreads, as well as live music on weekends, charity fundraisers, and a wine harvest series in the fall. The facilities may be rented for private functions or weddings. Children and pets are welcome.

Sparkling Wines: Dawn.

White Wines: Chardonnay, Sunset White, Viognier.

Rosé Wines: Cabernet Franc Rosé, Sunset Rosé.

Red Wines: Cabernet Franc, Merlot, Mosaic, Nebbiolo, Petit Verdot, Sunset Red, Tannat.

Dessert Wines: Nettare di Tramonto.

Fortified Wines: Dusk *(port-style)*.

Price Range: $22–$60

Tastings: $10 per person.

Groups: Reservations required for groups of 11–20, $15 per person fee.

Purchasing: Shipping to CA, CO, DC, FL, MD, MN, NC, NY, PA, TX, VA, WV, and WY.

Directions: From Route 7, merge onto Route 9 West (Charles Town Pike). Drive 5.7 miles to the Berlin Turnpike (Route 287). Turn left and drive 2.6 miles. Turn left again onto Fremont Overlook Lane (unpaved) to the winery parking lot on the right.

Terra Nebulo
39892 Old Wheatland Road
Waterford VA 20197

Hours: Sa–Su 12:00–6:00
Closed New Year's, Easter, Christmas

703-622-9117
www.terranebulo.com
E-mail: info@terranebulo.com

Michael and Cheryl Morrison opened their winery in August 2015 on a hill just outside the historic Quaker village of Waterford. The winery is housed in an Amish-built replica of a two-story nineteenth-century barn in Maryland. Wines are made by Randy Phillips (*Cave Ridge*) and are sourced from a vineyard in the Shenandoah Valley. Terra Nebulo offers wood-fired pizzas and light snacks. Adults only, please.

White Wines: Chardonnay, Riesling, Traminette, Viognier.

Red Wines: Cabernet Franc, Chambourcin.

Fortified Wines: Chambourcin *(port-style)*.

Price Range: $17–$33

Tastings: $5 per person.

Restrictions: Adults (21 and older) only; no pets.

Directions: From Leesburg, take Route 7 and merge onto Route 9 West (Charles Town Pike). Drive ½ mile, then turn right onto Clarks Gap Road. In the village of Waterford, turn left onto Water Street, which quickly merges into Main Street. Make a slight left onto Old Wheatland Road and continue 0.4 miles to the winery entrance on the right.

Two Twisted Posts
12944 Harpers Ferry Road
Purcellville VA 20132

Hours: Th–M 11:00–6:00
Closed New Year's, Thanksgiving, Christmas

540-668-6540
www.twotwistedposts.com
E-mail: contact@twotwistedposts.com

Two Twisted Posts was founded by Theresa and Brad Robertson, who planted their vineyard in 2008 on their scenic property at the base of the Short Hills, naming it after the Two Twisted Posts Tavern in Theresa's native town of Colchester, England. Seating is offered indoors or outside next to the winery's large red barn. Light snacks are available for purchase. The winery sponsors live music on many weekends as well as special events, such as Paint-N-Sips. Dogs are welcome.

White Wines: Chardonnay, Sweet Life, Vidal Blanc.

Red Wines: Cabernet Franc, Cabernet Sauvignon, Petit Verdot, Thomas Great *(Bordeaux-style blend)*.

Price Range: $17–$33

Tastings: $5 per person.

Groups: Reservations required for groups of 8 or more, $15 per person.

Directions: From Route 7, merge onto Route 9 West (Charles Town Pike). Drive 9.8 miles and turn right onto Harper's Ferry Road (Route 671). Continue 3.1 miles to the winery entrance on right.

Walsh Family Wine
16031 Hillsboro Road
Purcellville VA 20132

Hours: Daily 12:00–6:00
Closed New Year's, Thanksgiving, Christmas

540-668-6248
www.walshfamilywine.com
E-mail: info@walshfamilywine.com

Nate and Sarah Walsh founded Walsh Family Wines in 2014, ultimately purchasing the former North Gate Vineyards four years later. The Walshes produce all their wines from grapes grown on the estate or vineyards that Nate manages. The winery offers special dinners, bar takeovers with winemakers from elsewhere in Virginia, and wine-focused educational events. Cheese and charcuterie picnic baskets and other light food is available at the winery. Seating is available both indoors as well as on the patio; tables are also scattered on the grounds. The facilities can be rented for private events. Children and leashed dogs are welcome.

White Wines: Chardonnay, Petit Manseng, Sauvignon Blanc, Viognier.

Rosé Wines: Rosé.

Red Wines: En Passant, Loudoun County Cuvée, Merlot, Petit Verdot, Tannat, What Will The Women Drink.

Price Range: $28–$35

Tastings: $10 per person for a self-guided flight.

Groups: Reservations required for groups of 8 or more.

Restrictions: No smoking permitted; no groups on Saturdays.

ADA accessible.

Purchasing: Online to AK, AL, AZ, CA, CO, DC, FL, GA, HI, IA, ID, IL, IN, KS, LA, MA, MD, ME, MN, MO, NC, ND, NE, NH, NM, NV, NY, OH, OR, PA, SC, TN, TX, VA, WA, WI, WV, and WY.

Directions: From Route 7, merge west onto Route 9 (Charles Town Pike). Drive 7.6 miles and turn left onto Hillsboro Road (Route 690). The winery will be on the right in 1.7 miles.

The Wine Reserve At Waterford
38516 Charles Town Pike
Waterford VA 20197

Hours: F 2:00–6:00, Sa–Su 11:30–6:00
Closed New Year's, Easter, Christmas

540-692-9463
www.waterfordwinereserve.com
E-mail: contact@waterfordwinereserve.com

Jon and Cori Phillips purchased the former Loudoun Valley Vineyards, one of the oldest in Loudoun County, in late 2016, and reopened under its current name. Self-guided tastings feature their own Virginia-grown wines as well as wines from elsewhere in Virginia or from out-of-state. Both the tasting room and deck offer beautiful views of the valleys and hills to the west. The Wine Reserve often sponsors live music and light snacks; guests may also bring their own food. Supervised children and leashed pets are welcome. Reservations recommended for indoor seating.

White Wines: Chardonnay, First Harvest *(Petit Manseng)*, Home Sweet Home.

Red Wines: Leap *(Cabernet Franc)*, Meritage, Tenacity *(Petit Verdot)*.

Price Range: $24–$38

Tastings: $12 per person for a self-guided flight.

Groups: Reservations required for groups of 8 or more.

Directions: From Route 7, merge onto Route 9 West (Charles Town Pike). Drive 5 miles to the winery's gravel drive on the right.

Handy Guide to Virginia Wineries

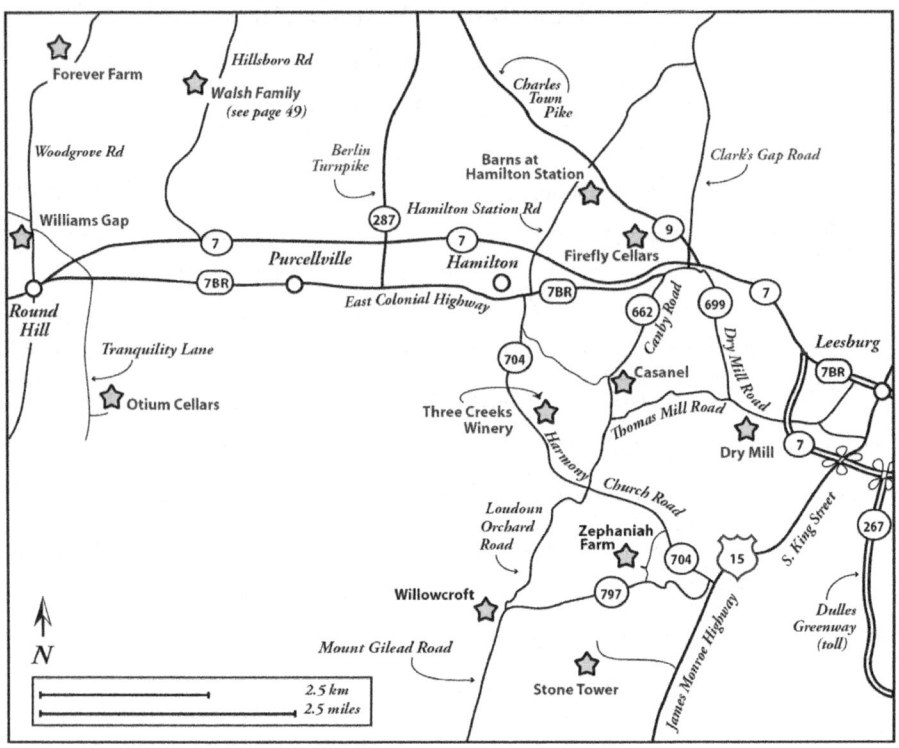

Map 3.4. Leesburg West

LEESBURG WEST

The Barns at Hamilton Stations
16804 Hamilton Station Road
Hamilton, VA 20158

Hours: Th –Su, holiday M 11:00–5:30
Closed New Year's Eve & Day, Easter,
Thanksgiving, Christmas Eve & Day

540-338-5309
www.thebarnsathamiltonstation.com
E-mail: info@thebarnsathamiltonstation.com

    The Barns at Hamilton Station is under the ownership of Andrew and Marianne Fialdini, with Michael Shaps as winemaker. Located on an old dairy farm, the winery's tasting room is in a restored two-story barn that can be rented for weddings and parties. Wines are made from their own vineyards and from a leased vineyard near Charlottesville. The Barns features live music on select Friday evenings and offers a range of cheeses, spreads, and meats for purchase in the tasting room. Leashed dogs are welcome.

White Wines: Bank Barn White, Cascina, Chardonnay, Petit Manseng, Viognier.

Rosé Wines: Rosé.

Red Wines: Bank Barn Red, Harmony, Meritage, Petit Verdot.

Price Range: $24–$42

Tastings: $10–$15 per person for self-guided tasting flights.

Groups: Reservations required for groups of 8 or more; $15 per person fee.

Restrictions: No limo or bus parking; no groups over 15 without rental.

ADA accessible.

Purchasing: Online to AL, AK, AZ, CA, CO, DC, FL, GA, HI, IA, ID, IL, IN, KS, LA, MA, MD, ME, MN, MO, NC, ND, NE, NH, NM, NV, NY, OH, OR, PA, SC, TN, TX, VA, WA, WI, WV, and WY.

Directions: From Leesburg, take Route 7 West and drive 7 miles. Take the Hamilton exit and then turn left onto VA Route 704. Drive 0.7 miles to the winery entrance on the right.

Casanel Vineyards
17956 Canby Road
Leesburg VA 20175

Hours: F–M 11:00–5:30 (Apr–Nov)
F–M 12:00–5:00 (Dec–Mar)
Closed New Year's, Easter, July 4th, Thanksgiving, mid-Dec to mid-Jan

540-751-1776
www.casanelvineyards.com
E-mail: info@casanelvineyards.com

Nelson and the late Casey DeSouza opened Casanel Vineyards to the public in 2008, several years after Nelson, a native of Brazil, retired as head of DeSouza Construction. Casanel's 40 scenic acres include a winery pond and tranquil picnic area overlooking the vines. Casanel also sponsors special events, including live music on summer weekends, food trucks, and occasional Paint-N-Sip classes. Children and leashed pets are welcome; children must remain with adults. Military service personnel receive a 10% discount. Adults only at the yellow barn's Dawson Room and side decks.

Sparkling Wines: Red Spark *(Norton)*.

White Wines: Chardonnay, Elleana, Patricia Marie.

Rosé Wines: José Rosé.

Red Wines: Cabernet Sauvignon, K2, Petit Verdot, Red Blend.

Fortified Wines: The Full Nelson (*port-style*).

Price Range: $20–$50

Tastings: $10–$15 per person.

Groups: Reservations required for groups of 8 or more (including children); deposit required. Reservations required for buses and limos.

ADA accessible.

Purchasing: Online to AL, AK, AZ, CA, CO, DC, FL, GA, HI, IA, ID, IL, IN, KS, LA, MA, MD, ME, MN, MO, NC, ND, NE, NH, NM, NV, NY, OH, OR, PA, SC, TN, TX, VA, WA, WI, WV, and WY.

Directions: From Leesburg, drive on Route 7 West and take the Route 9 exit (Charles Town Pike). At the roundabout, take the exit onto East Colonial Highway (Business Route 7). Drive ½ mile and turn left onto Canby Road (portions unpaved). The winery will be 1.4 miles on the left.

Dry Mill Vineyards & Winery
18195 Dry Mill Road
Leesburg VA 20175

Hours: Tu–W 1:00–5:00; F–Sa 12:00–7:00; Su 12:00–6:00
Closed New Year's, Easter,
Thanksgiving, Christmas

703-737-3930
www.drymillwine.com
E-mail: info@drymillwine.com

Dry Mill Vineyards & Winery opened its doors in early 2009 in the renovated stable and barn of the former Loudoun Hunt Club. Owners Dean and Nancy Vanhuss source their wines from the Short Hill Vineyards near Lovettsville, with winemaking under the guidance of Karen Reed. The tasting room offers a pleasant setting in which to enjoy Dry Mill's wines, including a fireplace, verandas overlooking the grounds, and a patio that seats up to 30. Light fare is available for purchase. The winery offers live music on weekends. Leashed dogs are welcome.

White Wines: Chardonnay, Traminette, Viognier.

Rosé Wines: Chambourcin Rosé.

Red Wines: Cabernet Sauvignon, Chambourcin, Merlot, Norton.

Sweet/Dessert Wines: Sweet Stallion.

Price Range: $18–$25

Tastings: $14 for a flight.

Groups: Reservations required for groups of 6 or more.

ADA accessible.

Directions: From Leesburg, drive south on U.S. Route 15 (King Street) and turn west onto Catoctin Circle SE. Drive about ½ mile and turn left onto Dry Mill Road SW. The winery entrance will be two miles on the left.

Firefly Cellars
40325 Charles Town Pike
Hamilton VA 20158

Hours: Th 12:00–6:00; F 12:00–7:00;
Sa 11:00–7:00; Su 12:00–6:00
Closed New Year's, Christmas

703-314-5650
https://fireflycellars.com
E-mail: andrea@fireflycellars.com

Longtime Loudoun County business owners Andrea Zaidi and brother Zach Pierleonardi purchased the former Hunters Run Wine Barn in late 2020, converting it into Firefly Cellars and renovating the tasting room and cellar. All the wines are estate-grown, with Randy Phillips (*Cave Ridge Vineyard*) serving as winemaker. Firefly has expanded the outdoor seating available, with tables and chairs scattered across the property. The winery features live music and food trucks on many weekends. Charcuterie and cheese boards are available for sale. Children and well-behaved dogs are welcome.

Firefly Cellars offers a one-bedroom cottage for rental on AirBNB; see the website for more details.

White Wines: Chardonnay, Riesling, Traminette, Viognier.

Rosé Wines: Rosé.

Red Wines: Cabernet Franc, Chambourcin, Gypsy Red, Wine Barn Red.

Fortified Wines: Todd's *(port-style)*.

Price Range: $26–$35

Tastings: $11 per person.

Groups: Reservations recommended for groups of 8 or more.

Directions: From Route 7, merge onto Route 9 West (Charles Town Pike) and drive 1.2 miles to the winery entrance on the left.

Forever Farm and Vineyard
15779 Woodgrove Road
Purcellville VA 20132

Hours: Sa–Su 12:00–6:00 (late spring–early fall)
Closed late fall–early spring

540-822-0954
www.foreverfarmandvineyard.com
E-mail: winery@foreverfarmandvineyard.com

Bob and Teri Riggs opened their farm winery near Hillsboro after Bob retired from a 40-plus-year career as an executive in the canning industry. Forever Farm offers wines made mostly from estate- and Virginia-grown grapes, with Bob as winemaker. Their signature Boykin Blend red is named in honor of their beloved Boykin Spaniels; one dollar from each bottle sold goes to benefit the Boykin Spaniel Rescue. Children are welcome but must be accompanied by an adult at all times. Special dog days and events are also scheduled; see the winery's Facebook page for dates. Some seating is available inside the tasting room, with multiple tables and chairs scattered under the trees and verandas.

White Wines: Chardonel, White Oak Blend.

Rosé Wines: Forever Blush.

Red Wines: Boykin Blend, Cabernet Franc, Chambourcin, Pinot Noir.

Price Range: $23–$30

Tastings: $12 per person for self-guided; $25 for winemaker-guided.

Directions: From Purcellville, take Route 7 (Business) west for 6.5 miles to the village of Round Hill. Turn right onto Evening Star Drive and continue about one mile to Woodgrove Road (VA Route 719). Drive 2.8 miles to the winery entrance on the left.

Otium Cellars
18050 Tranquility Lane
Purcellville VA 20132

Hours: Th–M 11:00–5:00 (6:00 in summer) 540-338-2027
Closed New Year's, Thanksgiving, Christmas www.otiumcellars.com
E-mail: contact@otiumcellars.com

Originally founded by Gerhard Bauer in May 2012, Otium Cellars is now owned by Anita Tanamala, a longtime Loudoun County resident and horse lover, with Max Bauer as winemaker. The two-story tasting room offers seating on both levels indoors, with a two-sided wood stove that adds a cozy touch on chilly days. Outdoor seating is available on the patio and grounds, as well as the outdoor pavilion. Sandwiches and hot pretzels are offered on weekends. The pavilion next to the tasting room may be rented for parties or special events. Leashed dogs are welcome outdoors. Adults only, please.

White Wines: Chardonnay, Grüner Veltliner, Pinot Gris.

Red Wines: Blaufränkisch, Cabernet Sauvignon, Dornfelder, Malbec, Merlot.

Price Range: $20–$36

Tastings: $12 per person.

Groups: Reservations required; groups of 8 or more.

ADA accessible (some limitations).

Directions: From Route 7, take the Route 7 Business exit at Round Hill. Drive east for 1.3 miles toward Purcellville and turn right at Tranquility Road (portions unpaved). Continue another 1.8 miles to the winery entrance on the left.

Stone Tower Winery
19925 Hogback Mountain Road
Leesburg VA 20175

Hours: Th–M 11:00–6:00
Closed Easter, Thanksgiving, Christmas

703-777-2797
www.stonetowerwinery.com
E-mail: reservations@stonetowerwinery.com

Stone Tower is on a 300-acre estate owned by Michael and Kristi Huber, who opened their winery in 2013. The winery has an expansive events building as well as a two-story tasting room that are both popular weekend destinations for wine lovers who may purchase a range of light snacks and food. The tasting room opens onto a sloping lawn with a beautiful view of the winery's vineyards. The winery may be rented for weddings or private events. The Tower View Tasting Room is for adults only (reservations recommended), while the Harvest Barn is family-friendly. Leashed dogs are welcome on the grounds.

Sparkling Wines: Rosé Cuvée, Wild Boar Blanc de Blanc.

White Wines: Chardonnay, Riesling, Sauvignon Blanc, Viognier.

Rosé Wines: Rosé.

Red Wines: Cabernet Franc, Cabernet Sauvignon, Hogback Mountain, Nebbiolo, Petit Verdot, Pinot Noir, Pursuit, Wind Swept Hill.

Price Range: $28–$69

Tastings: $15 per person.

Groups: Reservations required; no groups over 6.

Purchasing: Shipping to many states; see website for details.

Directions: From Leesburg, drive south on Route 15 for 4.5 miles. Turn right onto Hogback Mountain Road and continue 1.4 miles to the winery on the left.

Three Creeks Winery
18548 Harmony Church Road
Hamilton VA 20158

Hours: Th–Su 11:00–5:30 (Apr to mid-Dec)　　540-369-4655
Closed mid-Dec to early Mar　　www.3creekswinery.com
　　E-mail: 3creekswinery@gmail.com

Three Creeks Winery was opened in 2020 by John and P-J Lawrence on their Loudoun County farm overlooking the three creeks that inspired the winery's name. After working with Ashton Lough at Vint Hill Farms for several years, the Lawrences decided to branch out and establish a winery of their own, with Lough as winemaker. All their wines are made from Virginia-grown fruit, including a Rappahannock County vineyard the Lawrences manage. Well-behaved leashed dogs are welcome but may not play in the water. Reservations are recommended on weekends. Adults only, please.

White Wines: Chardonnay, Petit Manseng, Vidal Blanc, Viognier.

Rosé Wines: Rosé.

Red Wines: Cabernet Franc, Cabernet Sauvignon, GSM *(Grenache, Syrah, Mourvèdre)*, Mélange Rouge, Petit Verdot, Pinot Noir.

Price Range: $26–$42

Tastings: $10 per person.

Purchasing: Shipping to Virginia only.

Directions: Take U.S. Route 15 South from Leesburg for 3 miles. Turn right onto Harmony Church Road (Route 704). After 3.5 miles, turn right onto Yellowwood Road and the winery entrance on the left.

Williams Gap Vineyards
35521 Sexton Farm Lane
Round Hill VA 20141

Hours: F–Su, hol M 11:00–7:00;
Th 12:00–6:00 (Aug)
Closed New Year's, Christmas

540-440-1933
www.williamsgapvineyard.com
E-mail: info@williamsgapvineyard.com

Jack and Jeanne Sexton opened Williams Gap Vineyards in mid-2021 after selling grapes from their 30-acre vineyard for over a decade. The two-story tasting room offers seating both indoors as well as outside on the veranda and covered pavilion. Visitors can choose a cheese or charcuterie board, or a catered Sunday brunch on the first Sunday of each month. Williams Gap hosts a range of events, including live music on many weekends and winemaker dinners. The facilities may be rented for private events.

White Wines: Petit Manseng, Vidal Blanc, White Blend.

Red Wines: Cabernet Franc, Merlot, Red Blend.

Price Range: $26–$40

Tastings: $15–$20 per person for a wine flight.

Groups: Reservations required for groups of 10 or more.

Directions: From Purcellville, take Route 7 (Business) west for 6.5 miles to the village of Round Hill. Turn right onto Evening Star Drive and continue about one mile. Turn right onto Woodgrove Road (VA Route 719), then left into the winery drive (portions unpaved) on the left. Continue 0.75 miles to the tasting room.

Willowcroft Farm Vineyards
38906 Mount Gilead Road
Leesburg VA 20175

Hours: F–M 11:00–5:30
Closed New Year's, Christmas

703-777-8161
www.willowcroftwine.com
E-mail: visit@willowcroftwine.com

Willowcroft, the oldest winery in Loudoun County, was founded in 1979 by owner-winemaker Lew Parker. The tasting room is in a weathered barn that predates the Civil War; light food is available for purchase. The winery grounds include picnic tables and a one-mile walking trail with beautiful views of Loudoun Valley. Willowcroft offers occasional events, such as turkey chili weekends and an Oktoberfest. Supplies and seminars for home winemakers are also available. Children and pets are welcome.

Fruit Wines: Applause.

Handy Guide to Virginia Wineries

White Wines: Albariño, Chardonnay, Harmony, Petit Manseng, Riesling-Muscat, Seyval Blanc, Traminette, Vidal Blanc.

Rosé Wines: Rose of Sharon.

Red Wines: Assemblage *(Bordeaux-style blend)*, Cabernet Franc, Cabernet Sauvignon, Chambourcin, Merlot, Petit Verdot.

Price Range: $20–$42

Tastings: $10 per person for a wine flight.

Groups: Reservations required for groups of 7 or more, $15 per person fee; groups of 10 or more, $15 per person plus $50 per hour. No groups after 2:00 p.m.

Purchasing: Online to AL, AK, CA, CO, DC, FL, GA, HI, IA, ID, IL, IN, KS, LA, MD, ME, MN, MO, NC, ND, NE, NH, NM, NV, NY, OH, OR, PA, SC, TN, TX, VA, WA, WI, WV, and WY.

Directions: Take U.S. Route 15 South from Leesburg for 3 miles. Turn right onto Harmony Church Road (Route 704) and drive 2.3 miles. Turn left on Loudoun Orchard Road (portions unpaved) and drive another 2.3 miles. Turn right onto Mt. Gilead Road and the winery on the right.

Zephaniah Farm Vineyard
19381 Dunlop Mill Road
Leesburg VA 20175

Hours: F–Su 12:00–5:30 (Apr to mid-Dec)
Closed mid-Dec to early Mar

703-431-1994
http://zephwine.com
E-mail: bonnie@zephwine.com

Zephaniah Farm Vineyard is on a 376-acre working farm that has been in the Hatch family for three generations. Owners Bill and Bonnie Hatch planted their first vines in 2002 and produced their first vintage six years later; Bill and son Tremaine are the winemakers. Zephaniah's tasting barn is next to the family's historic manor house that was constructed by the builder of President James Monroe's Oak Hill. Tastings are held in the barn as well as on the shaded outdoor seating next to the facilities. Adults only, please.

White Wines: Adeline, Chardonnay, Steamship White, Vermentino, Viognier.

Rosé Wines: Rosé.

Red Wines: Cabernet Franc, Cabernet Sauvignon, Chambourcin, Three Captains Red.

Price Range: $20–$27

Tastings: $15 per person.

Groups: No groups over 6.

Purchasing: Online to AL, AK, CA, CO, DC, FL, GA, HI, IA, ID, IL, IN, KS, LA, MD, ME, MN, MO, NC, ND, NE, NH, NM, NV, NY, OH, OR, PA, SC, TN, TX, VA, WA, WI, WV, and WY.

Directions: Take U.S. Route 15 South from Leesburg for 3 miles. Turn right onto Harmony Church Road (Route 704). After one mile, turn left onto Dunlop Mill Road (portions unpaved) and the winery ½ mile on the right.

Handy Guide to Virginia Wineries

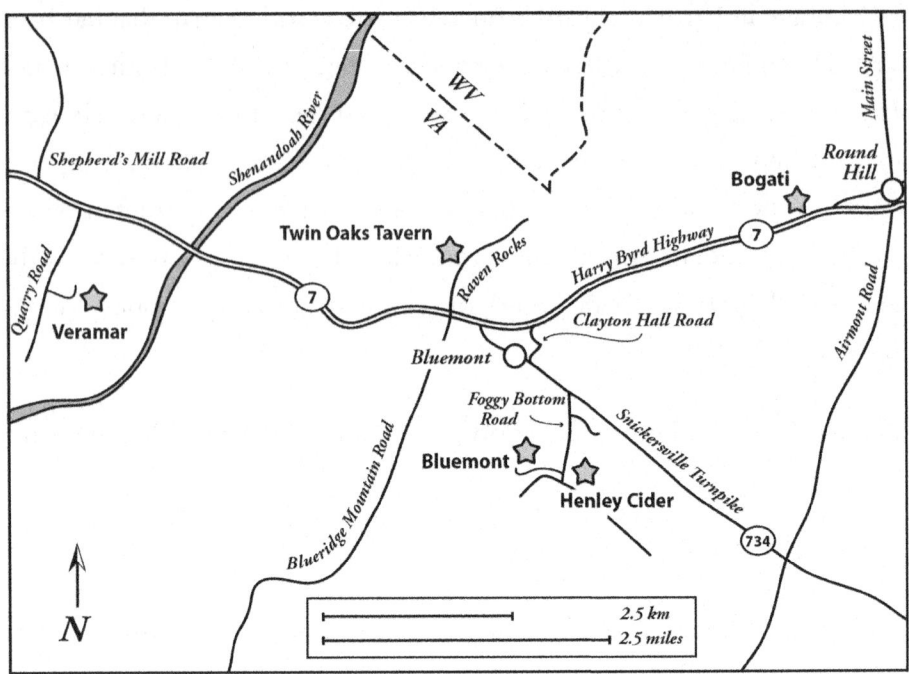

Map 3.5. Bluemont

Northern Virginia Region & Middleburg AVA

BLUEMONT

Bluemont Vineyard
18755 Foggy Bottom Road
Bluemont VA 20135

Hours: Daily 11:00–7:00 (F, Sa to 9:00) (Apr–Oct)
Th–Su 11:00–5:00 (Nov–Mar)
Closed New Year's, Thanksgiving, Christmas

540-554-8439
www.bluemontvineyard.com
E-mail: cheers@bluemontvineyard.com

Bluemont Vineyard is Loudoun County's highest winery, located on the eastern side of the Blue Ridge Mountains at 951 feet above sea level. The winery sources its grapes both from its own vines and from other vineyards in the area. The main tasting area is upstairs in the two-story tasting room and features a wide deck with panoramic views toward Leesburg and Washington, D.C. The winery offers gourmet snacks and flatbreads, as well as early brunch on weekends; outside food is not permitted inside the facilities. Children and leashed pets are welcome. Reservations required on weekends, two-hour limit.

Bluemont has four cottages for rent on the property, from a studio to a three-bedroom house. Check the website for rental details.

Sparkling Wines: Sparkling Rosé *(Chambourcin)*, Peach *(with Vidal Blanc)*.

White Wines: Albariño, Ascent White, Chardonnay, Petit Manseng, Vidal Blanc, Viognier.

Rosé Wines: Rosé.

Red Wines: Ascent Red, Cabernet Franc, Cabernet Sauvignon, Chambourcin, Meritage, Merlot, Petit Verdot.

Sweet/Dessert Wines: Petit Manseng.

Fortified: Norton *(port-style)*.

Price Range: $25–$40

Tastings: $15 per person.

Groups: Maximum group size of 10, $30 table reservation fee.

Restrictions: No full-sized buses; club members only on front decks.

Purchasing: Online to AL, AK, CA, CO, DC, FL, GA, HI, IA, ID, IL, IN, KS, LA, MD, ME, MN, MO, NC, ND, NE, NH, NM, NV, NY, OH, OR, PA, SC, TN, TX, VA, WA, WI, WV, and WY.

Directions: From Route 7, turn onto Clayton Hall Road (Route 760 South) toward the town of Bluemont. Take the first left onto Snickersville Turnpike and then turn at the first right onto Foggy Bottom Road to the winery driveway, ½ mile on the right. Continue up the hill to the parking lot.

Bogati Winery
35246 Harry Byrd Highway
Round Hill VA 20142

Hours: M–Th 1:00–5:00 (6:00 in summer);	540-338-1144
F 12:00–8:00, Sa 12:00–7:00, Su 12:00–5:00	www.bogatiwinery.com
Closed New Year's, Easter, Thanksgiving, Christmas	E-mail: info@bogatiwinery.com

Bogati Winery was established in 2010 by the Bogaty family, which also owns Veramar and James Charles. Justin Bogaty serves as winemaker for all three, using grapes grown at Veramar for production. The Bogatys decided to open the Bogati Winery after a family trip to Argentina, where they were inspired by that wine-producing country. Bogati Winery also sells a range of small plates, including charcuterie platters, truffle fries, and flatbread pizzas. Guests can choose between indoor seating and outdoors on the deck. The tasting room is available for rental for parties and special events.

White Wines: Seyval Blanc, Tango Blu, Vidal Blanc.

Rosé Wines: JB Rosé.

Red Wines: Fat*ss Red, Terracotta, Malbec.

Price Range: $23–$38

Tastings: $12 per person for classic; $8–$10 for self-guided flights.

Groups: Reservations required for groups up to 10.

ADA accessible.

Purchasing: Online purchasing available to AK, CA, DC, FL, and VA.

Directions: From Leesburg, take Route 7 West for 15 miles. The winery will be on the right at the Hill High Orchard Building, about ¾ mile past Airmont Road/Main Street in the village of Round Hill.

Henway Hard Cider
18780 Foggy Bottom Road
Bluemont VA 20135

Hours: Daily 11:00–6:00
Closed New Year's, Thanksgiving, Christmas

540-837-4000
www.henwayhardcider.com
E-mail: cheers@henwayhardcider.com

Henway Hard Cider was launched in 2019 by the Zurschmeide family to complement their nearby Bluemont Vineyards. Visitors can choose a tasting flight as well as foods from the "Bird Bites" menu, which features charcuterie, pretzels, cheese, and crackers, as well as soft drinks and non-alcoholic cider. Henley sponsors public events on weekends, including cider festivals and live music. The property is available for rental for private events. Children and well-behaved dogs are welcome.

Hard Ciders: Brut, Blood Orange, Blueberry Lavender, Coop, Peach, Strawberry, Strawberry Hibiscus.

Price Range: $7–$25, depending on size

Tastings: $12 per person.

Restrictions: No outside foods.

From Route 7, turn onto Clayton Hall Road (Route 760 South) toward the town of Bluemont. Take the first left onto Snickersville Turnpike and then turn at the first right onto Foggy Bottom Road. The cidery will be 0.7 miles on the left.

Twin Oaks Tavern Winery
18035 Raven Rocks Road
Bluemont VA 20135

Hours: Th–M 1:00–6:00, (F–Sa til 7:00 in summer) 202-255-5009, 540-554-4547
Closed New Year's, Thanksgiving, Christmas   www.twinoakstavernwinery.com
                               E-mail: info@twinoakstavernwinery.com

Twin Oaks Tavern Winery is housed in a restored 100-year-old stone tavern of the same name at the northern edge of the Blue Ridge. Owner Donna Evers and her late husband Bob first planted their vineyard in 1999, opening to the public in 2008. The tasting room is in a small restored outbuilding next to a comfortable deck where visitors can enjoy wine and food over a magnificent view of the Shenandoah Valley below. Events include live music on Saturday afternoons. The property is available for rental for small private events and weddings. Children and pets are welcome.

Fruit Wines: Raspberry.

White Wines: Chardonnay, Vidal Blanc, White Nights.

Red Wines: Cabernet Sauvignon, Merlot, Raven Rocks Red.

Price Range: $26–$28

Tastings: $12 per person.

Groups: Reservations required for groups over 6.

Directions: From Leesburg, drive west on Route 7 about 15 miles. Just past the village of Bluemont, turn right onto Raven Rocks Road to the winery, ⅓ mile on the left.

Veramar Vineyard
905 Quarry Road
Berryville VA 22611

Hours: Daily 12:00–5:00 (Sa to 7:00)   540-955-5510
Closed New Year's, Thanksgiving, Christmas   www.veramar.com
E-mail: info@veramar.com

Jim and Della Bogaty opened Veramar Vineyard in 2001 on their 100-acre property bordering the Shenandoah River. Veramar's estate-grown wines are produced under the supervision of son Justin Bogaty. The tasting room opens onto a covered deck overlooking a pond and the hills beyond, with ample outdoor seating. The winery is named after the Vera-Mar Steakhouse in North Carolina, where Jim and Della dined during their honeymoon. Veramar hosts various special events, including Friday evening "Wine Downs" and an annual Taste of Tuscany. Breads, cheeses, and other snacks are available for purchase. The facilities are available for weddings and private events. Children and pets are welcome.

White Wines: Chardonnay, Riesling, Seyval Blanc, Viognier.

Rosé Wines: Pink Chicken.

Red Wines: Cabernet Franc, Merlot, Rooster Red *(Bordeaux-style blend)*.

Sweet/Dessert Wines: D'Oro *(Vidal Blanc)*.

Price Range: $24–$36

Tastings: $10 per person; $15 for reserve tasting with food pairings (first Saturday of each month only, reservations requested).

Groups: Reservations and prepayment required for groups of 10 or more; $18 per person fee.

Purchasing: Online to AK, CA, DC, FL, IN, KS, MO, NV, and VA.

Directions: From Leesburg, take Route 7 West for 22 miles. Past the Shenandoah River, turn left onto Quarry Road (Route 612). Continue one mile to the winery driveway (portions unpaved) on the left.

PHYLLOXERA

While Europe's grapes are from *Vitis vinifera*, native American grapevines are members of different *Vitis* species, including *Vitis labrusca*, *Vitis aestivalis*, or *Vitis riparia*. American grape varieties excel at producing table grapes or grape juice, but not all are well-suited for wine. Many have strong flavors, and some have a smell that professional wine tasters refer to as "foxiness," a colorful and self-explanatory term.

Native American rootstocks were at the origin of Europe's greatest vineyard crisis though they also proved to be the salvation of *V. vinifera*.

The mid-nineteenth century was a time of expanding interest in science, including botany, and wealthy Europeans brought back samples of American rootstocks for gardens and greenhouses. Unfortunately, those rootstocks also brought with them the almost microscopic phylloxera louse, which was (and still is) endemic to much of the United States. American grapevines had built up a resistance to phylloxera, but *V. vinifera* is highly vulnerable to phylloxera infestation. Europe's vineyards soon began dying off in an agricultural disaster second only to the Irish potato blight of the 1840s in terms of its impact.

In the 1870s, an American and a French scientist together found a solution. French scientist Jules Planchon was the first to identify the tiny phylloxera louse as the cause of the devastation spreading throughout European vineyards. Missouri state entomologist Charles Riley then uncovered a vital link by identifying the French louse as identical to the American one. Planchon came to Missouri in 1873 to study under Riley's guidance, and the two developed a new approach of grafting *vinifera* vines onto American rootstocks.

Today, roughly 85 percent of *vinifera* vines worldwide have been grafted onto native American rootstocks. Because phylloxera finds very dry and/or sandy soils inhospitable, however, ungrafted vines are still cultivated in such regions as South Australia, New Zealand, and Chile.

Handy Guide to Virginia Wineries

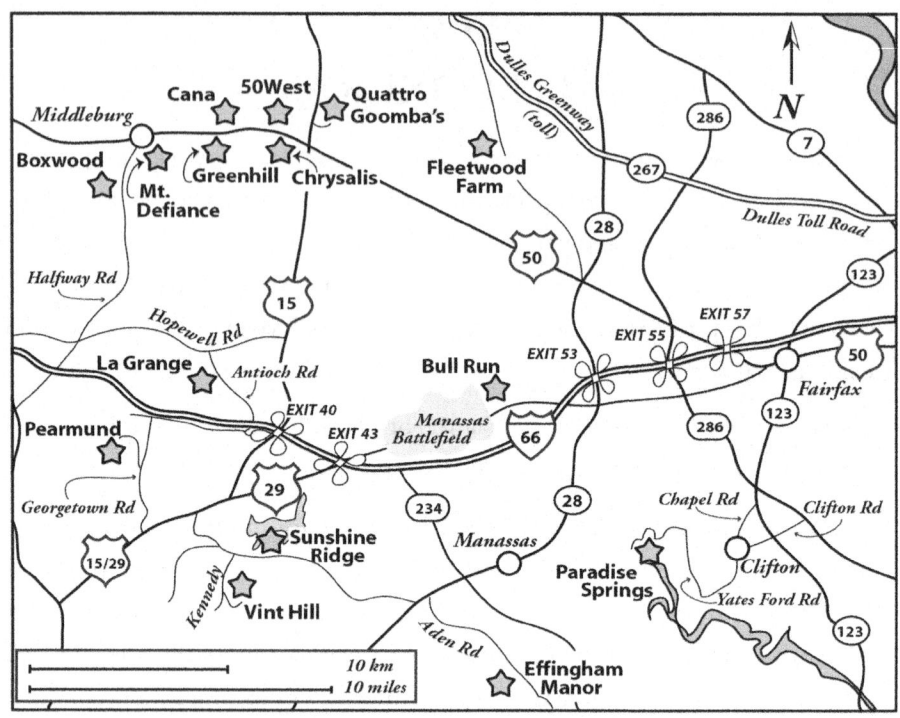

Map 3.6. Middleburg-Fairfax

MIDDLEBURG-FAIRFAX

50 West Vineyards
39060 John Mosby Highway
Middleburg VA 20117

Hours: F 12:00–6:00, Sa–Su 11:00–6:00
Closed New Year's, Christmas

571-367-4760
www.50westvineyards.com
E-mail: information@50westvineyards.com

50 West Vineyards is the sister winery to Sunset Hills, opening in August 2015 on the slopes of a hill just east of Middleburg. The primary tasting room is in a renovated two-story stable, called the Tack Room, with seating and tasting bars on both levels; the downstairs opens onto a broad patio with tables overlooking the vineyards and Bull Run Hills beyond. Light fare is offered for purchase at the winery. Children and leashed dogs are welcome.

White Wines: Piedmont, Sauvignon Blanc, Petit Manseng.

Rosé Wines: Rosé.

Red Wines: Aldie Heights Cuvée, Chambourcin, Tannat.

Price Range: $25–$40

Tastings: $10 per person for flights.

Groups: Reservations required for groups over 8; no groups over 20.

Directions: From I-66 West, take Exit 57B onto U.S. Route 50 West toward Fair Oaks/Winchester. Continue on U.S. Route 50 for almost 20 miles and turn right into the winery driveway.

Boxwood Winery
2042 Burrland Road
Middleburg VA 20118

Hours: Th–Su 11:00–6:00 (Mar–Nov)
F–Su 11:00–6:00 (Dec–Apr)
Closed New Year's, Thanksgiving, Christmas

540-687-8778
www.boxwoodwinery.com
E-mail: contact@boxwoodwinery.com

Boxwood Winery was founded by John Kent Cooke at the historic Boxwood Estate, one of the earliest farms established in the Middleburg area. Boxwood's wines are all Bordeaux-style reds made with grapes from its 19-acre vineyard; its first white, a Sauvignon Blanc, was introduced in 2017. Tastings are held either inside the small tasting room or outdoors on the patio; club members also can opt for the members-only pavilion on the hill amidst the vines. Cheese plates and bottled water are available for purchase.

White Wines: Sauvignon Blanc, Sauvignon Gris.

Rosé Wines: Rosé.

Red Wines: Reserve, Topiary, Trellis.

Price Range: $22–$45

Tastings: $10 per person for flights.

Groups: Reservations required for groups of 6 or more, $20 per person.

Restrictions: No tour buses permitted; no smoking; no pets.

Purchasing: Online to CA, CO, DC, FL, MD, NC, and VA.

Directions: From I-66, take Exit 40 onto U.S. Route 15 North. Drive about 10 miles and turn onto U.S. Route 50 West. Continue 5 miles into

Middleburg and turn left onto Loudoun Road, which will become Halfway Road. Drive about 1 mile to the winery entrance on the right.

Cana Vineyards & Winery
38600 John Mosby Highway
Middleburg VA 20117

Hours: Th–F, Su–M 12:00–6:00 (F til 8:00 in summer) 703-348-2458
Sa 11:00–6:00   www.canavineyards.com
Closed Thanksgiving, Christmas Eve & Day   E-mail: info@canavineyards.com

First established in 2012 on the grounds of a 47-acre farm just outside of Middleburg, Cana Vineyards is now owned by the Petty and Grant families. The tasting room is sited on a hill, offering a nice view and cooling breezes from the pavilion and decks. Winemaker Melanie Natoli makes Cana's production from estate- and Virginia-grown fruit. Visitors may bring their own picnic lunches to enjoy on the grounds or purchase snacks in the tasting room. The winery sponsors live music on Saturday and Sunday afternoons. The facilities are available for weddings and private parties. Children and leashed dogs are welcome.

Fruit Wines: Blueberry-Apple.

White Wines: Albariño, Chardonnay, Rhapsody in White, Riesling.

Rosé Wines: Rosé.

Red Wines: Cabernet Franc, Chambourcin, Le Mariage, Merlot, Miracle, Rhapsody in Red, Tempranillo.

Fortified Wines: Porta Bella *(port-style)*, Sweet Vermouth.

Price Range: $20–$32

Tastings: $12 per person for self-guided flight.

Groups: Private rental required for groups of 15 or more.

Purchasing: Online to CA, DC, FL, MD, NY, and VA.

ADA accessible.

Directions: From I-66 West, take Exit 57B onto U.S. Route 50 West toward Fair Oaks/Winchester. Continue on U.S. Route 50 for 20 miles and turn right into the winery driveway.

Chrysalis Vineyards
39025 John Mosby Highway
Middleburg VA 20117

Hours: M–Th 12:00–6:00, F–Sa 12:00–8:00, Su 12:00–7:00 (Apr–Oct)   540-687-8222
Daily 12:00–5:00 (Nov–Mar)   www.chrysaliswine.com
Closed New Year's, Thanksgiving, Christmas   E-mail: info@ChrysalisWine.com

Founded in 1998 by Jennifer McCloud, Chrysalis has over 70 acres of vineyards with plantings in over 20 varieties. McCloud has long had a special interest in the Norton grape and actively works to promote a greater appreciation of this native American variety; indeed, Chrysalis has the largest planting of Norton in the country. Tastings of their mostly estate-grown wines are held indoor or outside at five covered stations. On weekends (F–Su), visitors can choose from several wood-fired pizzas, with a panini menu available on weekdays; charcuterie and cheeses from Chrysalis's own Locksley Farm are on offer every day. Last pours begin thirty minutes before closing. The winery's Champe Ford property may be rented for private events.

Sparkling Wines: Buttorfleoge *(Norton)*.

White Wines: Albariño, Petit Manseng, Sarah's Patio White, Snobby Bitch White Sangria, Viognier.

Rosé Wines: Mariposa, Sarah's Patio Red *(Norton)*, Tximeleta.

Red Wines: Nebbiolo, Norton, Petit Verdot, Rubiana, Tannat.

Fortified Wines: Borboleta *(port-style Norton)*.

Price Range: $19–$48

Tastings: $15 per person.

Groups: Reservations required for groups of 8 or more.

Restrictions: Reservations required for tour buses.

ADA accessible.

Directions: From I-66 West, take Exit 57B onto U.S. Route 50 West toward Fair Oaks/Winchester. Continue on U.S. Route 50 for almost 20 miles and turn left into the winery's gravel driveway. Cross the ford and drive up the hill to the tasting room.

Effingham Manor
14325 Trotters Ridge Place
Nokesville VA 20181

Hours: Daily 11:00–6:00   703-594-2300
Closed New Year's, Thanksgiving, Christmas   www.effinghammanor.com

Chris Pearmund founded Effingham Manor in September 2017 on the grounds of a historic 1767-era manor house, with winemaking under the guidance of Ashton Lough, who also serves as winemaker at Three Creeks and The Winery at Bull Run. The winery currently offers both indoor and outdoor seating options. In addition to crackers, meats, and spreads, Effingham sponsors food trucks and catered dinners on select weekends. The property may be rented for weddings and private events.

Sparkling Wines: Sparkling.

White Wines: Celebration, Chardonnay, Traminette, Viognier.

Rosé Wines: Cameo Rosé.

Red Wines: King's Ransom (*Bordeaux-style blend*), Meritage, Merlot, Norton, Tannat.

Price Range: $25–$39

Tastings: $10–$12 for a self-guided flight.

Restrictions: Adults only; no dogs; no buses or large vans.

Directions: From Manassas City at the Prince William Parkway, take Route 28 South for 2.8 miles. Turn left onto Aden Road (VA 646). Continue to follow Route 646 for 6.5 miles in all. Turn right onto Trotters Ridge Place. The winery entrance will be 0.5 miles on the left.

Fleetwood Farm Winery
23075 Evergreen Mills Road
Leesburg VA 20175

Hours: Th, Su 12:00–6:00, F–Sa, 12:00–8:00 (summer)   703-722-2124
F–Su 12:00–6:00 (winter)   www.fleetwoodfarmwinery.com
Closed New Year's, Thanksgiving, Christmas   E-mail: jeff@fleetwoodfarmwinery.com

Fleetwood Farm opened in 2018 on the grounds of a manor house dating from the mid-1700s. The large, modern tasting room offers seating both indoors as well as on the wraparound porch and surrounding patios. The winery offers light snacks and frequently has food trucks on weekends. In addition to hosting private parties and weddings, Fleetwood Farm also sponsors a range of creative workshops.

White Wines: Pinot Blanc, Riesling, Tempête Blanche, Viognier.

Red Wines: Cabernet Franc, Cabernet Sauvignon, Ellsey Red.

Price Range: $29–$32

Tastings: $14 per person for a flight.

Groups: Reservations required for groups of 7 or more.

Restrictions: Adults only; no pets, no buses or limos.

Purchasing: Online for winery pickup.

Directions: From the Dulles Greenway (Route 267), take Exit 7 onto the Loudoun County Parkway. Drive south for 1.7 miles, then turn right onto Ryan Road. Continue 3.3 miles before turning left onto Evergreen Mills Road. The winery will be 0.2 miles on the right.

Greenhill Vineyard
23595 Winery Lane
Middleburg VA 20117

Hours: Daily 12:00–6:00 (F–Su until 7:00, May–Sep)
Closed New Year's, Thanksgiving, Christmas

540-687-6968
www.experiencegreenhill.com
E-mail: info@greenhillvineyard.com

David Greenhill purchased the historic 128-acre Valley View Estate, home to the former Swedenburg Estate Winery, and opened to the public in mid-2013. Ben Comstock serves as the winemaker. The tasting room offers seating both indoors and out, with cheeses, cold cuts, and crackers available for purchase. The outdoor tables offer splendid views of the vineyards as well as of the original manor house that now serves as a space for wine club members only. Leashed dogs are welcome outdoors. Adults only, please.

Sparkling Wines: Blanc de Blancs.

White Wines: Chardonnay, Intuition, Petit Manseng, Riesling, Seyval Blanc, Viognier.

Red Wines: Merlot, Petit Verdot, Superstition.

Price Range: $30–$60

Tastings: $14 per person.

Groups: Reservations required for groups of 6 or more; reservations required for buses and limousines at least 48 hours in advance.

Restrictions: Adults only.

Purchasing: Online for all states *except* AL, AR, KY, ME, MO, MT, OK, PA, and SD.

Directions: From I-66, take Exit 57B onto U.S. Route 50 West and drive 21 miles to the winery driveway on the left.

Mt. Defiance Cider
495 E. Washington Street
Middleburg VA 20117

Hours: Tu–Su 12:00–6:00
Closed New Year's, Thanksgiving, Christmas

540-883-3176
www.mtdefiance.com
E-mail: info@mtdefiance.com

Mt. Defiance was launched by Marc Chretien and offers both classic and craft ciders in its Cider Barn, located high on a hilltop on the eastern edge of the historic town of Middleburg. The cider barn offers ample outdoor seating, as well as well-spaced tables indoors. Guests can purchase light snacks or, on select weekends, opt for a food truck menu. Children and leashed pets are welcome.

Mt. Defiance also operates a distillery nearby at 207 W. Washington Street in Middleburg.

Ciders: Farmhouse Style, General's Reserve Hard Cider, Ginger Cider, Blueberry Cider, Old Volstead's Homemade Cider, Summer Shandy.

Fortified Wines: Sweet Vermouth.

Price Range: $7–$18

Tastings: $10–$15 per person, depending on flight selection.

Groups: Reservations required for groups of 10 or more; reservations also required for buses and limousines at least 48 hours in advance.

Purchasing: Online for DC, IL, and VA.

Directions: From I-66, take Exit 57B onto U.S. Route 50 West and drive 22.4 miles to the cider barn on left.

Paradise Springs Winery & Vineyard
13219 Yates Ford Road
Clifton VA 20124

Hours: Daily 11:00–7:00 (F to sunset, Apr–Dec only)
F–Su 11:00–6:00 (Jan–Mar)
Closed New Year's, Easter, Thanksgiving, Christmas

703-830-9463
www.paradisespringswinery.com
E-mail: wine@paradisespringswinery.com

Paradise Springs was founded in 2007 by Jane Kincheloe and her son Kirk Wiles and opened to the public in 2009. The winery sponsors Friday happy hours, live music on weekends, and a pumpkin carving festival in October. The spacious tasting room offers light fare to have either inside or on the covered deck, which features an outdoor fireplace. The facilities are available for rental for private parties and dinners. Leashed dogs are welcome. Please note that last pours begin thirty minutes before closing.

Sparkling Wines: Après *(Viognier)*, Blanc de Blancs.

White Wines: Chardonnay, Petit Manseng, Sommet Blanc, Vidal Blanc, Viognier.

Rosé Wines: Nana's Rosé.

Red Wines: Cabernet Franc, Cabernet Sauvignon, Mélange, Meritage, Norton, Petit Verdot, The Moment, PVT, Tannat.

Fortified Wines: Late Harvest Vidal Blanc, Swagger *(port-style)*.

Price Range: $29–$55

Tastings: $15 per person for a flight.

Groups: Reservations required for groups over 10; and for buses, vans, and limos.

ADA accessible.

Restrictions: Adults only; no groups over 10 indoors; no groups over 30 outside; no buses or large vans after 3:00.

Purchasing: Online to AK, AL, CA, DC, FL, ID, IL, LA, MN, MO, NC, ND, NE, NH, NM, NV, OH, OR, VA, WV, and WY..

Directions: From I-66, take Exit 55 onto southbound Fairfax County Parkway (Route 286 South). Drive about 5 miles and take the exit for Route 123 South. Turn right at the second traffic light onto Clifton Road (Route 645). Turn left onto Yates Ford Road before entering the village of Clifton and drive 1.7 miles to the winery on left.

Pearmund Cellars
6190 Georgetown Road
Broad Run VA 20137

Hours: Daily 10:00–6:00   540-347-3475
Closed New Year's, Easter, Thanksgiving, Christmas   www.pearmundcellars.com
                               E-mail: info@pearmundcellars.com

Chris Pearmund founded Pearmund Cellars in 2003 after selling grapes to regional wineries from his 25-acre Meriwether Vineyard for a number of years. All of Pearmund's wines are made from Virginia-grown fruit. The winery sponsors a number of special events, including TGIF nights, Girls Night Out, winemaker dinners, and an SPCA fundraiser. The barrel room is available for rental for parties and dinners. Adults over 21 only, except at the Farmstore, a 19th-century house next to the winery.

White Wines: Chardonnay, Palindrome, Petit Manseng, Riesling, Viognier.

Rosé Wines: Cameo Rosé.

Handy Guide to Virginia Wineries

Red Wines: Ameritage, Black Ops, Cabernet Franc, Merlot, Petit Verdot.

Sweet/Dessert Wines: Late Harvest Petit Manseng, Late Harvest Traminette.

Price Range: $20–$39

Tastings: $12 per person for a flight; $15 per person for guided tastings.

Groups: Reservations required for groups of 6 or more.

ADA accessible.

Directions: From I-66, take Exit 43A (Gainesville/Warrenton) onto U.S. Route 29 South. Drive 7.5 miles and take a right onto Old Alexandria Turnpike, staying straight to go onto Georgetown Road (Route 674) after ¼ mile. The long winery driveway (portions unpaved) will be one mile on the left.

Quattro Goomba's Winery
22860 James Monroe Highway
Aldie VA 20105

Hours: W–M 12:00–6:00 (F to 9:00 in summer) 703-327-6052
Closed New Year's, Thanksgiving, Christmas www.goombawine.com
E-mail: qgw@goombawine.com

Quattro Goomba's is a micro-commercial winery that sources its wines from Virginia and other grape-growing states and countries. After sampling wines, visitors can stay over a glass or bottle and enjoy freshly baked Sicilian-style pizza by the slice at one of the winery's indoor tasting tables or outdoors on the grounds. Quattro Goomba's offers live music on weekends and can be rented for weddings and private parties. Children and leashed dogs are welcome. The winery also offers a brewery on site.

White Wines: Piney River White, Sorelle *(Washington state)*, Viognier.

Rosé Wines: Piney River Rosé.

Red Wines: Curico *(Chile)*, Petit Verdot, Piney River Red, Red Blend, Tradizione, Vino di Nonni *(California)*.

Sweet/Dessert Wines: Vino Dolce.

Price Range: $26–$35

Tastings: $30 per group of 2–8 people, by reservation only.

ADA accessible.

Restrictions: No large groups, buses, or limos with prior rental reservations.

Purchasing: Online ordering for CA, DC, FL, MN, NC, and VA.

Directions: From I-66, take Exit 57B onto U.S. Route 50 West. Follow U.S. Route 50 West for 17 miles through one roundabout. At the second roundabout, take the exit onto James Monroe Highway (U.S. Route 15 North) and drive 1.2 miles to the winery on right.

Vint Hill Craft Winery
7150 Lineweaver Road
Warrenton VA 20187

Hours: W–Su, holiday M 12:00–6:00
Closed New Year's, Thanksgiving, Christmas

540-351-0000
www.vinthillcraftwinery.com
E-mail: info@craftwinery.com

Vint Hill is a custom-crush winery that offers customers a unique opportunity to design and produce a half or full barrel of wine under the guidance of experienced winemakers. Founded in 2009 by Chris Pearmund (Pearmund Cellars) and Ray Summerell, the winery is housed in a restored 1900 dairy barn at Vint Hill Farms, once a secure listening post run by the U.S. military from World War II until the 1990s. Guests may try flights or bottles at one of Vint Hill's outdoor tables; reservations recommended.

Price Range: $22–$29 for a bottle under production

Tastings: $10 per person for a flight.

Groups: Reservations requested for groups of 6 or more.

Directions: From I-66, take Exit 43A (Gainesville/Warrenton) onto U.S. Route 29 South. Drive 5.2 miles and turn left onto Vint Hill Road (Route 215). After 1.6 miles, turn right onto Kennedy Road (Route 652). Turn left at the stop sign onto Aiken Road; drive ¼ mile. Turn left onto Bludau Drive and then right onto Lineweaver Road to the entrance.

The Winery at Bull Run
15950 Lee Highway
Centreville VA 20120

Hours: Sa–W 11:00–7:00, Th 11:00–8:00, F 11:00–9:00
Closed New Year's, Easter, Thanksgiving, Christmas

703-815-2233
www.wineryatbullrun.com

Jon and Kim Hickox opened The Winery at Bull Run on a historic property bordering the Manassas National Battlefield Park; display cases in the tasting room feature Civil War relics found during construction, while historical walking tours are offered on weekends. Winemaker Ashton Lough uses all Virginia- and estate-grown fruit for the wines. The tasting room features indoor and outdoor seating on the veranda and grounds, including covered tables in the Generals' Quarters (reservation only). The winery has live music on weekends with light fare and food trucks, and may be rented for parties and weddings. Children must be supervised at all times. Bull Run offers discounts for military personnel, police, and firefighters.

Sparkling Wines: Stonebridge.

Fruit Wines: Cannonshot Hard Cider, Peach.

White Wines: Chardonnay, Delaney, Petit Manseng, Pinot Gris, Riesling, Vidal Blanc, Viognier.

Rosé Wines: Rosé of Chambourcin.

Red Wines: Cabernet Franc, Cabernet Sauvignon, Long Tom Red, Malbec, Meritage, Merlot, Norton, Petit Verdot, Reconciliation, Syrah.

Price Range: $28–$42

Tastings: $15 per person for a tasting flight.

Groups: Reservations required for groups of 8 to 20; tastings held before 3:00, $20 per person.

ADA accessible.

Purchasing: Online ordering available to most states.

Directions: From I-66, take Exit 52 onto U.S. Route 29 South. Drive 2.8 miles to the winery entrance on the right.

Winery at La Grange
4970 Antioch Road
Haymarket VA 20169

Hours: Daily 11:00–6:00 (Sa, Su to 8:00 in summer)
Closed New Year's, Easter, Thanksgiving, Christmas

703-753-9360
www.wineryatlagrange.com
E-mail: info@wineryatlagrange.com

Originally founded in 2006 by Chris Pearmund, the Winery at La Grange is now owned by private Chinese investors, with Seth Chambers serving as winemaker. It is located on the 20-acre historic La Grange estate, whose manor house dates from the 1790s and has several interesting ghost stories associated with it. The parlor and downstairs lounge offer comfortable indoor seating, with tables and chairs available on the patios. La Grange sponsors a number of special activities and events, including movie nights, Sangria Saturdays, and winemaker dinners. The facilities are available to rent for private parties and weddings.

White Wines: Catherine's Blend, Cuvée Blanc, Gewurztraminer.

Red Wines: Antioch Red, Barbera, Cabernet Franc, Cabernet Sauvignon, General's Battlefield Red, GSM, Meritage, Merlot, Petite Sirah, Zinfandel.

Fortified Wines: Snort *(port-style)*.

Price Range: $24–$43

Tastings: $13 per person with souvenir glass.

Groups: Reservations required for groups of 6 or more.

ADA accessible.

Purchasing: Online to AK, AL, AZ, CA, CO, DC, FL, GA, HI, IA, ID, IL, IN, KS, LA, MA, MD, ME, MN, MO, NC, ND, NE, NH, NM, NV, NY, OH, OR, PA, SC, TN, TX, WA, WI, WV, and WY.

Directions: From I-66, take Exit 40 (Haymarket) onto U.S. Route 15 South. Turn right at the second light onto Route 55 and drive about one mile. Turn right onto Antioch Road and continue 3 miles to the winery on left.

Winery at Sunshine Ridge Farm
15850 Sunshine Ridge Lane
Gainesville VA 20155

Hours: W–Sa 11:00–8:00, Su 11:00–6:00
Closed New Year's, Easter, Thanksgiving, Christmas

703-753-9500
www.thewineryatsunshineridgefarm.com
E-mail: info@twsrf.com

Located on twenty acres on the banks of Lake Manassas, The Winery at Sunshine Ridge Farm was opened in 2019 by Maria Rafferty and Tom Schrade, who are working with The Winery at Bull Run while their own vineyard matures. The tasting room has indoor and outdoor seating on both levels, as well as numerous tables scattered around the grounds. Sunshine Ridge Farm hosts live music and food trucks on many weekends. The facilities are available to rent for private parties and weddings. Leashed dogs are welcome. Visitors must be 16 or older.

Sunshine Ridge Farm also operates an onsite brewery, with a taproom immediately adjacent to the wine tasting room.

White Wines: Chardonnay, Pinot Gris, Riesling.

Rosé Wines: Rosé.

Red Wines: Cabernet Franc, Meritage, Norton.

Price Range: $29–$36

Tastings: $12 per person.

Groups: Reservations required for groups of 6 or more.

Restrictions: Guests 16 and older only.

Directions: From I-66, take Exit 43A (Gainesville/Warrenton) onto U.S. Route 29 South toward Charlottesville. Drive 3.7 miles and turn left onto Buckland Mill Road. Continue another 1.6 miles to the winery driveway on the left.

READING A VIRGINIA WINE LABEL

All wine labels must be approved by the federal Bureau of Alcohol, Tobacco, Firearms, and Explosives (BATFE), which determines the specific guidelines governing each element on those wine labels, down to the font size of the print.

Let's decipher the label of an imaginary Virginia winery.

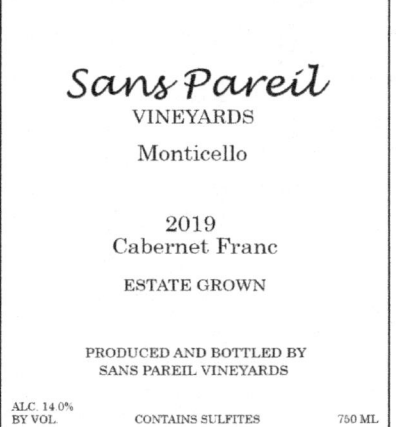

Below the winery name is the name of an American Viticultural Area (AVA). This means that at least 85 percent of the grapes in this particular wine were grown in that AVA. If a county name is included instead, at least 85 percent of the grapes must have come from that county. If the label reads simply "Virginia," then 75 percent or more of the grapes are from Virginia. Look (or ask) for "100% Virginia grown" if you are seeking a pure Virginia wine.

The vintage year and varietal name will also be displayed on the label, although even wines labelled as varietals may include up to 25% of another grape variety, according to U.S. guidelines. If the wine is a blend, the label will show the name of the wine, but the specific grape varieties and their proportions may or may not be listed, depending on the winery's preferences. And "estate grown" means that all the grapes for this wine were grown on the winery's property.

This particular wine was produced and bottled at the winery itself. Many small Virginia wineries work with a larger winery or a "custom crush" facility to produce their wines. In these instances, the winery owners work closely with an expert winemaker to customize the wine and blend it to the winery's specifications.

Handy Guide to Virginia Wineries

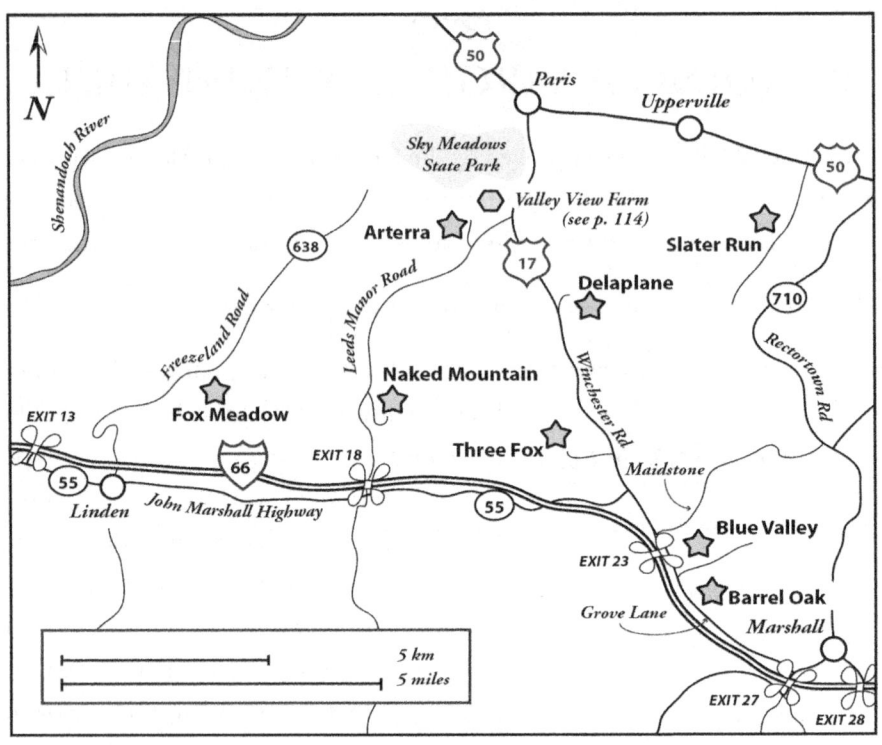

Map 3.7. Delaplane

DELAPLANE

Arterra Vineyard
1808 Leeds Manor Road
Delaplane VA 20144

Hours: F–Su, holiday M 12:00–6:00
Closed New Year's Eve & Day, Christmas

540-422-3443
www.arterrawines.com
E-mail: arterrawines@gmail.com

Arterra was opened in 2015 by Jason Murray and Sandy Gray-Murray to showcase Jason's Virginia-grown wines as well as Sandy's Hawkmoth Art Studio. Arterra's tasting bar features river-tumbled rocks under a glass top, and the winery's indoor and outdoor tables offer a zen view of the surrounding trees and vineyards. Jason centers his winemaking on organically grown fruit, fermented with natural yeasts; some of the wines are fermented in amphoras. Light snacks may be purchased at the winery. Leashed dogs are welcome.

Fruit Wines: Blueberry-Apple.

White Wines: Chardonnay, Chenin Blanc, Roussanne.

Red Wines: Cabernet Franc, Malbec, Petit Verdot, Petite Sirah, Seven Oaks, Tannat, Trilogy.

Sweet/Dessert Wines: Hawkmoth.

Price Range: $29–$49

Tastings: $15 per person for 5 wines (groups of 6 or fewer only).

Groups: Bottle or glass sales only for groups from 6-10; no groups over 10; no limos or buses.

Purchasing: Online for AL, AK, AZ, CA, CO, DC, FL, GA, IA, ID, IL, IN, KS, LA, MA, MD, ME, MN, MO, NE, NV, NH, NM, NC, ND, NY, OH, OR, PA, SC, TN, TX, VA, WA, WI, WV, and WY.

Directions: From I-66, take exit 23 (Delaplane/Paris). Drive north on Winchester Road (U.S. Route 17) for 5.8 miles. Turn left onto Leeds Manor Road (Route 688). Drive 1.4 miles to the winery's long gravel drive on the right and continue up the hill.

Barrel Oak Winery
3623 Grove Lane
Delaplane VA 20144

Hours: M–Th 12:00–5:00, F–Su 11:00–6:00 (Dec–Apr)
(F to 9:00, Sa to 8:00, May–Nov only)
Closed New Year's, Thanksgiving, Christmas

540-364-6402
www.barreloak.com
E-mail: info@barreloak.com

Barrel Oak, originally founded in 2008 by Brian and Sharon Roeder, has become a popular dog-friendly weekend wine destination. Most seating is outdoors on the grounds, with reservations available for limited indoor seating or to hold an outdoor table; no groups over 10, please. In addition to live music and TGI Sunsets, Barrel Oak sponsors a range of special food vendors on weekends. Children and leashed dogs are welcome. Barrel Oak now features an onsite brewery, the Farm Taproom.

White Wines: Albariño, BowHaus White, Chardonnay, Dogwood, Petit Manseng, Seyval Blanc, Traminette, Viognier.

Rosé Wines: Rosé, Peanut's Petit Cuvée.

Red Wines: BowHaus Red, Cabernet Franc, Cabernet Sauvignon, Meritage, Merlot, Norton, Petit Verdot, Petite Sirah, Syrah.

Sweet/Dessert Wines: Chocolate Lab, Goldie, Late Harvest Vidal Blanc.

Fortified Wines: Declaration *(Madeira-style)*.

Price Range: $29–$60

Tastings: $8 per person for self-guided flight of four wines.

ADA accessible.

Purchasing: Online for AL, AK, CA, DC, FL, ID, IL, LA, MN, MO, NE, NV, NH, NM, NC, ND, OH, OR, VA, WV, and WY.

Directions: From I-66, take Exit 27 (Marshall). Turn north in the direction of Marshall onto Free State Road (Route 55). Make an immediate left onto Grove Lane. The winery entrance will be about 2 miles on the right.

Blue Valley Vineyard & Winery
9402 Justice Lane
Delaplane VA 20144

Hours: Daily 11:00–5:00 (F–Sa to 7:30, Su to 6:00, Apr–Oct)   540-364-2347
M–Th 11:00–5:00, F–Su 11:00–6:00 (Nov–Mar)   www.bluevalleyvineyardandwinery.com
Closed New Year's, Thanksgiving, Christmas   E-mail: reservations@BlueValleyVA.com

John and Helen Zissios opened their tasting room high on a hill with views of vineyards and hilltops from the spacious stone patios that surround the facilities. Blue Valley's wines are made with fruit from their 14-acre vineyard as well as from elsewhere in the United States. Breads, cheeses, and dips are available for purchase in the tasting room. The facilities may be rented for special events and weddings. Children and dogs are welcome.

White Wines: Chardonnay, Heritage, Memories, Sauvignon Blanc, Viognier.

Rosé Wines: Rosé, Chambourcin Rosé.

Red Wines: Cabernet Franc, Celebration, Remembrance, Sangiovese, Tradition.

Price Range: $25–$49

Tastings: $15 per person.

Groups: Reservations required for groups of 8 or more.

Purchasing: Online to AK, AL, AZ, CA, CO, DC, FL, GA, HI, IA, ID, IL, IN, KS, LA, MA, MD, ME, MN, MO, NC, ND, NE, NH, NM, NV, NY, OH, OR, SC, TN, TX, VA, WA, WI, WV, and WY.

Directions: From I-66, take Exit 27 (Marshall). Turn north in the direction of Marshall onto Free State Road (Route 55). Make an immediate left onto Grove Lane. Drive 3.1 miles and turn right onto Justice Lane (narrow, portions unpaved). The winery entrance will be about 0.3 miles on the left.

Delaplane Cellars
2187 Winchester Road
Delaplane VA 20144

Hours: M–Th 11:00–5:00, F–Su 11:00–6:00 (Mar–Dec); F–Su 11:00–5:00 (Jan-Feb) Closed New Year's, Thanksgiving, Christmas Eve & Day

540-592-7210
www.delaplanecellars.com
E-mail: wine@delaplanecellars.com

Originally founded by Jim and Betsy Dolphin, Delaplane Cellars is now owned by Daniel and Katie Gomez, Nicholas Jordan, and Thomas Duckenfield. The winery offers visitors a lovely view of the Crooked Run valley from its tasting room and decks. Light food is available for purchase; guests may also bring their own. In summer, Delaplane sponsors Al Fresco wine brunches and dinners (reservation only), as well as live music on select weekends. The winery is certified Virginia Green. Outdoor seating only.

White Wines: Chardonnay, Mélange Blanc, Petit Manseng.

Red Wines: Cabernet Franc, Cinq7, Duet, Left Bank, Mélange Rouge, Merlot, Piedmont Station, Springlot, Tannat, Williams Gap.

Price Range: $28–$60

Tastings: $8 per person for self-guided flights.

ADA accessible.

Restrictions: No buses or limos; no groups over six; adults only.

Purchasing: Online purchasing available for CA, CO, DC, Fl, and VA.

Directions: From I-66, take Exit 23 onto Winchester Road (U.S. Route 17 North) toward Delaplane and Paris. Continue on U.S. Route 17 North for 4 miles and turn right onto the winery's single-lane gravel driveway.

Fox Meadow Winery
3310 Freezeland Road
Linden VA 22642

Hours: M–F 11:00–5:00, Sa–Su 11:00–6:00 540-636-6777
Closed New Year's, Easter, Thanksgiving, Christmas www.foxmeadowwinery.com
E-mail: info@foxmeadowwinery.com

Perched on a hillside over 1,700 feet above sea level, Fox Meadow Winery offers guests a spectacular vista of vineyards and the Blue Ridge from its tasting room and outdoor deck. Originally part of the Freezeland Orchards, Fox Meadow was launched by Dan and Cheryl Mortland and opened to the public in 2006. The tasting room offers visitors two tasting bars as well as limited table setating. A side tasting room may be rented for small events. Fox Meadow is available for weddings or private parties. Well-behaved leashed dogs are welcome.

White Wines: Blue Mountain Mist, Chardonnay, Freezeland White, Le Renard Gris, Pinot Grigio.

Rosé Wines: Rosé.

Red Wines: Cabernet Franc, Cabernet Sauvignon, Freezeland Red, Le Renard Rouge *(Bordeaux-style blend)*, Meritage.

Price Range: $25–$37

Tastings: $15 per person for flights.

Groups: No groups over 6.

ADA accessible.

Purchasing: Online for DC, FL, GA, MD, NC, PA, TX, and VA.

Directions: From I-66 West, take Exit 18 (Markham) and turn south onto Leeds Manor Road. Turn west onto John Marshall Highway (Route 55) and drive 4 miles toward Linden. Turn right onto Freezeland Road (Route 638) and continue 3 miles to the winery up the hill and on the right.

Naked Mountain Vineyard
2747 Leeds Manor Road
Markham VA 22643

Hours: Daily 11:00–5:00 (F–Su to 6:00, Apr–Oct) 540-364-1609
Closed New Year's Eve & Day, Thanksgiving, www.nakedmountainwinery.com
Christmas Eve & Day E-mail: drinknaked@nakedmountainwinery.com

Founded in 1982, Naked Mountain is now owned by Randy and Megan Morgan. Located on 41 acres on the eastern Blue Ridge, it produces over 6,000 cases of wine each year. The tasting room includes a fireplace for chilly days and opens onto a deck offering a splendid view of mountains, valleys, and vines. Light snacks are available in the tasting room, or guests may bring their own to enjoy out on the grounds. The winery hosts winemaker dinners and open houses, as well as live music on weekends. Pets are welcome.

White Wines: Albariño, Chardonnay, Chardonnay-Riesling, Riesling.

Rosé Wines: Make Me Blush.

Red Wines: Cabernet Franc, Cabernet Sauvignon, Catamount Run Red, Raptor Red, Talon.

Sweet/Dessert Wines: Old Vine Riesling, Soar.

Price Range: $22–$36

Tastings: $10 per person for a self-guided flight.

Groups: Reservations required for groups of 6 to 15 (maximum size), $15 per person fee; long vehicles and stretch limos will find it difficult to maneuver around the driveway's blind curve.

Purchasing: Online to AK, AL, AZ, CA, CO, DC, FL, GA, IA, ID, IL, IN, KS, LA, MA, MD, ME, MN, MO, NC, ND, NE, NH, NJ, NM, NV, NY, OH, OR, PA, SC, TN, TX, VA, WA, WI, WV, and WY.

Directions: From I-66, take exit 18 (Markham) and drive north on Leeds Manor Road (Route 688) for 1.6 miles. The long winery driveway will be on the right (but watch out for the blind curve!).

Slater Run Vineyard
1500 Crenshaw Road
Upperville VA 20184

Hours: Th–M 11:00–5:00
Closed New Year's Eve & Day, Thanksgiving, Christmas Eve & Day

540-878-1476
www.slaterrun.com
E-mail: info@slaterrun.com

Chris and Kerry Slater Patusky established their winery on 300 acres that have been in Kerry's family since the early 1700's; they planted the first vines in 2010, with an initial vintage four years later. Slater Run produces all estate-grown wines under winemaker Katell Griaud. The airy tasting room is sited on a hill overlooking the vines with ample outdoor seating from which to enjoy the breezes and the view. A menu of various cheeses, charcuterie, and bread is available. The winery offers special dinners and tasting events, and may be rented for special occasions. Adults only, please.

White Wines: Chardonnay, Pinot Gris.

Rosé Wines: Rosé.

Red Wines: Cabernet Franc, First Bridge, Merlot, Pit Jumper, Roots.

Sweet/Dessert Wines: Chateau Kalian Monbazillac.

Price Range: $24–$58

Tastings: $10 per person.

Groups: Reservations requested for groups of 8 or more.

ADA accessible.

Restrictions: No pets; adults only.

Purchasing: Online to AL, AK, AZ, CA, CO, DC, FL, GA, HI, IA, ID, IL, IN, KS, LA, MA, MD, ME, MN, MO, NC, ND, NE, NH, NM, NV, NY, OH, OR, PA, SC, TN, TX, VA, WA, WI, WV, and WY.

Directions: From I-66, take Exit 57B onto U.S. Route 50 West. Drive 27.5 miles and turn left onto Crenshaw Road, just past Goose Creek. The winery driveway will be ½ mile on the right.

Three Fox Vineyards & Brewery
10100 Three Fox Lane
Delaplane VA 20144

Hours: F–Su 11:00–5:00
Closed New Year's Eve & Day,
Christmas Eve & Day

540-364-6073
www.threefoxvineyards.com
E-mail: info@threefoxvineyards.com

Three Fox Vineyards acquired its name when founders Holli and Jon Todhunter spotted three foxes on a hill while first visiting the property. Now owned by Tim and Emily Faltemier, the winery sits on 50 acres of gently rolling hills with over 15 acres of vines. Three Fox sponsors a range of events, including yoga in the vines, teacher appreciation days, and Dog & Cat of the Month drawings. Children and dogs are welcome. Three Fox also has a craft brewery onsite.

White Wines: Calabrese Pinot Grigio, Gatto Bianco, La Bohème Viognier, La Giocosa Chardonnay, Leggero Chardonnay, Pinot Gris, Seyval Blanc.

Rosé Wines: Triality Rosé.

Red Wines: Alouette Cabernet Franc, La Trovatella Merlot, Piemontese Nebbiolo, Signor Sangiovese Reserve, Volpe Sangiovese.

Fortified Wines: Rosso Dolce Chambourcin.

Price Range: $27–$45

Tastings: $10 per person.

Groups: Reservations required for groups over 8.

Restrictions: No buses after 3:00 p.m.

Purchasing: Online to AL, AK, AZ, CA, CO, DC, FL, GA, HI, IA, ID, IL, IN, KS, LA, MA, MD, ME, MN, MO, NC, ND, NE, NH, NM, NV, NY, OH, OR, PA, SC, TN, TX, VA, WA, WI, WV, and WY.

Directions: From I-66, take Exit 23 (Delaplane/Paris). Turn onto U.S. Route 17 North and continue about one mile. After crossing the railroad tracks, turn left onto Three Fox Lane and continue up the hill to the winery on the right.

WINE CLOSURES

Since ancient times, winemakers have sealed the vessels containing wine to keep oxygen away from the liquid inside. A successful seal must be reliable, inert to the wine, easy to remove, and low cost. Today, the most common closures used are corks (whether from natural or synthetic materials), screwcaps, and, less frequently, crown caps.

Cork was often used in ancient Greece and Rome. Early Roman authors, for instance, described how cork plugs were inserted into the neck of a clay amphora, then coated with pitch to make them airtight. Cork faded as a closure during the Middle Ages when it became harder to acquire for several centuries and was replaced by wood stoppers hammered into barrel openings.

Natural cork rose again in popularity in the 17th century after glass wine bottles were developed and the glass stoppers made for them proved expensive. These natural corks led to the development of a new tool: the corkscrew, which was developed at the end of the 17th century.

Because cork is subject to degradation that can taint the flavor of the wine, synthetic corks have been increasingly used in recent decades. Types include agglomerate corks (cork crumbs pressed together), technical corks (combination of cork flour and a synthetic compound), or plastic corks (inert synthetic materials).

Screwcaps were first introduced in 1959 by the French. They were embraced by Australian and New Zealand winemakers beginning in 2001; by 2010, some 94 percent of New Zealand wines and 80 percent of Australian wines were being sealed with screwcaps, according to the *Oxford Companion to Wine*. Long-term tests have shown that screwcaps preserve wine better than all but the very best natural corks.

Crown caps—the small metal caps on beer and soda bottles—are mainly used in sealing sparkling wines made in the pétillant naturel ("pet nat") style.

Handy Guide to Virginia Wineries

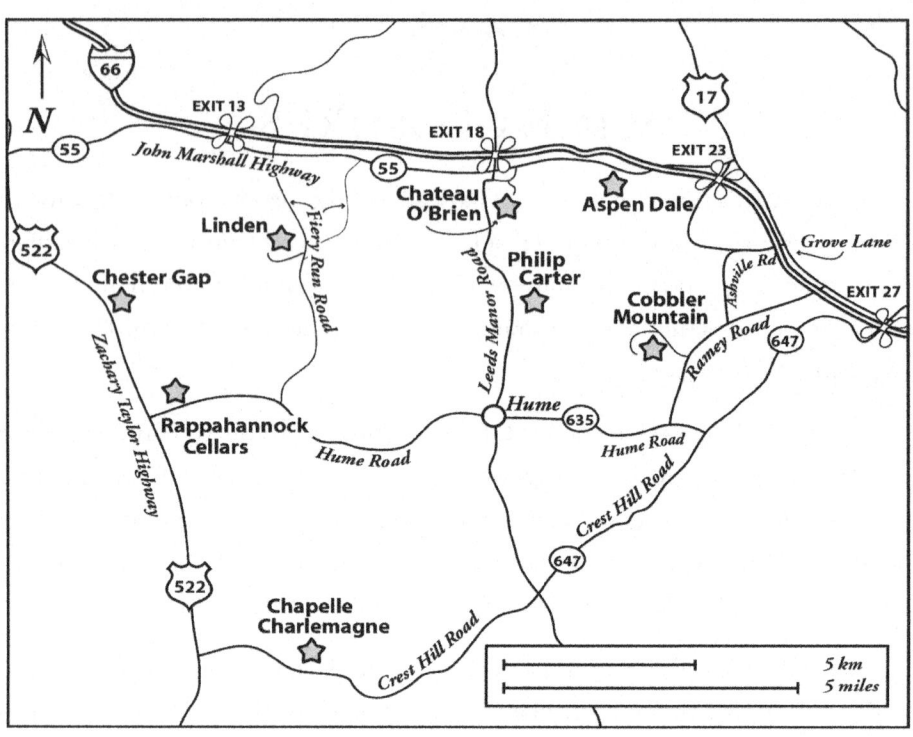

Map 3.8. Northern Blue Ridge

NORTHERN BLUE RIDGE

Aspen Dale Winery at the Barn
11083 John Marshall Highway (GPS address)
Delaplane VA 20144

Hours: M–Th 11:00–5:00, F–Sa 11:00–6:00, Su 12:00–6:00   540-364-1722
Closed New Year's, Thanksgiving,   www.aspendalewinery.com
Christmas   E-mail: info@aspendalewinery.com

Aspen Dale Winery, owned by Larry and Kelly Carr, is located on a 200-year-old country estate that once belonged to the family of 19th-century Supreme Court Chief Justice John Marshall. The tasting room is in a restored barn, with tables, sofas, and wing chairs adjoining the tasting bar; the grounds are home to several animals, including three miniature horses. Cheeses and sausages are offered for purchase, while quiches and food trays may be pre-ordered; guests are also welcome to bring their own picnics. The winery facilities can be rented for private parties and weddings. Children and dogs are welcome.

White Wines: E.B.'s White, Mosby's Gold, North Lawn Viognier.

Rosé Wines: Mary Madeleine's Rosé.

Red Wines: Bridgetown Red, Chambeau Nouveau, Rockawalkin *(Bordeaux-style blend)*, Smokehouse Red.

Price Range: $22–$42

Tastings: $15 per person for a flight with food bites.

Groups: Reservations required for groups of 8 or more.

Directions: From I-66, take Exit 23 (Paris/Delaplane) onto U.S. Route 17 North for ½ mile. Turn west onto John Marshall Highway (Route 55). Drive 2.4 miles to the winery entrance on the left.

Chapelle Charlemagne Vineyards
13453 Crest Hill Road
Flint Hill VA 22627

Hours: Sa 12:00–5:00
Closed New Year's, Christmas

703-598-5073
http://chapellecharlemagne.com
E-mail: info@chapellecharlemagne.com

Chapelle Charlemagne is the work of three generations of the Schmitz family, who planted their first vines in the mid-1990s on their 60-acre estate. After selling grapes to other Virginia wineries, the family decided to reserve some for their own production, working with nearby Rappahannock Cellars to bottle wine under their own label. The name of the vineyard was inspired by their grandfather, a history buff who was fascinated by the Emperor Charlemagne and his chapel at Aachen, Germany. Chapelle Charlemagne currently has outdoor seating only. Guests can bring their own snacks to have after their tasting. Well-behaved dogs are welcome.

White Wines: Chardonnay.

Rosé Wines: Rosé.

Red Wines: Cabernet Franc.

Price Range: $27–$30

Purchasing: Online for DC, MD, and VA.

Directions: From I-66, take Exit 18 (Markham). Turn south onto Leeds Manor Road (Route 688) and cross John Marshall Highway (Route 55).

Continue following Leeds Manor Road for 9.5 miles. Turn right onto Crest Hill Road (Route 647) and drive 5 miles to the winery entrance on the right. Continue about 0.1 mile along the gravel and grass lane up the hill to the parking area on the right, next to the small tasting room.

Chateau O'Brien at Northpoint
3238 Rail Stop Road
Markham VA 22643

Hours: Daily 11:00–5:00 by appointment
Closed New Year's, Easter,
Thanksgiving, Christmas Eve & Day

540-364-6441
www.chateauobrien.com
E-mail: howard@chateauobrien.com

Howard O'Brien opened his winery and vineyard to the public in 2006, four years after purchasing the property. Chateau O'Brien's French-style farmhouse is on a hilltop south of I-66 that visitors can see long before they reach the parking lot. The facilities include three separate tasting rooms and a covered deck with sweeping views of the countryside and vines. Chateau O'Brien has hosted murder mystery dinners, an annual crab boil, and various festivals in the past. Active duty military receive a 15 percent discount. The winery is currently open for tastings by reservation only.

Fruit Wines: Virginia Apple Wine, Blueberry Apple.

Sparkling Wines: Gosset Brut, Ruinart Blanc to Blanc.

White Wines: Chardonnay, Northpoint White, Petit Manseng.

Rosé Wines: April's Apple Rosé, Ruinart Rosé, Tannat Rosé.

Red Wines: Buddy's Bistro Red, Cabernet Franc, Cabernet Sauvignon, Luigi's Luscious Red, Malbec, Mourvèdre, Northpoint Red, Padlock Red, Petit Verdot, Tannat, Vintner's Reserve.

Sweet/Dessert Wines: Ice Apple Wine, Late Harvest Tannat.

Price Range: $25–$79

Tastings: $20-$50 per person, depending on package chosen.

Groups: Reservations required.

ADA accessible.

Restrictions: No one under 21 permitted in the tasting room or on the winery grounds; buses, vans, and limos by appointment only. No pets.

Purchasing: Online ordering available for most states; see website for details.

Directions: From I-66, take Exit 18 (Markham). Turn south onto Leeds Manor Road (Route 688) and cross John Marshall Highway (Route 55). Turn left onto Old Markham Road and then make a hairpin right onto Rail Stop Road. Drive up the hill to the winery entrance.

Chester Gap Cellars
4615 Remount Road
Front Royal VA 22630

Hours: F–Su 11:00–5:00 (to 6:00 in summer) 540-636-8086
Memorial Day & Labor Day 11:00–5:00 www.chestergapcellars.com
Closed Jan–mid Feb, Christmas E-mail: info@ChesterGapCellars.com

Chester Gap is located near the Shenandoah National Park at over 1,000 feet in elevation, with a lovely view from the winery decks of Rappahannock County and of the gap for which the winery is named. First established in 2000, Chester Gap has been owned since 2017 by Jeff Seese and Travis Patton; Jeff serves as winemaker and produces all Virginia-grown wines from their eight-acre vineyard. Visitors can buy light snacks from the tasting room or bring their own to have at the many tables on the grounds. Chester Gap sponsors occasional events, such as movie and wine nights. Leashed pets are welcome.

Chester Gap's Idle Hour, a three-bedroom house adjacent to the winery, may be rented for overnight stays; see the website for details.

White Wines: Roussanne, Petit Manseng, Viognier.

Rosé Wines: Rosé.

Red Wines: Cabernet Franc, Merlot, Petit Verdot, Vintner Red.

Price Range: $26–$32

Tastings: $10 per person for a flight.

Restrictions: Reservations required for groups over 6; no buses or limos.

Purchasing: Online to AK, AL, AZ, CO, DC, FL, GA, HI, IA, ID, IL, IN, KS, LA, MA, MD, ME, MI, MN, MO, NC, ND, NE, NH, NM, NV, NY, OH, OK, OR, PA, SC, TN, TX, VA, VT, WA, WI, WV, and WY.

Directions: From I-66, take Exit 13 (Linden). Turn south onto Apple Mountain Road (Route 79) and then right onto John Marshall Highway (Route 55). Drive 4.7 miles and turn left onto U.S. Route 522 (Remount Road/Zachary Taylor Highway). The winery entrance will be 4.7 miles on the left; continue along the drive to the parking lot.

Cobbler Mountain Cider
10363 Moreland Road (GPS address)
5909 Long Fall Lane (street address)
Delaplane VA 20144

Hours: Th–M 11:00–5:00 (Sa to 6:00 in summer)
Closed New Year's,
Thanksgiving, Christmas

540-364-2802
www.cobblermountain.com
E-mail: shop.cobbler@gmail.com

Jeff and Laura McCarthy Louden established Cobbler Mountain Cellars on a 90-acre farm Laura's father had originally purchased in 1959. Located on a hilltop overlooking Little Cobbler Mountain, the cidery offers seating on the patio at the side of the house and on the lawn. Several signs along the long driveway point guests to a creekside picnic area and a hiking trail. Bread and artisanal cheeses are available for purchase. Cobbler Mountain also features live music on many weekends. The facilities may be rented for weddings. Well-mannered children and pets are welcome.

Ciders: Ginger Peach, Hard Apple Cider, Harvest Pumpkin, Jammin' Cranberry Ginger, Kickin' Cinnamon, Maple Stout, Mountaintop Hop, Original Honey, Smackin' Orange, Traditional Jeffersonian, Wild Blackberry Hop.

Price Range: $10–$14.

Tastings: $10 per person

Purchasing: Online to DC, MD, VA, and WV.

Restrictions: No smoking; no styrofoam.

Directions: From I-66, take Exit 27 (Marshall) and turn north in the direction of Marshall onto Free State Road (Route 55). Make an immediate left onto Grove Lane. Take the first left onto Ramey Road. Drive 3.2 miles and turn right onto Moreland Road (portions unpaved). Cobbler Mountain's driveway (also unpaved) will be about ⅓ mile on the left; continue up the hill to the tasting room entrance on the left side of the house.

Linden Vineyards
3708 Harrels Corner Road
Linden VA 22642

Hours: F–Su 11:00–5:00 by reservation (Apr–Nov)
Sa–Su 11:00–5:00 by reservation (Dec–Mar)
Closed Easter, mid-Dec–6 Jan

540-364-1997
www.lindenvineyards.com
E-mail: wine@lindenvineyards.com

Owner-winemaker Jim Law founded Linden Vineyards in 1983 and opened to the public five years later. A highly respected vintner, Law is considered a mentor by many fellow Virginia winemakers and offers a two-year wine apprenticeship program. Visitors may opt for a tasting flight and stay for a bottle on the grounds (club members only on the deck on weekends). Guests may bring their own food if the kitchen is closed (call first). Adults only, please. The winery is currently open by reservation only.

White Wines: Chardonnay, Sauvignon Blanc.

Rosé Wines: Rosé.

Red Wines: Avenius Red, Claret, Hardscrabble Red, Petit Verdot.

Sweet/Dessert Wines: Late Harvest Petit Manseng, Late Harvest Vidal.

Price Range: $22–$65

Tastings: $15 per person for tasting flight.

Restrictions: No limos, buses, or groups over 4; Case Club members only on the deck and grounds on weekends.

Purchasing: Online ordering for DC and VA residents.

Directions: From I-66, take Exit 18 (Markham) and turn south on Leeds Manor Road (Route 688). Turn right onto John Marshall Highway (Route 55) and drive 4.2 miles to the village of Linden. Turn left onto State Route 638 which will become Harrels Corner Road. The winery's gravel driveway will be 2.2 miles on the right.

Philip Carter Winery
4366 Stillhouse Road
Hume VA 22639

Hours: M, Th 12:00–6:00, F 12:00–9:00,
Sa 11:00–7:00, Su 11:00–6:00 (May–Oct)
M, Th–Su 12:00–5:00 (Nov–Apr)
Closed New Year's, Thanksgiving, Christmas

540-364-1203
www.pcwinery.com
E-mail: info@pcwinery.com

Philip Carter Strother purchased the former Stillhouse Winery in 2008, renaming it in honor of the Carter family's long role in Virginia's history. The winery sponsors a range of events, including live music, summertime Sunset in the Vineyards evenings, an annual Crab Fest, and book signings for local authors. The winery facilities, which are rated Virginia Green, are available to rent for private dinners and weddings. Children and leashed dogs are welcome. The Strother family also operates Valley View Farm (www.valleyviewva.com) in Delaplane, a locavore market and orchard.

The winery also offers a guest suite for rent at its Valley View Farm; check the website for details.

White Wines: Chardonnay, Governor Fauquier Vidal Blanc, Sabine Hall Viognier, Valley View White, Vihdal Verde.

Rosé Wines: Rosewell.

Red Wines: Cleve, Merlot, Nomini Hall, Ten Vines Red.

Sweet/Dessert Wines: Sweet Danielle.

Fortified Wines: 1762 *(port-style)*.

Price Range: $27–$39

Tastings: $12–$20 per person for a flight

Groups: Reservations required for groups of 8 or more, $12 per person.

Purchasing: Online to AK, AL, CA, DC, FL, ID, IL, LA, MN, MO, NC, ND, NE, NH, NM, NV, OH, OR, VA, WV, and WY.

Directions: From I-66, take Exit 18 (Markham) and turn south onto Leeds Manor Road. After crossing John Marshall Highway, continue 4 miles and turn left onto Stillhouse Road (portions unpaved) to the winery on right.

Rappahannock Cellars
14437 Hume Road
Huntly VA 22640

Hours: Daily 11:30–5:00 (Sa to 6:00) 540-635-9398
Closed New Year's, Easter, Thanksgiving, Christmas www.rappahannockcellars.com
E-mail: info@rcellars.com

John and Marialisa Delmare founded Rappahannock Cellars in 1998 after selling their Saratoga Vineyards in California's Santa Cruz Mountains. Light food is available for purchase, and live music and food trucks are often featured on weekends, with seating indoors or outside on the grounds. The winery is available for rental for private parties and weddings. The tasting room includes a children's corner with books and games. Dogs are welcome. Rappahannock Cellars also has a distillery and offers some of its products on the grounds; see the website for more details.

Sparkling Wines: Charmat Blanc de Blanc, Fizzy Rosé, Sparkling Red, Sparkling Muscat.

White Wines: Chardonnay, Chard/Vio, Seyval Blanc, Viognier, Vx2 (*Vidal Blanc, Viognier*).

Rosé Wines: Rosé.

Red Wines: Cabernet Franc, Eighteen, Meritage, New World Red, Petit Verdot.

Sweet/Dessert Wines: Late Harvest Vidal, Solera *(sherry style)*.

Fortified Wines: Red Dessert *(port-style)*, Tawny Red Dessert *(port-style)*.

Price Range: $28–$75

Tastings: $15 per person for a flight.

Groups: Reservations required for groups of 8 or more.

ADA accessible.

Purchasing: Online to AK, AL, CA, FL, ID, IL, LA, MO, ND, NE, NH, NM, NV, OH, OR, VA, WV, and WY.

Directions: From I-66, take Exit 13 (Linden/Front Royal) and turn south onto Apple Mountain Road (Route 79) and then right onto John Marshall Highway (Route 55) toward Front Royal. Drive 4.7 miles and turn left onto U.S. Route 522 South (Remount Road). Drive 6.9 miles and turn left onto Hume Road (Route 635). The winery will be on the left.

SPARKLING WINES

Few things add a more festive and elegant touch to any celebration than sparkling wine. Sparkling wine as we know it originated and was perfected in France's Champagne region by, as tradition has it, the Benedictine monk Dom Perignon. Only sparkling wines made in Champagne may be called by that name; all others are more correctly termed "sparkling" wines although they may indicate on their labels if they were made using the champagne (or traditional) method.

In this process, sparkling wine gets its bubbles through a second fermentation in the bottle. After the grapes have been pressed and the base wine fermented and blended, a sugar-yeast mixture is added to the wine, which is then put into the familiar thick, dark bottles we see on wine store shelves. After this second fermentation has finished, the yeast sediments are frozen and removed through a process called disgorgement, and the bottles are then corked and sealed.

Sparkling wine may also be made by the tank (or charmat) method. Here, the second fermentation takes place in a large pressurized tank, resulting in larger bubbles in the wine. Prosecco is made in this way.

More recently in Virginia, some sparkling wines are being made using the "pétillant naturel" (or "pét-nat") process, an ancient method in which fermenting wine is put into individual bottles that are sealed (nowadays, with a crown cap). This traps the carbon dioxide that naturally occurs during fermentation inside the bottle, producing a sparkling wine.

Sparkling wine may be made from many different grapes, but the classic ones used for champagne are a blend of Chardonnay, Pinot Noir, and Meunier (also called Pinot Meunier). If the label includes the phrase "blanc de blancs" (French for "white from white"), the wine was made solely from Chardonnay grapes, while "blanc de noirs" ("white from black") means only Pinot Noir (or, more rarely, Meunier) was used.

Handy Guide to Virginia Wineries

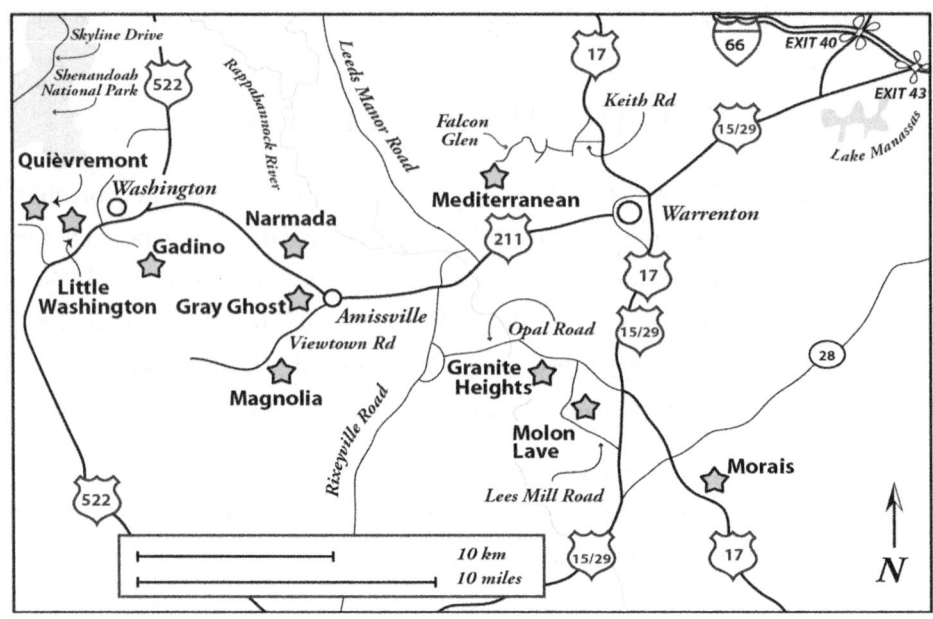

Map 3.9. Warrenton

WARRENTON

Gadino Cellars
92 Schoolhouse Road
Washington VA 22747

Hours: F, Su–M 11:30–5:00, Sa 11:30–6:00 (Feb–Dec) 540-987-9292
Closed January, Easter, Thanksgiving, Christmas www.gadinocellars.com
E-mail: info@gadinocellars.com

Longtime wine enthusiasts Bill and Aleta Saccuta Gadino first planted their fifteen-acre vineyard in 1989. Sixteen years later, the couple opened Gadino Cellars to the public outside the historic town of Little Washington, with Bill and daughter Stephanie serving as winemakers. The tasting room offers cheese and sausage for purchase to enjoy inside or on the trellised deck overlooking the vines and gardens. Guests can also test their skills on the two regulation-size bocce ball courts. Gadino sponsors a number of special events, including fundraisers, live music, and harvest picnics. Gadino is a certified Virginia Green winery. Pets and children are welcome.

White Wines: Chardonnay, Luminoso, Petit Manseng, Pinot Grigio, Sunset, Vidal Blanc, Viognier.

Rosé Wines: Moonrise.

Red Wines: Cabernet Franc, Cabernet Sauvignon, Delfino Rosso, Merlot, Nebbiolo, Petit Verdot.

Sweet/Dessert Wines: Dolce Sofia *(Petit Manseng, Vidal Blanc)*.

Fortified Wines: Finale *(port-style)*.

Price Range: $18–$49

Tastings: $10 per person for a flight.

Handy Guide to Virginia Wineries

Groups: Reservations required for groups of 7 or more.

ADA accessible.

Purchasing: Online to AK, AZ, CA, CO, DC, FL, GA, HI, IA, ID, IL, IN, KS, LA, MA, MD, ME, MN, MO, MT, NC, ND, NE, NH, NM, NV, NY, OH, OK, OR, PA, SC, TN, TX, VA, VT, WA, WI, WV, and WY.

Directions: From Warrenton, take U.S. Route 29 South. Turn onto U.S. Route 211 West toward the Shenandoah National Park. Drive 23.3 miles and turn left onto Schoolhouse Road (Route 636). The winery driveway (portions unpaved) will be about ½ mile on the left.

Granite Heights Vineyards
8141 Opal Road
Warrenton VA 20186

Hours: F 1:00–6:00, Sa–Su Noon–5:00 (Apr–Nov)
Closed Dec–Mar

540-349-5185
www.ghwine.com
E-mail: TR@gh.wine

Granite Heights was started by Luke and Toni Kilyk on a working farm and orchard that has now expanded to 53 acres. Granite Heights produced its first vintage in 2010 and opened to the public two years later. Luke serves as the winemaker for the winery's all-Virginia grown wines, with a focus on red Bordeaux-style blends. The tasting room is in a restored farmhouse with several indoor tasting areas and a number of outdoor tables and chairs, shaded by old magnolia trees. Sandwiches and other light fare are available for purchase, as are jams from Granite Heights Orchard fruit and honey from beehives on the property. Well-behaved children are welcome.

White Wines: Chardonnay, Petit Manseng, Shadow White.

Rosé Wines: Rosé.

Red Wines: Barbera, Cabernet Franc, Cabernet Sauvignon, Evening Serenade, Humility, Lomax Reserve, Merlot.

Sweet/Dessert Wines: Intemporel *(Petit Manseng)*.

Fortified Wines: Ashby *(port-style)*.

Price Range: $17–$29

Tastings: $10 per person.

Groups: Reservations required for groups over 8.

Restrictions: No buses, limos, or vans.

Purchasing: Online to AK, AZ, CO, DC, FL, GA, HI, IA, ID, IL, IN, KS, LA, MA, MD, ME, MN, MO, NC, ND, NE, NH, NM, NV, NY, OH, OK, OR, PA, SC, TN, TX, VA, VT, WA, WI, WV, and WY.

Directions: From Warrenton, drive south on U.S. Route 15/17/29 about 7 miles to the village of Opal. Turn right onto Opal Road and continue 2.7 miles to the winery driveway on the left.

Gray Ghost Vineyards & Winery
14706 Lee Highway
Amissville VA 20106

Hours: W–Th 1:00–5:00, F–Su, M holidays 11:00–5:00 (Mar–Dec),   540-937-4869
Sa-Su, M holidays 11:00-5:00 (Jan-Feb)   www.grayghostvineyards.com
Closed New Year's, Easter, Thanksgiving, Christmas

Gray Ghost was founded in 1994 by Al and Cheryl Kellert, who now produce about a dozen estate-grown wines. Seating is available upstairs on the top floor of the tasting room or outdoors on the deck, gazebos, or tables. Visitors can buy cheese and crackers at the winery or bring their own to have on the grounds. Gray Ghost offers a range of activities, including a Valentine's Day tasting, a volunteer harvest program, an annual food drive, and a Civil War authors day. In December, the winery also puts on a Holiday Open House that features statues and scenes made from over 60,000 wine corks. Children and well-behaved leashed dogs are welcome.

White Wines: Chardonnay, Gewurztraminer, Riesling, Seyval Blanc, Victorian White, Vidal Blanc.

Red Wines: Cabernet Franc, Cabernet Sauvignon, Petit Verdot, Ranger Reserve *(Bordeaux-style blend)*, Victorian Red.

Sweet/Dessert Wines: Adieu *(late-harvest Vidal Blanc)*.

Price Range: $17–$50

Tastings: $5 per person.

Groups: Reservations required for groups of 8 or more.

Directions: From Warrenton, take U.S. Route 29 South and turn onto U.S. Route 211 West toward the Shenandoah National Park. Drive 11.5 miles to Woods Edge Lane at the Amissville Volunteer Fire & Rescue. Make a U-turn on the highway to return to the winery entrance on the right.

Little Washington Winery & Brewery
65 Clark Lane
Washington VA 22747

Hours: Th–M 11:00–5:00
Closed New Year's, Christmas

540-987-3300
www.littlewashingtonwinery.com
E-mail: info@littlewashingtonwinery.com

Little Washington Winery is located just outside the historic town of "little" Washington. Opened in 2011 by Carl and Donna Henrickson, the winery is on a 25-acre farm with scenic views from its decks. Visitors may bring their own picnic lunches to enjoy on the grounds. Art and jewelry by local artists are often available in the tasting room. Light fare is available in the certified Virginia Green winery. Children and pets are welcome. Little Washington also operates a brewery on-site as well as an 18-hole disc golf course on the grounds.

White Wines: Chardonnay, Solstice, Viognier.

Rosé Wines: Pink.

Red Wines: Cabernet Franc, Chateauneuf du Shenando Merlot, George *(Bordeaux-style blend)*, Merlot Cabernet, Que Syrah.

Price Range: $18–$34

Tastings: $15 per person.

Groups: Please call ahead for groups for 8 or more.

ADA accessible.

Purchasing: Online to AK, AL, AZ, CA, CO, DC, FL, GA, HI, IA, ID, IL, IN, KS, LA, MA, MD, ME, MN, MO, NC, ND, NE, NH, NM, NV, NY, OH, OK, OR, PA, SC, TN, TX, VA, VT, WA, WI, WV, and WY.

Directions: From Warrenton, take U.S. Route 29 South. Turn onto U.S. Route 211 West toward the Shenandoah National Park. Drive 24 miles and turn right onto Clark Lane. The winery driveway will be about ½ mile on the right.

Magnolia Vineyards
200 Viewtown Road
Amissville VA 20106

Hours: Th–M 11:30–5:30
Closed New Year's, Easter, Christmas

703-785-8190
www.magnoliavineyards.com
E-mail: info@magnoliavineyards.com

Magnolia Vineyards was founded by Glenn and Tina Marchione who planted the first vines on the 50-acre property in 2008. The tasting room offers a beautiful view of the vineyard and of Hawkins Run in the distance. Seating is available indoors and outside on the veranda and large deck, as well as on the grounds under a splendid black walnut tree. The Marchiones' two rescue dogs are likely to be on hand to welcome visitors; one dollar from each sale of Hawkins Run Red is donated to the Rappahannock animal shelter in their honor. Magnolia sponsors various events, including Paint-N-Sips and live music. Children and leashed dogs are welcome.

White Wines: Black Walnut White, Viognier.

Red Wines: Cabernet Franc, Cabernet Sauvignon, Hawkins Run Red *(Bordeaux-style blend)*, Petit Verdot.

Sweet/Dessert Wines: Pazzo.

Price Range: $18–$24

Tastings: $10 per person.

Groups: Reservations required for groups of 6 to 15.

Restrictions: No buses, no groups over 15.

Purchasing: Online to AK, AL, AZ, CA, CO, DC, FL, GA, HI, IA, ID, IL, IN, KS, LA, MA, MD, ME, MN, MO, NC, ND, NE, NH, NM, NV, NY, OH, OR, PA, SC, TN, TX, VA, WA, WI, WV, and WY.

Directions: From Warrenton, take U.S. Route 29 South and turn onto U.S. Route 211 West toward the Shenandoah National Park. Drive 11 miles to Viewtown Road and turn left. Continue 3.2 miles on Viewtown Road to the winery driveway on the left.

Mediterranean Cellars
8295 Falcon Glen Road
Warrenton VA 20186

Hours: Daily 11:00–5:00 (Sa–Su to 6:00 in summer)   540-428-1984
Closed New Year's, Thanksgiving, Christmas   www.mediterraneancellars.com
E-mail: info@mediterraneancellars.com

Mediterranean Cellars was opened in 2003 by Louis Papadopoulos, who first began making wine in his native Greece before moving to Virginia in 1984. The winery is located on a hillside that offers visitors a charming view of the valley and vineyards below from its stone patio. Inside the tasting room are a small tasting bar and larger tasting room with several tables and chairs for seating. In addition to its wide selection of mostly estate-grown varietals, Mediterranean offers a retsina-style white wine in a tribute to the Papadopoulos family's ancestral origins as well as a range of olive oils. Light fare is available for purchase. Children and pets are welcome.

White Wines: Belleview Blanc, Chardonnay, Meteorana, Moscato, Pinot Grigio, Rechina *(retsina-style)*, Riesling, Vidal Blanc, Viognier.

Rosé Wines: Calypso, Matina's Rosé.

Red Wines: Cabernet Sauvignon, Chambourcin, Corinthian Summer, Kerasounta, La Fos, Mejortage, Nostalgia, Pinot Noir, Romance.

Sweet/Dessert Wines: Sweet Lucia, Sweet Romance Reserve.

Price Range: $16–$95

Tastings: $10 per person.

Groups: Reservations requested for groups for 8 or more.

ADA accessible.

Purchasing: Online to AK, AZ, CO, DC, FL, GA, HI, IA, ID, IL, IN, KS, LA, MA, MD, ME, MN, MO, NC, ND, NE, NH, NM, NV, NY, OH, OK, OR, PA, SC, TN, TX, VA, VT, WA, WI, WV, and WY.

Directions: From Warrenton, take U.S. Route 17 North for about 3 miles. Turn left onto Keith Road (Route 628) and drive 1.1 miles. At the end of the road, turn left onto Cannonball Gate Road and drive about 1 mile. Turn right onto Falcon Glen Road (portions unpaved) to the winery driveway ½ mile on the left.

Molon Lave Vineyards
10075 Lees Mill Road
Warrenton VA 20186

Hours: Daily 11:00–5:30   540-439-5460
Closed New Year's, Easter, Thanksgiving, Christmas   www.molonlavevineyards.com
E-mail: info@molonlavevineyards.com

Molon Lave was founded by Louis Papadopoulos, son of the owner of nearby Mediterranean Cellars. The winery's name is rooted in ancient Greek history: at the battle of Thermopylae, Persian King Xerxes called on Spartan King Leonidas to surrender his greatly outnumbered force, but Leonidas replied, "Come and take them" [*molon lave*]. The tasting room includes two spacious areas with several tasting bars as well as a wraparound patio and outdoor pavilion. Tastings also include small food pairings. Snacks are available for purchase at the winery, which may be rented for weddings and private events. Kosher wine tastings are available by reservation. Leashed dogs are welcome.

White Wines: Autumn Nectar, Chardonnay, Petit Manseng, Riesling, Vidal Blanc.

Rosé Wines: Kokineli *(retsina-style)*.

Red Wines: Cabernet Franc, Cabernet Sauvignon, Chambourcin, Kate's Charm, Merlot.

Price Range: $22–$38

Tastings: $10 per person.

Groups: Reservations required for groups of 8 or more and all buses, limos, and vans; $15 per person.

ADA accessible.

Purchasing: Online to AK, AZ, CO, DC, FL, GA, HI, IA, ID, IL, IN, KS, LA, MA, MD, ME, MN, MO, NC, ND, NE, NH, NM, NV, NY, OH, OK, OR, PA, SC, TN, TX, VA, VT, WA, WI, WV, and WY.

Directions: From Warrenton, drive south onto U.S. Route 15/17/29 about 7 miles to the village of Opal. Turn right onto Opal Road. After one mile, turn left onto Lees Mill Road. The winery will be on the left in 0.7 miles.

Morais Vineyards
11409 Marsh Road
Bealeton VA 22712

Hours: F 1:00–7:00, Sa–Su 12:00–6:00
Closed New Year's, Easter, Thanksgiving, Christmas

540-326-6336
www.moraisvineyards.com
E-mail: hello@moraisvineyards.com

José and Josephine Morais [*more-ice*] established Morais Vineyards in 2004, when they planted the first vines on their 100-acre property. The winery opened to the public eight years later, offering all estate-grown wines. Several of the wines honor the family's Portuguese heritage, such as Verdelho and a tawny port. Visitors can relax in the tasting area around a fireplace or outside on the patios, which feature a view of the vines. The facilities include a ballroom for weddings and other events. Children and leashed dogs are welcome at the main tasting facilities.

Morais also offers a satellite tasting room, Aroma, in Manassas (9249 Center Street, W–Th 4:00–7:00, F 4:00–9:00, Sa 1:00–8:00, Su 1:00–6:00).

Fruit Wines: Cherry.

White Wines: Battlefield White, Sauvignon Blanc, Verdelho.

Rosé Wines: Rosé.

Red Wines: Cabernet Franc, Comendador, Merlot, Touriga Nacional.

Sweet/Dessert Wines: Moscatel *(Muscat)*.

Fortified Wines: Tawny Port.

Price Range: $23–$34

Tastings: $8 per person.

Groups: Reservations required for groups of 6 or more, and for buses, limos, and vans.

ADA accessible.

Directions: From Warrenton, drive south onto U.S. Route 15/17/29 about 7 miles to the village of Opal. Turn left to continue following U.S. Route 17. Drive 4.9 miles and make a U-turn at the Sunoco station; the winery driveway will be 0.1 mile on the right.

Narmada Winery
43 Narmada Lane
Amissville VA 20106

Hours: Th–F, M–Su 12:00–5:00, Sa 11:00–7:00
Closed New Year's, Thanksgiving, Christmas

540-937-8215
www.narmadawinery.com
E-mail: info@narmadawinery.com

Narmada brings a taste of India to Virginia's wine country. The winery was established by Sudha and the late Pandit Patil, who planted their first vines in 2005, naming the winery in honor of Pandit's mother, Narmada. In addition to cheeses, cold cuts, and breads, Narmada also offers small plates that may feature Indian specialties on weekends (reservations recommended). Guests can sit indoors or outside on the spacious grounds. The winery is available for rental for private parties of up to a hundred people and offers occasional yoga events. Children and pets are welcome.

White Wines: Chardonel, Chardonnay, Dream *(Traminette)*, MOM *(Chardonel, Vidal Blanc)*, Viognier.

Rosé Wines: Gulabi *(Chambourcin, Chardonel)*

Red Wines: Cabernet Franc, Cabernet Sauvignon, Jubilee, Malbec, Mélange *(Bordeaux-style blend)*, Merlot, Midnight *(Chambourcin)*, Reflection *(Chambourcin)*, Tannat, Yash-Vir *(Bordeaux-style blend)*.

Sweet/Dessert Wines: Lotus *(Vidal Blanc)*, Primita *(Chambourcin, raspberry)*.

Fortified Wines: Allure *(port-style)*.

Price Range: $20–$36

Tastings: $15 per person for a flight.

Groups: Reservations required for groups of 8 or more, $20 per person.

ADA accessible.

Purchasing: Online to AL, AK, AZ, CA, CO, DC, FL, HI, ID, IL, IN, KS, LA, MA, MD, MN, MO, NC, ND, NE, NM, NV, NY, OH, OR, PA, SC, TN, TX, VA, WA, WI, WV, and WY.

Directions: From Warrenton, take U.S. Route 29 South. Turn onto U.S. Route 211 West toward the Shenandoah National Park and drive 13 miles to the winery entrance on the right.

Quièvremont Winery
162 Gidbrown Hollow Road
Washington VA 22747

Hours: Th–Su 12:00–6:00 (F, Sa to 7:00, Apr–Oct)
Closed New Year's, Thanksgiving, Christmas

540-827-4579
www.quievremont.com
E-mail: info@quievremont.com

John and Teri Guevremont established their winery next to the 250-year-old Reality Farm property they purchased after John retired from a long career as a Marine Corps aviator. The couple opened Quièvremont [*KEE-ver-mont*] several years later and named it in honor of the family name's ancient origins in Normandy, France. The spacious tasting room includes multiple tables for seating indoors as well as a wide back deck that overlooks the winery pond and hills beyond. A range of crackers and various cheeses are available for purchase, and food trucks are hosted on some weekends. The winery frequently offers live music on weekends and may be rented for private events. Children and leashed dogs are welcome.

White Wines: Chardonnay, Petit Manseng, Q Table White.

Rosé Wines: Rosé.

Red Wines: Cabernet Sauvignon, Q Table Red, Rouge de Ferme, Vin de Maison.

Price Range: $20–$50

Tastings: $16 per person.

Purchasing: Online to AK, AL, CA, DC, FL, ID, IL, LA, MD, MN, MO, NC, ND, NE, NH, NM, NV, OH, OR, VA, WV, and WY.

Directions: From Warrenton, take U.S. Route 29 South. Turn onto U.S. Route 211 West toward the Shenandoah National Park. Drive 24.8 miles and turn right onto Gidbrown Hollow Road. The winery entrance will be about ½ mile on the right.

Handy Guide to Virginia Wineries

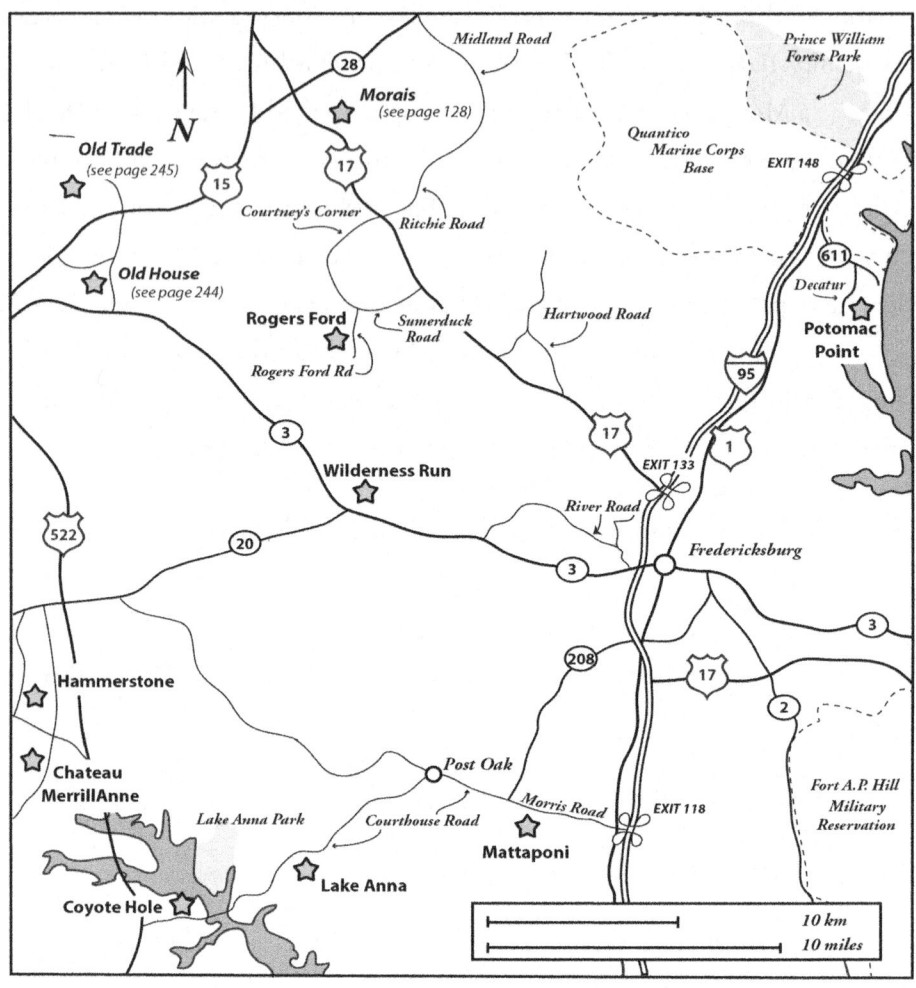

Map 3.10. Fredericksburg

FREDERICKSBURG

Chateau MerrillAnne
16234 Marquis Road
Orange VA 22960

Hours: F–Sa, M holidays 11:00–5:00, Su 12:00–5:00 (Mar–Nov)
(Open also Th 11:00–5:00, Jun–Aug only)
Closed Dec–Feb, Easter, Thanksgiving

540-656-6177
www.chateaumerrillanne.com
E-mail: ChateauMerrillAnne@gmail.com

Kenny and Emily White transformed the 117-acre farm inherited from Kenny's father into a vineyard in 2010 when they began planting vines, with their first harvest two years later. The winery is named to honor Kenny's parents, Merrill and Anne, and the black cat on the wine labels was inspired by a cat on the property. The tasting room is in a renovated barn, with seating inside and out; guests can bring their own snacks for a picnic outdoors. The winery hosts various events, such as potluck dinners, special tastings, and game nights. Supervised children and leashed dogs are welcome.

White Wines: Chardonnay, Palace White, Viognier.

Rosé Wines: Vin Gris.

Red Wines: Cabernet Sauvignon, Founded 1734, Governor Spotswood *(Bordeaux-style blend)*, Marquis Rouge, Merlot, Palace Red, Petit Verdot.

Price Range: $19–$28

Tastings: $10 per person.

Groups: Reservations required for groups of 8 or more.

Restrictions: No buses; limos only before 1:00.

Directions: From Culpeper, take U.S. Route 522 South and drive 16 miles. Turn right onto Independence Road (VA 650), then turn left after ½ mile onto Marquis Road (VA 669). The winery will be 5.6 miles on the right.

Coyote Hole Ciderworks
225 Oak Grove Drive
Mineral VA 23117

Hours: W–Th 4:00–8:00, F–Sa 12:00–8:00, Su 11:00–5:00
Closed New Year's, Thanksgiving, Christmas

540-894-1053
www.coyotehole.com
E-mail: info@coyotehole.com

Coyote Hole was launched in 2016 by Chris and Laura Denkers as the next step in Chris's longstanding interest in cider and beer-making. Located on a 20-acre farm, the cidery is named for blast holes (called "coyote holes") made by prospectors who worked in the area's gold, zinc, and lead mines. The ciders are made from 100% Virginia-grown apples and other local fruits, and are available on tap in the tasting room. The cidery has a wide variety of events, including comedy shows, trivia nights, and monthly LGBTQ Sunday field days. Snacks and light fare may be purchased on-site. Coyote Hole is kid- and pet-friendly.

Flagship Ciders: Sangria, Sunset Sangria, Sister Sangria, HPA (hopped-pressed apple), Oma Smith's.

Seasonal Ciders: Orange Lite, Lemon Lite, 1630 (pear), Bel-Hole (whiskey-aged), Berry Lite, Ciderita, Slopeside, Roasted (coffee-aged), Citrus Spring, Coyo-Tea (chai tea-infused), Pine-Apple, Apparition (pumpkin), Sour Cascade, Sweet Summer, Cherry, Prospect Peach.

Price Range: $13–$17 per four-pack.

Northern Virginia Region & Middleburg AVA

Directions: From I-95, take Exit 126 (Spotsylvania). Merge onto U.S. Route 1/U.S. Route 17 South and drive 1 mile. Turn right onto Spotsylvania Parkway and drive 2 miles; after the road becomes Smith Station Road, continue another 1.7 miles. Turn left onto Courthouse Road (Route 208) and drive 21 miles, crossing over Lake Anna. Turn right onto Oak Grove Drive to the cidery entrance after 0.2 miles.

Hammerstone Cellars
14035 Kendall Road
Orange VA 22407

Hours: Sa–Su 12:00–5:00 (Apr–mid-Nov)
Closed Easter

540-395-1656
www.hammerstonecellars.com
E-mail: hammerstonecellars@gmail.com

Hammerstone's five acres of grapes were first planted in 2014, and the winery opened to the public three years later, with Ashton Lough as winemaker. Visitors can opt for indoor seating (limited) or outdoors on the grounds. Hammerstone features occasional live music and food trucks on select weekends; guests are also invited to bring their own picnics to enjoy on the grounds. Children and well-mannered leashed dogs are welcome.

White Wines: Chardonel, Chardonnay, Cuvée Blanc, Marquis Muse, Petit Manseng, Vidal Blanc, Viognier.

Rosé Wines: Rosé.

Red Wines: Cabernet Franc, Merlot, Norton, Petit Verdot, Berry Run *(Petit Verdot, Tannat)*.

Price Range: $22–$26

Tastings: $5 per person.

Directions: From Culpeper, drive south on U.S. Route 522 South for 14 miles. Turn right onto Constitution Highway (Route 20) and continue 3.7 miles. Turn left onto Kendall Road (Route 600). The winery entrance will be 3.2 miles on the left.

Lake Anna Winery
5621 Courthouse Road
Spotsylvania VA 22551

Hours: W–Sa 11:00–5:00, Su 1:00–5:00
Closed New Year's, Thanksgiving, Christmas

540-895-5085
www.lawinery.net
E-mail: info@lawinery.net

Lake Anna Winery was started as a vineyard in 1983 by Bill and Ann Heidig, who decided seven years later to produce their own wines. Now run by sons Jeff and Eric, Lake Anna produces about 7,000 cases of wine annually. The tasting room includes a tasting bar, indoor tables, and a gift shop, with extra seating outdoors on the grounds. The winery also offers free Wi-Fi and special events, including live music, a "Wine and Whiskers" SPCA fundraiser, and annual Octoberfest. The facility may be rented for private events and weddings. Children and pets are welcome.

White Wines: Chardonnay, Lake Side White, Seyval Blanc, Totally White.

Rosé Wines: Eros, Lake Side Sunset.

Red Wines: Cabernet Franc, Lake Side Red, Morgan Merlot, Petit Verdot, Spotsylvania Claret, Tannat.

Sweet/Dessert Wines: Concerto (*Chambourcin, cherry*), Essensual (*Vidal Blanc*).

Price Range: $18–$42

Tastings: $5 per wine flight.

ADA accessible.

Directions: From I-95, take Exit 118 (Thornburg) and turn west onto Morris Road (Route 606) which will become Courthouse Road (Route 208). At the Post Oak community, turn left to continue following Courthouse Road and drive 7.5 miles to winery entrance on left.

Mattaponi Winery
7530 Morris Road
Spotsylvania VA 22551

Hours: W–Su 10:00–6:00 (summer/fall),
W–Su 11:00–6:00 (winter)
Closed New Year's, Thanksgiving, Christmas

540-582-2897
www.mattaponiwinery.com
E-mail: mattaponiwinery@aol.com

Mattaponi *(matta-poe-NIGH)* is one of only two Native American-owned wineries in the United States (North Carolina's Native Vines is the other). Owners Mike and Janette Evans began as home winemakers 30 years ago and eventually opened their winery on the grounds of their Christmas tree farm near Fredericksburg. The Evanses chose Algonquin names for several wines to honor the Native Americans who originally settled Virginia. Proceeds from their Tibik-Kizismin wine support the Avon Cancer Foundation.

Fruit Wines: Kizismin *(peach)*, Makadewamin *(blackberry)*, Odeimin *(strawberry)*, Pow Wow *(chocolate, strawberry)*, Tibik-Kizismin *(blueberry)*, Wematin *(strawberry, grapefruit)*, Wojape *(strawberry)*.

White Wines: Chardonnay, Wabamin *(Niagara)*, Riesling.

Red Wines: Cabernet Franc, Cabernet Sauvignon, Chambourcin, Freedom *(Cabernet Franc, White Moore's Diamond, Concord)*, Merlot, Miskwamin *(Concord)*.

Price Range: $15–$20

Tastings: $5 per person.

Groups: Reservations required for groups of 10 or more.

Directions: From I-95, take Exit 118 (Thornburg) and turn west onto Morris Road (Route 606). Drive 4 miles to winery entrance on left and follow the gravel driveway to the tasting room entrance.

Potomac Point Vineyard & Winery
275 Decatur Road
Stafford VA 22554

Hours: W–Th, Su 11:00–6:00, F 1:00–9:30, Sa 11:00–8:00 (reservations required)
Closed New Year's, Thanksgiving, Christmas

540-446-2266
www.potomacpointwinery.com
E-mail: info@potomacpointwinery.com

Since opening in 2007 under the ownership of Skip and Cindi Causey, Potomac Point has become a popular venue for weekend wine tourism. The winery's tasting room opens onto an outdoor courtyard, with more seating on a rooftop patio and a large gazebo next to the vines. The winery hosts a number of special events, such as Ladies' Nights and live music on Fireside Fridays and Sundays (with cover charge). Children are welcome to play in the "Little Buds" room. The in-house bistro menu offers small plates, soups, and salads. The facilities, including a ballroom, may be rented for special occasions. Leashed pets are welcome. Reservations required.

White Wines: Chardonnay, La Belle Vie White, Petit Manseng, Viognier.

Rosé Wines: La Belle Vie Rosé.

Red Wines: Abbinato, Cabernet Franc, Coyote Cave Red, Richland Reserve *(Bordeaux-style blend)*, Merlot, Norton, Petit Verdot.

Sweet/Dessert Wines: Dolce Rubus, Moscato Dolce.

Fortified Wines: Rabelos Port *(port-style)*.

Price Range: $15–$33

Tastings: $14–$18 for tasting flights.

Groups: Reservations required for groups of 10 or more.

ADA accessible.

Purchasing: Online to AK, AZ, CA, CO, DC, FL, GA, MD, MN, MO, NY, NC, PA, TX, VA, and WA.

Directions: From I-95, take Exit 148 toward Quantico. Turn east onto Russell Road and merge onto U.S. Route 1 South. Drive 1.4 miles. Turn left onto Telegraph Road (Route 637). After ½ mile, turn left onto Widewater Road (Route 611). Drive 2.8 miles and turn right onto Decatur Road. The winery driveway (portions unpaved) will be 1 mile on the left.

Rogers Ford Farm Winery
14674 Rogers Ford Road
Sumerduck VA 22742

Hours: F 2:00–7:00, Sa 12:00–7:00,
Su 12:00–6:00 (Mar–Dec)
Closed Jan–Feb, Christmas

540-439-3707
www.rogersfordwine.com
E-mail: john@rogersfordwine.com

Rogers Ford Farm Winery is located on a 55-acre property that has been a working farm since 1825. Owner-winemaker John Puckett is happy to share his knowledge of the farm's Civil War history with visitors and welcomes those who arrive on horseback (a hitching post is outside). The farmhouse tasting room has a tasting bar and seating upstairs; snacks are also available for purchase. The property extends to the Rappahannock River, with outdoor seating for visitors. Rogers Ford collaborates with a nearby equestrian center to offer wine trail rides and with the Inn at Kelly's Ford to hold murder mystery dinners and wine tastings. Children and well-behaved leashed dogs are welcome.

Sparkling Wines: Cuvée Julia.

White Wines: Jacob Christopher Chardonnay, Goldvein, Vidal Blanc.

Rosé Wines: Sumerduck Rosé.

Red Wines: Cabernet Franc, Cabernet Sauvignon, Petit Verdot.

Sweet/Dessert Wines: Brandy Station Dulce, First Frost Vidal Blanc.

Fortified Wines: Snake Castle *(port-style)*.

Price Range: $20–$40

Tastings: $10 per person.

Groups: Reservations required for groups of 8 or more; $14 per person.

Purchasing: Online to AK, AZ, CO, DC, FL, GA, HI, IA, ID, IL, IN, KS, LA, MA, MD, ME, MN, MO, NC, ND, NE, NH, NM, NV, NY, OH, OR, PA, SC, TN, TX, VA, WA, WI, WV, and WY.

Directions: From Fredericksburg, drive 12.5 miles on U.S. Route 17 North. Turn left onto Sumerduck Road (Route 651). After 3.7 miles, turn left onto Rogers Ford Road. The winery is 2 miles on the right.

Wilderness Run Vineyards
11109 Plank Road
Spotsylvania VA 22553

Hours: M–W 2:00–8:00, Th, 2:00–9:00,
F–Sa 12:00–10:00, Su 12:00–8:00
Closed New Year's, Thanksgiving, Christmas

540-847-0199
www.wildernessrunvineyards.com
E-mail: harry@wildernessrunvineyards.com

Harry Pagan and his father, Robert, were inspired by a trip to Tuscany to start a vineyard on their 150-acre working farm on the outskirts of the historic Wilderness Battlefield where General Ulysses Grant began the long campaign against Confederate General Robert E. Lee that ended the Civil War. Wilderness Run's tasting list includes wines made from its own vineyards as well as from other Virginia wineries. Seating is available both inside the tasting room and outside, with food available for purchase. The winery sponsors live music on weekends; it also offers a cigar lounge and the 1781 Brewery on-site. Children and leashed pets are welcome; an adults-only area is also available.

Fruit Wines: Orchard Peach *(Niagara)*.

White Wines: Chardonnay.

Rosé Wines: Pink Chair Rosé *(Concord)*.

Red Wines: Cabernet Sauvignon, Field Blend, Merlot, Petit Verdot, Tool Shed Red.

Price Range: $17–$32

Tastings: $8 per person.

Groups: Please call ahead for groups over 6.

Directions: From I-95, take Exit 133 (Warrenton) onto U.S. Route 17 North. Drive 12.6 miles to the winery entrance on the right.

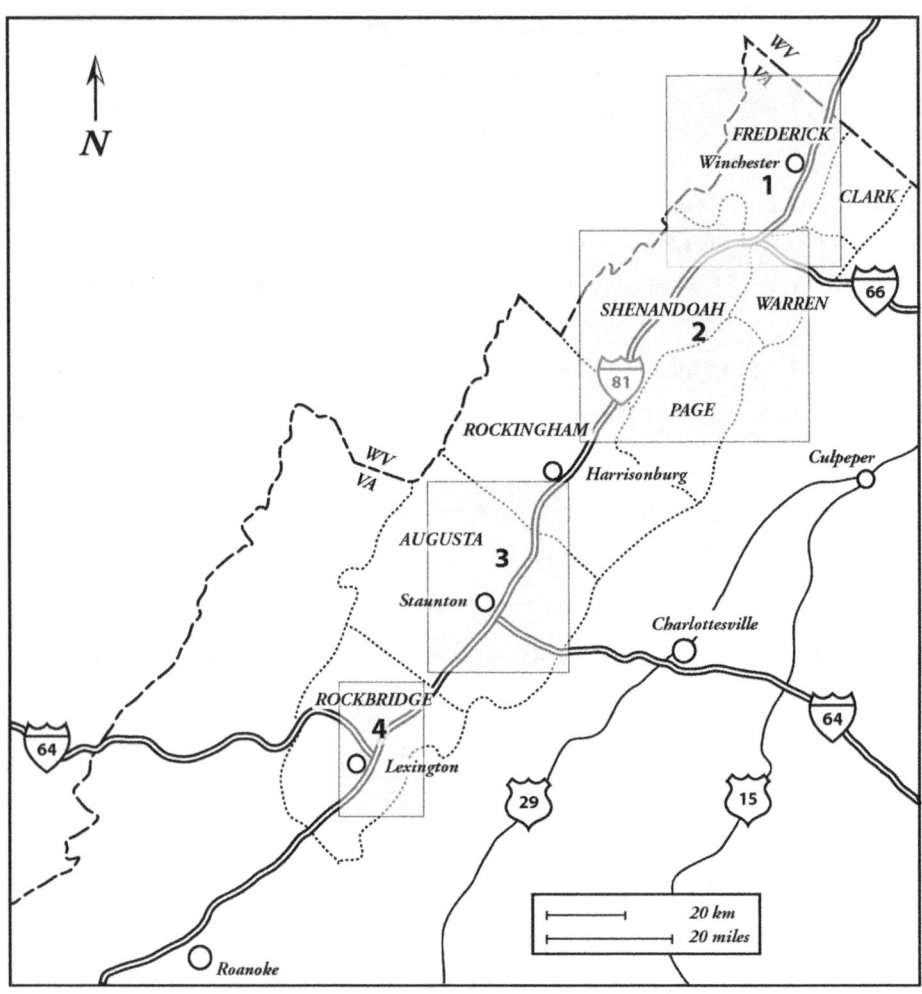

Map 4.0. Shenandoah Valley Region & Shenandoah AVA: (1) Winchester; (2) Edinburg-Mt. Jackson; (3) Harrisonburg-Staunton; (4) Lexington.

4. SHENANDOAH VALLEY REGION & AVA

The Shenandoah Valley offers visitors both rich history and stunning scenic beauty. Stretching from the Virginia-Maryland line to just past the town of Lexington, it is bordered on the east by the Blue Ridge Mountains and on the west by the Alleghany and Appalachian Plateaus. Much of the region is underlain by limestone, and the entire valley is pockmarked by numerous caverns. Sitting in the rain shadow of the Appalachians, the summers here are drier than elsewhere in Virginia, although winters can be snowy and quite cold at times.

The Shenandoah region has over two dozen wineries scattered along the length of the valley. Large or small, all combine a serene wine tasting opportunity with picturesque natural settings. The valley is bisected by I-81, a busy north-south highway that provides easy access to wineries and other sites. Visitors with more time may prefer instead to take U.S. Route 11 which parallels the interstate but is a more tranquil way to experience the small towns and scenic countryside of the Shenandoah.

Things to see and do: There is something for nature lovers of all ages here: caverns for exploring, trails for hiking and camping, mountains for skiing, and lakes and rivers for fishing. Predictably, underground caverns are particularly numerous. Visitors can explore Luray Caverns, Shenandoah

Caverns, or the granddaddy of them all, Grand Caverns, which has been open to the public since 1806. All three are open year-round and are great places for adults and children alike.

The 50-mile-long Massanutten Mountain splits the valley from Strasburg to Harrisonburg and offers hiking and skiing, depending on the season. The numerous hiking trails include the Stony Man Mountain Hike near Luray and the Massanutten Storybook Trail, the latter accessible even for children. Further south, visitors can explore the Natural Bridge, an ancient twenty-story-high natural arch that was a sacred site for the Native American Monacan tribe. Some historians believe the teenaged George Washington visited the site around 1750 on his surveying trip for Lord Fairfax.

As the breadbasket of Virginia, the Shenandoah is also rich in Civil War history. The area saw frequent clashes as General Thomas "Stonewall" Jackson led his troops in an extended campaign up and down the Valley in 1862, while Union General Phil Sheridan headed the 1864 effort to push Confederate forces out of the valley and deprive Southern forces of the rich agricultural resources that had sustained them, a campaign known as The Burning. Among the battlefields are New Market, where Virginia Military Institute (VMI) cadets participated; Cedar Creek, near Middletown; and Kernstown, near Winchester. Self-guided driving tours can be downloaded at www.civilwartraveler.com/EAST/VA [case sensitive].

The town of Lexington is home to both VMI and to Washington and Lee University, the ninth oldest university in the country. Originally founded in 1749 as the Augusta Academy, the institution's leaders changed its name to Washington Academy in appreciation for George Washington's gift of stock in the James River Canal. In 1865, Robert E. Lee became president of then-Washington College, serving for five years before his death in 1870. The college then changed its name to add Lee, who is entombed on the campus; his favorite horse, Traveller, is buried just outside the Lee Chapel.

Visitors may also experience the region's cultural history in Staunton *[STAN-ton]* at the open-air Frontier Culture Museum, a living history site that includes farmsteads from England, Germany, Ireland, and West Africa, as well as from a traditional Shenandoah Valley farm showing how all four origins influenced the typical Valley farmstead. Check the website (www.frontiermuseum.org) for details on events and openings. For theater lovers, the American Shakespeare Center offers year-round performances at its Blackfriars Playhouse, a reproduction of the first indoor theater in the English-speaking world. The ASC website provides more information on its plays and events (www.americanshakespearecenter.com).

<u>Wine Trails</u>: Several wine trails center around the Shenandoah Valley, including the Blue Ridge Whiskey Wine Loop, the Shenandoah County Wine Trail, the Shenandoah Spirits Trail, and the Shenandoah Valley Wine Trail. Portions of the Skyline Wine-Whiskey-Beer Trail are also in the Shenandoah. See Appendix 1 for more details.

Handy Guide to Virginia Wineries

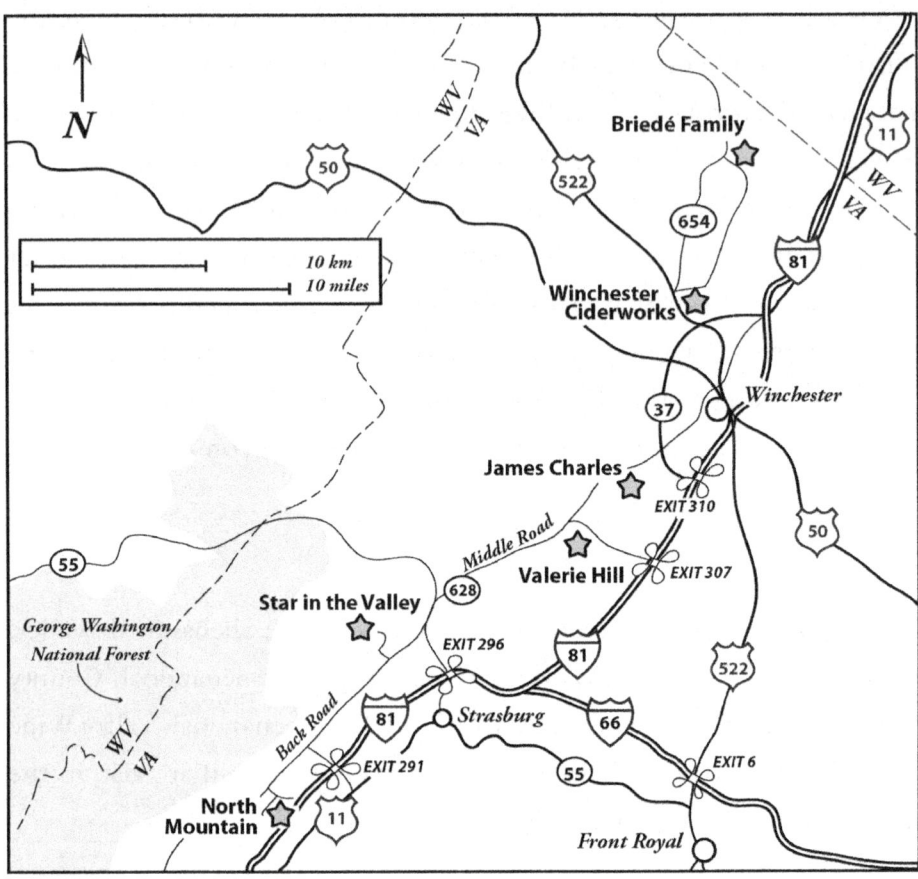

Map 4.1. Winchester

NORTHERN SHENANDOAH VALLEY

Briedé Family Vineyards
450 Green Spring Road
Winchester VA 22603

Hours: Sa–Su 12:00–5:00
Closed New Year's, Christmas

540-664-2048
www.briedevineyards.com
E-mail: info@briedevineyards.com

Longtime Winchester residents Paul and Loretta Briedé established their winery in 2013 on a farm originally purchased for Loretta's horses. Winemaker Nate Walsh (*Walsh Family Wines*) uses fruit from Briedé's own vines and other area vineyards, including varieties such as Arandell that are new to Virginia. Limited indoor seating is available; a range of outdoor seating options are offered on the stone terrace or at the nearby covered pavilion. Light snacks can be purchased, and guests are welcome to bring their own. Briedé sponsors special events, including dinners and dancing. The grounds may be rented for weddings or special events. Leashed dogs are welcome.

Sparkling Wines: Sparkling Winchester.

White Wines: Plié (Cayuga), Duet, La Crescent.

Rosé Wines: The Bloom.

Red Wines: Arandell, Cabernet Franc, Tannat.

Price Range: $24–$47

Tastings: $5 per person for a flight.

Groups: Reservations requested for groups over six.

Purchasing: Online to AK, AZ, CO, DC, FL, GA, HI, IA, ID, IL, IN, KS, LA, MA, MD, ME, MN, MO, NC, ND, NE, NH, NM, NV, NY, OH, OK, OR, PA, SC, TN, TX, VA, VT, WA, WI, WV, and WY.

Directions: From I-81, take Exit 321 (Clearbrook/Brucetown). Turn west onto Hopetown Road (VA 672) and drive 2 miles. Turn right onto Welltown Road (VA 671). After 1 mile, turn left onto Cedar Hill Road (VA 671) which will become White Hall Road and then Green Spring Road. Drive 2.5 miles to the winery driveway on the right.

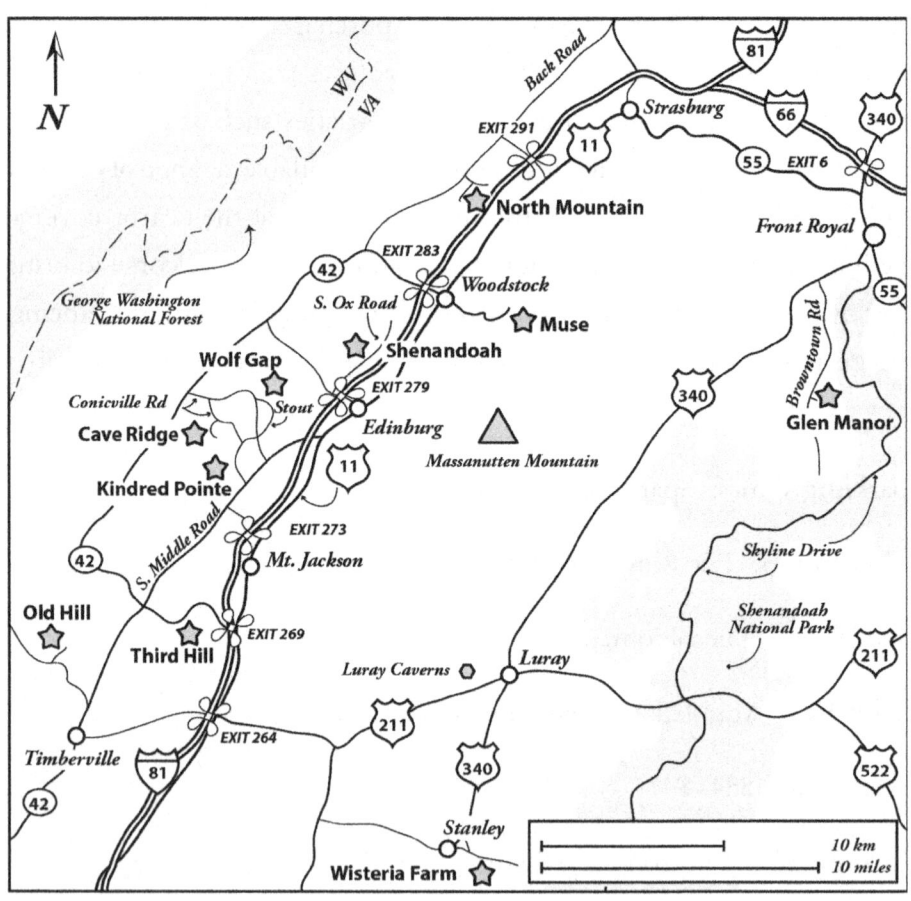

Map 4.2. Edinburg-Mt. Jackson

❖ ❖ ❖

Cave Ridge Vineyard
1476 Conicville Road
Mt. Jackson VA 22842

Hours: M–F, Su 12:00–6:00, Sa 12:00–7:00
Closed New Year's, Thanksgiving, Christmas

540-477-2585
www.caveridge.com
E-mail: caveridgewines@caveridge.com

Owner and winemaker Randy Phillips established Cave Ridge in 2000, opening the winery to the public six years later. The winery name comes from a cave on the property; some of the wine labels feature a photo of a large fossil uncovered when the vines were being planted. Visitors can relax over one of the estate-grown wines on the deck or the cobblestoned courtyard outside the tasting room and may either bring their own food or purchase snacks on site. The winery may be rented for dinners, weddings, and special events. Cave Ridge sponsors live music, chili Saturdays, and holiday open houses. Children and leashed dogs are welcome.

Sparkling Wines: Cuvée Select, Fille des Étoiles, Le Bon Minou, Raspberry Noir.

White Wines: Chardonnay, Traminette, Riesling, Viognier.

Rosé Wines: Rose.

Red Wines: Cabernet Franc, Cabernet Sauvignon, Chambourcin, Fossil Hill Reserve, Mount Jackson Rouge, Petit Verdot, Red Silk, Syrah.

Sweet/Dessert Wines: La Petite Traminette.

Fortified Wines: Fandango *(port-style)*.

Price Range: $17–$42

Tastings: $12–$18 per person for a flight.

ADA accessible.

Reservations requested for groups of 6 or more.

Purchasing: Online to AK, AZ, CO, DC, FL, GA, HI, IA, ID, IL, IN, KS, LA, MA, MD, ME, MN, MO, NC, ND, NE, NH, NM, NV, NY, OH, OK, OR, PA, SC, TN, TX, VA, VT, WA, WI, WV, and WY.

Directions: From I-81, take Exit 283 (Woodstock) and turn west onto Reservoir Road (Route 42). Continue for 10.4 miles and turn left onto Conicville Road. The winery's single-lane gravel drive is on the right after 1.6 miles (be careful at the semi-blind curve at the end!).

Glen Manor Vineyard
2244 Browntown Road
Front Royal VA 22630

Hours: W–Th, Su 11:00–5:00, F–Sa 11:00–6:00 (Apr–Nov)
F–M 11:00–5:00 (Dec–Mar)
Closed Easter, Thanksgiving, Christmas–New Year's Day

540-635-6324
www.glenmanorvineyards.com
E-mail: gmvwine@glenmanorvineyards.com

Glen Manor Vineyards, on the western flank of the Blue Ridge, is a 212-acre working farm, recognized by Virginia as a Century Farm for having been owned and farmed by the same family for over 100 years. Jeff White planted his first vineyards in 1995, opening his winery in 2008 after working with neighboring Linden Vineyards for twelve years. Jeff's niece, Ashleigh White, has joined her uncle in working the vineyards and making Glen Manor's award-winning estate-grown wines. While no food is available for sale, visitors are welcome to bring their own. Leashed dogs are welcome.

White Wines: Petit Manseng, Sauvignon Blanc.

Rosé Wines: Morales Rosé.

Red Wines: Cabernet Franc, Hodder Hill, Petit Verdot, St. Ruth, Vin Rouge.

Sweet/Dessert Wines: Raepheus *(late-harvest Petit Manseng)*.

Price Range: $21–$35

Tastings: $10 per person.

Restrictions: No groups over 4 (including non-drinkers); no limos or buses.

ADA accessible.

Directions: From I-66, take Exit 6 (Front Royal) and follow U.S. Route 340 South for 4.5 miles. Just after passing the entrance to Skyline Drive and the Shenandoah National Park, turn left onto Browntown Road and continue 5.2 miles to the winery's gravel driveway on the left.

James Charles Winery & Vineyard
4063 Middle Road
Winchester VA 22602

Hours: M–Th 12:00–6:00, F 12:00–8:00 (to 9:00 in summer) 540-931-4386
Sa 12:00–7:00 (to 8:00 in summer), Su 12:00–5:00 www.jamescharleswine.com
Closed New Year's, Thanksgiving, Christmas E-mail: info@jamescharleswine.com

James Charles is the third endeavor by the Bogaty family, which also owns Veramar and Bogati Wineries. Named after the family patriarch, James Charles offers wines made by son Justin Bogaty using Virginia-grown grapes from the family's vineyards as well as others in the area. The winery offers seating indoors as well as on a patio with sweeping views of vines and hills. Breads, cheeses, and spreads are available for purchase. The facilities may be rented for weddings or private parties. Leashed pets are welcome.

White Wines: Chardonnay, Cuvée de la Reine, Riesling, Sauvignon Blanc, Vidal Blanc, Viognier.

Rosé Wines: JB Rosé.

Red Wines: 1913 Ameritage, Cabernet Franc, Cabernet Sauvignon, Terracotta.

Price Range: $25–$40

Tastings: $15 per person.

Groups: Reservations required for groups of 8 or more.

Directions: From Winchester, drive south on Middle Road (Route 628) south for 5 miles to the winery entrance on the left.

Muse Vineyards
16 Serendipity Lane
Woodstock VA 22664

Hours: Su–W 12:00–6:00, Th–Sa 12:00–8:00
Closed Thanksgiving, Christmas (early closing
Christmas Eve, New Year's Eve, New Year's Day)

540-459-7033
www.musevineyards.com
E-mail: info@musevineyards.com

Robert Muse and Sally Cowel first bought the property that was to become Muse Vineyards in 2003, opening officially in late 2016. Working with winemaker Tim Rausse, Robert produces mainly blends from estate-grown grapes, including Teroldego, Sangiovese, and Rhone varieties. Muse offers a range of small plates and cheese & charcuterie platters for purchase in the tasting room. Visitors can also explore the 1.8-mile nature trail that meanders through the vines. Children and leashed dogs are welcome.

White Wines: Chardonnay, Erato *(Muscat)*, Thalia.

Red Wines: Cabernet Franc, Clio, Gamay, Petit Verdot, Urania.

Price Range: $21–$35

Tastings: $15 per person for a flight.

Groups: Groups limited to 10 people.

Purchasing: Online to AK, AZ, CO, DC, FL, GA, HI, IA, ID, IL, IN, KS, LA, MA, MD, ME, MN, MO, NC, ND, NE, NH, NM, NV, NY, OH, OK, OR, PA, SC, TN, TX, VA, VT, WA, WI, WV, and WY.

Directions: From I-81, take Exit 283 (Woodstock) and turn east onto Reservoir Road (VA 610). After 1.5 miles, turn right onto Hollingsworth (Route 609) just past the Shenandoah Animal Hospital. Follow Route 609 through a hairpin curve to a single-lane concrete bridge across Shenandoah River. Turn right into the winery drive on the right.

North Mountain Vineyard & Winery
4374 Swartz Road
Maurertown VA 22644

Hours: W–Su 11:00–5:00
Closed New Year's, Thanksgiving, Christmas

540-436-9463
www.northmountainvineyard.com
E-mail: wine@northmountainvineyard.com

North Mountain was founded in 1983, when its vineyards were first planted. The tasting room includes picture windows that open onto decks, where visitors can enjoy the view over a glass of wine. The winery offers barrel room tours and tastings with advance reservations. North Mountain sponsors live music on weekends, chili cook-offs, winemaker's dinners, and an annual Oktober Wein Festival. The facilities are available for weddings and private parties. Children and pets are welcome.

Fruit Wines: Apple.

White Wines: Chardonnay, Grüner Veltliner, Oktoberfest, Riesling, Vidal Blanc.

Rosé Wines: Zweigelt Rosé.

Red Wines: Cabernet Franc, Cabernet Sauvignon, Chambourcin, Claret, Petit Verdot, Tom's Brook Red, Zweigelt.

Sweet/Dessert Wines: Mountain Midnight, Virginia Sweet Reserve.

Price Range: $19–$39

Tastings: $15 per person.

Groups: Reservations required for groups of 8 or more.

Directions: From I-81, take Exit 291 (Tom's Brook) and turn west onto Mount Olive Road. Drive 1.4 miles and turn left onto Back Road (Route 623). Continue 2 miles and turn left onto Harrisville Road (Route 655). After 0.4 miles, turn right onto Swartz Road and the winery entrance.

❖ ❖ ❖

Old Hill Hard Cider
17768 Honeyville Road
Timberville VA 22853

Hours: M–Sa 11:00–5:00 (opens at 9:00 in summer)
Closed New Year's, Thanksgiving, Christmas

540-896-7582
www.oldhillcider.ecwid.com
E-mail: info@showaltersorchard.com

Sharon and Shannon Showalter were inspired to open their cidery after purchasing the Showalter Orchard from Shannon's father, who had started the orchard 50 years earlier. In addition to cider tastings, Old Hill has an annual apple harvest festival and an apple school. Seating is offered both indoors in a glass-walled solarium and outside on the grounds, both offering a view of the mountains. Children and leashed dogs are welcome.

Ciders: Betwixt, Farmhand, Heritage, Off The Press, Yesteryear.

Sweet/Dessert Ciders: Season's Finish.

Price Range: $18–$20

Tastings: $5 per person.

Groups: Reservations requested for groups of 8 or more.

Directions: From I-81, take Exit 264 (New Market) and turn west onto Old Cross Road (Route 211). Drive 5.6 miles into the town of Timberville and turn right onto South Main Street. Continue 0.7 miles and make a left onto Orchard Drive. Drive another 2.6 miles and turn right onto Honeyville Road and the orchard entrance.

Shenandoah Vineyards
3659 South Ox Road
Edinburg VA 22824

Hours: Daily, 10:00–5:00 (to 6:00 in summer)   540-984-8699
Closed New Year's, Thanksgiving, Christmas   www.shenandoahvineyardsva.com
E-mail: info@shenandoahvineyardsva.comt

Shenandoah Vineyards was founded in 1976 by Jim and Emma Randal, and is Virginia's second oldest winery still in operation. Now owned by Michael Shaps since 2018, Shenandoah is expanding its vineyards, including with Alsatian varietals such as Pinot Blanc. The tasting room is in a Civil War-era barn that features two balcony decks from which to appreciate the views of the vineyards and nearby Massanutten Mountain. Shenandoah offers pizza lunches and light food on weekends, and sponsors live music and winemaker dinners. The facilities may be rented for private events. Well-behaved leashed dogs are welcome.

White Wines: Blanc, Chardonnay, Cuvée Emma, Pinot Gris, Riesling.

Red Wines: Cabernet Franc, Cabernet Sauvignon, Chambourcin, Petit Verdot, Reserve Red.

Price Range: $15–$38

Tastings: $15 per person for a flight.

Groups: Reservations required for groups of 8 or more.

ADA accessible.

Purchasing: Online to AK, AZ, CO, DC, FL, GA, HI, IA, ID, IL, IN, KS, LA, MA, MD, ME, MN, MO, NC, ND, NE, NH, NM, NV, NY, OH, OK, OR, PA, SC, TN, TX, VA, VT, WA, WI, WV, and WY.

Directions: From I-81, take Exit 279 and turn west onto Stoney Creek Road. Make an immediate right onto South Ox Road. The winery will be 1.6 miles on the left.

Star in the Valley Estate Winery
33 Amos Lane
Strasburg VA 22657

Hours: F 3:00–8:00,
Sa 12:00–6:00, Su 12:00–5:00
Closed New Year's, Thanksgiving, Christmas

540-514-1687
www.starinthevalley.com
E-mail: wine@starinthevalley.com

Cara and Shane Waller opened Star in the Valley in 2019 on the foothills of Little North Mountain at 1,300 feet in elevation. The airy tasting room offers some indoor seating and features a lovely mural of a starry night sky, made from a photo taken by the owners. Food trucks are sponsored on many weekends, and guests are also welcome to bring their own to have on the deck or grounds while they soak in the views and enjoy the live music. Private two-hour tours of the vineyard and winery may be available by reservation. Children and leashed dogs are welcome.

White Wines: Chardonel, Field Star White.

Rosé Wines: Dry Rosé.

Red Wines: Atlas, Cabernet Franc, Field Star Red Reserve.

Price Range: $24–$35

Tastings: $16 per flight.

Purchasing: Online to AK, AZ, CO, DC, FL, GA, HI, IA, ID, IL, IN, KS, LA, MA, MD, ME, MN, MO, NC, ND, NE, NH, NM, NV, NY, OH, OK, OR, PA, SC, TN, TX, VA, VT, WA, WI, WV, and WY.

Directions: From I-81, take Exit 296 (Strasburg) and turn west onto John Marshall Highway (U.S. Route 58 W/ VA 55 W) toward Wardensville. After 2.3 miles, turn left onto Back Road (VA 623) and continue 1.5 miles. Turn right onto Junction Road (VA 638) and drive 0.4 miles. Turn left onto White Rock Land and then make an immediate right onto Woods Lane. The winery entrance will be ahead in 0.2 miles; continue another 0.2 miles up the long driveway to the tasting room.

Third Hill at DeMello Vineyards
2110 Quicksburg Road
Quicksburg VA 22847

Hours: Th–Sa–M 1:00–5:00 (Sa to 6:00), F 3:00–7:00 (Jun–Oct);   540-740-8464
Sa–Su 1:00–5:00 (fall–spring)   www.demellovineyardsthirdhillwinery.com
Closed New Year's, Thanksgiving,   E-mail: wecrushred@gmail.com
Christmas, mid-Feb–mid-Mar

Edward and Wendy DeMello opened their winery in late 2016 when they returned to Wendy's native Washington D.C. area after many years in California. The winery is named for Third Hill, a peak visible from the winery's windows and that served as a signal station during the Civil War. The tasting room offers cheese plates that visitors can have on the winery deck and grounds while enjoying the view of the mountains. Third Hill offers live music on weekends, weather permitting. Leashed dogs are welcome.

De Mello now offers River Run Cottage, a two-bedroom riverfront cottage, for overnight rentals; see the website for more details.

White Wines: Chardonel, Riesling, Vidal Blanc.

Rosé Wines: Rosé.

Red Wines: Cabernet Franc, Cabernet Sauvignon, Chambourcin, Petite Pearl, Petit Verdot, Triage.

Fortified Wines: Aurora.

Price Range: $25–$32

Tastings: $5 to $10 per person.

Directions: From I-81, take Exit 269 (Shenandoah Caverns) and turn west onto Caverns Road which bends sharply to the right. After 1.2 miles, turn left onto Turkey Knob Road (Route 698) and continue 1.3 miles. After crossing Holmans Creek, turn right onto Quicksburg Road (Route 767) and drive 0.7 miles to the entrance on the left.

Valerie Hill Winery
1687 Marlboro Road
Stephens City VA 22655

Hours: M–Th 11:00–6:00, F 11:00–8:00 (9:00 in summer), Sa 11:00–7:00, Su 11:00–5:00
Closed New Year's Eve & Day, Thanksgiving, Christmas Eve & Day

540-869-9567
www.valeriehillwinery.com
E-mail: info@valeriehillwinery.com

Valerie Hill opened to the public in 2012 on an 18-acre property just south of Winchester. The tasting room is housed in an early nineteenth-century manor house featuring a stone patio and fire pit to warm chilly afternoons. Winemaker Justin Bogaty (*Veramar*) produces Valerie Hill's wines from all Virginia-grown grapes. A selection of cheeses, cold cuts and spreads is available on a café menu. Live music is featured on many weekends; brunch is also available on select Sunday afternoons. Children and pets are welcome; some areas are reserved for adults only.

Sparkling Wines: Sparkling Rosé.

White Wines: Antebellum, Chardonnay, Manor House White, Seyval Blanc, Vidal Blanc.

Red Wines: Cabernet Franc, Merlot, Petit Verdot, Stone Chimney Red.

Price Range: $27–$29

Tastings: $10 per flight.

Groups: Reservations required for groups of 8 or more.

Directions: From I-81, take Exit 307 (VA Route 277) toward Stephens City/Route 340. Turn right after 0.3 miles onto Fairfax Pike which will become Marlboro Road. Drive 3.7 miles in all to the winery entrance on the left.

Winchester Ciderworks
2504 North Frederick Pike
Winchester VA 22603

Hours: W-Th 4:00–8:00, Fr–Sa 12:00–9:00,
Su 12:00–7:00
Closed Thanksgiving, New Year's, Christmas

540-686-7632
www.winchesterciderworks.com
E-mail: stephen@winchesterciderworks.com

Stephen Schuurman began making ciders for his own enjoyment after arriving in Virginia in 2004 from his native England, eventually deciding to expand his efforts after meeting fifth-generation orchardist Diane Kearns of Fruit Hill Orchard. Stephen's ciders are made in the eastern English style (slightly off-dry) and all are from Virginia fruit, including some aged in barrels. The cidery sponsors live music on some weekends.

Ciders: 522, Malice, Pious Pear, Va-Ginga, Wicked Wiles *(aged in bourbon or rye barrels)*, Wyld Cide.

Price Range: Varies depending on size of container

Tastings: $6–$8 per person.

Directions: From I-81, take Exit 310 (Kernstown) and turn onto Route 37 North after 0.2 miles. Continue 6.7 miles and take the exit for U.S. 522 (Berkeley Springs), which becomes North Frederick Pike. Drive 2.5 miles and turn into the entrance on the right.

The Winery at Kindred Pointe
3575 Conicville Road
Mt. Jackson VA 22842

Hours: F–Su 12:00–6:00 (summer)
Sa–Su 12:00–6:00 (winter)
Closed New Year's, Thanksgiving, Christmas

540-447-3570
www.kindredpointe.com
E-mail: winery@kindredpointe.com

Kindred Pointe, owned and operated by Amy and Bruce Helsley, started out as Kindred Pointe stables but morphed into a winery after the Helsleys planted five acres of vines on the 58-acre property. The couple converted the horse barn into a tasting room with two fireplaces to keep visitors warm on chilly days and a heated outdoor pavilion, with fire pits and picnic tables on the grounds. The winery sells snacks; guests may also bring their own. Kindred Pointe sponsors live music on weekends. The facilities may be rented for private parties and weddings. Well-behaved children and dogs are welcome.

Handy Guide to Virginia Wineries

Ciders: Cider Master's Cut, Cherry Bomb, Cinnifool, Hard Core, Hard Luck, Hard Times, Hard Up, Hoppy.

White Wines: Chardonnay, Oscar *(Vidal Blanc)*, Petit Manseng, Seyval Blanc.

Rosé Wines: Run for the Rosé.

Red Wines: Chambourcin, Malbec, Merlot, Petit Verdot, Picasso.

Price Range: $23–$32

Tastings: $10 per person.

Purchasing: Online to AK, DC, FL, ID, LA, MN, MO, NC, ND, NE, NH, NM, NV, OH, OR, VA, WV, and WY.

Directions: From I-81, take Exit 273 (Mt. Jackson). Turn west onto Mt. Jackson Road (VA Route 703) for 1.3 miles. Turn right onto South Middle Road (VA Route 614) and drive 0.9 mile. Turn left onto Conicville Road, continuing for 1.5 miles to the winery entrance on the left.

Wisteria Farm & Vineyard
1126 Marksville Road
Stanley VA 22851

Hours: F–Su 12:00–6:00 (Mar–Dec)
Closed Thanksgiving, Christmas, Jan–Feb

540-742-1489
www.wisteriavineyard.com
E-mail: info@wisteriavineyard.com

Wisteria Vineyard is part of a working farm owned by Sue and Moussa Ishak, a native of Lebanon. The tasting room is next to the farm's Victoria-era farmhouse, with an outdoor deck and firepits. Guests may bring their own picnics and snacks. The winery hosts a number of special events, such as animal rescue fundraisers, live music, an annual Blessing of the Vines, and Wine & Ewe Shearing Days. Wisteria Farm is a certified Virginia Green winery. Children and well-behaved dogs are welcome. Wisteria also offers yarn and free-range eggs for sale from their farm.

White Wines: Chardonnay, Pinot Gris, Seyval Blanc, Traminette, Viognier.

Red Wines: Adonis, Carmine, Merlot, Norton, Velvet.

Sweet/Dessert Wines: Sweet Daisy.

Price Range: $16–$18

Tastings: $8 per person.

Groups: Reservations requested for groups of 8 or more; no groups over 20.

ADA accessible.

Directions: From Luray, take U.S. Route 340 South for 6 miles and bear left onto Hawksbill Road. After ½ mile, turn left onto Marksville Road. The winery will be on the right after about ¼ mile.

Wolf Gap Vineyard & Winery
123 Stout Road
Edinburg VA 22824

Hours: F–M 12:00–7:00 (Apr–Oct),
Sa, Su 12:00–5:00 (Nov–Feb)
Closed New Year's, Easter, Christmas, March

540-984-3306
www.wolfgapvineyard.com
E-mail: admin@wolfgapvineyard.com

Wolf Gap Winery was opened in 2007 by Will and Diane Elledge, who named it after the Wolf Gap that can be seen to the west along the Virginia-

West Virginia state line. The two-story winery has a tasting deck and events patio for warm weather seating and scenic views of the Allegheny Mountains. Private winery and vineyard tours are available with advance reservations. The facilities may be rented for special events and weddings. Wolf Gap offers discounts for active-duty military personnel.

Fruit Wines: Blueberry Wine.

White Wines: Chardonnay, Traminette, Viognier-Traminette.

Rosé Wines: Lobo Loco.

Red Wines: Cabernet Franc, Cabernet Sauvignon, Chambourcin, Mariage.

Price Range: $16–$34

Tastings: $10 per person.

Groups: Reservations required for groups of 8 or more.

Purchasing: Online to AK, AZ, CA, DC, DE, FL, GA, KS, MN, MO, NC, NJ, NM, RI, and TX.

Directions: From I-81, take Exit 279 east onto Stoney Creek Road (Route 185). Drive 1 mile. Turn right onto South Main Street (U.S. Route 11 South). Drive 1.7 miles and turn right onto South Middle Road. After 2.8 miles, turn right onto Headquarters Road. Drive 2.4 miles; turn right onto Stout Road; the winery will be on the left.

WHITE, RED, AND PINK WINES

Peel back the skin of a *V. vinifera* grape, and you will find, with few exceptions, that the fruit underneath is light, regardless of the color of the grape skins. It is easy to see that white wines get their color from the grape itself. The color for red and pink wines comes from a different step in the winemaking process.

The juice for red wines becomes red by keeping the grape skins in contact with the juice. This skin contact may range from less than a day to a week or more, depending on the wine being made. In addition to color, the skins also convey flavor and tannins, helping give the finished wine body and structure.

This also means that white wines may be made even from dark-skinned grapes as long as the juice does not come in contact with the skins. The most well-known such wine is Champagne, which is made from Pinot Noir and Pinot Meunier (both black grapes) as well as from Chardonnay (a white grape).

Rosé, or pink, wines are made through various methods. In direct press, the grapes are crushed, and the must (juice, pulp, skins, stems) is put in a fermentation tank;. the juice remains in contact with the skins, a process called maceration, for a very short time before being drained off. In the saignée method, black grapes are barely crushed and the resulting free-run juice is bled off (*saignée* means "bled" in French). Sometimes the saignée method is used to drain off excess juice before continuing to process the grapes to make red wine. Both methods produce wines that range from pale blush to a deeper pink.

Another practice can be to blend white and red wines after fermentation. This approach is generally frowned on in France, though French winemakers can co-ferment white and black grapes or blend a light rosé with a darker one.

Virginia winemakers are increasingly growing black grapes with the specific intent of making rosé. Grapes are harvested earlier than for red wines, giving the resulting wine a bright acidity and refreshing crispness.

Handy Guide to Virginia Wineries

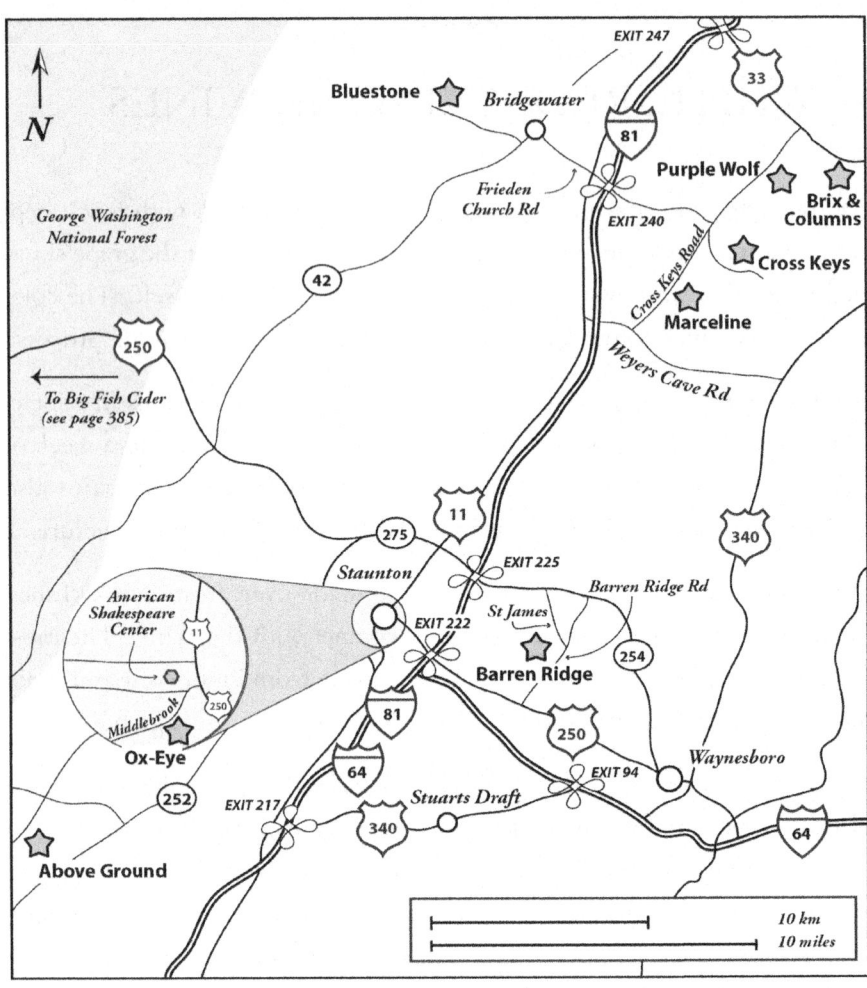

Map 4.3. Harrisonburg-Staunton

SOUTHERN SHENANDOAH VALLEY

12 Ridges Vineyard
24981 Blue Ridge Parkway
Vesuvius VA 24483

Hours: F 12:00–7:00, Sa 11:00–7:00, Su 12:00–5:00
Closed Thanksgiving, Christmas, Jan–Feb

434-996-4252
www.12ridges.com
E-mail: info@12ridges.com

12 Ridges opened to the public in 2019 on the grounds of the former Skylark Farm on a ridgetop 3,300 feet in elevation. The winery is selling wines from other producers while their own 12-acre vineyard matures. Their focus will be on cool climate grapes, including Riesling and Pinot Noir, from which they plan to make sparkling wines. Crackers and cheeses are available for purchase on-site. Seating is available inside the tasting room as well as on the huge outdoor patio with panoramic views of the Blue Ridge. The facilities may be rented for weddings and other private events. Well behaved children and leashed dogs are welcome.

Tastings: $12 per person for five wines.

Reservations recommended for groups of 8 or more.

ADA accessible.

Directions: From I-81, take Exit 205 (Raphine) and turn east on Raphine Road (VA 606). After 1.6 miles, turn left onto U.S. Route 11 North. Take the second right onto Tye River Turnpike (VA 56 East) and drive 1.7 miles. At the village of Vesuvius, turn right to stay on VA 56 East and continue another 3.7 miles before turning onto the Blue Ridge Parkway. The winery entrance will be 2.2 miles on the right.

Above Ground Winery
975 McKinley Road
Middlebrook VA 24459

Hours: Sa–Su 10:00–5:00
Closed New Year's, Christmas

540-430-4394
www.agwinery.com
E-mail: marybeth@agwinery.com

After operating Above Ground in Loudoun County's Purcellville for several years, Mark and Mary Beth Barbagello decided to move further south, launching their new seven-acre vineyard high on a Shenandoah mountainside southwest of Staunton. Above Ground's tasting room is in a former barn, which also houses its production facilities. Seating is available both indoors and outside on the grounds. Adults only, please.

Fruit Wines: Dividing Ridge Red *(with raspberry)*, Dividing Ridge White *(with apple)*, Wild River Red *(with elderberry)*.

White Wines: Chardonnay.

Red Wines: Karma.

Price Range: $16–$26

Tastings: $10 per person.

Reservations recommended for groups of 8 or more.

Restrictions: No children or dogs.

Directions: From Staunton and the Woodrow Wilson Parkway, drive south on Middlebrook Road (Route 252) for 10 miles. Turn right onto Cales Spring Road (Route 603) and continue ½ mile. Turn left onto Shemariah Road (Route 677). Continue another 2 miles; take a left onto Summerdean Road (Route 602). After another 2 miles, turn left again onto McKinley

Road (Route 682). The winery entrance will be about ⅓ mile on the left, next to Redeemer Lutheran Church; look for the directional signs.

Barren Ridge Vineyards
984 Barren Ridge Road
Fishersville VA 22939

Hours: M–Th 12:00–6:00, F–Sa 12:00–8:00, Su 1:00–6:00
Closed New Year's, Easter, Thanksgiving, Christmas

540-248-3300
www.barrenridgevineyardsva.com
E-mail: info@barrenridgevineyards.com

Barren Ridge was established by John and Shelby Higgs on an apple orchard that has been in John's family since 1934. The tasting room, housed in the orchard's renovated apple barn, offers scenic views of the Alleghany Mountains, including some of Virginia's highest peaks. Guests may buy cheese and sausage plates to have inside or on the patio while enjoying the view of the vines surrounding the tasting room. In addition to live music on weekends, the winery holds an annual Swedish Fire Festival in winter and a Pork & Cork Festival on the 4th of July. The facilities may be rented for private parties or weddings. Children and leashed dogs are welcome.

Fruit Wines: Alma-Ata *(apple)*.

White Wines: Chardonnay, Harmony, Riesling, Tinkling Spring, Traminette, Vidal Blanc, Viognier.

Rosé Wines: Rosé.

Red Wines: Cabernet Franc, Meritage, Merlot, Petit Verdot, Red Barren, Touriga Nacional.

Sweet/Dessert Wines: Christof *(Traminette, Vidal Blanc)*.

Fortified Wines: Port *(Chambourcin)*.

Handy Guide to Virginia Wineries

Price Range: $20–$42

Tastings: $16 per person for a flight.

Groups: Reservations required for groups of 8 or more.

Purchasing: Online to AK, AL, AZ, CA, CO, DC, FL, GA, HI, IA, ID, IL, IN, KS, LA, MA, MD, ME, MN, MO, NC, ND, NE, NH, NM, NV, NY, OH, OR, PA, SC, TN, TX, VA, WA, WI, WV, and WY.

Directions: From I-81, take Exit 225 onto Woodrow Wilson Parkway (Route 275) east toward Fishersville. After 1 mile, the road becomes Hermitage Road (Route 254). Continue 1.2 miles and turn right onto St. James Road. Drive 2.3 miles and turn right onto Barren Ridge Road and then to the winery entrance on the right.

Bluestone Vineyard
4828 Spring Creek Road
Bridgewater VA 22812

Hours: M–Sa 11:00–6:00, Su 1:00–6:00
Closed New Year's, Thanksgiving, Christmas

540-828-0099
www.bluestonevineyard.com
E-mail: rc@bluestonevineyard.com

Bluestone Vineyard was opened to the public in 2011 by Curt and Jackie Hartman, several years after Curt retired. Son Lee Hartman serves as Bluestone's winemaker, producing all Virginia-grown wines from the estate's own vines or from other vineyards nearby. The tasting room offers seating indoors or on a spacious patio with a fireplace and fire pits. Small bites can be purchased in the tasting room, but guests may bring their own snacks. Bluestone sponsors live music, charity benefits, and a summer concert series. Leashed dogs are welcome.

Sparkling Wines: Blanc de Blancs.

White Wines: Bridgewater Gold, Chardonnay, Golden Hour, Petit Manseng, Traminette, Vidal Blanc, Viognier, Wilton White.

Rosé Wines: Dry Rosé.

Red Wines: Bridgewater Crimson, Cabernet Franc, Cabernet Sauvignon, Cadenza, Houndstooth, Local Chop & Grill Valley Red, Merlot, Petit Verdot, Quartz Hill Red, Steep Face.

Sweet/Dessert Wines: Beau, Blue Ice *(Traminette)*, Crooked and Weedy, Moscato.

Fortified Wines: Dry Dock *(port-style)*.

Price Range: $15–$26

Tastings: $10 per person for a flight.

Reservations required for groups of 8 or more.

ADA accessible.

Purchasing: Online for AK, AZ, CA, CO, DC, FL, GA, HI, IA, ID, IL, IN, KS, LA, MA, MD, ME, MN, MO, NC, ND, NE, NH, NM, NV, NY, OH, OK, OR, PA, SC, TN, TX, VA, VT, WA, WI, WV, and WY.

Directions: From I-81, take Exit 240 and turn west onto Friedens Church Road (Route 257). Drive 3.3 miles into the town of Bridgewater and turn left onto North Main Street (Route 42). After ½ mile, turn right onto Spring Creek Road. Continue 1.7 miles to the winery on the right.

Brix & Columns Vineyards
1501 Dave Berry Road
McGaheysville VA 22840

Hours: M–Th 11:00–6:00, F 11:00–6:00 (to 9:00 Mar–Nov),
Sa 11:00–5:00, Su 12:00–6:00
Closed New Year's, Thanksgiving, Christmas

540-810-0566
www.brixandcolumns.com
E-mail: brix.columns@gmail.com

Shenandoah natives Stephanie and Steve Pence opened Brix and Columns in early 2017 on the grounds of their 160-acre Six Penny Farm near Massanutten Mountain. They planted their first vines in 2016 and currently work with Michael Shaps (*Michael Shaps Wineworks*) to produce their wines. Brix and Columns sponsors live music on weekends, as well as outdoor yoga and zumba sessions, weather permitting. The facilities are available for rental for weddings and private events. Leashed dogs are welcome; children must be accompanied at all times.

Sparkling Wines: Sparkling White, Sparkling Rosé.

White Wines: Chardonnay, Viognier, Petit Manseng, White Brix.

Rosé Wines: Rosé.

Red Wines: Cabernet Franc, McGahey Reserve Red, Merlot, Petit Verdot.

Sweet/Dessert Wines: Lil Em, Kerus, Sweet W.

Fortified Wines: Six Penny Postscript.

Price Range: $20–$35

Tastings: $12 per person for a flight.

Reservations required for groups of 7 or more.

Purchasing: Online for several states; contact the winery for details.

Directions: From I-81, take Exit 247A (Elkton) east onto E. Market Street (U.S. Route 33 East). Drive 9.6 miles and turn right onto New Hope Road. Make an immediate left onto McGaheysville Road, then take the first right onto Dave Berry Road. The winery will be 1.2 miles **on the left.**

CrossKeys Vineyards
6011 East Timber Ridge Road
Mt. Crawford VA 22841

Hours: Daily 11:00–7:00 (Apr–Oct),
11:00–5:00 (Nov–Mar)
Closed New Year's, Thanksgiving, Christmas

540-234-0505
www.crosskeysvineyards.com
E-mail: info@crosskeysvineyards.com

CrossKeys was founded by Bob and Nikoo Bakhtiar, who came to the US from their native Iran as university students. They planted their first vines in 2002 and opened the winery to the public six years later. The winery's 25-acre vineyard is under the supervision of winemaker Steve Monson. CrossKeys offers "Grape to Glass" tours each day at 12:00, 2:00, and 4:00. The winery's various events rooms can be rented for private parties or weddings. CrossKeys also hosts a variety of special programs, including live music, special festivals, a holiday illumination in December, and a New Year's Eve party. Dogs are welcome.

White Wines: Chardonnay, Joy White *(Vidal Blanc)*, Viognier.

Rosé Wines: Fioré.

Red Wines: Cabernet Franc, Cabernet Sauvignon, Joy Red *(Chambourcin)*, Meritage, Merlot, Petit Verdot, Pinot Noir, Touriga.

Sweet/Dessert Wines: Ali d'Oro *(Chardonel)*, Scarlet.

Fortified Wines: Tavern *(Touriga Nacional)*.

Price Range: $20–$38

Tastings: $15 per person for a flight.

Groups: Reservations required for groups of 10 or more.

ADA accessible.

Directions: From I-81, take Exit 240 and turn east onto Friedens Church Road (Route 682). Drive 4 miles and turn right onto Cross Keys Road (Route 276). Continue ½ mile to East Timber Ridge Road and turn left. The winery will be 1.2 miles on the left.

Ecco Adesso Vineyards
340 Ecco Adesso Lane
Fairfield VA 24435

Hours: Th–Su 11:00–5:00
Closed New Year's, Easter, Thanksgiving, Christmas

540-817-0419
http://eccoadesso.com
E-mail: info@eccoadesso.com

    Cierra and Michael Weatherly decided to launch Ecco Adesso while weathering the 2020 lockdown in their Nelson County cabin. They bought the 350-acre property that now is Ecco Adesso (Italian for "here now") and began planting their vineyards, which will have both familiar varieties and less common ones, such as Saperavi and Lagrein. The winery sponsors Wine & Oyster Thursdays as well as live music on weekends; light food bites are also on sale though guests are welcome to bring their own snacks. While their vineyards fully mature, Ecco Adesso is offering wines from other Virginia wineries and other countries. Children and leashed dogs are welcome.

Shenandoah Valley Region & AVA

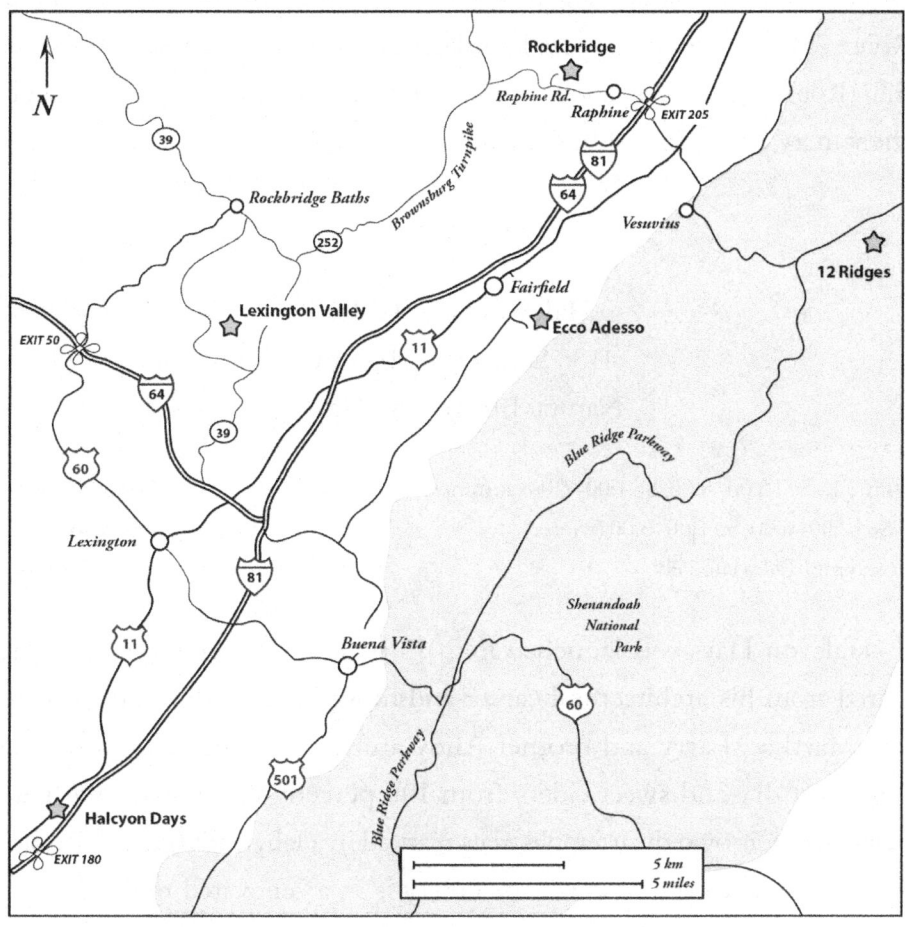

Map 4.4. Lexington

Ecco Adesso has four guest houses on the property for overnight stays: a 5-bedroom farmhouse dating from 1819, a guest house, a barn loft, and a one-bedroom cabin nestled in the woods. See the website for details.

Price Range: $24–$40

Tastings: $14–$20 per person for a flight.

Directions: From I-81, take Exit 200 (Fairfield) and turn east onto Sterrett Road (Route 710) in the direction of Fairfield. After 1/2 mile, turn right onto U.S. Route 11 South and drive 2.7 miles. Turn left onto Mackeys Lane (Route 714). Continue another 1.3 miles and turn right onto Borden Grant Trail (Route 706). Drive about ½ mile and turn left onto Sheep Creek Lane. The winery entrance will be 0.2 miles on the left.

Halcyon Days Cider
4135 South Lee Highway
Natural Bridge VA 24578

Hours: F–Sa 12:00–8:00, Su 1:00–6:00 (summer)
F–Sa 12:00–6:00, Su 1:00–5:00 (winter)
Closed mid-Dec–late Feb

540-291-1340
www.halcyondayscider.com
E-mail: kirin@halcyondayscider.com

Halcyon Days was launched in 2015 by Larry Krietemeyer after he retired from his architectural career and moved to the Shenandoah with wife Martha. Larry and brother Andy are the cidermakers, producing a range of dry and sweet ciders from 100 percent Virginia-grown fruit, including their own dwarf apple trees planted in a labyrinth that is 1.7 miles from the start to the center. The cidery is in a renovated milking barn, while the tasting room is housed in an 1860-era log cabin with indoor and outdoor seating.

Dry Ciders: Baker's Batch, Eureka, Eventide, Harkening, Labyrinth, Midas Touch, Occam's Razor.

Semi-Dry Ciders: Fickle, Tom's Thumb *(pear)*, Whimsy.

Price Range: $16–$20

Tastings: $8 per person.

Directions: From I-81, take Exit 180B (Fancy Hill) and turn right onto South Lee Highway (U.S. Route 11 North). Drive 0.7 miles to the cidery.

Lexington Valley Vineyards
80 Norton Way
Rockbridge Baths VA 24473

Hours: Sa 12:00–5:00, Su 12:00–4:30 (Mar–Oct),
Sa–Su 12:00–4:30 (Nov–Feb)
Closed New Year's, Christmas

540-462-2974
www.lexingtonvalleyvineyard.com
E-mail: info@lexingtonvalleyvineyard.com

Lexington Valley Vineyard is located on 67 acres on the rolling hills northwest of the historic town of Lexington. Owners Calvin and Janet Hale launched their vineyard with a planting of Norton in 2000, expanding over the years to include such varieties as Grüner Veltliner and Maréchal Foch. In summer, the winery sponsors occasional "Wine and Wags" where guests are invited to bring a picnic and their favorite four-legged friends. Snacks are available for purchase in the tasting room, which offers free Wi-Fi. Children and pets are welcome.

White Wines: Catawba, Grüner Veltliner, Traminette, Vidal Blanc.

Rosé Wines: Rosé of Cabernet Franc.

Red Wines: Cabernet Franc, Maréchal Foch, Norton.

Price Range: $18–$25

Tastings: $14 per flight.

Restrictions: No pets allowed.

Directions: From I-64, take Exit 50 (Kerr's Creek) onto U.S. Route 60 East toward Lexington. Turn left almost immediately onto Big Spring Road (VA 631). Continue 1 mile and turn left onto Bethany Road (VA 625). After 2.7 miles, bear left onto Turkey Hill Road (VA 602) at Bethany Church. Drive another 1.3 miles and turn right into the winery entrance at Norton Way.

Marceline Vineyards
5887 Cross Keys Road
Mt. Crawford VA 22841

Hours: W–Sa 11:00–6:00, Su 1:00–7:00 (Mar–Oct),
W–Sa 11:00–5:00, Su 1:00–5:00 (Nov–Feb)
Closed New Year's, Thanksgiving, Christmas

540-212-9798
www.marcelinevineyards.com
E-mail: info@marcelinevineyards.com

Susan Rudolph Pleasant and her family opened Marceline [*mar-seh-leen*] Vineyards in December 2016, ten years after planting their first vines. Named for Susan's mother, Marceline's tasting room is in a restored barn atop a hill overlooking the vineyards. Tim and Peter Rausse are consultants, with Tim serving as winemaker for Marceline's all-Virginia wines. The winery offers crackers and cheeses for purchase; guests may enjoy these either inside the tasting room or out on the deck with its views of Massanutten Mountain. The facilities may be rented for private events or weddings.

Marceline also offers the Log Home Loft on the top floor of the tasting room barn for overnight rentals; see the website for details.

White Wines: Chardonnay, Vidal Blanc.

Rosé Wines: Rosé.

Red Wines: Cabernet Franc, Cabernet Sauvignon.

Sweet/Dessert Wines: L'Amore di Notte, White Dessert.

Price Range: $21–$25

Tastings: $14 per flight.

Restrictions: No dogs or pets allowed.

Directions: From I-81, take Exit 247A (Elkton) and turn east onto East Market Street (U.S. Route 33 East). Drive 4 miles, then turn right onto Cross Keys Road (Route 276). The winery will be 5.7 miles on the left.

Ox-Eye Vineyards
44 Middlebrook Avenue
Staunton VA   24401

Hours: M–Th 12:00–6:00, F 12:00–7:00 (to 8:00 in summer),
Sa 10:00–7:00 (to 8:00 in summer), Su 12:00–5:00
Closed New Year's, Easter, Thanksgiving, Christmas

540-849-7926
www.oxeyevineyards.com
E-mail: info@oxeyevineyards.com

Ox-Eye Vineyards was founded by John and Susan Kiers, who opened to the public in 2011 after selling grapes for many years to other wineries. They named their winery after the ox-eye daisies that proliferate in the valleys around the village of Swoope where their vineyards are located. The tasting room is in a restored 1904 railroad weigh station in Staunton's historic restaurant and tourism district. After tasting Ox-Eye's estate-grown wines, visitors can relax over a glass or bottle at one of the tables upstairs or outside on the patio. The tasting room features exhibits by local artists on the walls. Light fare is offered for purchase. Free Wi-Fi is available.

Sparkling Wines: Ox-Eye Sparkling (*Chardonnay*).

White Wines: Chardonnay, Grü-V *(Grüner Veltliner)*, Riesling, Traminette, White Ox.

Rosé Wines: Shy Ox.

Red Wines: Cabernet Franc, Lemberger, Pinot Noir.

Fortified Wines: Ruby Ox *(port-style)*.

Price Range: $18–$35

Tastings: $10 per person.

Purchasing: Online to AK, AL, AZ, CA, CO, DC, FL, GA, HI, IA, ID, IL, IN, KS, LA, MA, MD, ME, MN, MO, NC, ND, NE, NH, NM, NV, NY, OH, OR, PA, SC, TN, TX, VA, WA, WI, WV, and WY.

Directions: From I-81, take Exit 222 onto U.S. Route 250 West. Drive two miles into Staunton. Bear right onto Greenville Avenue, where U.S. Route 250 and U.S. Route 11 merge. Take the first left onto Commerce Road to continue following U.S. Route 250. Take the third left onto Middlebrook Avenue. The winery will be on the left in 0.1 mile; parking is available on the street or in the town parking lot across from the tasting room.

Purple Wolf Vineyards
2644 Cross Keys Road
Harrisonburg VA 22801

Hours: M–Sa 12:00–6:00, Su 1:00–6:00
Closed New Year's, Easter, Thanksgiving, Christmas

540-421-6345
www.purplewolfvineyard.com
E-mail: whiteoaklavender@gmail.com

Purple Wolf, the winery side of the White Oak Lavender Farm, offers several Virginia-grown wines, some infused with lavender. Opened in 2015 by Julie Houshalter, Purple Wolf's wines are made by Randy Phillips of nearby Cave Ridge Vineyard. After tasting, visitors can either linger over a glass or bottle of wine or check out the many lavender-based products in the farm store.

White Wines: Imperial Gem, Riesling, Thumbelina, Traminette, Viognier.

Rosé Wines: Butterfly Kisses.

Red Wines: Cabernet Franc, Chambourcin, Pardon My Purple, Petit Verdot.

Fortified Wines: Royale Velvet.

Price Range: $18–$24

Tastings: $10 per person.

Purchasing: Online to AK, AZ, CO, DC, FL, GA, HI, IA, ID, IN, KS, LA, MA, MD, ME, MN, MO, NC, ND, NE, NH, NM, NV, NY, OH, OR, PA, SC, TN, TX, VA, WA, WI, WV, and WY.

Directions: From I-81, take Exit 247A (Elkton) and turn east onto East Market Street (U.S. Route 33 East). Drive 4 miles, then turn right onto Cross Keys Road (VA 276). The winery will be 2.4 miles on the right.

Rockbridge Vineyard & Brewery
35 Hill View Lane
Raphine VA 24472

Hours: Tu–Sa 10:00–6:00, Su–M 12:00–5:00
Closed New Year's Eve & Day, Thanksgiving,
Christmas Eve & Day

540-377-6204
www.rockbridgevineyard.com
E-mail: rockbridgewine@gmail.com

Rockbridge Vineyard was established in 1992 by Shepherd Rouse and Jane Millott-Rouse. Shep, who serves as the winemaker, worked at several California wineries, including Chateau St. Jean, Schramsburg, and Carneros Creek, before returning to his native Virginia. Rockbridge's name comes from the county in which it is located as well as from the county's most famous natural feature, the Natural Bridge, whose depiction adorns many of the winery's labels. The DeChiel label of some of Rockbridge's wines is in honor of Shep's French Huguenot lineage. The winery and tasting room are in a large, red barn, with a small deck just outside the tasting room entrance. Light fair is available for purchase. The facilities can be rented for private parties and weddings. Rockbridge frequently sponsors live music, winemaker dinners, and harvest festivals. Children and dogs are welcome.

Rockbridge is also home to a brewery offering pale ales, lagers, and porters. The brewery is open Th–Sa 12:00–6:00 and Su 12:00–5:00.

Fruit Wines: Vin de Pomme *(apple)*.

White Wines: Chardonnay, St. Mary's Blanc, Traminette, Tuscarora White, Vignoles, Viognier, White Riesling.

Rosé Wines: Rose Hill Rosé, Jeremiah's Blush *(Concord, Vidal Blanc)*, Pinot Noir Blanc.

Red Wines: Cabernet Franc, Chambourcin, Meritage, Merlot, Pinot Noir, Syrah, Virginia Claret *(Norton)*, Lexington & Concord, Tuscarora Red.

Sweet/Dessert Wines: V d'Or.

Price Range: $12–$25

Tastings: $10–$12 per person for a flight.

Groups: Reservations required for groups of 8 or more for indoor seating.

Purchasing: Online purchasing is available for AZ, CA, CO, DC, FL, GA, HI, IA, ID, IL, IN, KS, LA, MO, NC, NM, OH, OR, TX, VA, WA, WI, WV, and WY.

Directions: From I-81, take Exit 205 (Raphine) onto Route 606 West. The winery will be one mile on the right, past the village of Raphine.

RED BORDEAUX-STYLE BLENDS

Bordeaux, Bordeaux-style, Meritage—do these terms all mean the same thing? Well, yes and no.

True Bordeaux wines are only from the area around Bordeaux, France. The Bordeaux region encompasses vineyards along both banks of France's Gironde River, which flows through the city of Bordeaux, and its tributaries, the Garonne and Dordogne. Wine grapes have been cultivated here since at least the 1st century AD, when Roman aristocrat and naturalist Pliny the Elder wrote about the grape-growing and wines he encountered in the area.

Also called Claret, red Bordeaux is a blend of Cabernet Sauvignon, Merlot, Cabernet Franc, Petit Verdot, and Malbec; a sixth grape, Carmenère, is used only rarely. In 2019, four more grapes were approved: Touriga Nacional, Castets, Marselan, and Arinarnoa. Each grape variety is first fermented separately and aged in oak barrels for over a year before being blended and bottled. High-quality Bordeaux wines age beautifully, becoming more complex and refined over time.

Wines said to be "Bordeaux-style" are blends of two or more of these red wine varieties. Because Bordeaux reds rank among the world's greatest wines, a winery's Bordeaux-style wine will often be held up as its finest. The specific grapes and proportions in the blend vary from year to year, depending on the vintage quality, and the winery may or may not reveal its specific blend.

Meritage (rhymes with "heritage") is a trademarked name for Bordeaux-style American wines. Coined in 1981, the name is a combination of "merit" to signify grape quality and "heritage" to denote the historical tradition of wine blending. To use the term Meritage on the label, the wine must be a blend of two or more of the six classic Bordeaux varieties. No single grape variety may account for more than 90% of the blend. The winery must also join the Meritage Alliance and pay an annual licensing fee to the group.

Handy Guide to Virginia Wineries

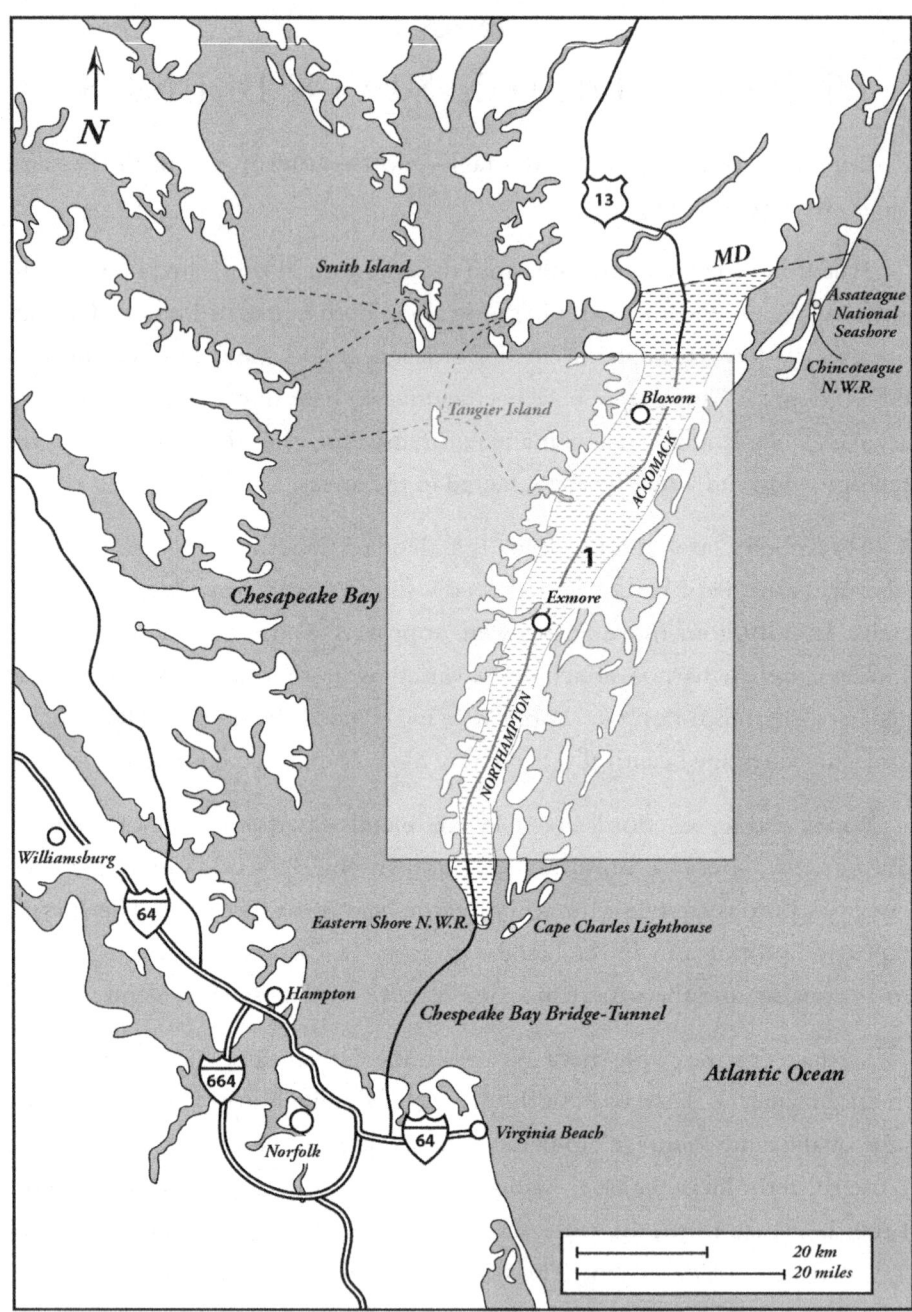

Map 5.0. Eastern Shore

5. EASTERN SHORE REGION & AVA

The Eastern Shore of Virginia is a narrow finger of land directly accessible from Virginia only by way of the 17.6-mile Chesapeake Bay Bridge-Tunnel (CBBT) or by passenger ferry across the Chesapeake Bay. (For drivers with a fear of bridges, a CBBT employee can drive your car across the bridge with advance reservations.) With the Atlantic Ocean on one side and the Chesapeake Bay on the other, the region is marked by sandy, well-drained soils and a temperate climate. At its broadest point, the peninsula is only 22 miles wide and stretches seventy miles from the Maryland border down to its southern tip.

The Eastern Shore's sole remaining winery produces AVA-designated wines, allowing wine aficionados to conduct their own horizontal tastings at home to compare the range of character and personality in wines from across Virginia.

<u>Things to see and do</u>: The Eastern Shore is blessed with exceptional natural beauty and offers numerous options for bird-watching, kayaking, boating, and fishing. Two of its national wildlife refuges (NWR)—the Eastern Shore of Virginia NWR and the Chincoteague NWR—along with the Assateague Island National Seashore and Virginia Coast Reserve all combined translate to perhaps the longest stretch of protected coastline on the Atlantic.

The Eastern Shore NWR at the southern tip of the peninsula is well known as a waystation for migratory birds, particularly in the autumn, as well as for raptors and butterflies. Bird lovers and photographers can use the observation decks and photography blinds in the refuge to observe and photograph birds in their habitat. The refuge's visitor center at Cape Charles has various displays and exhibits to introduce visitors to the region's wildlife. A "Please Touch" table is particularly popular with children, and the summertime Butterfly Garden is a photographer's delight.

The region also offers a number of biking trails, such as a self-guided walking and biking tour on Chincoteague, several trails at Kiptopeke State Park, and the recently opened Southern Tip Bike and Hike Trail. Special bike tours include the annual Between the Waters Bike Tour, a fundraiser hosted by Citizens for a Better Eastern Shore.

In addition, Assateague is famous for its wild ponies which can be seen wandering and grazing on the island. In the Chincoteague Pony Swim in late July, about 150 ponies swim across Assateague Channel in an annual event memorialized by Marguerite Henry in her 1947 children's book, *Misty of Chincoteague*. After some of the foals are sold, the ponies then swim back to Assateague, where visitors can see them in the wild on pony-watching cruises or kayak tours.

Eastern Virginia & Eastern Shore AVA

Handy Guide to Virginia Wineries

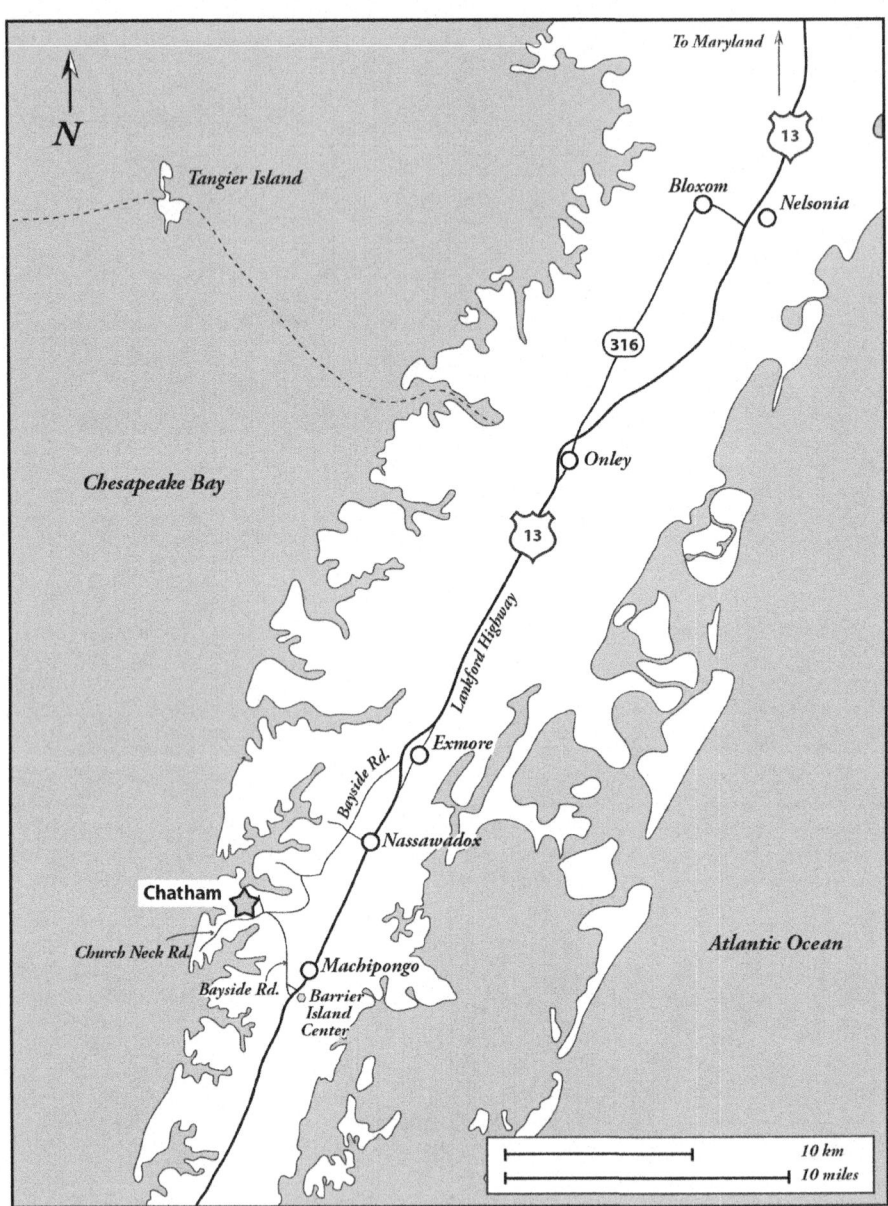

Map 5.1. Eastern Virginia

EASTERN VIRGINIA

Chatham Vineyards & Winery
9232 Chatham Road
Machipongo VA 23405

Hours: Daily 10:00–5:00 (Apr–Dec)
Th–Sa, M 10:00–5:00, Su 12: 00–5:00 (Jan–Mar)
Closed New Year's, Easter, Thanksgiving, Christmas

757-678-5588
http://chathamvineyards.net
E-mail: info@chathamvineyards.net

Chatham Vineyards is owned by second-generation vintner Jon Wehner who worked in his parents' Great Falls Vineyard while growing up in northern Virginia's Fairfax County. The wines are bottled under the Church Creek label, after the stream that flows next to the farm. Chatham hosts various special winery events, including kayak tours and "Girls Days Out." Bread and cheese selections are on offer at the tasting room. The winery may be rented for events and weddings. Children and pets are welcome.

White Wines: Chardonnay.

Rosé Wines: Rosé.

Red Wines: Cabernet Franc, Merlot, Vintner's Blend *(Bordeaux-style blend)*.

Sweet/Dessert Wines: Late Harvest Dessert Wine.

Price Range: $18–$25

Tastings: $8 for self-guided flight, $10 with souvenir glass

ADA accessible.

Purchasing: Online sales for AK, DC, FL, MD, MI, NY, and VA.

Directions: From U.S. Route 13, turn west at the Barrier Islands Center onto Young Street then right on Bayside Road. Drive 3 miles. Turn left onto Church Neck Road and right onto Chatham Road. The winery is on the left.

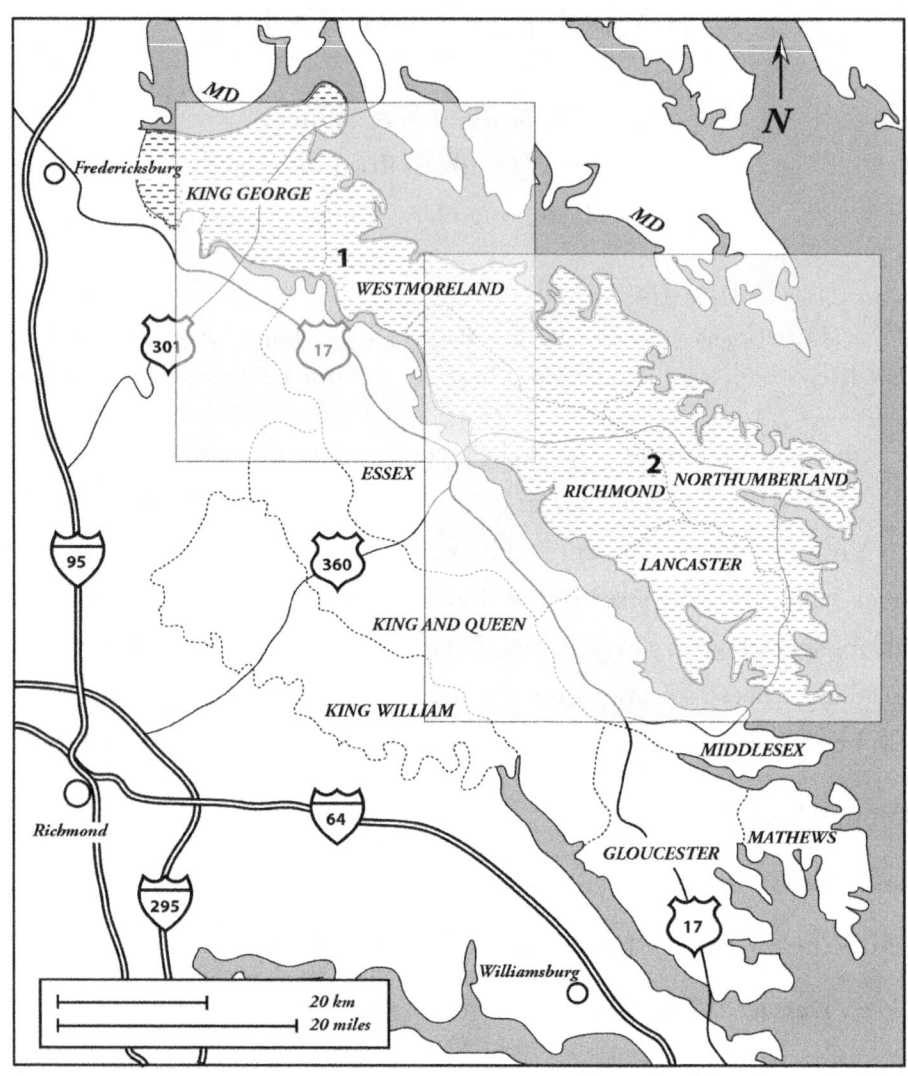

Map 6.0. Chesapeake Bay Region & Northern Neck-George Washington Birthplace AVA: (1) Northern Neck (northern section); (2) Northern Neck (southern section).

6. CHESAPEAKE BAY REGION & NORTHERN NECK-GEORGE WASHINGTON BIRTHPLACE AVA

Virginia's three long peninsulas jutting into the Chesapeake Bay were the first to be colonized by the English in the 17th century. The northernmost of these, the Northern Neck, is bounded on the north by the Potomac River and on the south by the Rappahannock. The Middle Peninsula is next, bounded by the Rappahannock to the north and the York River to the south.

The name of the AVA is generally given simply as Northern Neck, the original longer title having been a compromise between the names originally proposed. The AVA is characterized by relatively flat terrain and light, sandy, well-drained soils. It has a comparatively mild climate, especially during winter: the moderating influence of the Chesapeake Bay keeps frost days at a minimum, and river breezes help temper summertime heat and humidity.

The region's wineries produce the full range of wines, from sparkling to dry to dessert and even fortified. For their largely estate-grown production, Northern Neck wineries use varietals that are also grown elsewhere in Virginia, but the nature and essence of their wines will be distinctly different precisely because of the AVA's unique climate and soil combinations. Reds, for instance, can be lighter than those from central Virginia where the climate and soils are different.

<u>Things to See and Do</u>: The first recorded exploration of the Chesapeake Bay region by a European was in 1608 when Captain John Smith led two expeditions from Jamestown northward to map the Chesapeake and its native American settlements. Over the years, the region's agricultural and fishing resources attracted a growing number of planters and colonists from England who settled in the area.

A number of these families rose to prominence during the American War of Independence. Presidents George Washington, James Madison, and James Monroe were born on the Northern Neck, as were Francis Lightfoot Lee and Richard Henry Lee, signers of the Declaration of Independence. The Lee brothers' cousin, Henry Lee, was the grandfather of General Robert E. Lee, commander of the Confederate Army of Northern Virginia, who was born at Stratford Hall, the family plantation on the banks of the Potomac.

Local points of interest include the Steamboat Era Museum in Irvington, which highlights the economic impact of steamboats on previously isolated Northern Neck villages; the Morattico Waterfront Museum, housed in a century-old restored general store; and the Kinsale Museum, which features historic displays and exhibits by local artists.

The Northern Neck boasts a rich variety of outdoor activities for nature lovers to enjoy, including boating, camping, and hiking trails. For instance, Westmoreland State Park offers trails and riverside beaches over its 1,300 acres along the Potomac River. Fishing enthusiasts can take advantage of the various charter boats along the coast for a day of angling out on the nearby Chesapeake Bay. And wildlife lovers and birders can opt to visit the Northern Neck wetlands which welcome over 200 species of migratory birds each year and are home to one of the largest populations of bald eagles on the eastern U.S. coast, making the region a bird-watcher's paradise.

Wine Trails: The Chesapeake Bay Wine Trail includes all the wineries in the Northern Neck and Middle Peninsula. Please see Appendix 1 for more details.

Handy Guide to Virginia Wineries

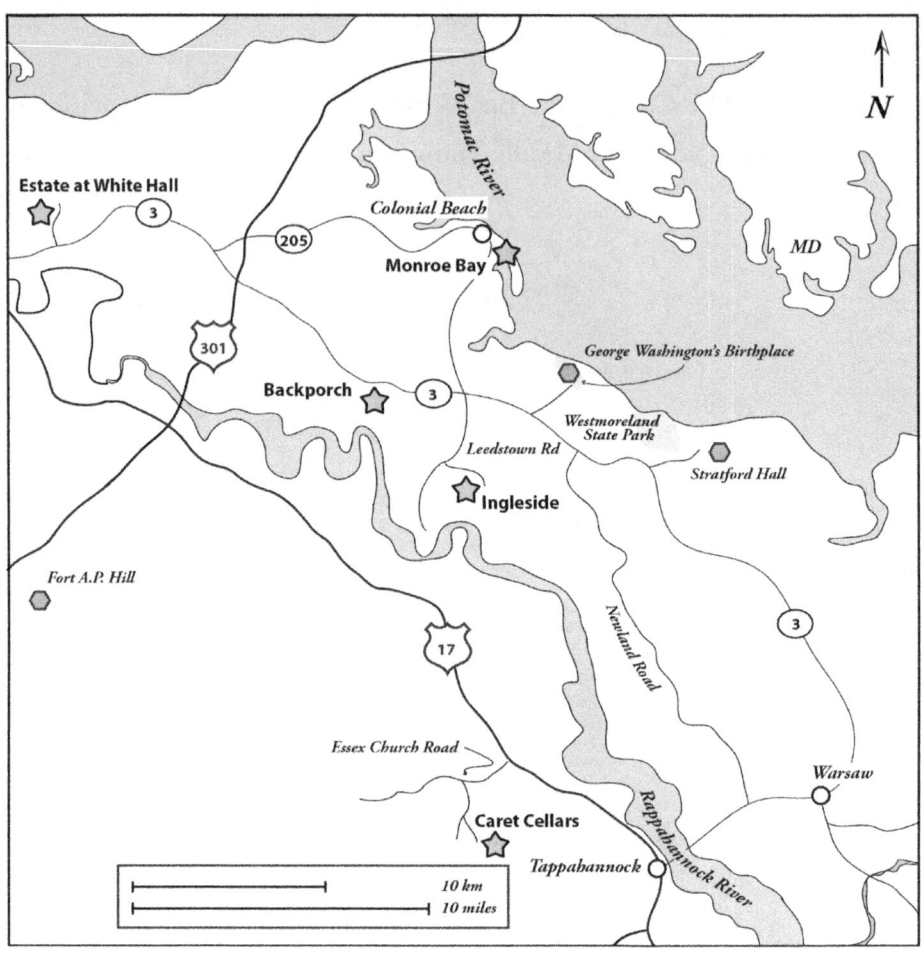

Map 6.1. Northern Neck (northern section)

NORTHERN NECK

Backporch Vineyard
16595 Wilmont Road
King George VA 22485

Hours: F 4:00–8:00, Sa 12:00–7:00, Su 12:00–6:00 (summer & fall)　　540-940-3939
F 4:00–8:00, Sa 12:00–6:00, Su 2:00–5:00 (winter)　　www.backporchvineyard.com
Closed New Year's, Easter, Christmas　　E-mail: backporchvineyard@gmail.com

Backporch was launched in 2019 by longtime Northern Neck friends and residents Lori and Rick Gump and Sherri Spillman, who opened their winery for business one year later. The tasting room is in an Amish-built barn that can be rented for private parties. The winery offers cheese and crackers for purchase and frequently has food trucks on-site; guests are also welcome to bring their own food. Backporch hosts occasional events such as Paint-N-Sips and live music.

White Wines: 77 Steps *(Riesling)*, Andrea's Flock *(Chardonnay)*.

Red Wines: Cabernet Sauvignon, Freeman's Red Oak, Sunset Red.

Price Range: $20–$30

Tastings: $6 per person.

Groups: Reservations encouraged for groups of 8 or more.

Directions: From Route 3, turn onto Rollins Fork Road at the hamlet of Rollins Fork, then onto Wilmont Road. The winery entrance will be 0.1 mile on the right.

Caret Cellars
495 Meadow Landing Lane
Caret VA 22436

Hours: F–Su 12:00–6:00
Closed New Year's, Thanksgiving, Christmas Eve & Day

540-413-6454
www.caretcellars.com
E-mail: info@caretcellars.com

Rich and Junghee Thompson opened Caret Cellars (*kah-rett*] in early September 2015 and produce all Virginia-grown wines, many from their own vineyards. The spacious tasting room has seating both indoors as well as outside where visitors can enjoy live music over their own picnics or selections from food trucks on weekends. Caret also sponsors special tastings, circumstances permitting. The facilities are available for private events. Children and leashed dogs are welcome.

White Wines: Chardonnay, Pinot Grigio, Viognier, White Merlot.

Rosé Wines: Rosato di Sangiovese.

Red Wines: Caret Sunset, Chambourcin, Merlot, Rivah Red, Sangiovese, Super Tuscan, .

Price Range: $15–$24

Tastings: $5 per person

Purchasing: Online to AK, AZ, CO, DC, FL, GA, HI, IA, ID, IN, KS, LA, MA, MD, ME, MN, MO, NC, ND, NE, NH, NM, NV, NY, OH, OR, PA, SC, TN, TX, VA, WA, WI, WV, and WY.

Directions: From U.S. Route 17, turn onto Essex Church Road (VA 624). Drive 0.5 mile and turn left onto Belmont Road (unpaved). After another half-mile, Belmont curves left and turns into Meadow Landing (unpaved). Continue on to the winery entrance on the left.

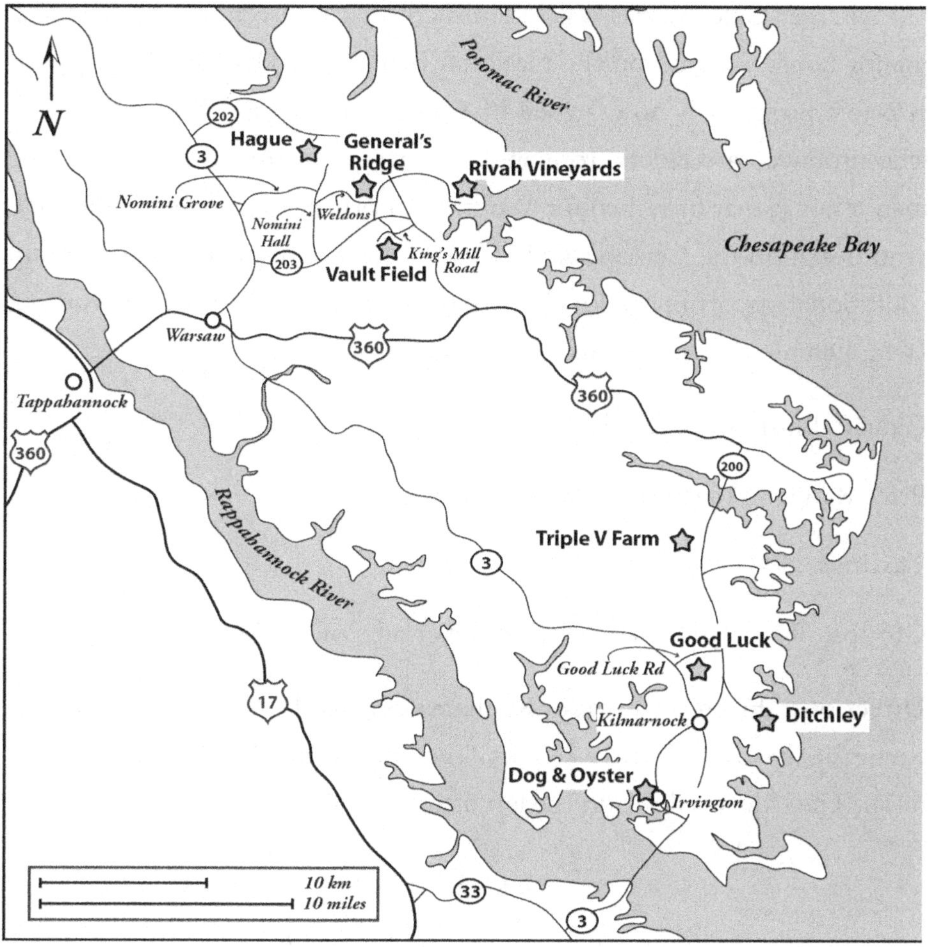

Chesapeake Bay Region & Northern Neck AVA

Map 6.2. Northern Neck (southern section)

❖ ❖ ❖

Ditchley Cider Works
1571 Ditchley Road
Kilmarnock VA 22482

Hours: Fr 4:00–6:00, Sa 1:00–5:00, Su 11:00–2:00
Closed New Year's, Easter, Christmas

804-435-3851
www.ditchleyciderworks.com
E-mail: Cathy@DitchleyCiderWorks.com

Ditchley Cider Works was established on a 17th-century estate whose manor house is listed on the National Register of Historic Places. The 162-acre property is now owned by Cathy Calhoun and Paul Grosklags, who produce hard ciders from apples grown in their own orchards. The manor house may be rented for weddings or private events, and has a small sand beach on the Chesapeake Bay. The cidery also puts on small group educational opportunities for children by reservation. As an active working farm, Ditchley has farm sausage and beef for sale.

Ciders: Blush, G-8, Rivah.

Price Range: $18 (bottle) – $38 (growler)

Tastings: $6 per person.

Groups: Reservations encouraged for groups of 8 or more.

Directions: From the town of Kilmarnock, take East Church Street (VA Route 200 North) and drive 2 miles. Turn right onto Ditchley Road (Route 607). The cidery will be on the left after 1.6 miles.

The Dog and Oyster Vineyards
65 Tavern Road
Irvington VA 22480

Hours: Daily 11:00–5:00 (May–Oct)
F-Su 11:00–5:00 (Apr, Nov)
Closed Dec–Mar

804-438-9463
www.hopeandglory.com/the-dog-oyster-vineyard
E-mail: info@dogandoyster.com

The Dog and Oyster is owned by Doug and Peggy Patterson who named the winery after their family rescue dogs and the oysters of the Chesapeake Bay. The winery is located on the grounds of the family's Hope & Glory Inn in the town of Irvington, not far from their original six-acre vineyard. The tasting room includes indoor and outdoor seating, including some overlooking a new one-acre vineyard planted to Petit Manseng. Visitors can choose from a light fare menu on weekdays, with daily oyster and crab specialties on weekends. Dogs are welcome. The facilities may be rented for private events.

Guests may stay at the Pattersons' Hope and Glory Inn, or the Tents at Vineyard Grove, about half a mile away.

White Wines: Oyster White *(Chardonel)*, Pearl *(Vidal Blanc)*.

Rosé Wines: Rosie.

Red Wines: Merlot, Shelter Dog Red.

Price Range: $28–$39

Tastings: $8 per person for a flight.

Groups: Call ahead for groups over six.

ADA accessible.

Directions: From U.S. Route 17 in the town of Kilmarnock, drive south on Irvington Road (VA Route 200) for 4 miles. Turn left onto White Fences Lane at the giant corkscrews and continue to the winery parking lot on the right.

The Estate at White Hall Vineyard
3668 White Hall Road
King George VA 22485

Hours: Fr 5:00–8:00, Sa 12:30–7:00, Su 1:00–7:00   540-656-6958
Closed New Year's, Easter, Christmas   www.theestateatwhitehall.com
E-mail: info@TheEstateAtWhiteHall.com

The Estate at White Hall Vineyards was launched in 2019 on a 250-year-old estate by owners Joel and Bethany Cassell, who dedicate a portion of tasting room sales for local non-profit and educational initiatives. Guests can sit indoors in the barn or outdoor on the grounds; firepits are available for chilly months (bring your own starter). Live music and food trucks are frequently sponsored on weekends. The winery facilities may be rented for weddings, including the 1850 Stable Chapel and 1907 Dairy Barn Cathedral. Discounts apply for military personnel and teachers.

White Wines: Cat's Meow, Lucky Goat, Soli Deo Gloria, Solus Christus.

Rosé Wines: Sola Gratia.

Red Wines: 1740 Reserve, Boergeaux Blend #1, Goats of Wrath, Sola Fide, Sola Scriptura, Wandering Goat.

Price Range: $22–$45

Tastings: $6 per person.

Groups: Reservations encouraged for groups of 8 or more.

ADA accessible.

Directions: From Route 3, turn onto Lambs Creek Church Road (Route 694) and drive 1.4 miles. Turn left onto White Hall Road and continue ½ mile to the winery entrance.

General's Ridge Vineyard & Winery
1618 Weldons Drive
Hague VA 22469

Hours: F 12:00–7:00, Sa 12:00–6:00, Su 12:00–5:00 804-472-3172
Closed New Year's, Thanksgiving, Christmas   http://generalsridgevineyard.com
E-mail: tastingroom@generalsridgevineyard.com

Founded by retired General Rick Phillips and his wife, Linda, General's Ridge began as a vineyard selling its production to nearby wineries. Ten years later, the couple decided to start their own winery and opened to the public in 2011. They currently have about 30 acres under vine and work with Michael Shaps Winery which handles their production. Snacks and light food may be purchased in the tasting room. General's Ridge offers various events, including wine pairings and murder-mystery dinners.

General's Ridge offers two guest houses for overnight stays, private parties, and weddings. The Manor House is a restored, two-story, 19th-century house; the smaller Carriage House can hold small conferences or wedding receptions. See the website for details.

Sparkling Wines: Semper Fi.

White Wines: Chardonnay, GRV White, Petit Manseng, Pinot Grigio, Viognier.

Rosé Wines: Rosé.

Red Wines: Cabernet Franc, GRV Red, Merlot, Petit Verdot, Westmoreland Red.

Sweet/Dessert Wines: General's Nightcap *(Petit Manseng)*.

Fortified Wines: General's Last Call *(port-style)*.

Handy Guide to Virginia Wineries

Price Range: $19–$28

Tastings: $9 per person for white or red flight, $14 for full tasting flight.

ADA accessible.

Directions: From U.S. Route 17, turn onto U.S. Route 360 East at the town of Tappahannock. Drive 6.6 miles and turn left onto Route 3 at the town of Warsaw. Continue following Route 3 for 6 miles. Turn right onto Nomini Grove Road (Route 621, which will become Route 600). Drive 3.7 miles until Nomini Grove Road until it ends at Nomini Hall Road and turn right. Take the second left onto Weldons Drive. The winery entrance will be about a mile on the left.

Good Luck Cellars
1025 Good Luck Road
Kilmarnock VA 22482

Hours: M, Th 11:00–5:00, F 11:00–7:00 (to 8:00 in summer), Sa 11:00–6:00 (to 8:00 in summer), Su 12:00–5:00 (Feb–Dec) F 11:00–7:00, Sa 11:00–6:00, Su 12:00–5:00 (Jan) Closed New Year's, Thanksgiving, Christmas

804-435-1416
www.goodluckcellars.com
E-mail: info@goodluckcellars.com

Good Luck Cellars was established by Katie and the late Paul Krop, longtime wine enthusiasts from Virginia Beach who planted their 12-acre vineyard on the site of a reclaimed sand and gravel pit. The winery, which opened in 2011, includes a tasting room with both indoor and outdoor seating, including a wrap-around veranda where visitors can linger. Good Luck offers food trucks on select days and Sangria Sundays. The facilities may be rented for special events.

White Wines: Baleen Beauty, Chardonel, Chardonnay, Seyval, Traminette, Vidal Blanc, Vignoles, Viognier.

Rosé Wines: Rip Rap Rosé.

Red Wines: Cabernet Franc, Cabernet Sauvignon, Chambourcin, Inheritage, Norton, Petit Verdot, Sweet Shamrock *(Chambourcin)*.

Price Range: $17–$32

Tastings: $5 per person.

ADA accessible.

Purchasing: Online to AK, AL, AZ, CA, CO, DC, FL, GA, HI, IA, ID, IN, KS, LA, MA, MD, ME, MN, MO, NC, ND, NE, NH, NM, NV, NY, OH, OR, PA, SC, TN, TX, VA, WA, WI, WV, and WY.

Directions: From the town of Kilmarnock, drive north on Main Street (VA Route 3) for 2 miles. Turn right onto Good Luck Road. The winery will be about one mile on the right.

The Hague Winery
8268 Cople Highway
Hague VA 22469

Hours: F–Su 11:00–5:00 (Apr–Nov) 804-472-7142
Closed Dec–Mar www.thehaguewinery.com
E-mail: chrlrmy@gmail.com

Stephen and Cynthia Madey established their five-acre vineyard on the grounds of the historic Buena Vista plantation, which dates to 1835, just outside the hamlet of Hague, Virginia. The first vines were planted in 2005, and the first estate-grown wines released in 2009 under the guidance of Lucie Morton, one of Virginia's pioneering viticulturists. The Hague's tasting room is in a renovated barn with several tables and chairs indoors as well as a covered patio outside where guests may enjoy light snacks over a glass or bottle of wine.

Visitors may rent The Cottage, a two-bedroom restored guest house on the property, for overnight stays; see the website for details.

White Wines: Chardonel, Chardonnay.

Rosé Wines: Rosé.

Red Wines: Cabernet Franc, Colonel's Red, Meritage, Merlot, Petit Verdot.

Dessert Wines: Cynthia *(Muscat Ottonel)*.

Price Range: $19–$29

Tastings: $6 per person.

Groups: Reservations encouraged for groups of 8 or more.

Purchasing: Online for AK, AZ, CA, CO, CT, DC, FL, GA, HI, IA, ID, IL, IN, KS, LA, ME, MI, MN, MO, NC, ND, NE, NH, NV, NY, OH, OR, SC, TN, TX, VA, VT, WA, WI, WV, and WY.

Directions: From U.S. Route 17, turn onto U.S. Route 340 East at the town of Tappahannock. Drive 6.6 miles and turn left onto Route 3 at the town of Warsaw. Continue following Route 3 for 3.3 miles and turn right onto Oldhams Road (Route 203). Drive 7.5 miles and turn left onto Cople Highway (Route 202). Drive 4.6 miles to the winery entrance on left.

Ingleside Vineyards & Winery
5872 Leedstown Road
Oak Grove VA 22443

Hours: M–Su 12:00–5:00 804-224-8687
(from Memorial Day to Labor Day, to 6:00 daily) www.inglesidevineyards.com
Closed New Year's, Easter, E-mail: info@inglesidevineyards.com
Thanksgiving, Christmas

One of Virginia's earliest wineries, Ingleside Vineyards is also among the largest in terms of acreage, with over 60 acres under vine. The property has been owned by the same family for over 100 years, making it a Virginia Century Farm. The winery sponsors a range of events, such as live music, barrel tastings, and harvest festivals, and is available for weddings or private parties for up to 150 guests on the grounds. The tasting room is in an old dairy barn and includes a patio with tables and chairs where visitors may enjoy a picnic lunch. Children will find a small natural history museum at one end of the patio. Pets are welcome.

Ingleside offers overnight stays at two waterfront guest houses: The Pointe and Summerton. Please check the website for rental details.

White Wines: Albariño, Blue Crab Blanc, Chardonnay, Coastal White, Pinot Grigio, Viognier.

Rosé Wines: Rosato di Sangiovese, Sweet Rose Mallow, Sweet Virginia Rosé.

Red Wines: Cabernet Franc, Cabernet Merlot, Coastal Red, Left Bank, Petit Verdot, Red Drum, Right Bank, Sangiovese.

Price Range: $17–$33

Tastings: $12 per person.

Groups: Reservations required for groups of 6 or more.

ADA accessible.

Purchasing: Online to AK, AL, AZ, CA, CO, DC, FL, GA, HI, IA, ID, IL, IN, KS, LA, MA, MD, ME, MN, MO, NC, ND, NE, NH, NM, NV, NY, OH, OK, OR, PA, SC, TN, TX, VA, WA, WI, WV, and WY.

Directions: From U.S. Route 301, turn south onto Route 3. Drive 10 miles and turn right onto Leedstown Road (Route 638). Drive 2.2 miles to the winery's gravel driveway on the left.

Monroe Bay Winery
4786 James Monroe Highway (Route 205)
Colonial Beach VA 22443

Hours: Sa–Su 12:00–5:00 (Jun–Aug);
Sa 12:00–5:00 (Apr–May, Sep–Dec)
Closed Jan–Mar

804-410-5628
www.monroebaywine.com
E-mail: info@monroebaywine.com

Monroe Bay Winery was launched by owner Kiki Apple who became a home winemaker after living in France and then sold wine at farmers markets. The winery offers live music and arts, and offers indoor seating and ample spaces outdoors, including chairs overlooking an inlet of the Potomac River where bald eagles and herons can be spotted. The facilities may be rented for weddings or private events. Monroe Bay also has a small tasting room in Colonial Beach at 10 Washington Avenue (Sa 5:00–8:00, summer only).

Ciders: Boardwalk, Hopped, Pumpkin Spice.

White Wines: Blue Heron White, Chardonnay, Petit Manseng, Viognier.

Rosé Wines: Blue Heron Rosé.

Red Wines: Blue Heron Red, Cabernet Franc, Petit Verdot.

Price Range: $17–$24

Tastings: $6 per person.

Directions: From Colonial Beach, take James Monroe Highway (Route 205) south. Drive one mile and turn left at the Colonial Beach Moose Lodge Center sign. The winery entrance will be about ¼ mile on the left.

Rivah Vineyards at the Grove
671 Kinsale Bridge Road
Kinsale VA 22488

Hours: Th, Su 12:00–5:00, F–Sa 1:00–8:00 (summer)
F–Su 12:00–5:00 (fall–spring)
Closed New Year's, Easter, Christmas

804-761-8344
www.rivahvineyards.com
E-mail: Rivahvines@gmail.com

Rivah Vineyards was the dream of Bryce Taylor, whose family has owned the historic property continuously since the 18th century; it is a Virginia Century Farm. Working with vineyard and wine consultant Floyd Oslin, Bryce produces a range of estate-grown wines and is happy to offer pairing suggestions for each. The tasting room is on a small bluff overlooking the Yeocomico River and has seating indoors as well as on the wrap-around deck; additional outdoor tables and chairs are under the trees surrounding the property. Guests may purchase cheeses and snacks or take advantage of the food trucks that are often present on weekends.

White Wines: Chardonel, Cool Breeze, Yeocomico White.

Red Wines: Chambourcin, Element, Stolen Kiss, Sweet Sue.

Price Range: $17–$30

Tastings: $6 per person.

Groups: Reservations encouraged for groups of 8 or more.

Directions: From the town of Warsaw, drive north on Route 3 for 2.5 miles, then turn right onto VA Route 203 North. Continue another 10 miles into the town of Kinsale. After crossing the Kinsale River, bear left onto Kinsale Bridge Road (Route 607) and drive ¼ mile. Turn left onto Browns Cove Road, then bear right to the winery entrance.

Triple V Farm Winery
3138 Jessie DuPont Memorial Highway
Heathsville VA 22473

Hours: F 3:00–dusk, Sa–Su 11:00–dusk (summer)
F 3:00–5:00, Sa–Su 12:00–5:00 (fall–spring)
Closed New Year's, Easter, Christmas

804-724-5765
www.triplevfarms.com
E-mail: camspirits@aol.com

Triple V Farm Winery was opened in 2020 by Craig Allshouse and Marti Moyer after purchasing the former Athena Vineyards and Winery. The couple offers wine (vines), vinegar, and vodka (the "triple V") for sale, as well as cheeses and crackers. The tasting room has a wraparound porch with seating for visitors who can also opt to sit on the grounds (fire pits available in cooler weather). Live music and food trucks are scheduled for many Saturdays.

White Wines: Chardonnay, Pinot Grigio, Seyval Blanc, Symphony, Viognier.

Rosé Wines: Sweet Rosé, Northern Neck Rosé, Reserve Rosé.

Red Wines: Cabernet Franc, Cabernet Sauvignon, Chambourcin, Merlot, Petit Verdot, Pinot Noir, Rip Tide.

Sweet/Dessert Wines: High Tide *(Symphony)*, Low Tide *(Symphony)*, White Caps Dolce *(Symphony)*, Wicomico Red.

Fortified Wines: Chesapeake Bay Port, Ebb Tide *(sherry-style)*.

Price Range: $17–$24

Tastings: $6 per person.

Groups: Reservations encouraged for groups of 8 or more.

Directions: From the town of Kilmarnock, drive north on VA Route 200 (Jessie DuPont Memorial Highway) for 9.5 miles to the winery entrance on the left.

Vault Field Vineyards
2953 Kings Mill Road
Kinsale VA 22488

Hours: Th–Su 11:00–5:00 (to 6:00 in summer) (Apr–Dec); 804-472-4430
Open most Saturdays, Jan–Mar (call first)   www.vaultfield.com
Closed Easter, Thanksgiving, Christmas   E-mail: info@vaultfield.com

After a career in the insurance industry, Keith and Joanne Meenan decided to purchase the historic Vault Field Farm and start a vineyard and winery. The Meenans and their son Dan manage all operations on the vineyard, with Keith also serving as winemaker. The tasting room is inside the winery building. The winery sponsors fall barrel tastings and a spring open house featuring music and light food; proceeds from the events are donated to the local volunteer fire department. Vault Field offers private tastings by appointment.

White Wines: Chardonnay, Conundrum *(Chardonnay, Chardonel, Vidal Blanc)*, Vidal Blanc.

Rosé Wines: Rosé.

Red Wines: Merlot, Red *(Merlot, Cabernet Sauvignon, Chambourcin)*, Reserve Red.

Price Range: $17–$22

Tastings: $5 per person.

ADA accessible.

Purchasing: Online for all states <u>*except*</u> AL, AK, AR, DE, HI, MA, MT, NJ, NM, OK, PA, SD, and UT.

Directions: From U.S. Route 17, turn onto U.S. Route 340 East at the town of Tappahannock. Drive 6.6 miles and turn left onto Route 3 at the town of Warsaw. Continue following Route 3 for 3.3 miles and turn right onto Oldhams Road (Route 203). Drive 7.5 miles and turn right onto Cople Highway (Route 202). Take the first right onto Kings Mill Road. The winery driveway will be about 1 mile on the right.

SWEET WINES

Sweet wines can range widely from lightly sweet, or "off dry," wines—enjoyed on their own or with food—to rich, almost voluptuous wines that are an exquisite finish to a fine meal.

While the sweetness of a wine is technically defined by its residual sugar (the percentage of sugar per liter of liquid), a wine's perceived sweetness depends on its acidity, tannins, alcohol strength, and serving temperature. This means that wines with as little as 1.5% residual sugar can be perceived as quite sweet.

Sweet wines are made by stopping fermentation before all the natural sugars have been consumed; by adding grape sugar (called "sweet reserve") after fermentation; or by concentrating the grapes' sweetness before fermentation.

While the first two methods are done after the process of making wine has begun, concentrating the fruit's natural sweetness takes place in advance. The three main ways of concentrating sweetness are by freezing the grapes, drying the grapes, or delaying harvest.

Ice wines are just what they sound like. Grapes are either allowed to freeze on the vine or are frozen through mechanical means after being harvested. Depending on the altitude of a vineyard and the climate of a given year, a few Virginia wineries are occasionally able to make true "frozen on the vine" ice wines.

Sweet wine may be made from grapes that have been spread on trays or mats and allowed to dry or "raisin" before the winemaking process begins. Potomac Point Winery, for instance, has on occasion offered a Vin de Paille as part of its selection of wines; *paille* means "straw" in French and refers to the straw mats traditionally used to dry grapes.

Late-harvest wines use grapes that have been left on the vine to the point of ultra-ripeness or even raisining before they are harvested. This concentrates the natural sugars of the grapes and gives their juice an added richness of flavor.

Handy Guide to Virginia Wineries

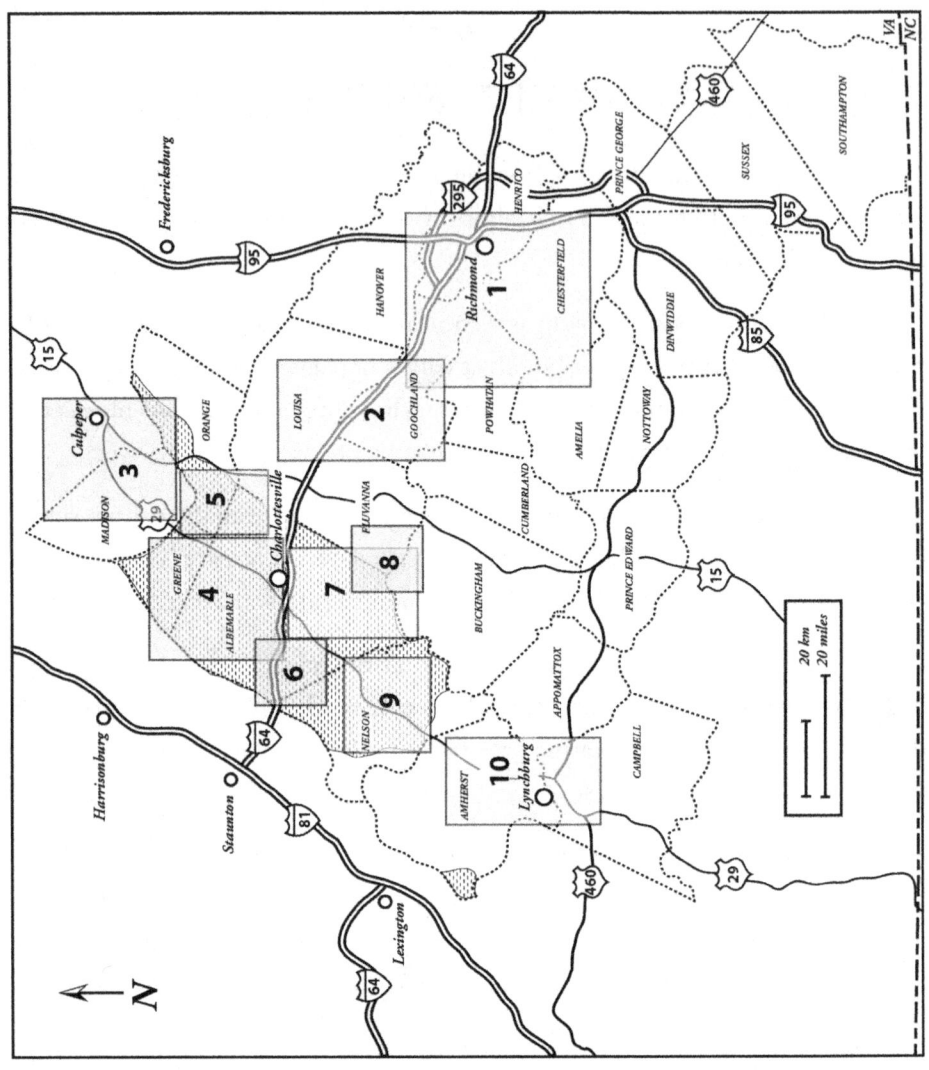

Map 7.0. Central Virginia Region & Monticello AVA: (1) Richmond; (2) Louisa; (3) Madison; (4) Free Union-White Hall; (5) Stony Point; (6) Afton-Crozet; (7) North Garden; (8) Scottsville; (9) Lovingston; (10) Lynchburg.

7. CENTRAL VIRGINIA REGION & MONTICELLO AVA

Bounded by the Blue Ridge on the west and Tidewater on the east, the Central Virginia Region is rich in history and natural attractions. The topography of this region varies considerably, rising from the flat terrain of the fall line at Richmond to the Blue Ridge Mountains in the west. The Monticello AVA is centered around Charlottesville in the western part of the larger region. While summers throughout Central Virginia are warm, the Blue Ridge tends to help moderate winter temperatures in the AVA, protecting it from the lower temperatures that can sometimes occur in the Shenandoah Valley immediately to the west.

The Central Virginia region is second only to Northern Virginia in the number of wineries, with nearly eighty that are regularly open to the public. Roughly two-thirds of these are in the Monticello AVA, whose vineyards produce twenty-four separate varieties of grapes, including less commonly known ones such as Rkatsiteli, Touriga Nacional, and Pinotage. As of 2016, 145 wines were labeled with the Monticello AVA designation, which means that 85 percent of the grapes used to produce them originated in the AVA itself. Soils here are generally clay underlain by granite and can produce quite full-bodied wines.

<u>Things to see and do</u>: There are numerous historical attractions spread throughout the region, ranging from homes of the American founders

(Thomas Jefferson's Monticello and James Monroe's Ash Lawn) to the central campus of the University of Virginia in Charlottesville, designed by Thomas Jefferson and the sole American university to be named a World Heritage Site.

Virginia's capital of Richmond offers a number of interesting sites for visitors. The Church Hill district, located immediately to the east of the downtown area, is a colonial-era neighborhood that includes the historic St. John's Church, where Patrick Henry gave his "Give me liberty or give me death!" speech in 1775. The Virginia state capitol building was designed by Thomas Jefferson, who used the Roman-era Maison Carrée in Nîmes, France, as his architectural inspiration. Near the Capitol is the Virginia Civil Rights Memorial that commemorates the student strike led by Barbara Rose Johns of Farmville, Virginia; the students' actions at their high school ultimately led to the Brown v. Board of Education lawsuit that mandated equal educational opportunities for all, regardless of race.

The entire region is particularly rich in Civil War history. The greater Richmond area includes, among other sites, the National Museum of the Civil War Soldier at the Pamplin Historical Park, located near Petersburg on the battlefield where General Ulysses S. Grant's forces shattered General Robert E. Lee's lines in April, 1865. The Sailor's Creek battlefield, just east of Farmville, was the last major battle of the Civil War in the Virginia theater. Three days after losing 7,700 men in combat there against Union forces, General Lee surrendered to General Grant at Appomattox Court House 46 miles to the west. The Lee's Retreat Trail is a self-guided driving tour that traces Lee's last moves as he was relentlessly pursued by Grant from Petersburg to Appomattox (www.varetreat.com/lee.asp).

Richmond's Jackson Ward neighborhood offers a walking tour where visitors may explore the area called the Harlem of the South that was home for many African-American entrepreneurs after the Civil War. Jackson Ward also was the residence of Maggie Walker, the first woman of any race to found and serve as the chief executive officer of a bank; her home is now a national historic site run by the National Park Service. Further south in Lynchburg is the home of Anne Spencer, the noted Harlem Renaissance poet who was the second African-American to be included in the Norton Anthology of Literature.

The region also includes part of Virginia's Civil Rights in Education Heritage Trail (www.varetreat.com/CivilRights.asp), a self-guided driving tour of key sites in the struggle of African-Americans, Native Americans, and women to attain greater access and rights to educational resources.

Visitors with children may want to add a side trip to King's Dominion, north of Richmond, a balloon ride over Albemarle County, or a kayak trip down the Rivanna River.

<u>Wine Trails</u>: There are several wine trails for Central Virginia wineries, among them the Heart of Virginia Wine Trail, the Monticello Wine Trail, the Foothills Scenic Wine Way, and Nelson 151. More details are available in Appendix 1.

Handy Guide to Virginia Wineries

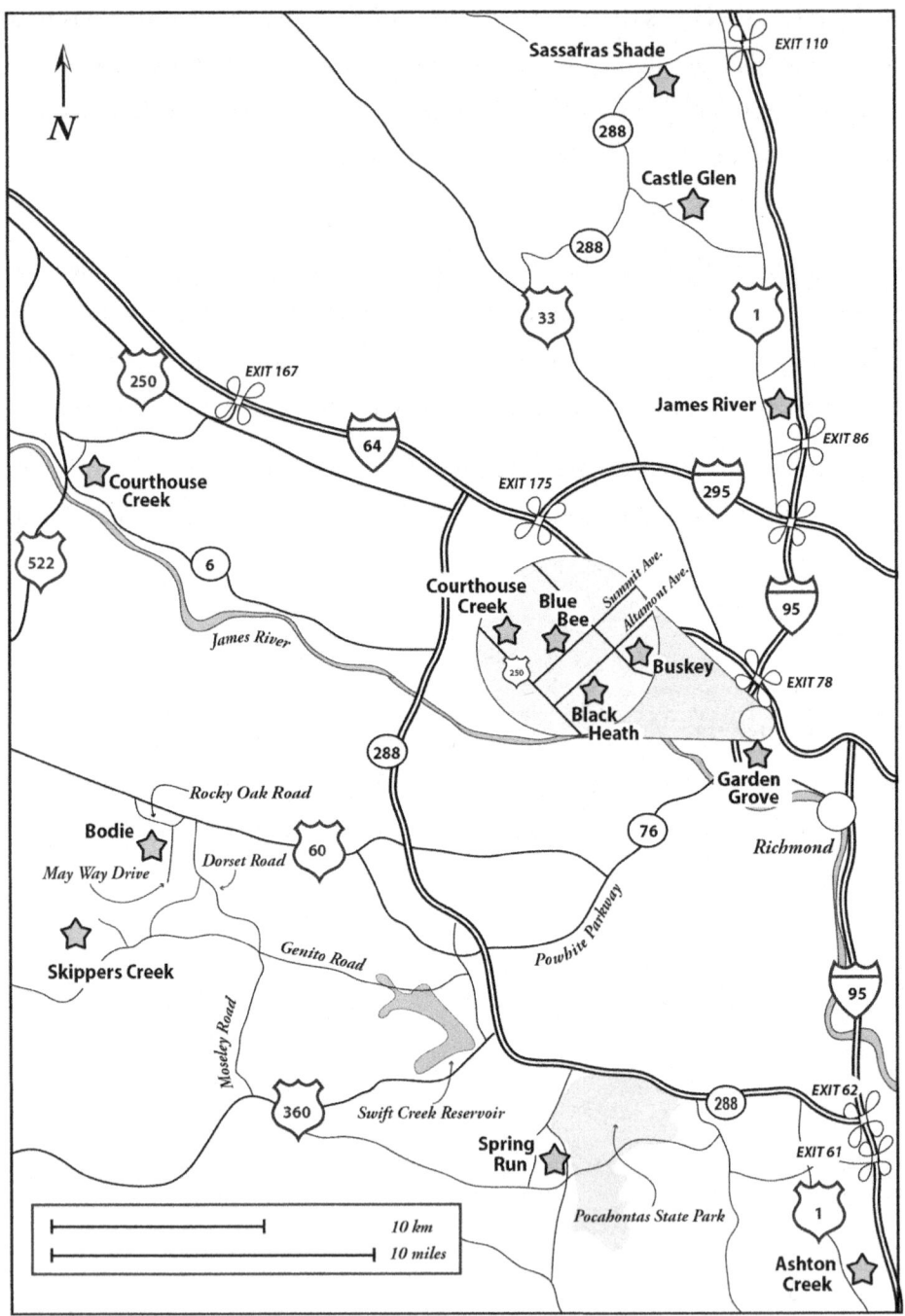

Map 7.1. Richmond

RICHMOND

Ashton Creek Vineyard
14501 Jefferson Davis Highway
Chester VA 23831

Hours: W–Sa 12:00–8:00, Su 12:00–6:00 (summer–fall)   804-896-1586
Closed New Year's, Thanksgiving, Christmas   www.ashtoncreekvineyard.com
E-mail: info@ashtoncreekvineyard.com

    Ashton Creek Vineyard was launched when Kirk and Lori Thibault decided to start a winery and tasting room on their Chesterfield County property. All wines are made with grapes from Virginia and Washington state, including from their vineyard near Lake Chesdin where they plan to open another tasting facility. Ashton Creek offers a range of food, from flatbreads to cheese platters and soups, as well as live music on weekends, yoga classes, and other events. The facilities may be rented on weekends for weddings. Well-behaved children are welcome.

Sparkling Wines: Celebration.

White Wines: Bluebird, Chardonnay, Star White, Twee Blanken, Vidal Blanc, Viognier, Willie's White.

Rosé Wines: Lady May.

Red Wines: After Hours, Bailey's Bold, Cabernet Franc, Cabernet Sauvignon, Cannonball Red, Gravity, Red Velvet, Side Ways.

Price Range: $22–$35

Tastings: $19 per person for a flight.

Purchasing: Online for VA and other states; check with the winery for details.

Directions: From Richmond, take I-95 Southbound for 13 miles to Exit 61B (Chester). Drive west on West Hundred Road (VA 10 West) for ½ mile. Turn left onto Jefferson Davis Highway (U.S. Route 1 South). The winery entrance will be 2.3 miles on the left.

Black Heath Meadery
1313 Altamont Avenue
Richmond VA 23230

Hours: Tu–F 4:00–9:00, Sa 1:00–9:00, Su 1:00–7:00
Closed New Year's, Thanksgiving, Christmas

804-998-7090
www.blackheathmeadery.com
E-mail: taproom@blackheathmeadery.com

Owner Bill Cavender launched Black Heath Meadery in Richmond's Scott's Addition neighborhood, building on his 24 years of experience as a home brewer of this ancient beverage. Cavender produces a wide range of meads, from traditional recipes to meads infused with hops, fruit, or peppers, or aged in gin barrels. All are made from honey and fruit from Virginia. The specific meads on the tasting line-up will vary, depending on availability.

Meads & Melomels: Armenian Reflection, Blue Angel, El Machete, Ficus Carica, Ginger Reflection, Heat of Passion, Krampus Kraft, Living Rose, Meadsaic, Montmorency Reflection, The Muse, Pompelmo Reflection, Respect, Santa Fe, Spicy Machete, Valhalla, Vanilla Angel.

Dessert Ciders: Firecracker, Harvest Ration.

Price Range: $5–$27

Tastings: $10 per person for a flight.

Purchasing: Online to VA and other states; call the meadery for details.

Directions: From Interstate 95, take Exit 78 onto Arthur Ashe Boulevard. Drive about one mile to Clay Street and turn right. Turn left onto Altamont Avenue; the meadery will be on the left.

Blue Bee Cider
1320 Summit Avenue
Richmond VA 23230

Hours: M, Th–F 1:00–9:00, Sa 12:00–9:00, Su 12:00–7:00 (summer)   804-231-0280
M, Th–F 1:00–8:00, Sa 12:00–8:00, Su 12:00–6:00 (winter)   www.bluebeecider.com
Closed New Year's, Thanksgiving, Christmas   E-mail: admin@bluebeecider.com

Blue Bee Cider, Virginia's first urban cidery, was founded in 2013 by Courtney Mailey who graduated from Cornell University's cider school and apprenticed at Albemarle Ciderworks. Named after Virginia's native blue orchard bees, Blue Bee is located in Richmond's historic Scott's Addition neighborhood just a short walk from Buskey Cider and Black Heath Mead. Blue Bee offers cheeses and charcuterie from the onsite Truckle Cheesemongers for visitors to enjoy over a cider after their tastings. The specific ciders on the tasting line-up will vary, depending on availability. Dogs are welcome outdoors.

Ciders: Aragon 1904, Charred Ordinary, Harrison, Hewe's Crab, Hops Addition, Hopsap Shandy, Petit Manchurian, Rocky Ridge Reserve, Trifecta.

Dessert Ciders: Firecracker, Harvest Ration.

Price Range: $11–$35

Tastings: $12 to $15 per person for a flight.

Purchasing: Online for AK, CA, CO, DC, FL, GA, IL, MD, MN, NC, NY, PA, TN, TX, VA, and WA.

Directions: From Interstate 95, take Exit 78 onto Arthur Ashe Boulevard. Drive about one mile to Clay Street and turn right. Turn left onto Summit Avenue; the cidery will be on the right.

Bodie Vineyards
1809 May Way Drive
Powhatan VA 23139

Hours: Sa 1:00–5:00 (until 6:00 in summer)   804-598-2240
Closed Nov–Mar   www.bodievineyards.com
E-mail: bodievineyards@rocketmail.com

Clyde and Mary Bodie are longtime home winemakers who established their small farm winery in 2008, opening it to the public two years later. The facilities include an outdoor pavilion and picnic tables, where guests are welcome to enjoy a picnic from home. The winery sponsors annual harvest festivals that welcome volunteers to help bring in the grapes. The facilities are available for private parties and events. Children and dogs are welcome.

White Wines: Michaux Blanc *(Cayuga)*.

Red Wines: Rochette Rouge *(Buffalo)*.

Price Range: $15–$20

Directions: From Route 288, turn west onto U.S. Route 60. Drive 8 miles and turn south onto Rocky Oak Road. After about half a mile, turn left onto May Way Drive. The winery driveway will be ⅓ mile on the right.

Buskey Cider
2910 West Leigh Street
Richmond VA 23230

Hours: M–Th 3:00–9:00, F–Sa 12:00–10:00, Su 12:00–9:00
Closed New Year's, Thanksgiving, Christmas

804-355-0100
www.buskeycider.com
E-mail: buskey@buskeycider.com

Will Correll, along with partner Matthew Meyer (head winemaker at Williamsburg Winery), opened Richmond's second cidery in 2016 in the historic Scott's Addition neighborhood that is becoming a hub for craft brewing and ciders. Cidermaker Alec Steinmetz uses organically-grown apples from an orchard near Harrisonburg in the Shenandoah Valley to make a range of ciders, including some infused with such ingredients as cherry, lemongrass, or jalapeño. The facilities may be rented for special events. The tasting room tables have slate tops and chalk for guests to use for doodling. The cidery name comes from an old Colonial American slang term for someone who is tipsy.

Buskey Cider also has a tasting room on the Eastern Shore at 109 Mason Avenue, Cape Charles; hours are F 4:30–8:00, Sa 12:00–8:00, Su 12:00–6:00.

Ciders: Blackberry Juniper, Buskey Brandy Barrel-Aged, Buskey Dry, Earl Grey Lemon Ginger, Guava Grapefruit, Heritage Blend, Jalapeño Lime, Peach Tea, RVA, Strawberry Rhubarb, Tart Cherry.

Price Range: Varies depending on size

Directions: From Interstate 95, take Exit 78 onto Arthur Ashe Boulevard. Drive about 0.9 mile to West Leigh Street and turn right. The cidery will be on the right.

Castle Glen Estates Farm & Winery
18185 Narrow Path Trail
Doswell VA 23047

Hours: F–Su 1:00–6:00
Closed New Year's, Easter, Christmas

804-763-9677
www.castleglenwine.com
E-mail: info@castleglenwine.com

Ed and Pamela Cowdrey opened Castle Glen in 2015 on their 10-acre property, five miles from King's Dominion, inspired by Ed's longtime fascination with winemaking. The winery offers tasting flights that can be enjoyed either indoors or out. Castle Glen holds a range of special events, such as cooking and wine-pairing presentations, happy hour live music, and even, on occasion, a baby goat-petting zoo. Well-behaved chidren and dogs are welcome.

White Wine: Sun Dress White, Vidal Blanc.

Rosé Wine: Cocktail Dress Rosé.

Red Wine: Cabernet Sauvignon, Chambourcin, Merlot, Sassy Sangria.

Price Range: $19–$29

Directions: From I-95, take Exit 98 (Doswell) and turn west. Take U.S. Route 1 toward Doswell. After 1.4 miles, turn left onto Verdon Road (Route 684) and drive 5.4 miles. Turn north onto Noel Road (Route 746) and continue 0.6 miles. Turn right onto Narrow Path Trail; the winery entrance will be on the right.

Courthouse Creek Cider
1581 Maidens Road
Maidens VA 23102

Hours: Sa–Su 12:00–6:00
Closed New Year's, Christmas

804-543-3157
www.courthousecreek.com
E-mail: info@courthousecreek.com

Californians Liza and Eric Cioffi were inspired to start a cidery after tasting a dry Virginia cider in 2012, eventually planting their four-acre orchard in 2014 and using fruit from other Virginia growers while their trees fully matured. Visitors can enjoy their all-natural ciders either inside the tasting area or on the covered deck and grounds, where they may see some of the Cioffis's chickens strolling around. Courthouse Creek hosts live music as well as special brunches and other events. The cidery also produces small-batch beers that are on tap at the Maidens location. Leashed dogs are welcome.

Courthouse Creek's Richmond location is in Scott's Addition at 3300 W. Broad Street, #106; hours are F 4:00–9:00, Sa 2:00–9:00, Su 12:00–5:00.

Ciders: Amuse Bouche, Bella Vita, Blackberry Lavender, Black Twig, Easy Breezy, Endless Summer, Hoppy Girl, Rustico, Samurai Sour.

Price Range: $17–$22

Tastings: $10 per flight

Purchasing: Online for AK, AZ, CO, DC, FL, GA, HI, IA, ID, IL, IN, KS, LA, MA, MD, ME, MN, MO, NC, ND, NE, NH, NM, NV, NY, OH, OK, OR, PA, SC, TN, TX, VA, VT, WA, WI, WV, and WY.

Directions: From Interstate 64, take Exit 167 south toward Oilville. Turn right onto U.S. Route 250 West and drive 0.8 miles. Make a left onto Fairgrounds Road (Route 632) and continue 3.5 miles. Turn left onto Maidens Road (Route 634). The cidery entrance will be 2 miles on the left.

Garden Grove Brewing & Urban Winery
3445 West Cary Street
Richmond VA 23221

Hours: M–Th 4:00–9:00, F–Sa 12:00 pm–12:00 am 804-918-6158
Su 12:00–8:00 www.gardengrovebrewing.com
Closed New Year's, Thanksgiving, Christmas

Garden Grove first launched as a craft brewery and expanded to become an urban winery in 2016. Owner Ryan Mitchell and team have partnered with Jason Murray's Arterra Vineyards to produce a range of classic wine varieties as well as meads, using mainly fruit from Garden Grove's Blue Ridge vineyard site and other Virginia locations. In addition to indoor seating in the bar and tasting area, the winery also has outdoor seating options.

Meads: Cold Front, Grandeur, Honesuckle, Refill.

White Wines: Chardonnay, Petit Manseng.

Red Wines: Adaptation, Petit Verdot.

Price Range: $16–$24

Tastings: $10

Directions: From Richmond's Scotts Addition neighborhood, drive south on Arthur Ashe Boulevard and take a left onto West Cary Street. Garden Grove will be ⅓ mile on the right.

James River Cellars
11008 Washington Highway
Glen Allen VA 23059

Hours: M–Th 11:00–6:00 (to 7:00 in summer), 804-550-7516
F–Sa, 11:00–7:00; Su 11:00–5:30 (to 6:00 in summer)
www.jamesrivercellars.com
Closed Easter, Thanksgiving, Christmas
E-mail: winery@jamesrivercellars.com

James River was founded by Ray Lazarchic in 2001 and is now owned by James and Mitzi Batterson, Ray's daughter and son-in-law, with James serving as winemaker. James River offers a picnic area and patio just outside the tasting room, where it holds Fridays on the Patio on the fourth Friday of every month, as well as a harvest wine festival. The winery hosts special events to support various charities, including the American Cancer Society and the Richmond SPCA, and can be rented for special events. Children and leashed dogs are welcome.

White Wines: Chardonel, Chardonnay, Gewurztraminer, Snowy White, Sunrise White, Traminette, Vidal Blanc.

Rosé Wines: Rosé.

Red Wines: Cabernet Franc, Cabernet Sauvignon, Chambourcin, Hanover, Merlot, Monitor vs. CSS Virginia, Petit Verdot, Rad Red, Sunset Red, Touriga Nacional.

Sweet/Dessert Wines: Hanover White, Montpelier Blush, Real Santa Red.

Price Range: $17–$45

Tastings: $15 per person.

Groups: Reservations required for groups of 10 or more, $15 per person.

ADA accessible.

Purchasing: Online ordering available to CA, DC, FL, MO, NC, and VA.

Directions: From I-95, take Exit 86B (Elmont) and drive west on Sliding Hill Road. Turn right at the second traffic light onto Washington Highway (U.S. Route 1 North). The winery will be on the right in about 1 mile.

Sassafras Shade Vineyard
4492 Ladysmith Road
Ruther Glen VA 22546

Hours: W-Su 11:00–5:00 (F to 7:00 late spring–early fall) 804-596-0179
Closed New Year's, Easter, www.sassafrasshade.com
Thanksgiving, Christmas E-mail: info@sassafrasshade.com

After growing grapes on their vineyards north of Richmond for 15 years, Gary and Ann Dudley decided to open a winery and tasting room of their own in 2014. The winery is named after the stand of sassafras trees that they found when they first cleared some of the brush from the property. All their wines are from Virginia-grown grapes, most from their own vineyards. Guests are welcome to bring snacks to enjoy on the porch after their tastings.

Fruit Wines: Granny Smith Apple, Old Fashioned Apple.

White Wines: Caroline White, Cayuga White, Chardonnay, Vidal Blanc, White Chambourcin.

Red Wines: Cabernet Franc, Caroline Red, Chambourcin.

Price Range: $14–$16

Tastings: $5 per person.

Directions: From Interstate 95, take Exit 110 (Ladysmith) and drive west onto Ladysmith Road. Continue 3.9 miles and turn left onto the winery's gravel driveway.

Skippers Creek Vineyard
965 Rocky Ford Road
Powhatan VA 23139

Hours: Sa–Su 1:00–5:00 (Apr–Oct) 804-598-7291
Closed Nov–Mar www.skipperscreekvineyard.com
E-mail: contact@skipperscreekvineyard.com

Chuck and Debbie Zacharias opened their winery west of Richmond after planting a five-acre vineyard on farmland that has been in Debbie's family for over 75 years. The couple plans to expand their plantings in the future, particularly after they retire from their careers in the medical field. Skippers Creek offers tours of the facilities as well as outdoor seating where guests may stay over a glass or bottle of wine.

White Wines: Blonde, Chardonnay, Viognier.

Rosé Wines: Lily (*Chardonnay, Viognier, Cabernet Franc*).

Red Wines: Cabernet Franc, Meriwether, Petit Verdot.

Price Range: $18–$22

Purchasing: Email ordering available for residents of AK, CA, DC, FL, NC, MD, MN, MO, NM, and VA.

Directions: From U.S. Route 60, drive west 7 miles and turn left onto New Dorset Road. Drive 0.8 miles. Turn left onto Dorset Road. After 1 mile, turn right onto Schroeder Road and drive 3.3 miles. Turn right again onto

Dorset Road (VA 604) and drive another 0.8 miles. Turn right onto Rocky Ford Road (VA 603) and continue 0.7 miles to the winery drive on the left.

Spring Run Vineyards
10700 Spring Run Road
Chesterfield VA 23832

Hours: First Sa 12:00–5:00, May – Nov only   804-382-4529
Closed Dec–Apr   www.springrunvineyards.com
                                            E-mail: springrunvineyards@yahoo.com

Opened as a self-described "nano" winery, Spring Run produces wine from its own vines as well as from other Virginia vineyards. Outdoor seating is offered, and guests may bring their own chairs. The winery sponsors live music and food trucks on select Saturdays, as well as craft workshops, such as painting or creating flower crowns. Children and leashed pets are welcome; however, please note that no outside food or coolers are allowed. Current and former military personnel receive a 10% discount.

Fruit Wines: Blackberry Rouge.

White Wines: Bright Hope Blanc, Villard Blanc.

Red Wines: Abyss.

Price Range: $18–$20

Tasting: $14

Directions: From Chesterfield, drive west on Beach Road (Route 655) for 5.5 miles. Turn right onto Spring Run Road and continue ½ mile to the winery entrance on the right.

FORTIFIED WINES

Fortified wines are those whose alcohol strength has been raised by adding some form of grape spirit, such as brandy. During fermentation, the grape juice's natural sugar is converted into alcohol through the action of yeasts. If left uninterrupted, this process will continue until all the sugar has been consumed. In fortified wine production, extra alcohol may be added before, during, or after fermentation.

The most well-known fortified wines are from the Iberian peninsula and the Portuguese island of Madeira.

Sherry originated in southwest Spain in the area around the city of Jerez, from which it draws its name. Made from the Palomino, Pedro Ximénez, and Muscat of Alexandria grapes, sherry is fortified after fermentation has occurred. Classic Spanish sherries are dry and range from the light and elegant Fino to the more concentrated Oloroso.

Port wines take their name from the Portuguese city of Oporto in the Douro region. Grape varieties traditionally used for port include Touriga Nacional, Touriga Francesa, Tinta Cão, Tinta Barroca, and Tinta Roriz. Because port wine is fortified during the fermentation process, the result is a sweet and strong wine.

Madeira is from the island of the same name. It originated by chance in the 17th century when merchants discovered that wine transported by ship across the tropics was transformed into a rich, sweet wine with an exceptional shelf life. Madeiras now are fortified during fermentation and then heated to caramelize the sugars. Madeira was very popular among American colonists in the 17th and 18th centuries. Indeed, participants at the Second Continental Congress toasted the signing of the Declaration of Independence in 1776 with glasses of madeira.

Handy Guide to Virginia Wineries

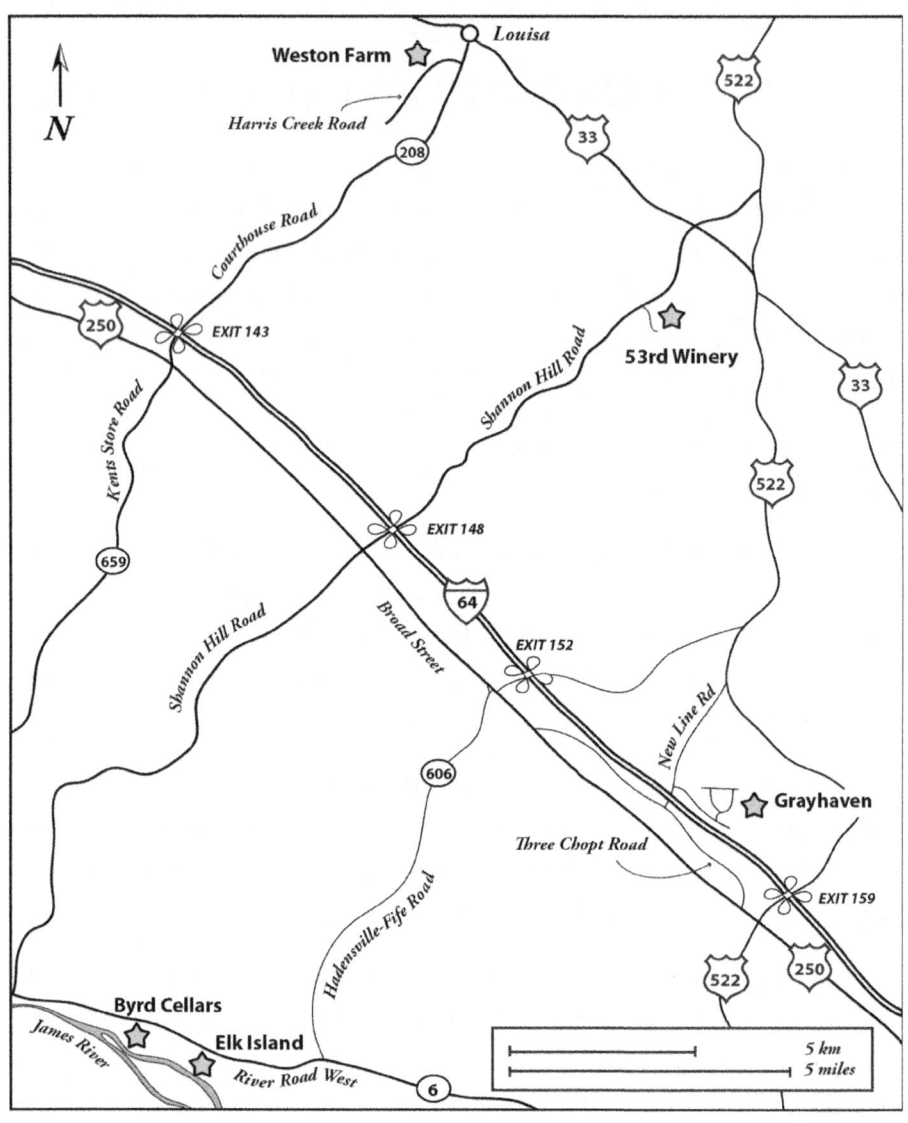

Map 7.2. Louisa

LOUISA

Byrd Cellars
5847 River Road West
Goochland VA 23063

Hours: Daily 12:00–5:00 (M–Th bottle sales only)
Closed New Year's, Christmas

804-652-5663
www.byrdcellars.com
E-mail: info@ByrdCellars.com

Byrd Cellars was established in 2008 by Bruce Murray initially as a collaborative venture with two other Goochland County vineyard owners (Murray now operates it alone). The tasting room offer visitors a light-filled space with scenic views of the James River; a new and larger tasting room is under construction and will open later in 2021. Byrd Cellars wines are all organically grown Virginia grapes, including from their own vineyards. Live music is hosted on select days. Guests are welcome to sit indoors or outside with a glass or bottle of wine. The facilities are available for small private events and parties. Children and pets are welcome.

Fruit Wines: Apple, Meadowsweet, Winter Solstice *(apple, cranberry)*.

White Wines: Chardonnay, Muscat, Sauvignon Blanc, White Cat.

Rosé Wines: Vin Rosé.

Red Wines: Cabernet Sauvignon, Dahlgren's Raid Red, Merlot, Norton, Pete's Red, Raven Red, Syrah.

Price Range: $14–$22

Tastings: $12 per person for a flight.

Purchasing: Online to VA residents; call for shipping to other states.

Directions: From I-64, take Exit 152 (Hadensville). Turn south onto Old Fredericksburg Road and drive 0.8 miles. Make a right onto Broad Street (U.S. Route 250 West) and an immediate left to stay on Old Fredericksburg Road which will become Three Chopt and then Hadensville-Fife Road. After 8 miles in all, turn right onto River Road West (VA 6) and drive 2.7 miles to the winery entrance on the left.

Elk Island Winery
5759 River Road West
Goochland VA 23063

Hours: Sa–Su 12:00–6:00 (spring–fall) 804-627-3929
Closed New Year's, Christmas www.elkislandwinery.com
E-mail: info@elkislandwinery.com

Named for a nearby 1,300-acre island in the James River, Elk Island Winery is owned and operated by Paul and Sue Anne Klinefelter whose winemaking venture began through their affiliation with Byrd Cellars. The Klinefelters ultimately opted to found their own winery and tasting room, where visitors are welcome to stay on the deck or enclosed porch. The facilities are available for private events and parties. The winery produces several wines under the Terroirier label, which was designed to honor their three rescue terriers; proceeds from their sale benefit terrier rescue organizations. Children and pets are welcome.

Fruit Wines: Blue *(blueberries)*, Cranberry, Eleanor's Red Currant, Ginger Green Tea Sangria, Island Sunset *(pear, pineapple)*, Wal-Tea *(Vidal Blanc, lemon, tea)*.

White Wines: Chardonnay, Merge White, Terroirier White, Vidal Blanc, Viognier.

Rosé Wines: Chambourcin Rosé.

Red Wines: Cabernet Sauvignon, Chambourcin, Norton, Petit Verdot, Ramey's Dream Dornfelder, Terroirier Red, Towpath.

Fortified Wines: Portamento PR *(Norton, Petit Verdot).*

Price Range: $14–$25

Tastings: $8 per person for a flight.

Groups: Reservations requested for groups of 8 or more.

Directions: From I-64, take Exit 152 (Hadensville). Turn south onto Old Fredericksburg Road and drive 0.8 miles. Make a right onto Broad Street (U.S. Route 250 West) and an immediate left to stay on Old Fredericksburg Road which will become Three Chopt and then Hadensville-Fife Road. After 8 miles in all, turn right onto River Road West (VA 6) and drive 2.2 miles to the winery entrance on the left.

Fifty-Third Winery & Vineyard
13372 Shannon Hill Road
Louisa VA 23093

Hours: Daily 11:00–5:00 (May–Dec only);
F–M 11:00–5:00 (Jan–Apr)
Closed New Year's, Thanksgiving, Christmas

540-894-5474
www.53rdwinery.com
E-mail: info@53rdwinery.com

Originally started by Geoffrey Cooper and Jacque Hogge (and named Cooper Vineyards), Fifty-Third Winery was purchased by David and Susan Drillock who renamed it in honor of its being the 53rd winery established in Virginia. Under winemaker Chelsey Blevins, Fifty-Third produces a range of wines including their Noche dessert wine, a blend of Norton and chocolate. Fifty-Third sponsors live music on weekends and often has food trucks on site for guests; graze boxes with cheese, charcuterie, and dips are also available for purchase. The two-story, LEED-certified tasting room includes an outdoor tasting area and veranda where guests are welcome to sit and enjoy the vineyard views. The facilities are available for private events and parties. Children and pets are welcome.

White Wines: Albariño, Chardonel, Chardonnay, Shannon Hill White, Vidal Blanc, Viognier.

Rosé Wines: Rosé.

Red Wines: Cabernet Franc, Cabernet Sauvignon, Chambourcin, Chelsey Red Mélange, Merlot, Norton, Petit Verdot, Shannon Hill Red, Two Springs.

Sweet/Dessert Wines: Noche *(Norton, chocolate)*, Red Genesis, Rhapsody, Sweet Louisa *(Concord)*.

Price Range: $17–$32

Tastings: $10 per person.

Purchasing: Online purchasing is available for DC, FL, MD, MN, NC, PA, and VA.

Directions: From I-64, take Exit 148 (Shannon Hill Road). Drive north on Shannon Hill Road (Route 605) about 8 miles to the winery's gravel driveway on right.

Grayhaven Winery
4675 E. Grey Fox Circle
Gum Spring VA 23065

Hours: Th–M 11:00–5:00 (Sa to 6:00 in summer)
Closed New Year's, Thanksgiving, Christmas

804-556-3917
www.grayhavenwinery.com
E-mail: max@grayhavenwinery.com

Established by Chuck and Lyn Peple and their daughters, Max and Mallory, Grayhaven was named after the Elvish port of Gray Havens in J.R.R. Tolkien's *Lord of the Rings* trilogy. The winery opened to the public in 1995 and offers a range of estate-grown wines; Grayhaven supplements its own production with wines from the owners' native South Africa. Visitors are welcome to linger over wine and a charcuterie platter to enjoy the grounds, which include a patio and small deck overlooking a koi pond. The winery hosts occasional special tastings, including a South Africa tasting weekend, and live music. The facilities may be rented for weddings and other special events. Children and leashed dogs are welcome.

White Wines: Chardonnay, Riesling, Sauvignon Blanc, Seyval Blanc.

Blush Wines: Eventide.

Red Wines: Cabernet Franc, Cabernet Sauvignon, Pinotage, Touriga, Trekker *(Bordeaux-style blend)*.

Fortified Wines: Rivercrest.

Price Range: $15–$35

Tastings: $10 per person.

Groups: Reservations required for groups of 8 or more, and all bus tours.

ADA accessible.

Purchasing: Online ordering for Virginia residents only.

Directions: From I-64, take Exit 159 (Gum Spring) and turn south onto Cross County Road (Route 522). Turn right onto Broad Street (U.S. Route 250 West) and make the first right onto Three Chopt Road (Route 700). Drive 2.3 miles and turn right onto New Line Road (Route 619). Make a right onto Sheppard Spring Road and then left onto Fox Chase Run. Turn right onto East Grey Fox Circle. The winery entrance will be on the right.

Weston Farm Vineyard & Winery
206 Harris Creek Road
Louisa VA 23093

Hours: W–Sa 11:00–5:00
Closed New Year's, Thanksgiving, Christmas

540-967-4647
www.westonfarmvineyardandwinery.webs.com
E-mail: pennymlouisa@aol.com

Bobby and Penny Martin first opened Weston Farm Vineyard to the public in 2010. They worked originally with Virginia vintner Gabriele Rausse and began making wine in 2009 after planting their vineyard four years earlier. Visitors are welcome to bring a picnic lunch to enjoy on the grounds after their tastings. Weston Farm has a number of animals on the property, with their winery dogs often on hand to greet visitors to the tasting room; rescue horses, miniature donkeys, and cows are also on the farm. The winery sponsors live music and fundraisers on selected weekends. Children and pets are welcome.

Fruit Wines: Peach, Raspberry, Strawberry, Watermelon.

White Wines: Petit Manseng, Pinot Grigio.

Rosé Wines: Rosé *(Norton)*.

Red Wines: Cabernet Franc, Cabernet Sauvignon, Meritage, Norton, Petit Verdot.

Sweet/Dessert Wines: Cherry.

Price Range: $19–$25

Tastings: $10 per person.

Directions: From I-64, take Exit 143 onto Courthouse Road (Route 208) north toward Louisa. Drive 8 miles and turn left onto Harris Creek Road (Route 630). The winery entrance will be on the right in ¼ mile.

Handy Guide to Virginia Wineries

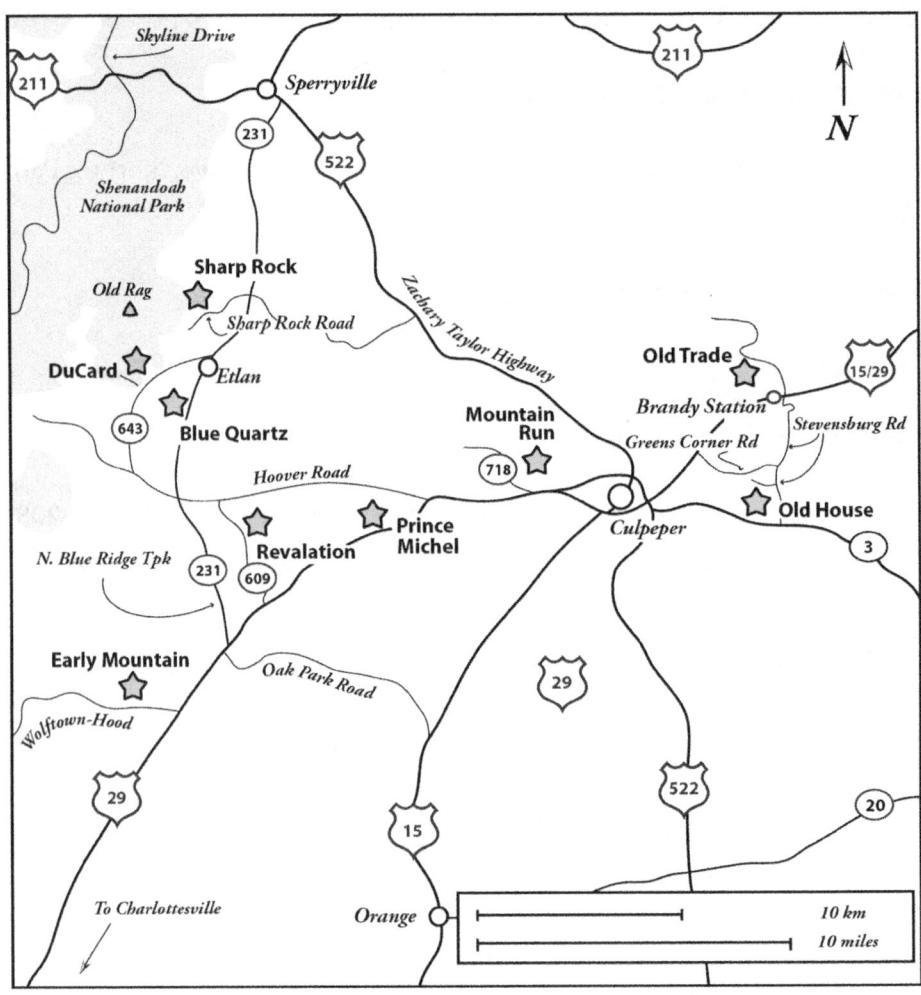

Map 7.3. Madison

Central Virginia Region & Monticello AVA

MADISON

Blue Quartz Winery
2585 S F T Valley Road
Sperryville VA 22719

Hours: Th 5:00–9:00, F 3:00–9:00,
Sa 12:00–9:00, Su 12:00–6:00
Closed New Year's, Christmas

540-923-4048
www.bluequartzwinery.com
E-mail: bluequartzwinery@gmail.com

Hal White and Chris Wallin opened Blue Quartz Winery in 2019, sharing their tasting room space with Shotwell Run Brewery. The tasting room provides indoor seating, with outdoor options available under two pavilions or on the grounds overlooking nearby Old Rag Mountain. Blue Quartz currently produces its wines in collaboration with Early Mountain Winery. The winery offers snacks and cheese platters for sale in the tasting room and hosts food trucks and live music on many weekends. Fieldstone Trails offers guided hour-long horseback rides through the vineyard in warmer weather. Children and dogs are welcome.

Ciders: Thornton River Cider.

White Wines: Chardonnay, Viognier.

Rosé Wines: Rosé.

Red Wines: Merlot, Petit Verdot.

Price Range: $21–$32

Tastings: $15 per person for a flight of four wines.

Purchasing: Online purchasing available to various states; contact the winery for details.

Directions: From Sperryville, drive south on S F T Valley Road (Route 231) for 12.7 miles to the winery entrance on the right.

From U.S. Route 29 at Madison, drive north on North Blue Ridge Turnpike (Route 231) for 7.9 miles to the winery entrance on the left.

DuCard Vineyard
40 Gibson Hollow Lane
Etlan VA 22719

Hours: M–Th 12:00–5:00, F 12:00–9:00, Sa–Su 12:00–6:00 (May–Nov)   540-923-4206
F–Su, M holidays 12:00–5:00 (Dec–Apr)   www.ducardvineyards.com
Closed Thanksgiving, 20 Dec–6 Jan   E-mail: scott@ducardvineyards.com

Scott and Karen Elliff started their vineyard on the site of an old apple orchard in Madison County, opening to the public in 2010. The Elliffs named their winery by flipping the name of Scott's favorite single malt scotch, Cardhu. The winery offers a scenic view of the Shenandoah National Park from the tasting room and the outdoor patios; the Elliffs donate a portion of the sale proceeds from their Shenandoah White to the park's trust. DuCard offers light snacks and sponsors occasional live music festivals; check the website for details. Pets and children are welcome.

Sparkling Wines: XOXO.

White Wines: Chardonnay, Cuvée 719, Decade One White, Gibson Hollow White, Pinot Gris, Shenandoah White, Viognier.

Rosé Wines: Decade One Rosé, Rosé.

Red Wines: Cabernet Franc, Decade One Red, Merlot, Norton, Petit Verdot, Popham Run Red, Triskele.

Fortified Wines: C'Est Trop *(Norton)*.

Price Range: $20–$59

Tastings: $24 per person for four half-glasses.

Groups: Reservations required for groups of 9 or more, $15 per person.

ADA accessible.

Purchasing: Online to AK, AL, AZ, CA, CO, DC, FL, GA, IA, ID, IL, IN, KS, LA, MA, MD, ME, MN, MO, MT, NC, ND, NE, NH, NM, NV, NY, OH, OR, PA, TN, TX, VA, WA, WI, WV, and WY.

Directions: From Sperryville, drive south on S F T Valley Road (Route 231) for 10 miles. At the village of Etlan, turn right onto Etlan Road (Route 643) and drive 2.7 miles. Turn right onto Gibson Hollow Road (Route 719). The winery will be immediately ahead on the right.

From U.S. Route 29 at Madison, drive north on North Blue Ridge Turnpike (Route 231) for 8.5 miles. At the village of Etlan, turn left onto Etlan Road (Route 643) and drive 2.7 miles. Turn right onto Gibson Hollow Road (Route 719). The winery will be immediately ahead on the right.

Early Mountain Winery
6109 Wolftown Hood Road
Madison VA 22727

Hours: Th–M 11:00–6:00
Closed New Year's Eve & Day, Easter,
Thanksgiving, Christmas Eve & Day

540-948-9005
http://earlymountain.com
E-mail: cheers@earlymountain.com

Early Mountain is owned by Jean Case who purchased the former Sweeley Estate Vineyards in 2011, renaming it in honor of Revolutionary

War patriot Joseph Early who was the original owner of the land on which the winery now stands. The tasting room offers extensive indoor seating and outdoor seating, a small gift shop, and an events room for weddings and private parties. Wine tastings feature Early Mountain's own production and select wines from other Virginia wineries. The winery sponsors various activities, including live music on Friday evenings, and has a tasting menu for onsite dining. Children and leashed pets are welcome.

Early Mountain's Guest Cottage next to the vineyard is available for overnight stays; see the website for details.

Sparkling Wines: EMV Estate Brut, Pet Nat Blanc.

White Wines: Chardonnay, Intention, Petit Manseng, Pur.

Rosé Wines: Rosé.

Red Wines: Cabernet Franc, Eluvium, Foothills, Rise, Soif.

Sweet/Dessert Wines: R.A.H. Series I.

Price Range: $25–$95

Tastings: $20 to $22 per person for a red, white, or mixed flight.

Groups: Reservations required for groups of 10 or more.

ADA accessible

Purchasing: Online to VA and many other states; see the website for details.

Directions: From U.S. Route 29 at Madison, turn west onto Wolftown Hood Road (Route 230). The winery will be 1.2 miles on the right.

❖ ❖ ❖

Mountain Run Vineyards
10753 Mountain Run Lake Road
Culpeper VA 22701

Hours: F–Su 12:00–sunset (Nov–Aug)
Th–M 12:00–sunset (Sep–Oct)
Closed New Year's, Easter, Christmas

703-638-5559
www.mountainrunwinery.com
E-mail: info@mountainrunwinery.com

David Foster launched Mountain Run after a career serving with the U.S. Army and teaching as a university professor, choosing Culpeper because of his deep family roots in the area. The tasting room is housed in a corn crib barn that includes a tasting bar and an adults-only section. Mountain Run features a Fall Harvest Festival, a Fall Crab Feast, an annual Volkswagen show, and live music. The facilities can be rented for private events and weddings. A small outdoor playground area is available for children; leashed dogs are also welcome.

White Wines: Chardonnay, Culpeper Love, Petit Manseng, Traminette, Viognier.

Rosé Wines: Dirt Road Rosé, Dog Rock Rosé.

Red Wines: Cabernet Franc, Cabernet Sauvignon, Chambourcin, Culpeper Crimson, Meritage, Petit Verdot, Shiraz.

Price Range: $24–$32

Tastings: $12 per person for a flight.

Groups: Reservations required for groups of 9 or more.

Purchasing: Online to AK, AZ, CO, DC, FL, GA, IA, ID, IL, IN, KS, LA, MA, MD, ME, MN, MO, NC, ND, NE, NH, NM, NV, NY, OH, OK, OR, PA, SC, TN, TX, VA, VT, WA, WI, WV, and WY.

Directions: From Culpeper, drive south one mile on U.S. Route 29. Turn right onto Mountain Run Lake Road (Route 718). The winery entrance will be 0.8 miles on the left.

Old House Vineyards
18351 Corkys Lane
Culpeper VA 22701

Hours: W–Th 12:00–5:00, F 12:00–8:00, Sa–M 12:00–6:00 (Apr–Sep) 540-423-1032
M, W–F, Su 12:00–5:00, Sa 11:00–6:00 (Oct–Mar) www.oldhousevineyards.com
Closed New Year's, Thanksgiving, Christmas E-mail: info@oldhousevineyards.com

Old House was founded in 1998 by Patrick and Allyson Kearney on a farm within the boundaries of the Brandy Station Civil War battlefield. Tastings are held in the main tasting room, which is in a restored 1800s-era farmhouse, as well as outdoors. Old House has ample seating on the grounds, which are open for family picnics; guests are also welcome to try their hand at a giant chessboard. The winery offers live music on weekends, fresh-baked pizzas, and annual chili cook-offs and Harvest Days festivals. Old House is also available for rental for private parties, weddings, and corporate events. Children are welcome. Old House also has a brewery and distillery onsite, with separate tastings available.

Sparkling Wines: Pétillante.

White Wines: Chardonnay, Clover Hill *(Pinot Grigio)*, Vidal Blanc.

Rosé Wines: Rosie's Rosé.

Red Wines: Bacchanalia, Cabernet Franc, Mélange de Maison, Petit Verdot, Wicked Bottom.

Sweet/Dessert Wines: Arctica *(Vidal Blanc)*.

Fortified Wines: Chambourcin Dessert.

Price Range: $18–$35

Tastings: $10 per person.

Groups: Reservations required for groups of 8 or more.

ADA accessible.

Purchasing: Online to AK, CA, FL, MN, and VA.

Directions: From U.S. Route 15/29 at Brandy Station, turn south onto Alanthus Road. Make an immediate left onto Brandy Road and take the first right onto Mount Dumpling Road, which will bend to the left and become Stevensburg Road. Drive 3.2 miles and turn right onto Corkys Road (narrow, gravel drive), which is the driveway to the winery. Continue about ½ mile to the winery parking lot.

Old Trade Brewery & Cidery
13270 Alanthus Road
Brandy Station VA 22714

Hours: Th 1:00–8:00, F 3:00–11:00,
Sa 12:00–10:00, Su 12:00–8:00
Closed New Year's, Thanksgiving, Christmas

540-729-1740
www.oldtradebrewery.com
events.oldtrade@gmail.com

Garrett and Sara Thayer first launched Old Trade as a farm brewery on their 20-acre property, then added ciders and wines. The tasting room is housed in a renovated barn, with porches and seating on the grounds with lovely views of the surrounding fields and hills. All their wines are made from Virginia-grown grapes, sourced from various vineyards across the state. Old Trade offers a core menu of pizzas, burgers, dips, and cheese plates to choose from and sponsors a wide range of events, from live music to happy hours to axe-throwing. A new events barn is planned and will be available for rental for private parties. Children have a fenced play area to explore; leashed pets are also welcome.

Ciders: Emmer Cider Wine, Rad Razz, Rocky Knoll (sparkling), Sunset Apricot.

White Wines: All Day Chardonnay, Wandering Cat (Petit Manseng).

Rosé Wines: Windy Rose.

Red Wines: Angry Rooster Red.

Price Range: $15–$22

Tastings: $10 per person.

Groups: Reservations required for groups of 8 or more, outdoors only.

Directions: From U.S. Route 15/29 at Brandy Station, turn north onto Alanthus Road (Route 663). Drive 1.5 miles to the winery entrance on the left.

Prince Michel Vineyard & Winery
154 Winery Lane
Leon VA 22725

Hours: Daily 11:00–7:00 (M to 8:00, W, F–Sa to 9:00) 1-800-800-WINE (9463)
M–Th 11:00–5:00, F–Su 11:00–6:00 (Jan–Mar) www.princemichel.com
Closed New Year's, Thanksgiving, Christmas E-mail: mhaney@princemichel.com

Established in 1982, Prince Michel is one of Virginia's largest wineries, producing well over 40,000 cases annually from Virginian and other American grapes. The tasting room includes a tasting bar in the middle of an extensive gift shop and free Wi-Fi; an on-site pub offers hot and cold dishes for purchase. The winery offers a free self-guided tour, as well as group tours (by reservation). Prince Michel has several suites for overnight stays. The facilities may be rented for weddings and private events. Prince Michel also has established a brewery on site, with a range of beers on tap.

Prince Michel wines are also available for tasting at the Carter Mountain Wine Shop at 1435 Carter's Mountain Trail in Charlottesville. The shop is open from June through November (M-Sa 11:00-6:00, Su to 5:00) and weekends from mid-April through May (F–M 11:00–5:00).

Fruit Wines: Rapidan River Apple-Blackberry, Rapidan River Peach, Rapidan River Raspberry.

Sparkling Wines: Prince Michel Pet Nat.

White Wines: Chardonnay, Mount Juliet Chardonnay, Mount Juliet Petit Manseng, Pinot Grigio, Rapidan River Chardonnay, Rapidan River Dry Riesling, Rapidan River Semi-Dry Riesling, Viognier.

Rosé Wines: Dry Rosé, Rapidan River Rosé.

Red Wines: Cabernet Franc, Cabernet Sauvignon, Merlot, Mountain View Cabernet Franc, Mount Juliet Petit Verdot, Quaker Run Farm Syrah, Symbius *(Bordeaux-style blend)*, Rapidan River Merlot.

Sweet/Dessert Wines: Trés Bien *(Petit Manseng)*, Prince Michel Dessert, Rapidan River Sweet White Reserve, Rapidan River Sweet Red Reserve, Rapidan River Chocolate.

Price Range: $14–$56

Tastings: $10 per person.

Groups: Reservations required for groups of 8 or more.

ADA accessible.

Purchasing: Online for CA, CO, DC, FL, GA, IA, LA, MD, MI, MN, MO, NC, ND, NH, NJ, NY, OH, PA, SC, TX, VA, WI, WA, and WY.

Directions: From Culpeper, take U.S. Route 29 South for 8 miles to the winery on right.

Revalation Vineyards
2710 Hebron Valley Road
Madison VA 22727

Hours: F 3:00–sunset, Sa 1:00–6:00, S–M 1:00–5:00 (May–Oct)   540-407-1236
F 1:00–sunset, Sa–Su 1:00–5:00 (Nov–Apr)   www.revalationvineyards.com
Closed New Year's, Christmas   E-mail: info@revalationvineyards.com

Revalation Vineyards was launched by Françoise Seillier-Moiseiwitsch and Julian Moiseiwitsch, who were inspired to plant their own 10-acre vineyard after falling in love with wine while working in California. The tasting room is in a beautiful log cabin dating from the 1830s, with a larger tasting room and production facility next to the original cabin. Visitors can soak in the scenic views of the nearby Hebron Valley over a tasting flight or bottle. Revalation sponsors special events, such as a monthly charity benefit for Literacy Madison, local artisanal pop-ups, and live music on many weekends.

Fruit Wines: Verjus *(grape, non-alcoholic)*.

White Wines: Petit Manseng, Pinot Gris, Quatre Blancs, Sauvignon Blanc, Vidal Blanc, Viognier.

Red Wines: Cabernet Franc, Mélange à Quatre, Merlot, Merlotage, Tannat, Village.

Price Range: $26–$43

Tastings: $10 per person.

Groups: Reservations required for groups of 8 or more.

Purchasing: Online for AK, AZ, CA, CO, DC, FL, GA, HI, IA, ID, IL, IN, KS, LA, MA, MD, ME, MN, MO, NC, ND, NE, NH, NM, NV, NY, OH, OK, OR, PA, SC, TN, TX, VA, VT, WA, WI, WV, and WY.

Directions: From Culpeper, take U.S. Route 29 South for about 11 miles. Turn right onto Hebron Valley Road (Route 603) and continue 2.8 miles to the winery entrance.

Sharp Rock Vineyards
5 Sharp Rock Road
Sperryville VA 22740

Hours: F–Su, M holidays 11:00–5:00 (mid-Feb–Dec)
Th–M 11:00–5:00 (Oct)
Closed Jan–mid-Feb, Christmas

540-987-8020
www.sharprockvineyards.com
E-mail: jeast@sharprockvineyards.com

Sharp Rock Vineyards is located at the base of Old Rag Mountain, one of the most popular hiking destinations in Virginia, and has been a working farm since the late 1700s. Owners Jimm and Kathy East first planted their vineyards in 1992 and now make about a dozen estate-grown wines. Tastings are held in the upper level of their restored barn. Breads and cheeses are available for purchase. There will generally be several winery dogs on hand out in the drive to greet visitors. The winery is available for rental for private parties and weddings. Children and pets are welcome.

Sharp Rock has two riverside cottages for overnight stays. Charges include a complimentary wine tasting and bottle of wine, breakfast, and snacks. The cottages are the closest accommodations available to Old Rag.

White Wines: Chardonnay, Chamois Blanc *(Chardonnay, Vidal Blanc)*, Pinnacle Blanc, Sauvignon Blanc.

Rosé Wines: Rosé, Rosé Noir.

Red Wines: Cabernet Franc, Cabernet Sauvignon, Chamois Rouge, Malbec, Old Rag Red, Petit Verdot, Pinnacle *(Bordeaux-style blend)*.

Price Range: $17–$28

Tastings: $10 per person.

Purchasing: Online to AL, AK, CA, CO, CT, DC, HI, ID, IL, IA, MN, MO, NE, NV, NM, ND, OH, OR, RI, VT, VA, WA, WV, and WI.

Directions: From Sperryville, drive south on Route 231 for 8 miles. Turn right onto Route 601 (Peola Mills Road which will become Nethers Road). Drive 1 mile to the intersection with Sharp Rock Road (Route 707) and turn right. The winery will be the farm on the right after crossing the Hughes River Bridge.

NORTON

One of Virginia's most noteworthy contributions to American wine was the Norton grape. Propagated by amateur horticulturist Dr. Daniel N. Norton on his farm near Richmond, the grape was first listed as Norton's Virginia Seedling in 1822 in the annual catalog of the Linnean Botanic Garden and Nurseries of Long Island, New York, perhaps the country's foremost horticultural institution at that time. The Princes' 1830 Treatise on the Vine described the grape as *Vitis nortoni* and credited the doctor with its cultivation.

It was through the efforts of German viticulturists—George Husmann, in particular—that the Norton grape rose to prominence as a wine grape in the United States. In 1846, German settlers in the central Missouri town of Hermann planted Norton cuttings, producing the first bottle of Norton wine two years later. As the Missouri wine industry grew, becoming at one point the largest producer in the United States, so also grew the cultivation and renown of the Norton grape.

Interest in the Norton peaked in 1870, when Hermann vintner Michael Röschel and business partner John Scherer entered their Norton wine in the 1873 Universal Exhibition in Vienna, Austria. The influential English wine critic Henry Vizatelly awarded a medal of merit to the Norton, one of only three American wines to be so decorated. It was also at this time that German vineyardists in Virginia established the Monticello Wine Company whose production was based heavily on Norton grapes.

The two Virginia winemakers who have been most influential in bringing Norton back to its native state are the late Dennis Horton of Horton Vineyards and Jennifer McCloud of Chrysalis. A Missouri native, Horton grew up in Hermann and was introduced to Norton in his college days. He first planted Norton cuttings in his Orange County vineyard in 1988. McCloud became fascinated by the Norton grape and its history after hearing Horton speak at a conference. After establishing Chrysalis, she began planting Norton in her vineyards and now has the single largest planting of this native Virginia grape in the country.

Handy Guide to Virginia Wineries

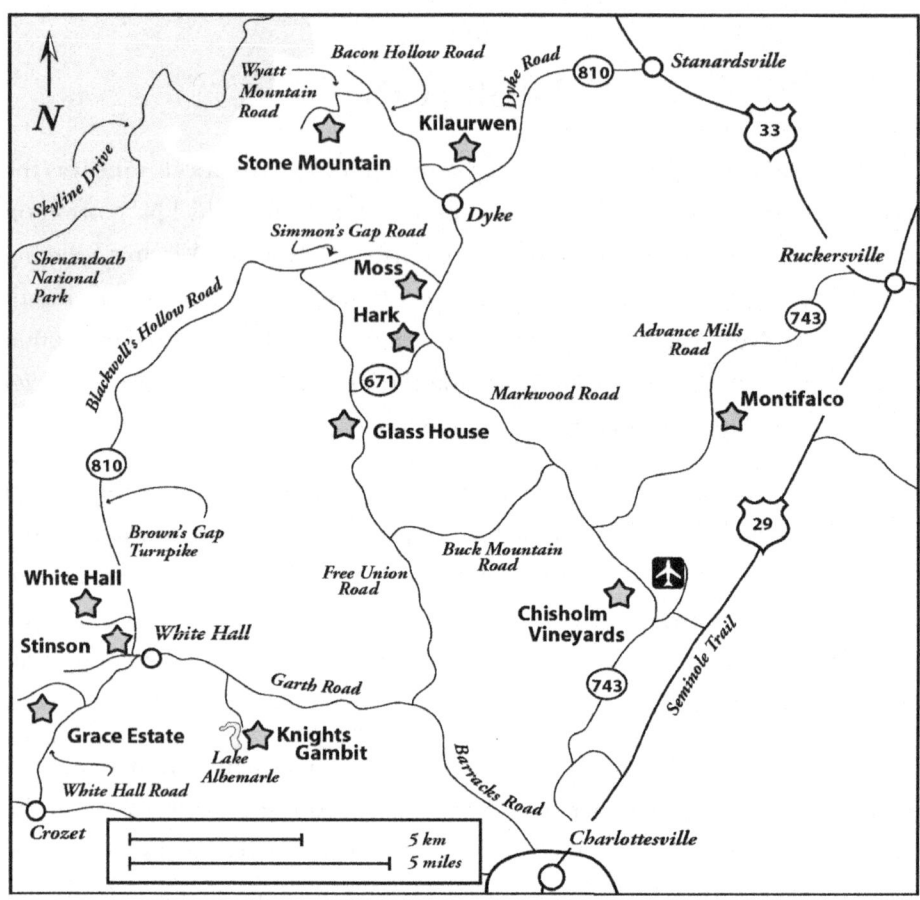

Map 7.4. Free Union-White Hall

UPPER MONTICELLO

Barboursville Vineyards
17655 Winery Road
Barboursville VA 22923

Hours: M–Sa 10:00–5:00, Su 11:00–5:00 540-832-3824
Closed New Year's, Thanksgiving, Christmas www.bbvwine.com
E-mail: bvvy@barboursvillewine.com

Barboursville Vineyards is one of the largest and oldest wineries in Virginia, established by the Zonin family who purchased the historic estate in 1976. Barboursville produces over 37,000 bottles of wine annually from its 185-acre vineyard under the guidance of winemaker Luca Paschina, a native of Italy. The tasting room looks onto the octagonal ruins of the Barbour family mansion that was destroyed by fire on Christmas Day 1884; a drawing of the ruins is featured on the label of the winery's flagship Octagon wine. Winery tours are available (Sa–Su), circumstances permitting. The Library 1821 offers tastings of library wines with optional food pairings. The facilities may be rented for private events and weddings.

The winery's Palladio Restaurant is open for lunch (W–Su) and dinner (F–Sa). The winery grounds also include two restored buildings—the 1804 Inn and Vineyard Cottage—that are available for overnight stays.

Sparkling Wines: Brut Blanc de Blancs, Brut Cuvée, Brut Rosé Cuvée.

White Wines: Chardonnay, Fiano, Pinot Grigio, Sauvignon Blanc, Vermentino, Viognier.

Rosé Wines: Allegrante Rosé.

Red Wines: Barbera, Cabernet Franc, Cabernet Sauvignon, Merlot, Nebbiolo, Octagon *(Bordeaux-style blend)*, Petit Verdot, Sangiovese.

Sweet/Dessert Wines: Paxxito, Philéo.

Price Range: $15–$55

Tastings: $15–$25 per person for a flight.

Groups: Reservations required for group tour buses and limos.

ADA accessible.

Purchasing: Online purchasing available for AK, AL, AZ, CA, CO, DC, FL, IL, KS, MD, MI, MN, MO, NC, NH, NM, NY, OR, PA, SC, TN, TX, VA, and WA.

Directions: From U.S. Route 33, turn south onto Route 20 (Constitution Highway). Make an immediate left onto Governor Barbour Street. Take the third right onto Mansion Road. After 0.75 mile, turn right onto Winery Road and the winery parking lot.

Burnley Vineyards
4500 Winery Lane
Barboursville VA 22923

Hours: Th–M 11:00–5:00 (May–Dec);
F–M 11:00–5:00 (Jan–Apr)
Closed: New Year's, Thanksgiving,
Christmas Eve & Day

434-960-4411
www.burnleywines.com
E-mail: burnleywines@gmail.com

Burnley Vineyard opened to the public in 1984 by the Reeder family, who first planted their vineyard in 1977. Visitors may purchase snacks, bread, and cheeses to enjoy with a glass or bottle of one of Burnley's estate-grown wines. Its Daniel Cellars label includes wines flavored by natural extracts and fruits. Burnley hosts a range of special winery events, such as wine and cheese weekends, a Thanksgiving Open House (F–Su), a holiday

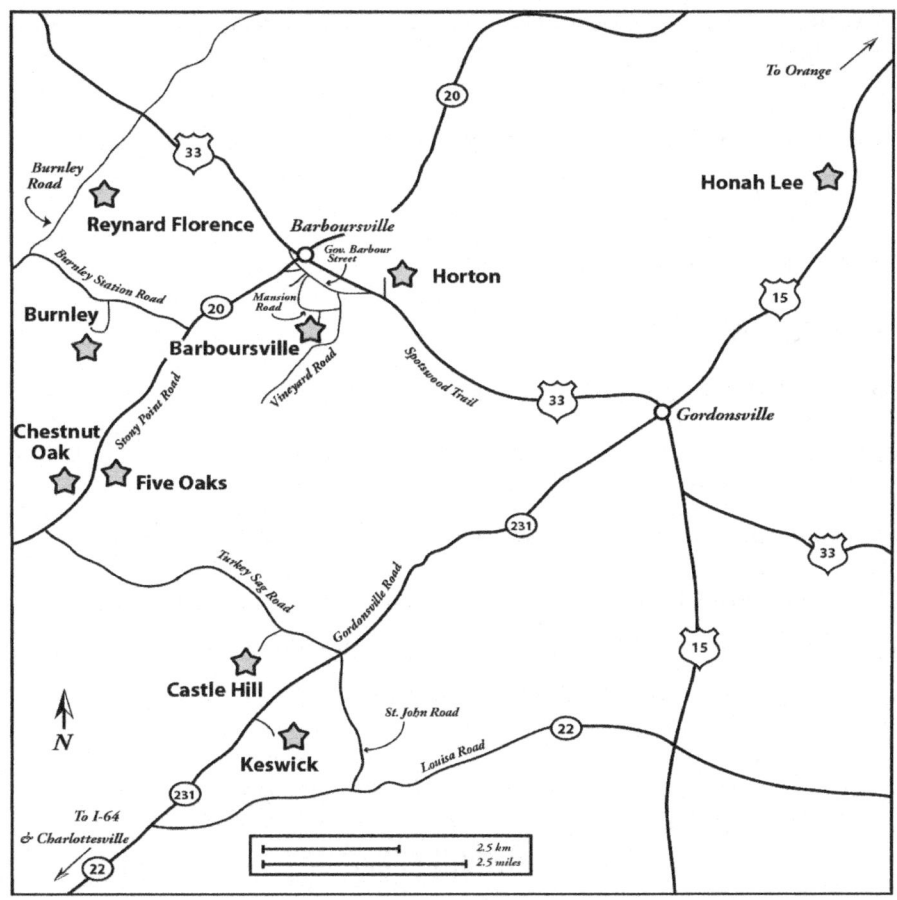

Map 7.5. Stony Point

open house in December, and special vertical tastings. The facilities may be rented for private parties. Children are welcome.

Burnley also offers overnight stays at Fernando's Hideaway, a furnished guest house with room for four; see the website for rentail details.

Fruit Wines: Peach Fuzz.

White Wines: Chardonnay, Rivanna White, Riesling.

Blush Wines: Rivanna Sunset *(Chambourcin)*.

Red Wines: Barbera, Cabernet Sauvignon, Chambourcin, Dog Gone Red, Norton, Rivanna Red.

Sweet/Dessert Wines: Aurora *(red wine with chocolate, raspberries)*, Somerset, Spicy Rivanna.

Fortified Wines: Rubix *(Norton port-style)*.

Price Range: $16–$20

Tastings: $10 per person.

ADA accessible.

Purchasing: Online ordering for many states; see website for details.

Directions: From U.S. Route 33, turn south onto Route 20 (Constitution Highway) and drive 2 miles. Turn right onto Burnley Station Road (Route 641). The winery entrance will be ⅓ mile on the left.

Castle Hill Cider
6065 Turkey Sag Road
Keswick VA 22947

Hours: Th 2:00–9:00, F–Su 12:00–7:00 (Apr–Oct); W–Su 12:00–5:00 (Nov–Mar)
Closed New Year's, Thanksgiving, Christmas

434-296-0047
www.castlehillcider.com
E-mail: info@castlehillcider.com

Castle Hill Cider opened to the public in 2011 on the grounds of the historic Castle Hill estate; the manor house was built in 1764 by Colonel Thomas Walker, who was appointed as Thomas Jefferson's guardian after his father's death. The cidery barn includes the tasting rooms and indoor seating; the grounds feature a pavilion and a range of seating options. Light snacks are available, and food trucks are often scheduled. Cidermaker Don

Whitaker uses kvevri terracotta vessels to make Castle Hill's Levity cider; kvevri originated over 8,000 years ago in the Republic of Georgia, where they are still used in traditional wine production. Castle Hill's facilities may be rented for weddings and private events.

Sparkling Ciders: Celestial, Celestial Merret, Levity, Serendipity, Terrestrial.

Still Ciders: Black Twig, Gravity.

Fortified Ciders: 1764 *(cider port)*, OG *(ginger-infused)*.

Price Range: $17–$305

Tastings: $14 per person for a flight.

Groups: Reservations requested for groups of 8 or more.

ADA accessible.

Purchasing: Online to AK, AL, AZ, CA, CO, DC, FL, GA, HI, IA, ID, IL, IN, KS, LA, MA, MD, ME, MI, MN, MO, NC, ND, NE, NH, NM, NV, NY, OH, OR, PA, SC, TN, TX, VA, WA, WI, WV, and WY.

Directions: From I-64, take Exit 124 onto U.S. Route 250 East (Shadwell). Drive 1.9 miles and turn onto Route 22 East. After 5.4 miles, stay straight to go onto Gordonsville Road (Route 231). Continue 3.3 miles and turn left onto Turkey Sag Road (Route 640). Drive ¾ mile and turn left into the cidery driveway between the white stone posts.

Chestnut Oak Vineyards
5050 Stony Point Road
Barboursville VA 22923

Hours: F–Su 12:00–5:00   434-964-9104
Closed New Year's, Easter, Christmas   www.chestnutoakvineyard.com
E-mail: info@chestnutoakvineyard.com

Chestnut Oak was opened by Janet Bolla on her vineyard between Charlottesville and Barboursville. The winery focuses on estate-grown production under the guidance of Michael Shaps. The winery offers indoor seating, with murals reminiscent of Latin American art in the tasting room; seating is also available outdoors. Chestnut Oak occasionally hosts local artisans and chocolate pairings. Well-behaved leashed dogs are welcome.

Sparkling Wines: Sparkling Wine *(Petit Verdot)*.

White Wines: Alba *(Viognier)*, Euclid, Petit Manseng.

Rosé Wines: Rosa Virginiana.

Red Wines: Cabernet Sauvignon, Chestnut One, Merlot, Petit Verdot, Red Table Wine, Virginia Blend.

Sweet/Dessert Wines: Dessert Wine *(Petit Manseng)*.

Price Range: $19–$40

Tastings: $10 per person for a flight.

Purchasing: Online to AK, AZ, CO, DC, FL, GA, HI, IA, ID, IN, KS, LA, MA, MD, ME, MN, MO, NC, ND, NE, NH, NM, NV, NY, OH, OK, OR, PA, SC, TN, TX, VA, VT, WA, WI, WV, and WY.

Directions: From Charlottesville, turn north onto Stony Point Road (VA Route 20) at the intersection of U.S. Route 250 and River Bend/Stony Point Roads. Drive 11.6 miles to the winery's drive on the left.

Chisholm Vineyards at Adventure Farm
1135 Clan Chisholm Lane
Earlysville VA 22936

Hours: F–Su 12:00–5:00 (F to 9:00 in summer)　　833-340-0086, 434-971-8796
Closed New Year's, Easter, Christmas　　　　　　www.chisholmvineyards.com
　　　　　　　　　　　　　　　　　E-mail: info@chisholmvineyards.com

The Chisholm family launched its winery on a 500-acre farm that has been in their family for over 60 years and on which they raise grass-fed beef cattle. Chisholm Vineyards made its first wines in 2013, with Michael Shaps as winemaker. It hosts food trucks and local bands on weekends, with visitors welcome to sit over a glass of wine out on the covered patio. Chisholm also offers an outdoor summer concert series, a pumpkin patch and fall festival in October, heritage-bred turkeys for sale in November, and Christmas trees (and a visiting Santa) in December. The facilities may be rented for weddings and private events. Supervised children and leashed dogs are welcome.

Chisholm Vineyards offers its four-bedroom Lake House for short-term rental; see the website for details.

Sparkling Wines: Sparkling Brut, Sparkling Rosé.

White Wines: Chardonnay, Viognier.

Rosé Wines: Rosé.

Red Wines: Cabernet Franc, Cabernet Sauvignon, Chambourcin, Gigi's Red Blend, Farmer's Red Blend, Petit Verdot.

Price Range: $22–$42

Tastings: $12 per person.

Groups: Reservations required for groups of 10 or more.

Purchasing: Online for AK, AZ, CO, DC, FL, GA, HI, IA, ID, IL, IN, KS, LA, MA, MD, ME, MN, MO, NC, ND, NE NH, NM, NV, NY, OH, OK, OR, PA, SC, TN, TX, VA, VT, WA, WI, WV, and WY.

Directions: From U.S. Route 29, turn west onto Town Center Road by the Charlottesville Airport. Drive 0.7 miles and turn left onto Dickerson Road (Route 606). After ½ mile, enter the roundabout and take the first exit onto Earlysville Road (Route 743). Drive 2.6 miles and turn left into the winery entrance on the left.

Five Oaks Vineyard
4574 Belle Vista Drive
Barboursville VA 22923

Hours: Sa–Su 1:00–6:00 (Jun–Sep),
Sa–Su 12:00–5:00 (Oct–May)
Closed New Year's, Easter, Christmas

434-563-3822
www.fiveoaksvineyard.com
E-mail: info@fiveoaksvineyard.com

Founded by Robert Shepherd, Five Oaks is on a working farm north of Charlottesville. Tastings are held either in the converted barn that serves as the main tasting room or out on the grounds, where guests are welcome to stay and enjoy the view of the surrounding vineyards. Five Oaks is using all estate-grown grapes for its wines, which feature various hybrid varieties. Well-behaved leashed dogs are welcome. Several RV spaces are available for overnight rental.

White Wines: Cayuga White, Mary Catherine, Vidal Blanc.

Rosé Wines: Five Oaks Blush.

Red Wines: Chambourcin.

Price Range: $21–$32

Tastings: $5 per person.

Purchasing: Online to AK, AZ, CO, DC, FL, GA, HI, IA, ID, IN, KS, LA, MA, MD, ME, MN, MO, NC, ND, NE, NH, NM, NV, NY, OH, OK, OR, PA, SC, TN, TX, VA, VT, WA, WI, WV, and WY.

Directions: From Charlottesville, turn north onto Stony Point Road (VA Route 20) at the intersection of U.S. Route 250 and River Bend/Stony Point Roads. Drive about 12 miles to the winery's drive on the right.

Glass House Winery
5898 Free Union Road
Free Union VA 22940

Hours: W–Th, Su 12:00–5:30, F 12:00–9:00, Sa 12:00–8:00 (summer)
W–Su, holiday M 12:00–5:30 (winter–spring)
Closed New Year's, Thanksgiving, Christmas

434-975-0094
www.glasshousewinery.com
E-mail: info@glasshousewinery.com

Glass House Winery was established by Jeff and Michelle Sanders who moved to Virginia after having spent five years in Honduras where Jeff operated a plant nursery. Glass House's six-acre vineyard is currently planted to eight varieties of grapes. The winery features a glass-enclosed tropical greenhouse that may be rented for weddings and private events. Michelle's hand-crafted gourmet chocolates are also on sale at the winery which hosts special events, such as live music on weekends. Leashed dogs are welcome.

Glass House offers a five-bedroom B&B for overnight stays; see the website for details.

White Wines: Chardonnay, Pinot Gris, Vino Signora, Viognier.

Rosé Wines: Brosé *(Barbera)*, Eville Pink Drink.

Red Wines: Amici, Audace, Barbera, Cabernet Franc, C-Villian, Estratto, Tannat, Twenty-First.

Sweet/Dessert Wines: Meglio Del Sesso.

Fortified Wines: Bellezza *(port-style)*.

Price Range: $19–$59

Tastings: $12–$32 per person for a flight.

Purchasing: Online to AK, AZ, CO, DC, FL, GA, HI, IA, ID, IN, KS, LA, MA, MD, ME, MN, NC, ND, NE, NH, NM, NV, NY, OH, OR, PA, SC, TN, TX, VA, WA, WI, WV, and WY.

Directions: From Charlottesville and U.S. Route 29 North, take Barracks Road West (becomes Garth Road) and drive about 4 miles. Turn right onto Free Union Road (Route 601) at the Hunt Country Market. Continue on Free Union Road for 7.9 miles. Turn left onto the winery's drive.

Grace Estate Winery
5273 Mount Juliet Farm Road
Crozet VA 22932

Hours: W–F, Su 11:00–5:00,
Sa 11:00–6:00 (to 7:00 May–Oct)
Closed New Year's, Thanksgiving, Christmas

434-823-1486
www.graceestatewinery.com
E-mail: graceestatewinery@gmail.com

Owned by the John Grace family, Grace Estate originally sold fourteen different varieties of grapes from their 50-acre vineyards to other Virginia wineries. The tasting room has ample indoor and outdoor seating, free Wi-Fi, and a large stone fireplace and windows with a view of the 550-acre property. The winery offers crackers, cheeses, and cold cuts for purchase or guests may bring their own; food trucks are also present on select weekends. Grace Estate sponsors live music on Friday evenings in summer and may be rented for weddings and private events. Leashed dogs are welcome.

Sparkling Wines: Herlève (*Chardonnay*).

White Wines: Chardonnay, Le Gras Cuve, Petit Manseng, Sauvignon Blanc, Viognier.

Rosé Wines: Le Gras Rosé.

Red Wines: Cabernet Franc, Cabernet Sauvignon, Merlot, Petit Verdot, Tannat.

Sweet/Dessert Wines: Adeliza *(Petit Manseng)*, Ice Wine.

Price Range: $19–$39

Tastings: $12 per person for flight.

Groups: Reservations required for groups of 5 or more.

ADA accessible.

Purchasing: Online to AK, AZ, CO, DC, FL, GA, HI, IA, ID, IL, IN, KS, LA, MA, MD, ME, MN, MO, NC, ND, NE, NH, NM, NV, NY, OH, OK, OR, PA, SC, TN, TX, VA, VT, WA, WI, WV, and WY.

Directions: From Charlottesville, take Barracks Road West (becomes Garth Road). Continue about 9 miles. Turn left on Browns Gap Turnpike (Route 614) at the Wyant Store. After 0.3 miles, keep straight to stay on White Hall Road (VA Route 789), then make the first right into the winery entrance.

Hark Vineyard
1465 Davis Shop Road
Earlysville VA 22936

Hours: F, Su 12:00–6:00, Sa 12:00–8:00
Closed New Year's, Easter, Christmas

434-964-9463 (WINE)
www.harkvineyards.com
info@harkvineyards.com

Candice and Aaron Hark fulfilled a dream of having a winery when they purchased a 70-acre property, ten years after moving to the Charlottesville area. Hark produces all estate-grown wines under the guidance of longtime Virginia winemaker Jake Busching. All seating is outdoors at the moment; visitors are also invited to bring their own chairs and blankets to spread on the lawn. Light food can be purchased in the tasting room; guests can also bring their own. Hark hosts live music on many weekends.

White Wines: Chardonnay, Fuse, Pinot Gris, Virginia Verde.

Red Wines: Cabernet Franc, Merlot, Petit Verdot, Spark.

Price Range: $20–$42.

Tastings: $10–$15 per person for a flight.

Groups: Reservations required for groups of 10 or more.

Directions: From U.S. Route 29, turn west onto Town Center Road by the Charlottesville Airport. Drive 0.7 miles and turn left onto Dickerson Road (Route 606). After ½ mile, enter the roundabout and take the first exit onto Earlysville Road (Route 743). Drive 2.6 miles and take a slight left onto Buck Mountain Road (Route 663). Continue another 1.8 miles and turn right onto Markwood Road (Route 664). Drive 4.3 miles and turn left onto Davis Shop Road. The winery entrance will be on the right.

Honah Lee Vineyard
13443 Honah Lee Farm Drive
Gordonsville VA 22942

Hours: Su–Th 11:00–5:00,
F–Sa 11:00–6:00 (F to 8:00 in summer)
Closed New Year's, Thanksgiving, Christmas

540-308-7724, 540-406-1313
www.honahleevineyard.com
info@.honahleevineyard.com

Wayne and Vera Preddy have long been known in Virginia's wine-growing community for their renowned Honah Lee vineyard, whose name came from the song *Puff the Magic Dragon*. After selling grapes for many years to other wineries, they launched their own label in late 2014. There is limited indoor seating, with tables and chairs available on the grounds overlooking the vines. Honah Lee sponsors food trucks on many weekends. The facilities may be rented for weddings or private events. Military personnel receive a discount on purchases. Dogs are welcome.

White Wines: Chardonnay, ENJoy, Petit Manseng, Viognier.

Rosé Wines: Rosé.

Red Wines: Captain, De la Merce, Malbec, Tannat.

Price Range: $20–$30.

Tastings: $12–$15 per person for a flight.

Groups: Reservations requested for groups of 10 or more.

Directions: From Orange, drive south on U.S. Route 15 for 5 miles. Turn right onto Honah Lee Farm and the BerryWood Farm store.
From Gordonsville, drive north on U.S. Route 15 for 4 miles and turn left onto Honah Lee Farm Road and the BerryWood Farm store.

Horton Vineyards
6399 Spotswood Trail
Gordonsville VA 22942

Hours: Daily 10:00–5:00
Closed New Year's, Thanksgiving, Christmas

540-832-7440
www.hortonwine.com
E-mail: info@hortonwine.com

Horton Vineyards had its origins in a home vineyard started by the late Dennis Horton who ultimately purchased 55 acres in Orange County in 1988, planting his vineyards the following year. Horton was the first in Virginia to plant Viognier and also was a key figure in reviving the Norton grape, first cultivated in Virginia and widely planted in Horton's home town of Hermann, Missouri. Horton Vineyards plants the widest range of grape varieties in the state, including lesser-known grapes such as Rkatsiteli and Pinotage. The winery hosts a number of events, such as a Mardi Gras festival, annual pig roasts, and a Thanksgiving weekend open house.

Fruit Wines: Blackberry, Blueberry, Cranberry, Eden *(apple)*, Peach, Pear, Raspberry, Strawberry.

Sparkling Wines: Erotes *(Touriga Nacional)*, Knotts & Shuttles *(Tannat)*, Sparkling Viognier.

White Wines: Albariño, Chardonnay, Freedom, Petit Manseng, Rkatsiteli, Roussanne, Stonecastle White, Vidal Blanc, Viognier.

Rosé Wines: Nebbiolo Rosé, Pinotage Rosé, Stonecastle Blush.

Red Wines: Cabernet Franc, Côtes d'Orange, Dio, Malbec, Nebbiolo, Norton, Petit Verdot, Pinotage, Route 33, Stonecastle Red, Tannat, TitforTat.

Sweet/Dessert Wines: Eclipse Red, Eclipse White, Late Harvest Petit Manseng, Late Harvest Rkatsiteli, Niagara, Sweet Concord, Xoco Blanco, Xoco Rojo.

Fortified Wines: Pear, Vintage Port.

Price Range: $14–$45

Tastings: $10–$25 per person for a flight.

Groups: Reservations required for groups of 8 or more.

ADA accessible

Purchasing: Online to AK, AL, AZ, CA, CO, DC, FL, GA, HI, IA, ID, IL, IN, KS, LA, MA, MD, ME, MN, MO, NC, ND, NE, NH, NM, NV, NY, OH, OR, PA, SC, TN, TX, VA, WA, WI, WV, and WY.

Directions: From U.S. Route 29, turn east onto U.S. Route 33 East at Ruckersville. Drive 8 miles to the winery entrance on the left.

Keswick Vineyards
1575 Keswick Winery Drive
Keswick VA 22947

Hours: Daily 10:00–5:00
Closed New Year's, Easter, Thanksgiving, Christmas

434-244-3341
www.keswickvineyards.com
E-mail: info@keswickvineyards.com

Al and Cindy Schornberg established Keswick Vineyards on the grounds of the historic Edgewood estate they purchased in 2000. South African native (and now son-in-law) Stephen Barnard serves as winemaker, focusing on high-quality classic varietals from the estate's 70-plus acres of vines. The winery patio offers ample outdoor seating for enjoying a flight or bottle, with cheese, bread, and crackers available for purchase; food trucks are also scheduled on many weekends. Keswick's events include comedy nights, live music, and occasional fundraisers. The facility may be rented for weddings and private events. Supervised children and pets are welcome.

Handy Guide to Virginia Wineries

Sparkling Wines: Amélie, Amélie Rosé.

White Wines: Chardonnay, Trevillian White, V2, Viognier.

Rosé Wines: Rosé.

Red Wines: Cabernet Franc, Cabernet Sauvignon, Heritage, Merlot, Petit Verdot, Rives Red, Trevillian Red.

Dessert Wines: Nektar *(Petit Manseng)*.

Price Range: $24–$75

Tastings: $5 per person for regular tasting.

Restrictions: No groups over 10.

ADA accessible

Purchasing: Online for AK, CA, CO, DC, FL, GA, MD, MA, MI, MN, MO, NH, NY, NC, OH, PA, SC, TX, VA, and WA.

Directions: From I-64, take Exit 124 onto U.S. Route 250 East (Shadwell). Drive 2 miles and turn onto Louisa Road (Route 22 East). After 5.4 miles, stay straight to go onto Gordonsville Road (Route 231). Continue 2.2 miles to Keswick Winery Drive and the winery on the right.

Kilaurwen Vineyards
1543 Evergreen Church Road
Stanardsville VA 22973

Hours: Sa–Su 12:00–6:00 (Apr–Nov),
holiday M 11:00-3:00
Closed Dec–Mar

434-985-2535
www.kilaurwenwinery.com
E-mail: info@kilaurwenwinery.com

Bob and Dorien Steeves opened Kilaurwen to the public fifteen years after first establishing their vineyard and supplying grapes to several other Virginia wineries. The couple named the winery after their three daughters, Kimberlee, Laura, and Wendy, who actively assist with winery operations. Light snacks are available in the tasting room. All their wines are from Virginia-grown grapes, most from their own vineyards. Children and pets are welcome.

Kilaurwen offers a two-bedroom guest house, The Loft, for short-term rentals; see the website for details.

White Wines: Fiesta White, Kilaurwen White, Riesling.

Rosé Wines: Dry Rosé.

Red Wines: Cabernet Franc, Cabernet Sauvignon, Chambourcin, Fiesta Red, Kilaurwen Red, Three Sisters Red *(Bordeaux-style blend)*.

Price Range: $20–$32

Tastings: $5 per person.

Directions: Take U.S. Route 29 to Ruckersville and turn onto U.S. 33 West to Stanardsville. Turn left onto Dyke Road (Route 810) and drive 5.1 miles. Turn right onto Evergreen Church Road. The winery entrance will be ⅓ mile on the right.

Knight's Gambit Vineyards
2218 Lake Albemarle Road
Charlottesville VA 22901

Hours: Th, 5:00–8:00, F 2:00–8:00, Sa 12:00–8:00 434-566-1168
Su 12:00–6:00   www.knightsgambitvineyard.com
Closed Nov–Mar   E-mail: jordan@knightsgambitvineyard.com

Paul and Jill Faulkner Summers first planted a small vineyard on their 400-acre farm west of Charlottesville at the encouragement of their son, Paul, who had worked at several wineries in Virginia, including Blenheim and Barboursville. The winery's name is both a chess move and the title of a short story by Jill's father, renowned American author William Faulkner. The winery offers live music and food trucks on many weekends, as well as light snacks, a picnic area, croquet field, and beanbag pitch overlooking the vines, with the winery dogs often on hand to greet visitors.

Knight's Gambit offers its vineyard farmhouse for overnight stays; see the website for details.

White Wines: Chardonnay, Pinot Grigio.

Rosé Wines: Rosé.

Red Wines: Cabernet Franc, Meritage, Petit Verdot.

Price Range: $24–$32

Tastings: $10 per person for a flight.

Groups: Reservations requested for groups of 8 or more.

Restrictions: No buses.

Directions: From Charlottesville and U.S. Route 29 North, take Barracks Road West, which becomes Garth Road after 2 miles. Continue another 7.5 miles and turn left onto Lake Albemarle Road. Drive 2 miles and stay straight at a sharp right-hand curve to enter the winery driveway.

Montifalco Vineyards
1800 Fray Road
Ruckersville VA 22968

Hours: Th–Su 12:00–5:00
Closed New Year's, Thanksgiving, Christmas

434-989-9115
www.montifalcovineyard.com
E-mail: visit@montifalcovineyard.com

Owner and winemaker Justin Falco brings experience in the Napa and Sonoma wine regions to his Montifalco Vineyards, using fruit from his own vineyards and others in the Monticello AVA. Guests can select from a menu of breads, cheeses, and charcuterie to enjoy indoors or outside on the covered patio overlooking the vineyard along with their tasting flights. Live music is featured on many weekends. Leashed pets are welcome. Adults only, please.

White Wines: Chardonnay, Estate Meritage, Resilient White, Sémillon.

Red Wines: Cabernet Franc, Coda Rossa, Malbec, Meritage, Petit Verdot, Resilient Red, Syrah, Tannat.

Price Range: $19–$42

Tastings: $14 per person for a flight.

Restrictions: Adults only.

Directions: From U.S. Route 29 at Ruckersville, turn west onto U.S. Route 33 West. After 1 mile, turn left onto Advance Mills Road (Route 743). Drive 3 miles to Fray Road. The winery is on the corner, with the entrance gates immediately on the left.

Handy Guide to Virginia Wineries

Moss Vineyards
1849 Simmons Gap Road
Nortonsville VA 22935

Hours: F–Su 12:00–5:00
Closed New Year's, Christmas

434-990-0111
www.mossvineyards.net
E-mail: mossvineyards@gmail.com

Barry and Ellen Moss opened Moss Vineyards to the public in 2012, three years after first planting the winery's vineyards. An architect, Barry has designed the tasting room to maximize scenic views of the winery's vineyards and the hills beyond. Seating is available inside the tasting room, where a fireplace inside helps warm chilly autumn afternoons, while the deck and grounds offers ample outdoor seating. Children and leashed dogs are welcome. Discounts offered for active-duty and retired military.

Moss offers a one-bedroom house in the woods near the winery for overnight stays; see the website for rental details.

Ciders: Moss Cider.

White Wines: Viognier.

Rosé Wines: Rosé.

Red Wines: Archittetura, Cabernet Franc, Vino Rosso.

Price Range: $28–$38

Tastings: $10 per person for a flight.

Groups: Reservations requested for groups of 7 or more.

Purchasing: Online for AK, AZ, CO, DC, FL, GA, HI, IA, ID, IN, KS, LA, MA, MD, ME, MN, MO, NC, ND, NE, NH, NM, NV, NY, OH, OK, OR, PA, SC, TN, TX, VA, VT, WA, WI, WV, and WY.

Directions: From U.S. Route 29 at Ruckersville, turn west onto U.S. Route 33. After 8.5 miles, turn left onto Dyke Road (Route 810). Drive 8 miles and turn right on Simmons Gap Road (Route 628). The winery will be ⅓ mile on the left.

Reynard Florence Vineyard
16109 Burnley Road
Barboursville VA   22923

Hours: Th–F & holiday M 12:00–5:00, Sa–Su 11:00–5:00
Closed New Year's, Easter, Thanksgiving, Christmas

540-832-3895
www.reynardflorence.com
E-mail: info@reynardflorence.com

Reynard Florence was established by Roe and Dee Allison, who planted their first vines in 2006 and produced their first vintage three years later, working with Michael Shaps. The winery's name combines the old French spelling for "fox" (Reynard) with Dee's first name (Florence). Roe and friends often are on hand for informal jam sessions on weekends, with the winery Corgis often in attendance. Firepits and outdoor seating, including a pergola, is available. Children and leashed pets are welcome.

White Wines: Chardonnay, Petit Manseng, Reynard Blanc.

Rosé Wines: Ti-Rey Rosé.

Red Wines: Cabernet Franc, Cabernet Sauvignon, Merlot, Petit Verdot, Recherché.

Price Range: $22–$30

Tastings: $12 per person for a flight.

Groups: Reservations required for groups of 8 or more.

Purchasing: Online for AK, AZ, CO, DC, FL, GA, HI, IA, ID, IN, KS, LA, MA, MD, ME, MN, MO, NC, ND, NE, NH, NM, NV, NY, OH, OK, OR, PA, SC, TN, TX, VA, VT, WA, WI, WV, and WY.

Directions: From U.S. Route 29, take U.S. Route 33 East at Ruckersville. Continue 3.6 miles and turn right onto Burnley Road. The winery entrance will be 1.6 miles on the left.

Stinson Vineyards
4744 Sugar Hollow Road
Crozet VA   22932

Hours: Th–Su, hol M 11:00–5:00
Closed New Year's, Easter, Thanksgiving,
Christmas Eve & Day

434-823-7300
www.stinsonvineyards.com
E-mail: info@stinsonvineyards.com

Scott and Martha Stinson opened Stinson Vineyards in 2011 on the grounds of the historic Piedmont House, which dates from 1796. Scott purchased the property planning to renovate it and was inspired to begin making wine after discovering an abandoned vineyard on the grounds; he and daughter Rachel Stinson Vrooman are the winemakers. The tasting room offers sandwiches and food platters for purchase, or guests may bring their own for a picnic on the patio. A range of seating is available outdoors. Leashed dogs are welcome.

Stinson offers several options for overnight stays, including a vineyard inn and rooms at a small hotel in downtown Charlottesville; see the website for booking information.

White Wines: Chardonnay, Petit Manseng, Sauvignon Blanc, Sugar Hollow White, Wild Kat (*Rkatsiteli*).

Rosé Wines: Rosé.

Red Wines: Cabernet Franc, Merlot, Meritage, Sugar Hollow Red, Tannat.

Fortified Wines: Imperialis *(port-style)*.

Price Range: $16–$38

Tastings: $10–$14 per person for a flight.

Groups: Reservations required for groups of 8 or more.

Purchasing: Online for AK, AZ, CO, DC, FL, GA, HI, IA, ID, IN, KS, LA, MA, MD, ME, MN, MO, NC, ND, NE, NH, NM, NV, NY, OH, OK, OR, PA, SC, TN, TX, VA, VT, WA, WI, WV, and WY.

Directions: From Charlottesville and U.S. Route 29 North, take Barracks Road, which becomes Garth Road. Drive 9 miles to the village of White Hall; stay straight in order to go onto Sugar Hollow Road when the main road bends to the right. The winery will be immediately on the right.

Stone Mountain Vineyards
1376 Wyatt Mountain Road
Dyke VA 22935

Hours: Th, M 12:00–5:00,
F–Su 11:00–6:00 (mid-Mar–mid-Dec)
Closed Easter, mid-Dec–mid-Mar

434-990-9463 (WINE)
www.stonemountainvineyards.com
E-mail: info@stonemountainvineyards.com

Stone Mountain, founded in 1986, is now owned by Jim and Deanna Gephart who produce estate-grown wines from their 20-acre vineyard. The tasting room includes an observation deck with sweeping views of the valley beneath its 1,700-foot elevation. Visitors are welcome to picnic on the grounds, either with snacks purchased at the winery or their own picnic lunches from home. Tours of the winery processing area are offered by reservation. The facilities may be rented for weddings and private events. Children and leashed well-behaved dogs are welcome.

White Wines: Chardonnay, Gewurztraminer, Pinot Grigio, Sauvignon Blanc.

Rosé Wines: Rosé.

Red Wines: Cabernet Franc.

Fortified Wines: Tribute.

Price Range: $24–$48

Tastings: $18 per person for a flight.

Purchasing: Online to multiple states; contact the winery for details.

Directions: From U.S. Route 29 at Ruckersville, take U.S. Route 33 West for 8.5 miles. Turn left onto Dyke Road (Route 810) and drive 6.5 miles. Take a right onto Bacon Hollow Road (Route 627) and drive 3.7 miles, then turn left onto Wyatt Mountain Road (Route 632) (unpaved). Drive up the winding and narrow gravel mountain road 2 miles to the winery entrance on left. (Note: Winery advises **not** following GPS unit directions.)

White Hall Vineyards
5282 Sugar Ridge Road
White Hall VA 22932

Hours: W–Su 11:00–5:00
Closed New Year's, Easter, Thanksgiving, Christmas Eve & Day

434-823-8615
www.whitehallvineyards.com
E-mail: tastingroom@whitehallvineyards.com

Tony and Edie Champ established White Hall in 1992, eventually expanding their vineyards to 45 acres. The winery tasting room includes a number of seating options and a large fireplace that invites visitors to linger after their tastings; both covered and open seating is also available outdoors on the grounds. The facilities include a large banquet room on the second floor with expansive views of the Blue Ridge that is available for private parties or weddings. Leashed dogs are welcome.

White Wines: Chardonnay, Petit Manseng, Soliterre, Sugar Ridge White, Viognier.

Rosé Wines: Breakheart Rosé, Vin Gris.

Red Wines: Cabernet Franc, Merlot, Petit Verdot.

Sweet/Dessert Wines: Edichi.

Price Range: $18–$30

Tastings: $10 per person.

Groups: Reservations required for groups of 7 or more.

ADA accessible.

Restrictions: No vehicles holding 14 or more occupants after noon.

Purchasing: Online for AK, AZ, CO, DC, FL, GA, HI, IA, ID, IN, KS, LA, MA, MD, ME, MN, MO, NC, ND, NE, NH, NM, NV, NY, OH, OK, OR, PA, SC, TN, TX, VA, VT, WA, WI, WV, and WY.

Directions: From Charlottesville and U.S. Route 29 North, take Barracks Road West, which becomes Garth Road. Continue to the village of White Hall, where the road curves to the right at the Piedmont Store and becomes Browns Gap Turnpike (Route 614). Take the first left onto Break Heart Road which will become Sugar Ridge Road (portions unpaved). The winery will be 1.5 miles on the right.

Handy Guide to Virginia Wineries

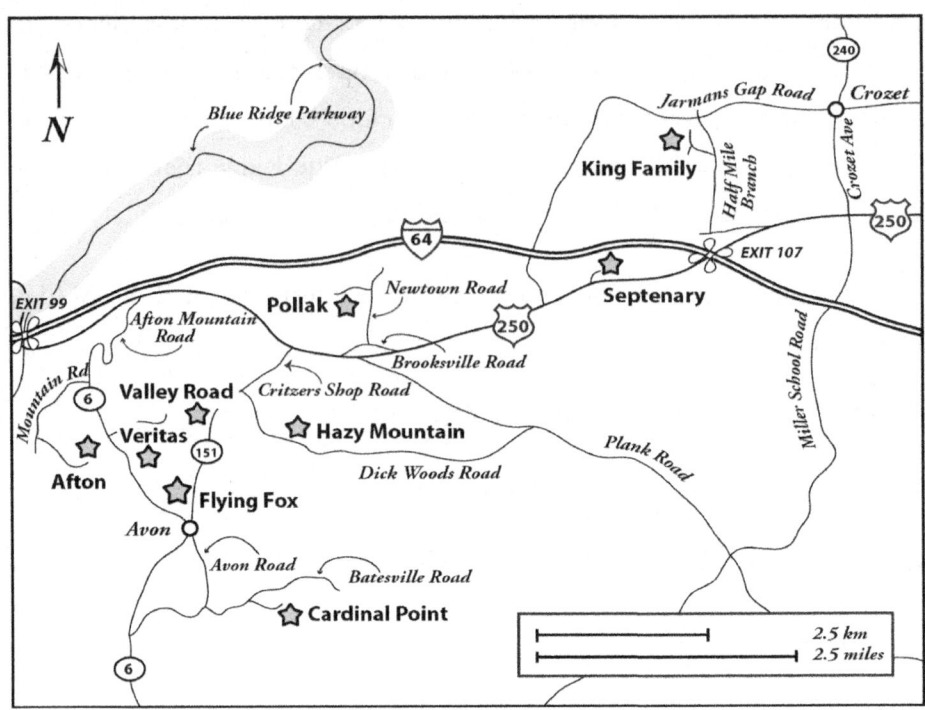

Map 7.6. Afton-Crozet

AFTON-CROZET

Afton Mountain Vineyards
234 Vineyard Lane
Afton VA 22920

Hours: Th–Su 11:00–5:00
Closed New Year's, Easter, Thanksgiving, Christmas Eve & Day

540-456-8667
www.aftonmountainvineyards.com
E-mail: info@aftonmountainvineyards.com

Nestled at the base of its namesake mountain, Afton Mountain Vineyards is located on the site of the former Bacchanal Vineyards, one of the pioneer vineyards of Virginia. Owned by Tony and Elizabeth Smith since 2009, Afton Mountain's production is under winemaker Damien Blanchon. Afton also offers several wines under the Monticello Wine Company label in tribute to this historic 1873 winery (now no longer in existance). Afton's picnic area offers a lovely view of the Virginia countryside and mountains. Picnic foods are available from the tasting room. The winery is available for weddings and private events. Dogs are welcome. Adults only, please.

Afton also has five guest cottages on the grounds for overnight stays; see the website for rental details.

Sparkling Wines: Bollicine.

White Wines: Chardonnay, Monticello Wineco Chardonnay, Muscat VDN.

Rosé Wines: Monticello Wineco Rosé, Rosé.

Red Wines: Cabernet Franc, Cabernet Sauvignon, Festa di Bacco *(Super Tuscan-style)*, Merlot, Monticello Wineco Doubtless, Monticello Wineco Cellar Red, Petit Verdot, Tannat, Tradition.

Fortified Wines: Port-Style VDN.

Price Range: $21–$55

Tastings: $12 per person for a flight; $25 for seated tasting (with reservation).

Restrictions: No groups over 6.

ADA accessible.

Directions: **From I-64 Westbound,** take Exit 107 onto U.S. Route 250 West. Drive 6.7 miles and turn left onto Afton Mountain Road (Route 6). Descend 1.6 miles and turn right onto Mountain Road (Route 631). Drive 1.2 miles to the winery's long driveway on the left.

From I-64 Eastbound, take Exit 99 onto U.S. Route 250 East; drive 1.9 miles and turn right onto Afton Mountain Road (Route 6). Descend 1.6 miles and turn right onto Mountain Road (Route 631). Drive 1.2 miles to the winery's long driveway on the left.

Cardinal Point Vineyard & Winery
9423 Batesville Road
Afton VA 22920

Hours: Daily 11:00–5:30 (Mar–Dec),
F–M 11:00–5:30 (Jan–Feb)
Closed New Year's, Easter,
Thanksgiving, Christmas

540-456-8400
www.cardinalpointwinery.com
E-mail: info@cardinalpointwinery.com

Cardinal Point was founded by Paul and Ruth Gorman, whose son Tim serves as the vineyard manager and winemaker. Visitors can watch a video tour of the winemaking process from the tasting room, which also includes a small gift area. The winery sponsors a number of special events, including an annual oyster roast and live music on the outdoor deck. The facilities may be rented for private events. Children and pets are welcome.

Guests may stay overnight at Cardinal Point's restored 19th-century farmhouse; see the website for details and reservations.

White Wines: A6, Aubaine, Chardonnay, Green, Hopped Chardonnay, Quattro.

Rosé Wines: Frai Rosé, Rosé *(Cabernet Franc)*.

Red Wines: Clay Hill Cabernet Franc, Petit Verdot, Rockfish Red, Union.

Price Range: $20–$40

Tastings: $10 per person for a flight; fee waived for teachers and military personnel with valid ID.

Groups: Reservations required for groups of 7 to 10.

ADA accessible

Restrictions: No groups over 10; no groups after 1:00.

Purchasing: Online for multiple states; contact the winery for details.

Directions: From I-64 Eastbound, take Exit 99 onto U.S. Route 250 East; drive 3.8 miles and turn right onto Critzers Shop Road (Route 151). Drive 2.5 miles and turn left onto Avon Road. Drive 1 mile and turn left onto Batesville Road. The winery will be ½ mile on the right.

From I-64 Westbound, take Exit 107 onto U.S. Route 250 West; drive 4.8 miles and turn left onto Critzers Shop Road (Route 151). Drive 2.5 miles and turn left onto Avon Road. Drive 1 mile and turn left onto Batesville Road. The winery will be ½ mile on the right.

Handy Guide to Virginia Wineries

Flying Fox Vineyard & Winery
10368 Critzer Shop Road
Afton VA 22920

Hours: Daily 11:00–5:30
Closed New Year's, Easter, Thanksgiving, Christmas

434-361-1692
www.flyingfoxvineyard.com
E-mail: flyingfoxtastingroom@gmail.com

Flying Fox Vineyard is located in the heart of scenic Nelson County. First established in 2001 by Rich Evans and Lynn Davis, it is now owned by the Hodson family (*Veritas Vineyards*). Flying Fox's production is estate-grown, using fruit from vineyards in the Monticello and Shenandoah AVAs. Light snacks are offered for sale in the tasting room, which has several indoor lounges for seating as well as tables and chairs outdoors. Dogs are welcome outdoors.

White Wines: Pinot Gris, Table White, Viognier.

Rosé Wines: Rosé.

Red Wines: Cabernet Franc, Merlot, Petit Verdot, Table Red, Trio.

Fortified Wines: Vermouth *(seasonal variations)*.

Price Range: $18–$35

Tastings: $10 per person.

Groups: Reservations required for groups of 6 or more.

Purchasing: Online for VA and multiple states; contact the winery for details.

Directions: From I-64 Westbound, take Exit 107 (Crozet) and turn onto U.S. Route 250 West. Drive about 4.8 miles and turn left onto Critzers Shop Road (Route 151). Continue 2.2 miles to the winery on the right.

From I-64 Eastbound, take Exit 99 (Afton Mountain) and turn onto U.S. Route 250 East. Drive 3.2 miles and turn right onto Critzers Shop Road (Route 151). Continue 2.2 miles to the winery on the right.

Hazy Mountain Vineyards & Brewery
8736 Dick Woods Road
Afton VA 22920

Hours: W–Su 11:00–6:00
Closed New Year's, Easter,
Thanksgiving, Christmas

540-302-2529
www.hazy-mountain.com
E-mail: info@Hazy-Mountain.com

Hazy Mountain Vineyards & Brewery is new to the Route 151 corridor, having opened in mid-2021. Owned and operated by Michael and Sandra McGinnis, Hazy Mountain produces all Virginia-grown wines from its two vineyards. The Italiante-style tasting room and event venue are sited on a hilltop, with covered verandas and terraces overlooking the vineyards and surrounding mountains. The kitchen offers cheese and charcuterie boards, pizzas, flatbreads, and hot pretzels. The facilities can be rented for private events and weddings. Hazy Mountain also has a craft brewery co-located with the winery that offers flights and beers on tap. Children are welcome.

White Wines: Chardonnay, Riesling.

Rosé Wines: Blaufränkisch Rosé, Rosé.

Red Wines: BDX, Cabernet Sauvignon, Pinot Noir.

Price Range: $18–$35

Tastings: $15 per person for a flight.

Groups: Reservations recommended for groups of 8 or more.

Restrictions: No dogs; no outside food.

ADA accessible

Directions: From I-64 Westbound, take Exit 107 (Crozet) and turn onto U.S. Route 250 West. Drive about 4.8 miles and turn left onto Critzers Shop Road (Route 151). After 0.8 mile, turn left onto Dick Woods Road and continue about one mile to the winery on the left.

From I-64 Eastbound, take Exit 99 (Afton Mountain) and turn onto U.S. Route 250 East. Drive 3.2 miles and turn right onto Critzers Shop Road (Route 151). After 0.8 mile, turn left onto Dick Woods Road and continue about one mile to the winery on the left.

King Family Vineyards & Roseland Polo Farm
6550 Roseland Farm
Crozet VA 22932

Hours: Daily 10:00–5:30 (W to 8:30, Apr–Nov)
Closed New Year's Eve & Day, Easter,
Thanksgiving, Christmas Eve & Day

434-823-7800
www.kingfamilyvineyards.com
E-mail: info@kingfamilyvineyards.com

King Family Vineyards was founded in 1998 by Texas natives Ellen and the late David King. The winery has two tasting rooms with indoor seating as well as tables and chairs on the patio and grounds. Wines offered include some produced at the family's Argentina vineyards. Winemaking is under the guidance of Mathieu Finot, a native of France's Rhône Valley. The winery hosts Sunday afternoon polo matches (summers only), live music, and Wednesday food truck nights. The facilities may be rented for private events and weddings. Cheeses, coldcuts, spreads, and bread are available for purchase, or guests may bring their own to have outdoors. Children and pets are welcome.

Sparkling Wines: Brut, Sparkling Rosé.

White Wines: Chardonnay, Mountain Plains White, Roseland, Sauvignon Blanc, Verde, Viognier.

Rosé Wines: Crosé.

Red Wines: Cabernet Franc, Meritage, Merlot, Mountain Plains, Petit Verdot.

Sweet/Dessert Wines: Loreley 'Late Harvest'.

Fortified Wines: Seven *(Merlot, aged in bourbon barrels)*.

Price Range: $22–$70

Tastings: $12 per person for a flight; $20 for reserved, reservations required.

Groups: Reservations recommended for groups of 8 or more.

ADA accessible

Purchasing: Online purchasing available for AL, CA, CO, DC, FL, GA, MD, MN, MO, NC, NY, OH, OR, PA, SC, TN, VA, and WA.

Directions: From I-64, take Exit 107 (Crozet) and turn onto U.S. Route 250 East. Drive ½ mile and make a left onto Hillsboro Lane (Route 797). Make the first right onto Half Mile Branch (Route 684) and drive one mile to the winery entrance on left.

Pollak Vineyards
330 Newtown Road
Greenwood VA 22943

Hours: W–Su 11:00–5:00
Closed New Year's, Easter, Thanksgiving, 21–29 Dec

540-456-8844
www.pollakvineyards.com
E-mail: info@pollakvineyards.com

Cincinnati residents Margo and David Pollak launched their winery in 2003 to fulfill their longstanding dream of owning a winery. Pollak is on a 98-acre farm at the base of a mountain, with over 30 acres currently under vine. The tasting room offers visitors scenic views of the vineyards, pond, and adjacent hills from its veranda and indoor tables, with a range of outdoor seating also available. Hot baguettes and cheese plates can be purchased to enjoy over a glass or bottle of wine. The winery may be rented for private events, dinners, and weddings. Well-behaved children and pets are welcome.

White Wines: Chardonnay, Durant White, Pinot Gris, Viognier.

Rosé Wines: Rosé.

Red Wines: Cabernet Franc, Cabernet Sauvignon, Meritage, Merlot, Petit Verdot.

Fortified Wine: Mille Fleurs *(Viognier, eau-de-vie)*.

Price Range: $24–$50

Tastings: $16 per person.

Restrictions: No groups over 6.

ADA accessible.

Purchasing: Ordering to AK, AZ, CO, DC, FL, GA, HI, IA, ID, IN, KS, LA, MA, ME, MN, MO, NC, ND, NE, NH, NM, NV, NY, OH, OR, PA, SC, TN, TX, VA, VT, WA, WI, WV, and WY.

Directions: From I-64, take Exit 107 (Crozet) and turn onto U.S. Route 250 West. Drive about 3 miles. Just past Ridgeley Estate, turn right onto Brooksville Road (Route 796) and drive ½ mile. Turn right again onto Newtown Road. The winery drive will be ½ mile on left.

Septenary Winery at Seven Oaks Farm
200 Seven Oaks Farm
Greenwood VA 22943

Hours: Th–Su 11:00–5:30
Closed New Year's Eve & Day, Easter, Thanksgiving, Christmas Eve & Day

434-996-6292
www.septenarywinery.com
E-mail: info@septenarywinery.com

Located on the historic Seven Oaks Farm, Septenary Winery was started in 2017 by Todd and Sarah Zimmerman after the couple returned to Virginia from Colorado. Their wines are made from estate-grown grapes or fruit from vineyards in other Virginia counties. The tasting room is in the estate's former pool house and features a fire pit and outdoor patio with a reflection pool. Cheese and charcuterie boards may be purchased from the tasting room and enjoyed on the spacious outdoor seating areas. Private tastings and tours may be available on request. Leashed dogs are welcome. Adults only, please.

Sparkling Wines: Sparkling Chardonnay, Sparkling Rosé.

White Wines: Chardonnay, Sauvignon Blanc.

Red Wines: Carriage House, Cloverplains, Coleman, Manor Reserve, Merlot.

Price Range: $30–$55

Tastings: $15 per person.

Groups: Reservations required for groups of 6 to 10; no groups over 10.

ADA accessible

Purchasing: Online to AK, AZ, CO, DC, FL, GA, HI, IA, ID, IN, KS, LA, MA, ME, MN, MO, NC, ND, NE, NH, NM, NV, NY, OH, OR, PA, SC, TN, TX, VA, VT, WA, WI, WV, and WY.

Directions: From I-64, take Exit 107 (Crozet) and turn onto U.S. Route 250 West. Drive about 1.5 miles and turn right onto Greenwood Station Road. The winery driveway will be about ½ mile on the right.

Valley Road Vineyards
9264 Critzers Shop Road
Afton VA 22920

Hours: M–Th 12:00–5:30, F 12:00–7:30, Sa–Su 10:30–5:30
Closed New Year's, Thanksgiving, Christmas

540-456-6350
www.valleyroadwines.com
E-mail: info@valleyroadwines.com

Valley Road Vineyards officially opened its doors in August 2016, founded by Stan Joynes who joined forces with several friends after a long career as a Richmond lawyer. Winemaking is done under the guidance of Mathieu Finot (*King Family Vineyards*), who is using fruit from Valley Road's vines supplemented by grapes from other Virginia vineyards. The winery sponsors live music on weekends and offers a range of artisanal cheeses, breads, and spreads for purchase. The facilities may be rented for weddings or private events. Leashed pets are welcome.

Sparkling Wines: Fête (*Viognier*), Joie (*rosé*).

White Wines: Chardonnay, Destana, Mountain Glen White, Sauvignon Blanc, Viognier.

Rosé Wines: Rosé.

Red Wines: Cabernet Franc, Meritage, Petit Verdot, Torn Curtain.

Sweet/Dessert Wines: Trillium.

Price Range: $22–$35

Tastings: $15 per person.

Groups: Reservations required for groups of 8 to 15 and for buses and vans.

Directions: **From I-64 Westbound,** take Exit 107 (Crozet) and turn onto U.S. Route 250 West. Drive about 4.8 miles and turn left onto Critzers Shop Road (Route 151). Continue one mile to the winery on the right.

From I-64 Eastbound, take Exit 99 (Afton Mountain) and turn onto U.S. Route 250 East. Drive 3.2 miles and turn right onto Critzers Shop Road (Route 151). Continue one mile to the winery on the right.

Veritas Vineyards & Winery
151 Veritas Lane
(GPS address: 145 Saddleback Farm)
Afton VA 22920

Hours: Daily 11:00–5:00 540-456-8000
Closed New Year's, Thanksgiving, Christmas www.veritaswines.com
E-mail: contact@veritaswines.com

Andrew and Patricia Hodson opened Veritas to the public in 2002; daughter Emily Pelton serves as the winemaker. The tasting room has a long tasting bar as well as armchairs and small sofas for visitors, while a covered veranda and tables on the grounds offer views of the vineyards and mountains beyond. Veritas sponsors a variety of special events, such as summertime "Starry Nights" and winter winemaker's dinners. Light fare and occasional pop-up menus are available for purchase; picnic foods brought by customers must be consumed outside. The facilities are available for private events and weddings. Children and pets are welcome.

Guests may stay overnight in one of the six suites at The Farmhouse, a restored farmstead originally built in 1836.

Sparkling Wines: Scintilla, Mousseux.

White Wines: Chardonnay, Sauvignon Blanc, Viognier, White Star.

Rosé Wines: Rosé.

Red Wines: Cabernet Franc, Merlot, Petit Verdot, Red Star, Vintner's Reserve *(Bordeaux-style blend)*.

Sweet/Dessert Wines: Kenmar, Petit Manseng.

Fortified Wines: Othello.

Price Range: $18–$45

Tastings: $10 per person.

Groups: Reservations required for groups of 8 to 15, $15 per person, M–F only. No groups over 15.

ADA accessible.

Purchasing: Online to AL, AK, AZ, AR, CA, CO, CT, DC, DE, FL, GA, HI, ID, IL, IN, KS, KY, LA, MA, MD, ME, MI, MN, MS, MO, MT, NC, NE, NM, NV, OH, OK, OR, PA, RI, SC, SD, TN, TX, VT, VA, WA, WI, and WY.

Directions: From **I-64 Westbound**, take Exit 107 onto U.S. Route 250 West; drive 6.7 miles and turn left onto Afton Mountain Road (Route 6). From **I-64 Eastbound**, take Exit 99 onto U.S. Route 250 East; drive 1.9 miles and turn right onto Afton Mountain Road (Route 6). Drive 2 miles and turn left onto Saddleback Trail. Continue to the parking lot on the right.

Handy Guide to Virginia Wineries

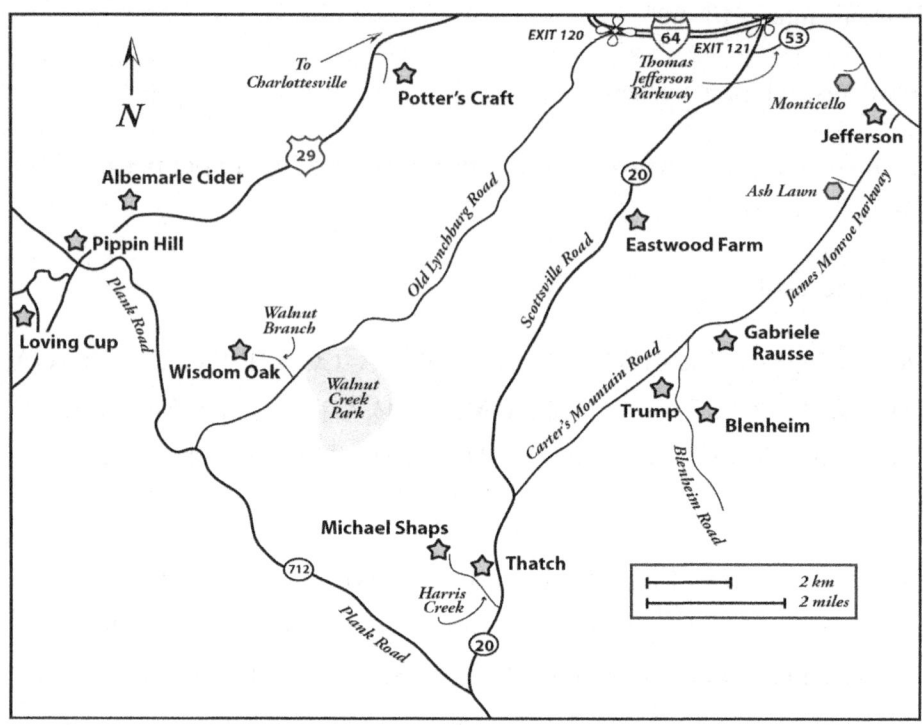

Map 7.7. North Garden

LOWER MONTICELLO

Albemarle Cider Works
2545 Rural Ridge Lane
North Garden VA 22959

Hours: W–Su 11:00–5:00 (Jan–Aug);
Daily 11:00–5:00 (Sep–Dec)
Closed New Year's, Thanksgiving, Christmas

434-297-2326, 434-979-1663
www.albemarleciderworks.com
E-mail: fruit@albemarleciderworks.com

Chuck and Charlotte Shelton opened Albemarle Cider Works in 2009 as a collateral line to their family's Rural Ridge Orchard, which has apple and other fruit trees for sale. All the ciders are made from classic and heirloom apple varieties. The cidery sponsors an apple festival as well as various workshops on apple growing and cider making. Live music and food trucks are featured on many weekends, and monthly Trivia in the Orchard lets guests test their knowledge. Guests may bring their own food or can purchase a range of snacks and locally-made cheeses and charcuterie inside the tasting room. Children are welcome but must be supervised at all times. Only limited seating is available indoors.

Albemarle Cider Works's Rural Ridge Cottage can be booked for overnight stays through the Crossroads Inn website *(www.crossroadsinn.com)*.

Ciders: Arkansas Black, Black Twig, Brut d'Albemarle, GoldRush, Jupiter's Legacy, Old Virginia Winesap, Pomme Mary, Red Hill, Ragged Mountain, Royal Pippin.

Price Range: $16

Tastings: $5–$10 per person, depending on range of ciders available.

Groups: No groups larger than 10.

Directions: From I-64, take Exit 118 onto U.S. Route 29 South. Drive 8 miles and turn right onto Rural Ridge Lane at the Rural Ridge Orchard.

Blenheim Vineyards
31 Blenheim Farm
Charlottesville VA 22902

Hours: Th–Su 11:00–5:30
Closed New Year's Eve & Day, Thanksgiving,
Christmas Eve & Day

434-293-5366
www.blenheimvineyards.com
E-mail: info@blenheimvineyards.com

Blenheim Vineyards was established in 2000 by Dave Matthews on the historic Blenheim estate that dates to a 1730 land grant. The tasting room offers a view of the lower-level winemaking facilities through paneled glass floors. Outdoor seating is available, including a covered tent area. Blenheim offers cheeses and snacks by pre-order; visitors are also welcome to bring their own. The winery sponsors live music and food trucks on weekends, as well as special brunches. The facilities may be rented for private events. Children are welcome.

White Wines: Chardonnay, Grüner Veltliner, On The Line White, Painted White, Rkatsiteli, Sauvignon Blanc, Viognier.

Rosé Wines: Rosé.

Red Wines: Cabernet Franc, Merlot, Painted Red, Petit Verdot.

Price Range: $19–$32

Tastings: $10 per person for a flight.

Groups: Reservations required for groups of 8 to 24.

Restrictions: No dogs; no groups over 24.

Central Virginia Region & Monticello AVA

Purchasing: Online to AZ, CA, CO, DC, FL, GA, ID, IL, IN, IA, KS, ME, MD, MI, MN, MO, NE, NV, NH, NM, NJ, NY, NC, ND, OH, OR, SC, TN, TX, VA, VT, WA, WI, WV, and WY.

Directions: From I-64 East, take Exit 121A (Scottsville) onto Route 20 South. Drive ½ mile and turn left onto Thomas Jefferson Parkway (Route 53). After 3.2 miles, make a slight right onto the James Monroe Parkway which will become Carters Mountain Road. Drive 4.8 miles and turn left onto Blenheim Road. The winery entrance will be ½ mile on the right.

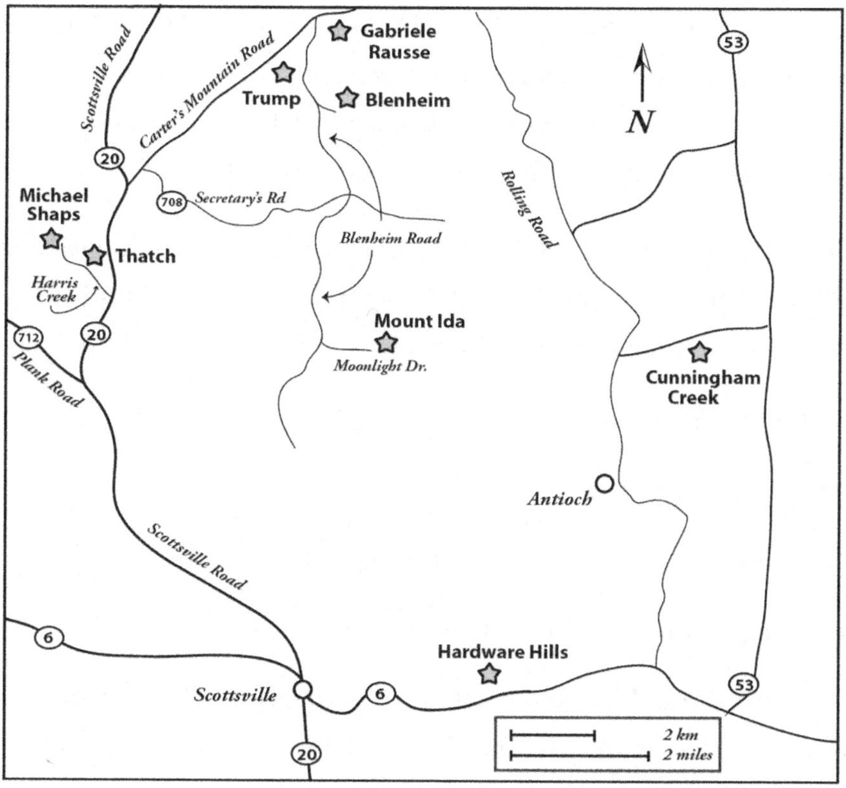

Map 7.8. Scottsville

Blue Toad Hard Cider
462 Winery Lane
Roseland VA 22967

Hours: Su–M, Th 11:00–6:00, F 11:00–7:00, Sa 11:00–8:00 434-760-9200
Closed New Year's, Thanksgiving, www.bluetoadhardcider.com
Christmas E-mail: ciderfarm@bluetoadhardcider.com

Blue Toad was founded in 2015 by Todd Rath, who partnered with his childhood best friends to launch cideries both in Virginia and Rochester, New York. Blue Toad's production facility and tasting room are located at the 28-acre farm that formerly housed Wintergreen Winery. All their hard ciders are produced from apples locally grown in Nelson County. Blue Toad offers food trucks and live music on weekends. Children are welcome. The range of ciders on tap and for sale changes seasonally.

Ciders: Barrel Aged, Black Cherry, Blue Raspberry, Blue Ridge Blonde, BlueToadenBerry, Cranny, Flannel Apple Amber, Granny Smith, Hoppin Toad, Local Mountain Apple, Orange Crush, Peach, ROC Hard Amber.

Price Range: $11–$13

Tastings: $6 per person.

Groups: Reservations requested for groups of 8 or more.

Purchasing: Online to Virginia residents.

Directions: From U.S. Route 250, turn onto Critzers Shop Road (Route 151) for 15 miles. Turn right onto Winery Lane and the cidery entrance ⅓ mile on the right.

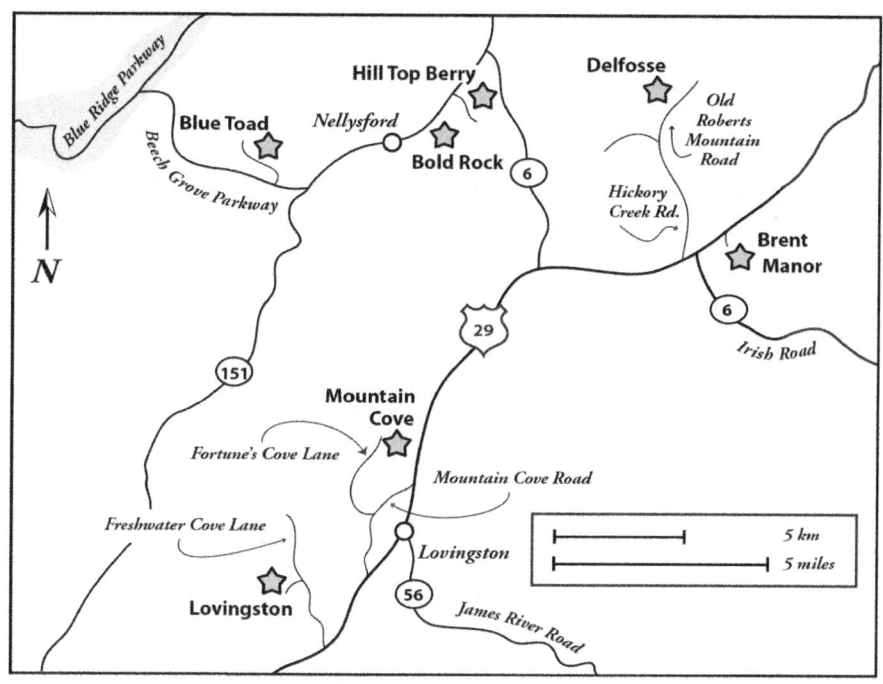

Map 7.9. Lovingston

Bold Rock Cider
1020 Rockfish Valley Highway
Nellysford VA 22958

Hours: M–Th 12:00–9:00, F–Sa 11:00–10:00, Su 11:00–8:00
Closed New Year's, Easter, Thanksgiving, Christmas

434-361-1030
www.boldrock.com
E-mail: info@boldrock.com

John and Robin Washburn opened their cidery upon returning to the U.S. from overseas, with New Zealand native Brian Shanks as cidermaker. The tasting room features the longest beam from a single tree in Virginia, a 50-foot Douglas Fir, as well as a glass-walled bottling room. Bold Rock has a rotating menu of dishes for visitors to enjoy either in the spacious indoor fireplace room or outside on the decks and patios, which offer lovely views of the Rockfish Valley. The upstairs features a cider history display from an observation deck looking down onto the bottling floor. Bold Rock sponsors Cider Cinema movie nights, weather permitting. Children and leashed dogs are welcome.

Ciders: Crimson Ridge Vat No. 1, Crimson Ridge Vintage Dry, IPA (India Pressed Apple), Pear Cider, Premium Dry, Virginia Apple, Virginia Draft.

Price Range: $9–$10

Directions: From U.S. Route 250, turn onto Critzers Shop Road (Route 151) for 12.5 miles to the cidery parking lot on the left.

Brent Manor Vineyards
100 Brent Manor Lane
Faber VA 22938

Hours: Sa 11:00–6:00, Su 11:00–5:00
Closed New Year's Eve & Day,
Christmas Eve & Day

434-826-0722
www.brentmanorvineyards.com
E-mail: wine@brentmanorvineyards.com

Jorge and Tracie Raposo opened Brent Manor in 2016 on a site they had originally planned as a bed-and-breakfast. Tastings are often led by the owners and include both Brent Manor's own wines as well as a varying selection of wines from Jorge's native Portugal. Seating is offered outside on a patio and grounds overlooking the vineyards. Live music and food trucks are routinely scheduled. Children and leashed dogs are welcome, though "Date Night" events are adults-only.

White Wines: Petit Manseng, Seyval Blanc, Vidal Blanc, Vinho Branco.

Rosé Wines: Rosé.

Red Wines: Cabernet Sauvignon, Chambourcin, Patio Red, Touriga Nacional, Vinho Tinto.

Fortified Wines: Vinho Abafado.

Price Range: $19–$39

Tastings: $12 per person.

Purchasing: Online to AK, AZ, CO, DC, FL, GA, HI, IA, ID, IL, IN, KS, LA, MA, MD, ME, MN, MO, ND, NE, NH, NM, NV, OH, OK, OR, PA, SC, TN, TX, VA, VT, WA, WI, WV, and WY.

Directions: From Charlottesville, take U.S. Route 29 South for 18 miles. At Irish Road (Route 6), make a U-turn. Drive north 0.7 miles to the winery entrance on the right.

Cunningham Creek Winery & Farm Store
3304 Ruritan Lake Road
Palmyra VA 22963

Hours: Th–F 1:00–8:00, Sa 1:00–9:00, Su 1:00–6:00 (summer)
Th–Su 1:00–6:00 (winter)
Closed New Year's, Thanksgiving, Christmas

434-207-3907
www.cunninghamcreek.wine
E-mail: info@middleforkfarm.net

Bruce and Debby Deal partnered with Rick and Sara Hernandez to open Cunningham Creek in 2016, five years after buying the property. They produce all Virginia-grown wines, including from their own 11-acre vineyard as well as others nearby. The winery features free Wi-Fi, live music on weekends, food trucks, and locally-made products, including cheeses and crackers; wine-pairing dinners and a harvest festival are also offered. Seating is available both indoors and outside. The facilities may be rented for weddings and special events. Children and leashed dogs are welcome.

White Wines: Chardonnay, Cycle 76, Middle Fork White, Viognier.

Rosé Wines: Rosé.

Red Wines: First Crush, Herd Dog Red, Petit Verdot, Meritage, Merlot, Rivanna Red.

Sweet/Dessert Wines: Petit Manseng.

Fortified Wines: Sweet Home, Tall & Strong.

Price Range: $17–$30

Tastings: $8 per person.

Groups: Reservation required for groups of 8 or more, $10 per person.

Directions: From I-64 East, take Exit 121A (Scottsville) onto Route 20 South. Drive ½ mile and turn left onto Thomas Jefferson Parkway (Route 53). After 15 miles, turn right at the village of Cunningham onto Ruritan Lake Road (Route 619). Continue 2 miles to the winery entrance.

Delfosse Vineyards & Winery
500 Delfosse Winery Lane
Faber VA 22938

Hours: W–Su 11:00–5:00
Closed New Year's, Thanksgiving, Christmas

434-263-6100
www.delfossewine.wine
E-mail: info@delfossewine.wine

Founded in 2002, Delfosse Vineyards was purchased in 2016 by Mike and Adrienne Albers who had long dreamed of owning a winery. Visitors can sit in the glass-walled tasting room or out on the grounds to sample Delfosse's estate-grown wines, either with food purchased at the winery or that they have brought from home. The winery has Crepe Sundays (by reservation) with sweet and savory French-style crepes. The grounds feature five miles of trails that guests can hike on the 318-acre property, which also includes a lake and waterfall. The facilities can be rented for private events. Leashed dogs are welcome.

Delfosse offers overnight stays at its restored Chestnut Log Cabin which dates from 1870; see the website for rental details.

Sparkling Wines: Joie de Vivre.

White Wines: Chardonnay, Deer Rock White, Grand Cru Reserve, Sauvignon Blanc.

Rosé Wines: Rosé.

Red Wines: 1870, Cabernet Sauvignon, Deer Rock Red, Grinning Fox Red, Hippie Chick Red, Malbec, Merlot, Petit Verdot, Screaming Hawk.

Fortified Wines: Meditation.

Price Range: $18–$40

Tastings: $15 per person.

Groups: Reservations required for groups of 8 or more.

Purchasing: Online for many states; contact the winery for details.

Directions: From I-64, take Exit 118A (Lynchburg) onto U.S. Route 29 South. Drive 18 miles and turn right onto Hickory Creek Road (Route 616). Continue 2.6 miles and bear right onto Old Roberts Mountain Road (Route 634). The winery will be about 1 mile further on the left.

Eastwood Farm & Winery
2531 Scottsville Road
Charlottesville VA   22902

Hours: W–F 4:00–8:00, Sa 12:00–8:00, Su 12:00–5:00
Closed New Year's, Easter, Christmas

434-264-6727
www.eastwoodfarmandwinery.com
E-mail: info@eastwoodfarmandwinery.com

Set on 77 acres on the scenic Carters Mountain range, Eastwood Farm and Winery opened in mid-2020. The family-run winery has a wide range of seating options, including picnic tables and adirondack chairs out on the terraced slopes, and indoor and covered seating at its tasting barn and veranda. Eastwood Farm sponsors live music and food trucks on many weekends, as well as yoga classes on some Wednesday afternoons and occasional brunches. The winery also has a marked hiking trail to explore and frequently has displays by local artists. The facilities can be rented for weddings and private events. Leashed dogs are welcome.

White Wines: Chardonnay, Viognier, White Blend.

Rosé Wines: Raspberry Rosé *(with 10% raspberries)*.

Red Wines: Cabernet Franc, Meritage, Merlot.

Price Range: $22–$35

Tastings: $10 per person.

Purchasing: Online for AK, FL, DC, GA, and VA.

Directions: From I-64, take Exit 121 (Scottsville) onto Route 20 South and drive 4 miles. Turn left into the winery entrance on the left.

Gabriele Rausse Winery
3247 Carter's Mountain Road
Charlottesville VA 22902

Hours: Th–F 11:00–5:00, Su 10–4:00
Closed New Year's, Easter, Thanksgiving, Christmas

434-981-1677
www.gabrieleraussewinery.com
E-mail: grwinery@gmail.com

Iconic winemaker Gabriele Rausse has been a fixture in the Virginia wine industry since first arriving from Italy to help start Barboursville Vineyards in the 1970s. He played a leading role in establishing a number of vineyards in central Virginia before founding his own winery in 1997, ultimately opening a tasting room to the public in 2015. Rausse and son Tim make all Virginia-grown wines using their own vines as well as fruit from established vineyards around the state. Most seating is outside, with limited spaces indoors. Leashed dogs are welcome.

Sparkling Wines: Capriccioso Sparkling Rosé.

White Wines: Chardonnay, Grüner Veltliner, Malvasia Bianca, Roussanne, Vin Gris de Pinot Noir.

Rosé Wines: Rosé de Tannat.

Red Wines: Cabernet Franc, Cabernet Sauvignon, Merlot, Nebbiolo, Rosso.

Price Range: $18–$35

Tastings: $12 per person.

Groups: Reservations required for groups of 8 or more.

ADA accessible.

Restrictions: No tour buses.

Directions: From I-64 East, take Exit 121A (Scottsville) onto Route 20 South. Drive ½ mile and turn left onto Thomas Jefferson Parkway (Route 53). After 3.2 miles, make a slight right onto the James Monroe Parkway which will become Carters Mountain Road. Drive 1.1 miles and turn left into the winery's gravel drive.

Hardware Hills Vineyard
5199 West River Road
Scottsville VA 24590

Hours: F 3:00–8:00, Sa 12:00–5:00, Su 1:00–5:00 (Mar–Dec)   434-286-4710
Closed Jan–Feb, Good Friday, Easter,   www.hardwarehills.com
Thanksgiving, Christmas   E-mail: admin@hardwarehills.com

Founded by George and Leslie Cushnie in 2008, Thistle Gate is now owned by Andrea and Rob Nickels who renamed it to commemorate the hills on which it is located and the hard work they are putting into the winery. Hardware Hills produces all-Virginia-grown wines, many with names with a local inspiration, including from Scottsville's riverine past. Guests may linger at one of the tables in the tasting room or on the wraparound deck with a lovely view of the vineyards. Live music is offered on most weekends. Children and leashed dogs are welcome.

Sparkling Wines: Sparkling Vidal Blanc.

White Wines: Chardonnay, Scott's Landing, Seyval Blanc, Thistle White.

Rosé Wines: Thistle Blush.

Red Wines: Batteau Red, Merlot, Petit Verdot, Psalterium Red, St. George Chambourcin, Thistle Red.

Fortified Wines: Highland Red *(port-style)*, Tartan Red *(port-style)*.

Price Range: $18–$33

Tastings: $5–$7 per person.

Groups: Reservations requested for groups of 10 or more.

Directions: From Charlottesville, take Route 20 south for 19 miles. At Scottsville, turn left onto Main Street (VA 6) and drive ½ mile. Turn left onto West River Road. Drive 5 miles to the winery entrance on the left.

Hill Top Berry Farm & Winery
2800 Berry Hill Road
Nellysford VA 22958

Hours: Daily 11:00–5:00 (summer), W–Su 11:00–5:00 (winter)　　434-361-1266
Closed New Year's, Easter, Thanksgiving,　　www.hilltopberrywine.com
Christmas Eve & Day　　E-mail: hilltop1@ntelos.net

Hill Top Berry has its roots in a pick-your-own blackberry farm begun by Marlyn and Sue Allen. Over the years, their interest in winemaking grew, with a special focus on "true to the fruit" wines and meads. The winery is now owned and operated by the couple's daughters, Kimberly Allen Pugh, Crystal Allen Brennan, and Marlo Gayle Allen. Hill Top's tasting room offerings vary because of its seasonal production. The winery offers a covered deck with a view of the farm and Rockfish Valley. Special events include a May Day celebration, a blackberry harvest festival, a fall foliage open house, and a holiday open house. Children and dogs are welcome.

Fruit Wines: Blackberry Delight, Blue Heeler *(blueberry)*, Cranberry, Little Heeler *(blueberry)*, Madison Peach Sangria, Mountain Apple, Pear, Plum Crazy, Sweet

Handy Guide to Virginia Wineries

Cherry, Sweet Melon, Sweet Vixen *(strawberry)*, Three Sisters Elderberry, Virginia Blackberry, Virginia Peach, Virginia Raspberry.

Meads: Dragon's Blood *(pomegranate, honey)*, Dragon's Breath *(smoked hot pepper)*, Eden, Forager *(pawpaw)*, Gladius *(pyment)*, Herald, Hunter's Moon Melomel *(pumpkin)*, Jolly Dragon *(blackberry, hot pepper)*, Lavender Metheglin, Matador *(blood orange)*, Nectarine Melomel, Oracle *(rose petal)*, Perry *(pear)*, Pounding Branch Persimmon, Tiger's Eye *(hibiscus)*, Voyage *(honey mead)*.

Red Wines: Raven's Roost Red.

Price Range: $17–$25

Tastings: $5 per person.

Groups: Please call ahead for groups of 6 or more.

Purchasing: Online to AK, AL, AZ, CA, CO, DC, FL, GA, HI, IA, ID, IL, IN, KS, LA, MA, MD, ME, MN, MO, NC, ND, NE, NH, NM, NV, NY, OH, OR, PA, SC, TN, TX, VA, WA, WI, WV, and WY.

Directions: From U.S. Route 250 East; turn right onto Critzers Shop Road (Route 151). Drive 10 miles and turn left onto Virginia Lane (Route 612). After 0.4 miles, turn right onto Berry Hill Road. Continue ⅓ mile across the bridge and up the hill to the winery on left.

Jefferson Vineyards
1353 Thomas Jefferson Parkway
Charlottesville VA 22902

Hours: W–Su 11:00–6:00   434-977-3042
Closed New Year's, Easter, Thanksgiving, Christmas   www.jeffersonvineyards.com
E-mail: info@jeffersonvineyards.com

Jefferson Vineyards is located midway between Thomas Jefferson's Monticello and James Monroe's Ash Lawn on the site of the vineyard originally planted by Filippo Mazzei for Jefferson. In 1981 owner Stanley Woodward began resurrecting the vineyard, which now includes 20 acres of vines, with Christopher Ritzcowan serving as winemaker. While seating indoors in very limited, outdoor seating is available on the grounds, with tables overlooking the vines and the English-style gardens. Guests are welcome to try the cheeses and crackers for sale at the winery or can bring their own. Jefferson Vineyards occasionally hosts formal winemaker dinners, including an annual Fête de la Bastille (14 July). Children and well-behaved leashed dogs are welcome.

Jefferson Vineyards has a 6-bedroom guest cottage, Colle, that can be rented; see the winery website for details.

White Wines: Chardonnay, Riesling, Vin Blanc, Viognier.

Rosé Wines: Rosé, Skin-Fermented Pinot Gris.

Red Wines: Cabernet Franc, Estate Reserve, Meritage, Merlot, Petit Verdot, Vin Rouge.

Price Range: $19–$52

Tastings: $12 per person for a flight.

Groups: No groups over 8;

ADA accessible.

Restrictions: No tour buses or vans; no groups over 8.

Purchasing: Online to CA, CO, DC, FL, IL, MD, NC, NY, OH, PA, TX, VA, and WA.

Directions: From I-64, take Exit 121A and turn onto Route 20 South. After ½ mile, turn left at the traffic light onto Thomas Jefferson Parkway (Route 53) and drive 3.3 miles to the winery entrance on the right.

Loving Cup Vineyard & Winery
3340 Sutherland Road
North Garden VA 22959

Hours: Sa–Su 11:00–5:00 (Apr–Dec)   434-984-0774
Closed Jan–Mar, Easter, Thanksgiving, Christmas   www.lovingcupwine.com
E-mail: info@lovingcupwine.com

Loving Cup was founded by Karl Hambsch on his family's 150-acre farm as an all-organic operation, using French-American hybrids that are more resistant to bugs and blight. Karl's interest in winemaking was sparked by making crabapple wine with his father; he later honed his skills at Prince Michel Vineyards. Visitors are welcome to relax on the wrap-around deck or grounds to enjoy the view of the vines and hills. Part of the proceeds from their Dudley Nose Rosé go to support the Almost Home Pet Adoption Center in Nelson County, a no-kill shelter committed to finding forever homes for abandoned pets. Children and leashed dogs are welcome.

Fruit Wines: Loving Cup Aronia.

Sparkling Wines: Sparkling White.

White Wines: Cayuga White, Loving Cup White, Rye Reserve White, Tellurian White.

Rosé Wines: Dudley Nose Rosé.

Red Wines: Loving Cup Red *(Marquette, Corot Noir)*, Rye Reserve Red, Tellurian Red.

Price Range: $8–$36

Tastings: $6 per person for a flight on the porch.

Groups: Advance notice appreciated for groups of 5 or more.

Purchasing: Online shipping available to AL, AZ, CO, DC, FL, GA, HI, IA, ID, IL, IN, KS, LA, MA, MD, ME, MI, MO, NC, ND, NE, NH, NM, NV, NY, OH, OK, OR, PA, SC, TN, TX, VA, VT, WA, WI, WV, and WY.

Directions: From I-64, take Exit 118 and turn onto U.S. Route 29 South. Drive 9.2 miles and turn right onto Sutherland Road, just after passing Plank Road. Continue 2.1 miles to the winery entrance on the right.

Lovingston Winery
885 Freshwater Cove Lane
Lovingston VA 22949

Hours: Sa–Su 11:00–5:00 (Apr–Nov)
Sa only 11:00–5:00 (Jan–Mar)
Closed New Year's, Christmas

434-263-8467
www.lovingstonwinery.com
E-mail: info@lovingstonwinery.com

Lovingston Winery, located just outside the old village of Lovingston, was opened to the public in 2010 by Ed and Janet Puckett. The couple had cultivated a vineyard in Georgia for several years before moving to Virginia when their daughter enrolled at the University of Virginia. Their tasting room is housed in the winery's production facility, allowing visitors a good view of the winemaking process in action from the second-floor level. Winemaker Riaan Rossouw currently oversees Lovingston's 8.5 acres of vines, which include Pinotage grapes from his native South Africa.

White Wines: Chardonnay, Petit Manseng, Seyval Blanc.

Red Wines: Cabernet Franc, Estate Reserve, Merlot, Pinotage, Rotunda Red *(Bordeaux-style blend).*

Price Range: $16–$30

Tastings: $10 per person for a flight.

Restrictions: No pets.

Purchasing: Online to AK, CA, DC, FL, MA, MN, NY, NC, OH, PA, TX, and VA.

Directions: From I-64, take Exit 118 onto U.S. Route 29 South. Drive 32.6 miles and turn right onto Freshwater Cove Lane (Route 653). The winery entrance will be on the left in 1 mile.

Michael Shaps Wineworks
1781 Harris Creek Way
Charlottesville VA 22902

Hours: Daily 11:00–5:00 434-296-3438
Closed New Year's, Thanksgiving, Christmas www.michaelshapswines.com
E-mail: tastingroom@virginiawineworks.com

Michael Shaps Wineworks was established by Virginia vintner Michael Shaps after he had spent several years working at both Jefferson Vineyards and King Family Vineyards as well as wineries in France where he has vineyards of his own. Located in the former Montdomaine winery, Shaps produces his wine under two labels, Wineworks and Michael Shaps, with all wines sourced only from Virginia vineyards. The winery also provides custom crush production for over 30 other Virginia wineries.

The winery also has a satellite tasting room in Charlottesville at 1585 Avon Street Extended (daily 1:00–7:00, 434-529-6848).

Sparkling Wines: Blanc de Franc, Méthode.

White Wines: Chardonnay, Odette, Petit Manseng, Viognier.

Rosé Wines: Rosie Rosé.

Red Wines: Cabernet Franc, Meritage, Petit Verdot, Tannat.

Sweet/Dessert Wines: Raisin d'Être Red, Raisin d'Être White.

Price Range: $25–$58

Tastings: $10–$15 per person for a flight.

Groups: Please call ahead for groups of 6 or more.

Purchasing: Online to AK, AZ, CA, CO, DC, FL, GA, HI, IA, ID, IL, IN, KS, LA, MA, MD, ME, MN, MO, NC, ND, NE, NH, NM, NV, NY, OH, OK, OR, PA, SC, TN, TX, VA, VT, WA, WI, WV, and WY.

Directions: From I-64, take Exit 121A and merge onto Route 20 South. Drive 10.4 miles and turn right onto Harris Creek Road (portions unpaved). Continue 1 mile to the winery at the end of the road.

Mountain Cove Vineyards
1362 Fortune's Cove Lane
Lovingston VA 22949

Hours: W–Su 12:00–6:00 (Apr–Oct)
W–Su 12:00–5:00 (Mar, Nov–Dec)
Closed Jan–Feb, Thanksgiving, Christmas

434-263-5392
www.mountaincovevineyards.com
E-mail: aweed1@juno.com

Founded in 1973 by Al and Suiling Weed, Mountain Cove Vineyards is the oldest winery still operating in Virginia. It is located in a scenic valley next to Fortune's Cove, a Nature Conservancy property with numerous hiking trails. As a small family-operated winery, one of the owners is likely to be on hand to greet visitors. Mountain Cove's wines are all vegan and, with the exception of its Chardonnay, all estate grown. While no indoor seating is available, the winery grounds include a pavilion for guests. The facilities may be rented for private events and weddings. Discounts offered for active or retired military personnel (with I.D.). RV parking is available.

Fruit Wines: Apple, Blackberry, Peach.

White Wines: Chardonnay, Skyline White *(Villard Blanc, Vidal Blanc)*.

Rosé Wines: Skyline Rosé.

Red Wines: Cabernet Franc, Chambourcin, Tinto.

Price Range: $12–$15

Tastings: $5

ADA accessible.

Directions: From I-64, take Exit 118 onto U.S. Route 29 South and drive 28 miles. Turn right onto Mountain Cove Road (Route 718) and drive 1.6 miles. Turn right onto Fortune's Cove Lane. The winery will be 1.4 miles on the right.

Central Virginia Region & Monticello AVA

Mount Ida Tasting Room & Taphouse
5800 Moonlight Drive
Charlottesville VA 24590

Hours: M–Th 12:00–6:00, F–Su 12:00–7:00
Closed New Year's, Thanksgiving, Christmas

434-286-4282
www.mountidareserve.com
E-mail: info@mountidareserve.com

Mount Ida Tasting Room & Taphouse is on a 7,000-acre sanctuary south of Charlottesville that has been owned by Gardner Larned and his family since 1999. Mount Ida's tasting room is housed a sprawling cedar and stone facility offering expansive views of the Blue Ridge to the west from its patios and observation deck. Guests can buy light snacks on weekdays, supplemented by pizzas, soups, and small plates on weekends, as well as wines by the glass and bottle. The facilities may be rented for weddings and private events. Mount Ida also has a brewery on-site, with several craft beers on tap. Children and leashed dogs are welcome (lawn area only).

Sparkling Wines: Over the Moon, Stargazer.

White Wines: Bell Mount Chardonnay, Moonlight White, Mount Pleasant Viognier, Petit Manseng.

Rosé Wines: Bell Mount Rosé.

Red Wines: Cabernet Franc, Cabernet Sauvignon, High Ridge 1810 Reserve Red, Moonlight Red, Petit Verdot.

Fortified Wines: Tannat 1795.

Price Range: $26–$38

Tastings: $12 per person.

Groups: Reservations suggested for groups of 6 or more.

Purchasing: Online to many states; contact the winery for details.

Directions: From I-64, take Exit 121A (Scottsville) and merge onto Route 20 South. Drive 8.6 miles and turn left onto Carters Mountain Road, then make an immediate right onto Secretarys Road. Continue 3.7 miles and turn right onto Blenheim Road. The entrance at Moonlight Drive will be on the left after 2.4 miles.

Pippin Hill Farm & Vineyards
5022 Plank Road
North Garden VA 22959

Hours: Tu–Th 11:00–5:00, F–Su 11:00–4:30
Closed Thanksgiving, Christmas Eve & Day, 1–15 Jan

434-202-8063
www.pippinhillfarm.com
E-mail: info@pippinhillfarm.com

Lynn and Dean Andrews opened Pippin Hill Farm to the public in 2011 with a focus on sustainable agriculture and eco-friendly practices. Seating is available both indoors and out, with a seasonal bistro menu available for purchase in the tasting room. Pippin Hill sources its wines from its own vineyards as well as from others in Albemarle County and elsewhere in Virginia; winemaking is under the guidance of Michael Shaps. The winery is available for rental for private parties and weddings. Children and pets are welcome. Reservations recommended for indoor and veranda seating.

Sparkling Wines: Blanc de Blanc, Sparkling Rosé.

White Wines: Chardonnay, Viognier, Zero White.

Rosé Wines: Rosé.

Red Wines: Cannon Red, Easton Blue, Petit Verdot, Red Pump, Wild Common.

Fortified Wines: Bin 21 *(port-style)*.

Price Range: $25–$38

Tastings: $20 per person for a seated flight (reservations needed); grab-and-go flights on the lawn.

Groups: Reservations required for groups of 8 to 16.

Purchasing: Online for CA, DC, FL, NC, and VA.

Directions: From I-64, take Exit 118 and turn onto U.S. Route 29 South. Drive 9 miles and turn right onto Plank Road. The winery entrance will be on the right in ¼ mile.

Potter's Craft Cider
1350 Arrowhead Valley Road
Charlottesville VA 22903

Hours: Th 3:00–9:00, F–Sa 12:00–9:00, Su 11:00–6:00
Closed New Year's, Thanksgiving, Christmas

434-244-2767
www.potterscraftcider.com
E-mail: info@potterscraftcider.com

Environmental engineer Daniel Potter got his start as a home brewer before moving on to craft ciders with friend Tim Edmond in 2011. Their tasting facility is housed in Neve Hall, a 100-year-old stone structure built as a manse and community center for the Archdeaconry of the Blue Ridge, and features a fireplace and seating on both levels as well as outdoors on the stone patio. Potter's Craft sponsors occasional charity benefits, such as for children's music education. The cidery hosts live music (reservations recommended) as well as food trucks on weekends, with bar snacks and small plates also on offer. The facilities may be rented for private parties and weddings. Well-behaved leashed dogs are welcome.

Ciders: Cider Nouveau, Dabinett, Deep See, Farmhouse Dry, Farmhouse Saison, Grapefruit Hibiscus Session, Harrison, Hewes Cuvée, Mangose's Revenge, Passionfruit Mosaic, Pelure, Pippin Cuvée, Strawberry Ginger, The Haven.

Price Range: $8–$22

Tastings: $10 per person.

Groups: Reservations recommended for groups of 12 or more.

Purchasing: Online for AK, AZ, CA, CO, DC, FL, GA, HI, IA, ID, IL, IN, KS, LA, MA, MD, ME, MN, MO, NC, ND, NE, NH, NM, NV, NY, OH, OK, OR, PA, SC, TN, TX, VA, VT, WA WI, WV, and WY.

Directions: From I-64, take Exit 118A and turn onto U.S. Route 29 South. After about 3 miles, make a left onto Arrowhead Valley Road. The cidery will be on the right.

Thatch Winery
1650 Harris Creek Road
Charlottesville VA 22902

Hours: Th–Su 11:00–5:00
Closed New Year's, Thanksgiving, Christmas

434-979-7105
www.thatchwinery.com
E-mail: info@thatchwinery.com

Founded in 2000 as First Colony Winery, Thatch Winery is now owned by David Fratkin and Jeff Miller. Renamed for its iconic thatched roof, the winery offers indoor and outdoor seating at its renovated tasting room, which includes fireplaces and three tasting bars; outdoor decks offer shaded seating under the trees that surround the building. Guests may purchase crackers and cheese for a snack on the grounds; groups under ten may also bring their own food from home for a picnic. Thatch also sponsors a range of weekend events and may be rented for private events, parties, and weddings. Children and pets are welcome.

White Wines: Chardonnay, Petit Manseng, Riesling, Thatch House White, Viognier, Zephyr.

Rosé Wines: Rosé.

Red Wines: Cabernet Sauvignon, Lemberger, Meritage, Tannat, Thatch House Red.

Fortified Wines: Thatch *(port-style)*.

Price Range: $19–$52

Tastings: $15–$35 per person for a flight; seated flights by reservation only.

Groups: Reservations required for groups of 10 or more.

Purchasing: Online for AK, CA, CO, DC, FL, IA, IL, IN, MD, MN, MO, NC, NY, OH, PA, TN, VA, and WI.

Directions: From I-64, take Exit 121A and merge onto Route 20 South. Drive 10.4 miles and turn right onto Harris Creek Road (portions unpaved). The winery will be on the right in ¾ mile.

Handy Guide to Virginia Wineries

Trump Winery
3550 Blenheim Road
Charlottesville VA 22902

Hours: W–M 11:00–5:00
Closed Tuesdays, New Year's Eve & Day, Easter,
Thanksgiving, Christmas Eve & Day

434-984-4855
www.trumpwinery.com
E-mail: cstrong@trumpwinery.com

Trump Winery is located on the slopes of Carter's Mountain in the Blue Ridge; purchased by Eric Trump in 2011, the winery was formerly known as Kluge Estate. Gourmet sandwiches, small plates, and salads are available for consumption on site, either indoors (limited seating) or on the covered patio and grounds where visitors can enjoy the sweeping views of vines and hillsides. The facilities are available for rental for special events, weddings, and dinners. The winery has over 200 acres under vine and is known for its sparkling wines made in the classic *méthode champenoise*. Last pours for tastings begin thirty minutes before closing.

Guests may stay at the luxury 45-room Albemarle Estate Hotel, visible across the valley and vineyards from the tasting room patio.

Sparkling Wines: Blanc de Blanc, Blanc de Noir, Rosé.

White Wines: Chardonnay, Sauvignon Blanc, Viognier.

Rosé Wines: Rosé.

Red Wines: Cabernet Sauvignon, Meritage, New World Reserve *(Bordeaux-style blend)*.

Fortified Wines: CRU *(Chardonnay, brandy)*.

Price Range: $19–$54

Tastings: $12–$18 per person.

Restrictions: Groups over 10 are seated on the grounds only.

Purchasing: Online ordering for all states *except* AL, AR, DE, HI, LA, MS, RI, and UT.

Directions: From I-64 East, take Exit 121A (Scottsville) onto Route 20 South and drive ½ mile. Turn left onto Thomas Jefferson Parkway (Route 53). After 3.2 miles, bend right onto James Monroe Parkway and drive 4.8 miles. Turn left onto Blenheim Road and the entrance ¼ mile on the right.

Wisdom Oak Winery
3613 Walnut Branch Lane
North Garden VA 22959

Hours: Th–Su 11:00–5:30 (Mar–Dec)
Closed New Year's, Easter, Thanksgiving, Christmas

www.wisdomoakwinery.com
E-mail: info@wisdomoakwinery.com

Wisdom Oak Winery is owned by Jason and Laura Lavallee on their farm several miles south of Charlottesville. The tasting room includes indoor and outdoor seating that offers a good vantage point of the vineyards and surrounding hills. Guests can choose from a seasonal menu of cheeses, charcuterie, sandwiches, and sides that go with Wisdom Oak's mostly estate-grown wines; food trucks are also hosted on select weekends. The facilities may be rented for private parties and weddings. Private tastings are offered (by reservation) in the barrel room. Leashed dogs are welcome.

Sparkling Wines: Blanc de Blanc.

White Wines: Chardonnay, North Garden White, Vidal Blanc.

Rosé Wines: Rosewood.

Red Wines: Cabernet Franc, Cabernet Sauvignon, Chambourcin, Meritage, North Garden Red.

Price Range: $20–$36

Tastings: $10 per person for a flight.

Groups: Reservations required for groups of 8 or more, $10 per person.

Purchasing: Online to AK, AL, AZ, CA, CO, DC, FL, GA, HI, IA, ID, IL, IN, KS, LA, MA, MD, ME, MN, MO, NC, ND, NE, NH, NM, NV, NY, OH, OR, PA, SC, TN, TX, VA, WA, WI, WV, and WY.

Directions: From I-64, take Exit 120 and turn onto Fifth Street Southwest, which eventually becomes Old Lynchburg Road. Continue on Old Lynchburg Road for about 7.5 miles. Turn right onto Walnut Branch Lane (narrow, portions unpaved) and drive 1.5 miles to the winery entrance.

FRUIT WINES, CIDERS, AND MEADS

While most wine is made from grapes, wine can also be made from many types of fruits, most often from apples, berries, and stone fruits such as pears or peaches. These wines may be made entirely from fruit or may contain a mixture of grape-based wine along with the fruit wine. Because many fruits lack enough natural sugars for fermentation to occur, the winemaker often must add sugar to the juice, and fruit wines can be slightly sweet as a result.

Like apple wine, hard cider is fermented apple juice but is lower in total alcohol strength than grape-based wine. Ciders range from 2% to 8.5% alcohol strength, while apple wines are higher in alcohol. Ciders may be either still or sparkling, depending on the cidermaker's wish. Cidermaking was brought to the United States by colonists from England, where hard cider is a traditional brew. Hard cider is considered to have been the most popular alcoholic beverage available in colonial America into the 19th century and was consumed by people from all levels of society. Presidents John Adams and Thomas Jefferson, for instance, both regularly drank and served hard cider.

Mead is a fermented beverage made from honey and has been produced since ancient times in Europe, the Middle East, Africa, and parts of Asia. Mead is often associated with old Germany and Scandinavia, where it was often drunk from horns. Key scenes in the great Anglo-Saxon epic *Beowulf* are set in the king's mead-hall, a large public room in the palace where warriors met to drink mead in the evenings and regale each other with stories of their deeds. A hopped mead, Tej, is considered the national drink of Ethiopia. It was first mentioned in 4th century A.D. writings by King Ezana and was well established when Portuguese priests arrived in the 16th century and described it as "wine of honey."

Meads made solely from honey may also be called hydromels, the name by which mead is known in France. Meads blended with fruit juice are known as melomels, while metheglin is mead flavored with herbs or spices.

Handy Guide to Virginia Wineries

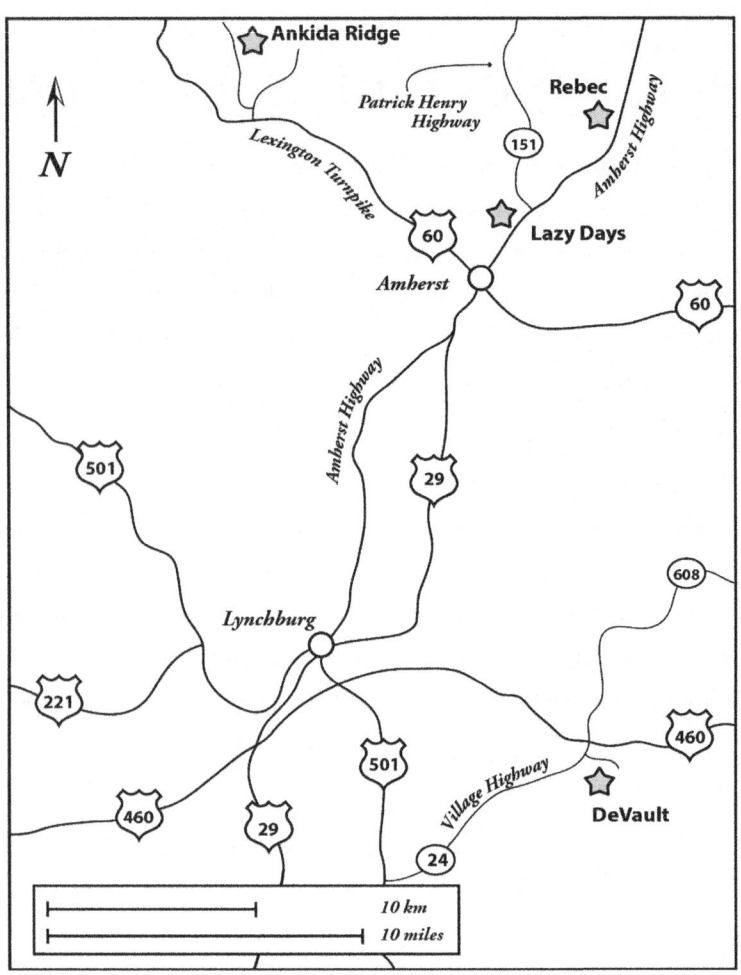

Map 7.10. Lynchburg

LYNCHBURG

Ankida Ridge Vineyards
1304 Franklin Creek Road
Amherst VA 24521

Hours: F–Su 12:00–5:00 (Apr–Oct), 434-922-7678
Sa–Su 12:00–5:00 (Nov–Mar) www.ankidaridge.com
Closed New Year's, Christmas E-mail: contact@ankidaridge.com

Named for a ancient Sumerian word that means "where the heavens and earth meet," Ankida Ridge Vineyards was founded by Dennis and Christine Vrooman on a mountainside property that reaches 1,800 feet in elevation. Son Nathan and daughter-in-law Rachel Stinson Vrooman serve as the winemakers. In addition to the winery's estate-grown Pinot Noir and Chardonnay, Nathan also produces wines under the Rockgarden label using grapes from nearby vineyards. Seating is available on the deck and grounds, with some indoor options. Ankida Ridge sponsors occasional events, including wine tastings and live music, and offers charcuterie and cheese boards for sale. Children are welcome.

Ankida Ridge offers a 5-bedroom house in Charlottesville's historic district for rent as an AirB&B; see the website for details.

Sparkling Wines: Blanc de Blancs Brut.

White Wines: Chardonnay, Rockgarden Vert.

Rosé Wines: Rosé of Pinot Noir.

Red Wines: Pinot Noir, Rockgarden Rouge.

Sweet/Dessert Wines: Patiné.

Fortified Wines: Rockgarden Vin Rouge.

Price Range: $20–$85

Tastings: $10–$12 per person for a flight.

Purchasing: Online to AK, AZ, CA, CO, DC, FL, GA, HI, IA, ID, IL, IN, KS, LA, MA, MD, ME, MN, MO, NC, ND, NE, NH, NM, NV, NY, OH, OK, OR, PA, SC, TN, TX, VA, VT, WA, WI, WV, and WY.

Directions: From Amherst, take U.S. Route 60 West for about 9 miles. Turn right onto Mount Pleasant Road (VA 631). Take the first left onto Franklin Creek Road (Route 632) just after the Liberty gas station and drive 3 miles. Pass the sign indicating the end of state maintenance, then drive through the gate on the right and continue 0.2 miles to the gray winery building on the left.

DeVault Family Vineyards
247 Station Lane
Concord VA 24538

Hours: Th–Sa 12:00–6:00 (Apr–Dec), 434-993-0722
Sa only 11:00–5:00 (Jan–Mar) www.devaultvineyards.com
Closed January, Thanksgiving, Christmas E-mail: devaultvineyards@hotmail.com

Terry and Sharon DeVault established their boutique winery on a 32-acre farm that is midway between Appomattox Court House and Lynchburg, with the wood-panelled tasting room housed in a restored barn. DeVault sponsors an annual holiday open house in December as well as live music and special events throughout the year. Visitors are welcome to bring their own food and picnic on the grounds. In addition to wine tastings, DeVault offers visitors a tennis court, basketball goal, stocked fishing pond, and an indoor pool. The facilities, including the pool, may be rented for parties and weddings. Children and pets are welcome.

Fruit Wines: Old Time Watermelon.

White Wines: Chardonel, Sweet Autumn Mist, Virginia Niagara.

Blush Wines: Lover's Blush.

Red Wines: Darien's Reserve *(Norton)*, Mr. D's Blend, Norton.

Price Range: $15–$24

Tastings: $5 per person.

ADA accessible.

Purchasing: Online to AK, AZ, CO, DC, FL, GA, IA, ID, KS, LA, MA, MD, ME, MN, MO, NC, ND, NE, NH, NM, NV, NY, OH, OR, SC, TN, TX, VA, WA, WI, WV, and WY.

Directions: From Lynchburg, take U.S. Route 460 East for 10 miles and turn right onto Village Highway (Route 24). Take the second left onto Station Lane (Route 741). Drive ⅓ mile and bear right to stay on Station Road. The winery entrance will be 0.2 miles on the right.

Lazy Days Winery
1351 North Amherst Highway
Amherst VA 24521

Hours: Th–Su, 11:00–5:00
Closed New Year's, Thanksgiving, Christmas

434-381-6088
www.lazydayswinery.com
E-mail: events@lazydayswinery.com

Bill and Marianne Fitzhugh established Lazy Days in 2007 when they planted the first vines in their three-acre vineyard; the winery opened to the public in 2010. The tasting room is a renovated livestock pavilion, which offers views of the vineyard from its covered patio. Visitors are welcome to bring a picnic lunch to enjoy on the grounds. Lazy Days sponsors several special events throughout the year, including a summer solstice festival and live music on select weekends. The facilities are available for private events and weddings. Children and pets are welcome.

Fruit Wines: Bill's Wild Blackberry, Sweet Peaches.

White Wines: Capuchin White *(Petit Manseng)*, Chardonnay, Sweet Lazy Days White.

Rosé Wines: Rosé.

Red Wines: Malbec, Petit Verdot, Sweet Lazy Days Red, Vintner's Reserve.

Price Range: $18–$42

Tastings: $12 per person for a flight.

Directions: From the town of Amherst, take U.S. Route 29 North and drive 5 miles in the direction of Charlottesville. Make a U-turn at the intersection with Route 151 North to circle back onto U.S. Route 29 South. The winery entrance will be on the right.

Rebec Vineyards
2229 North Amherst Highway
Amherst VA 24521

Hours: M–Th 11:00–5:00, F–Su 10:00–5:00
Closed New Year's, Thanksgiving, Christmas

434-946-5168
www.rebecwinery.com
E-mail: winery@rebecwinery.com

Richard and Lynn Hanson founded Rebec on their 70-acre farm at the edge of the Blue Ridge and began selling wines to the public in 1988. The winery was designed and built by Richard and son-in-law Mark Magruder, who used wood salvaged from old outbuildings on the property, including a 200-year-old tobacco barn. Rebec is now owned by its long-time winemaker Svetlozar Kanev, who makes a Bulgarian-style herbal sweet wine, Sweet Sofia, in honor of his native country. Visitors can picnic on the grounds or sit on the deck behind the tasting room. On the second weekend in October, Rebec hosts the annual Virginia Wine and Garlic Festival. The winery also sponsors a Summer Cooler festival (proceeds are donated to the American Cancer Society) and Third Thursday live music performances in summer. Children and pets are welcome.

Fruit Wines: Cherry.

White Wines: Chardonnay, Gewurztraminer, Landmark White, Pinot Grigio, Riesling, Viognier.

Rosé Wines: Sweet Briar Rosé.

Red Wines: Cabernet Franc, Cabernet Sauvignon, Landmark Reserve, Merlot, Pinot Noir.

Sweet/Dessert Wines: Autumn Glow, Landmark Sweet, Sweet Sofia.

Price Range: $18–$30

Tastings: $7 per person.

Groups: Please call ahead for groups of 8 or more.

Purchasing: Online to many states; contact the winery for details.

Directions: From I-64, take Exit 118 onto U.S. Route 29 South and drive 40.3 miles to the winery entrance on the right.

From the town of Amherst, drive 5 miles north on U.S. Route 29 to the winery on the left.

Handy Guide to Virginia Wineries

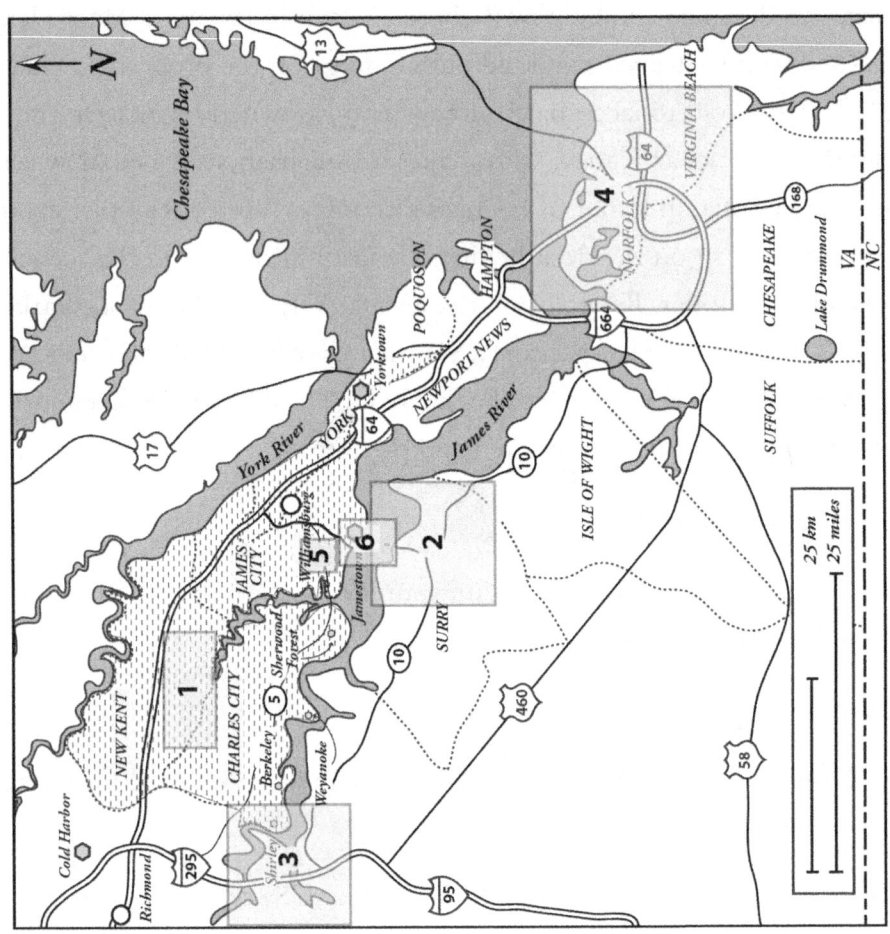

Map 8.0. Hampton Roads Region: (1) New Kent; (2) South of the James; (3) Hopewell-Upper Shirley; (4) Virginia Beach-Hampton Roads; (5) Silver Hand; (6) Williamsburg Winery

8. HAMPTON ROADS REGION

Located in the Tidewater of Virginia, this region is one of gentle, low hills and terrain crisscrossed with small creeks that flow into the James and York Rivers. The climate on the Virginia Peninsula and southeastern Virginia is the warmest in the state. Summers are hot and humid, while temperatures rarely dip below freezing in the winter. Soils in the region range from rich and loamy to downright swampy; indeed, the region is home to the Great Dismal Swamp which straddles the Virginia-North Carolina line. It also is the site of Lake Drummond, one of Virginia's only two natural lakes.

The Hampton Roads Region is home to Virginia's newest Agricultural Viticultural Area, the Virginia Peninsula AVA, which was approved by the federal government in 2021.

<u>Things to see and do</u>: Virginia's Hampton Roads Region is, in many ways, the heart of historic Virginia. It was here that English colonists first settled in 1607 at Jamestown and, after a shaky start, gradually began expanding their presence further into Virginia. This is also where Virginia's four original counties as an English colony were established in 1617: Henrico, James City, Bermuda Hundred, and Kecoughtan (the latter two no longer exist). Williamsburg was the colonial capital of Virginia from 1704 until 1799 and is just northwest of the site of the decisive Revolutionary War battle at Yorktown, where American forces defeated British troops and won America's struggle for independence.

Just across the James River from Williamsburg and Jamestown is Bacon's Castle, built in 1665 by Arthur Allen. The property is best known for its role in Bacon's Rebellion, a 1676 uprising led by Nathaniel Bacon against Royal Governor William Berkeley.

The John Tyler Memorial Highway (Route 5) is a scenic road that winds along the James River from Williamsburg to Richmond. There are a number of historic homes along its path for visitors to explore, including President John Tyler's Sherwood Forest, the Harrison family's Berkeley Plantation, and the Carter family's Shirley Plantation. More details are available at the James River Plantation website (http://www.jamesriverplantations.org).

Civil War history abounds here as well. McClellan's peninsula campaign of 1862 started at Fort Monroe, at the tip of Hampton Roads, and the army moved up the peninsula toward Richmond, where the Seven Days' Battles occurred. In 1864, General Ulysses Grant moved down from Spotsylvania and began his relentless pursuit of General Robert E. Lee. The battlefield at Cold Harbor, where Grant's army launched a headlong assault on Lee's fortified position, offers a vivid and moving glimpse into what soldiers faced on the field of war. Grant then moved his army across the James at Weyanoke, starting the final campaign that ultimately led to Lee's surrender at Appomattox Court House and the defeat of the Confederacy in 1865.

Visitors may also explore the numerous Black history sites in the area. Hampton University's museum is the oldest African-American museum in the United States, featuring art and artifacts from Africa and of Native American origins. The Virginia War Museum, the Casemate Museum at Fort Monroe, and the Virginia Air & Space Center all include exhibits on the role of Black Americans in the history of our country. The Great Dismal Swamp itself, though mostly in North Carolina, was a refuge for enslaved Blacks, who sought freedom and refuge in its wildness in the 18th and 19th centuries.

Nature lovers and biking enthusiasts will enjoy the Virginia Capital Trail, a 52-mile-long paved jogging and biking trail stretching from Richmond to Williamsburg alongside Route 5. The interactive trail map includes a range of key features for walkers and cyclists, including restaurants, bike rental and repair facilities, lodging, convenience stores, and picnic areas; see the website at http://virginiacapitaltrail.org for more details.

The Virginia Beach-Hampton Roads area offers numerous attractions for visitors, particularly those with children; these include the Virginia Aquarium and Marine Science Center, Mariner's Museum, and Nauticus. Those interested in spending time on the beach and boardwalk will find rich opportunities for food and fun at Virginia Beach.

<u>Wine Trails</u>: The wineries in the Hampton Roads Region are included in the Williamsburg Tasting Trail which focuses on wineries, breweries, and a meadery in and around Williamsburg. The Colonial Virginia Wine Trail features five wineries along the James River. See the Appendix for more details.

Handy Guide to Virginia Wineries

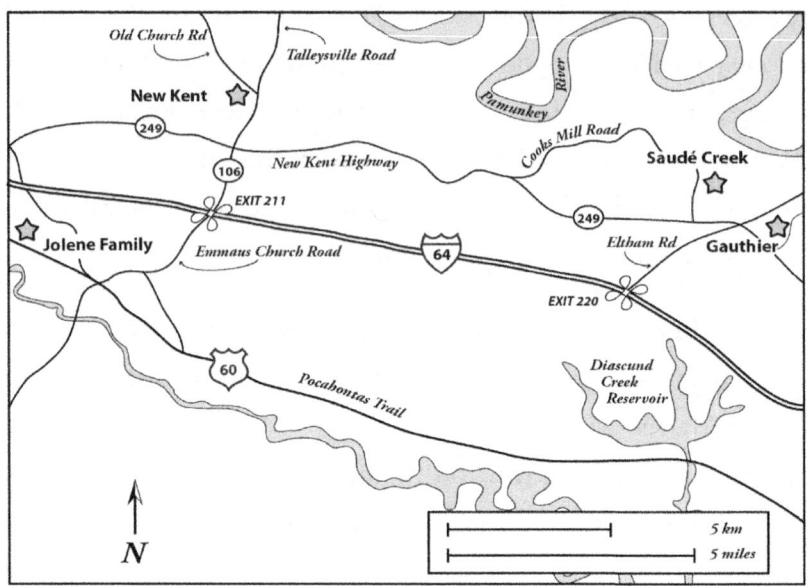

Map 8.1. New Kent

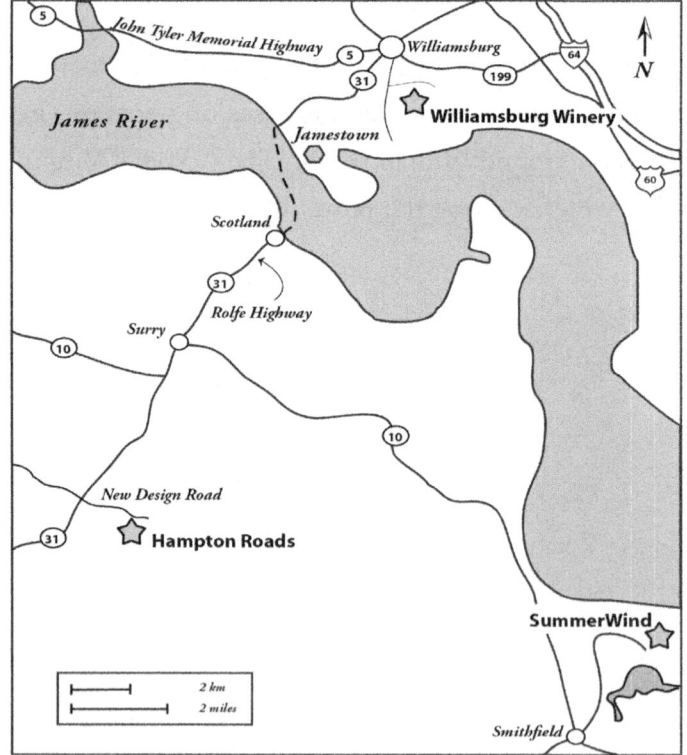

Map 8.2. South of the James

HAMPTON ROADS

Gauthier Vineyard
5000 Farmers Drive
Barhamsville VA 23011

Hours: F 4:00–8:00, Sa–Su 11:00–5:00 (to 6:00 in summer)   757-622-1107
Closed New Year's, Easter, Christmas   www.gauthiervineyard.com
E-mail: sandigauthier@aol.com

Maurice ("Mo") and Sandi Gauthier were inspired to start their own vineyard after visiting Cave Ridge Winery in the Shenandoah Valley. The Gauthiers planted their first vines in 2012 on the 110-acre farm that they purchased after retiring from the Navy. After sampling their Virginia-grown wines, visitors are welcome to linger inside the tasting room or outside on the wraparound veranda overlooking the winery pond. Gauthier Vineyards sponsors occasional live music and food trucks on weekends as well as charitable events to benefit first responders and wounded warriors. There is a 15% discount on purchases for active-duty or retired military. Leashed dogs are welcome.

Gauthier offers overnight stays at its Inn at Woodmont Plantation, adjacent to the winery; see the winery website for details.

Sparkling Wines: Sparkling Traminette.

White Wines: Chardonnay, Gazebo Blanc, Riesling, Traminette, Viognier.

Red Wines: Brick House Red, Cabernet Franc, Chambourcin, Estate Norton, Gazebo Rouge, Petit Verdot.

Sweet/Dessert Wines: Les Trois Mélanies.

Fortified Wines: Lafayette's Reserve, Rochambeau's Starboard, Sweet Beau.

Handy Guide to Virginia Wineries

Price Range: $15–$32

Tastings: $14 per person, with souvenir glass.

Groups: Reservations requested for groups of 8 or more.

Directions: From I-64, take Exit 220 and turn onto Eltham Road (Route 33 East). Drive 3 miles and turn right onto New Kent Highway (VA 249/VA 30). Continue 3.4 miles and turn left onto Farmers Drive (VA 273). The winery entrance will be 0.8 miles on the left.

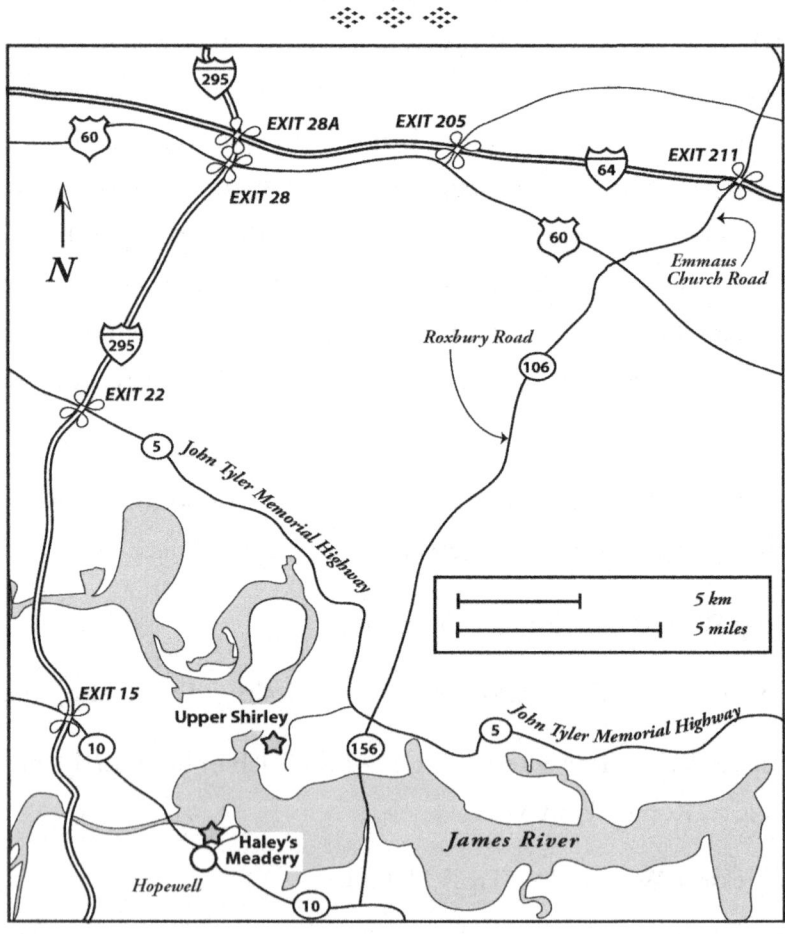

Map 8.3. Hopewell-Upper Shirley

Haley's Honey Meadery
235-237 East Broadway
Hopewell VA 23860

Hours: Th–F 4:00–8:00, Sa 11:00–8:00, Su 1:00–5:00
Closed New Year's, Christmas

804-668-5943
www.haleyshoneymeadery.com
E-mail: contact@haleyshoneymeadery.com

Tonya Haley, a second-generation beekeeper, and her husband Mike opened Haley's Honey after Tonya interned at a local meadery and then bought the business. She makes all her meads from pesticide-free honey from hives in Prince George County as well as from locally-sourced fruits. In addition to meads, Haley's sells bee pollen, honey-roasted peanuts, and a range of Virginia honeys, including raw and ginger or fruit-infused honey. Haley's also has a range of food items for sale, including sandwiches, dips, and snacks. Seating is available both inside the tasting room and outside. The meadery hosts live performances, trivia nights, and pop-up vendors.

Meads: Apple of My Eye, Berry Dust, Blue Line, Cherry Kisses, Cresent Moon, Dragon's Heart Cherry, Dusty Orchard, Five and Dime, Go-Sip, Liquid Silk, Midnight, Root 10, The Patriot, Traveller's Trough.

Price Range: $18

Tastings: $6 per person.

Directions: From I-295, take Exit 15 (Hopewell) onto Route 10 East. Drive 4 miles and turn left onto East Broadway in Hopewell. Make an immediate left onto Library Street. The meadery will be on the right.

Handy Guide to Virginia Wineries

Hampton Roads Winery
6074 New Design Road
Elberon VA 23846

Hours: Th–M 11:30–6:00
Closed New Year's, Easter,
Thanksgiving, Christmas

757-899-0203
www.hamptonroadswinery.com
E-mail: hamptonroadswinery@gmail.com

Hampton Roads is the dream project of David and Diane Shelton who opened their winery on the grounds of a lovely 1898 house just south of the James River. The large tasting room, built in the style of a horse barn, features a gift shop and, just outside, a paved patio and a goat tower for the family goats, inspired by the goat towers they saw during a trip to Portugal. Hampton Roads offers yoga classes in summer and live music on weekends; cheese and charcuterie boards are offered for sale in the tasting room. The facilities are available for rental for private parties and events.

White Wines: Chardonnay, Simply Seyval, White Oak White.

Red Wines: Cabernet Franc, Merlot, Petit Verdot.

Sweet/Dessert Wines: Hog Island Sweet Red, Hog Island Sweet White *(scuppernong)*.

Price Range: $18–$24

Tastings: $12 per person.

Groups: Reservations requested for groups up to 10; no groups over 10.

Purchasing: Online to AK, AZ, CO, DC, FL, GA, HI, IA, ID, IN, KS, LA, MA, MD, ME, MN, MO, NC, ND, NE, NH, NM, NV, NY, OH, OR, PA, SC, TN, TX, VA, WA, WI, WV, and WY.

Directions: From Williamsburg, cross the James River on the Jamestown-Scotland free ferry. After landing, continue straight on Rolfe Highway (VA 31 South) for 10 miles. At the hamlet of Elberon, turn left at the Dendron Fire Department onto New Design Road. The winery's gravel drive will be 0.4 miles on the right.

Jolene Family Winery
2750 Pocahontas Trail
Quinton VA 23141

Hours: Th–M 11:00–6:00 (F to 9:00)
Closed New Year's, Easter, Thanksgiving, Christmas

804-557-5316
www.jolenefamilywinery.com
E-mail: info@jolenefamilywinery.com

Jolene Family Winery was opened by siblings Cindy Mikelaites, Brian Mikelaites, and Sandy Lewis, who named their winery Jolene in honor of their parents, Joseph and Helene. Visitors can stay for a glass or bottle of wine after their tastings, including on the spacious deck and grounds overlooking Tom Brooks Lake. The winery offers light snacks and, on many weekends, has food trucks on-site. Jolene Family hosts a number of special events, such as yoga classes and live music. The winery may be rented for private events and weddings. Leashed pets are welcome.

Fruit Wines: Vasara Peach.

White Wines: Family White, Lake View White, Pinot Grigio.

Rosé Wines: Merlot Rosé.

Red Wines: Cabernet Franc, Chambourcin, Family Red, Lake View Red.

Price Range: $19–$29

Handy Guide to Virginia Wineries

Tastings: $6 per person for a flight.

Groups: Reservations required for groups of 10 or more.

Directions: From I-64, take Exit 205 (Bottoms Bridge/Quinton) and turn south onto Route 33. Drive 0.2 mile and turn left onto Pocahontas Trail (U.S. Route 60 East). After 0.6 mile; turn left into the winery drive and continue to the tasting room behind the Brianwood Business Park.

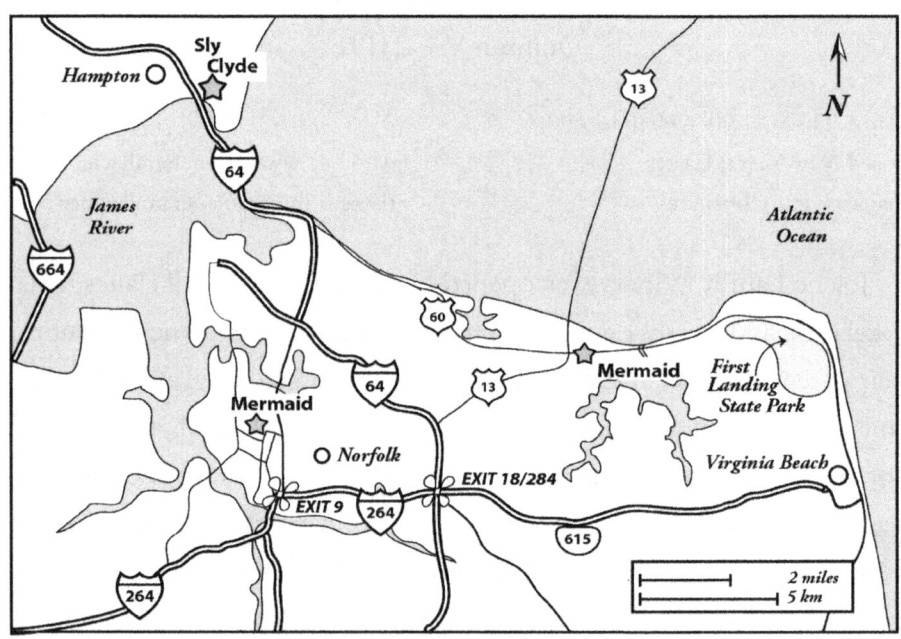

Map 8.4. Virginia Beach-Hampton Roads

Mermaid Winery
330 West 22nd Street, #106
Norfolk VA 23517

Hours: Tu–Th 12:00–9:00, F–Sa 12:00–10:00, Su 12:00–9:00
Closed New Year's, Thanksgiving, Christmas

757-233-4155
www.mermaidwinery.com
E-mail: info@mermaidwinery.com

Mermaid Winery is owned by Jennifer Doumar, who opened her urban winery in 2012 in Norfolk's Ghent neighborhood with a second location in Virginia Beach (4401 Beach Drive). The wines are sourced from vineyards in Virginia as well as other states and wine-growing regions. The winery hosts various events, including wine pairing dinners, and offers several tasting flights of wines in addition to its own production. Mermaid has lunch and dinner menus to enjoy, as well as a list of over 450 different wines from around the world.

Fruit Wines: My Beach Peach *(Viognier)*, Pink Claw *(dragonfruit, Moscato)*, Raspberry *(Zinfandel)*, Strawberry *(Merlot)*.

Sparkling Wines: Seaduction.

White Wines: Chardonnay, Siren's White.

Red Wines: Cabernet Franc, Cabernet Sauvignon, Malbec, Norfolk Express, Pinot Noir, Poseidon Red.

Price Range: $18–$40

Tastings: $5 per person.

Groups: Reservations required for groups of 10 or more.

ADA accessible.

Purchasing: Online for CA, DC, NC, and VA.

Directions: From I-264, take Exit 9 (Waterside Drive/St. Paul's Boulevard) onto St. Paul's Boulevard (U.S. Route 460 Alt East). Drive 1.5 miles and turn left onto East Princess Anne Road. Take the third right onto Llewellyn Avenue. After ½ mile, turn left onto 22nd Avenue. The winery is ¾ mile on the right at the Palace Station Shops.

New Kent Winery
8400 Old Church Road
New Kent VA 23124

Hours: Daily 11:00–5:00 (to 6:00 in summer)
Closed New Year's, Thanksgiving, Christmas

1-804-932-8240
www.newkentwinery.com
E-mail: info@newkentwinery.com

New Kent Winery opened in 2008 in the Viniterra community just east of Richmond, where winemaker Tom Payette oversees the production of New Kent's mostly estate-grown wines for the Dombroski family. After tasting, visitors can choose from New Kent's bistro menu, which features cheese and charcuterie boards, crab cakes, and dips, and then linger in the two-story tasting room or on one of the shaded patios with views of the vineyards. The winery sponsors a range of special events and may be rented for private parties and weddings. New Kent now has an on-site brewery, the Talleysville Brewing Company.

White Wines: Chardonnay, Vidal Blanc.

Rosé Wines: White Merlot, White Norton.

Red Wines: Cabernet Franc, Merlot, Meritage, Norton.

Sweet/Dessert Wines: Sweet Virginia.

Price Range: $20–$42

Tastings: $15 per person.

Groups: Reservations required for groups of 10 or more.

ADA accessible.

Purchasing: Online to AK, CA, CO, DC, FL, GA, HI, ID, IL, IA, KS, LA, MD, ME, MI, MN, MO, MT, NC, ND, NE, NH, NM, NV, NY, OR, SC, TN, TX, VA, VT, WA, WI, WV, and WY.

Directions: From I-64, take Exit 211 (Talleysville/Roxbury) north onto Emmaus Church Road (VA 106 North). At the third roundabout, take the second exit onto Old Church Road. The winery will be ⅓ mile on the left.

Saudé Creek Vineyards
16230 Cooks Mill Road
Lanexa VA 23089

Hours: M, W–Th 12:00–6:00, F 12:00– 8:30, Sa–Su 11:00–6:00 (summer); W–M 11:00–5:00 (winter) Closed New Year's, Thanksgiving, Christmas

804-966-5896
www.saudecreek.com
E-mail: info@saudecreek.com

Jason Knight and John Britt opened Saudé [*SAW-dee*] Creek Vineyards in 2011, building their tasting room on the former site of Frank's Ordinary, a colonial-era inn that counted George Washington and French General Count Rochambeau among its clientele; the winery's name is from a creek that ran behind the Alabama home of Jason's grandmother. The wines are mainly from Virginia-grown fruit, much of it from the owners' 40-acre vineyard in Halifax County. Saudé Creek offers seating indoors in its two-story tasting room as well as outside on the decks and covered porches, which provide a scenic view of the grounds and the Pamunkey River. The facilities are available for private parties and events, with several outdoor areas ideal for weddings. Children and leashed dogs are welcome.

Fruit Wines: Tavern White, Virginia Bluebelle.

White Wines: Chardonnay, Pamunkey Fall, Polaris, Riesling, Sauvignon Blanc, Traminette, Vidal Blanc, Viognier.

Rosé Wines: Pearl.

Handy Guide to Virginia Wineries

Red Wines: 1791, Barrel 76, Petit Verdot, Pinot Noir, Saudé Creek Red, Saudé Creek Red Reserve, Valor.

Sweet/Dessert Wines: Sweet Rebellion.

Price Range: $17–$48

Tastings: $18 per person for a flight.

Groups: Reservations required for groups over 10 (groups on Sa, Su only).

ADA accessible.

Purchasing: Online to VA residents only.

Directions: From I-64 East, take Exit 220 onto Eltham Road (Route 33 East). Drive 2.9 miles; turn left onto New Kent Highway (Route 249). After a mile, turn right onto Cooks Mill Road (Route 623). The winery entrance will be on the right after another mile.

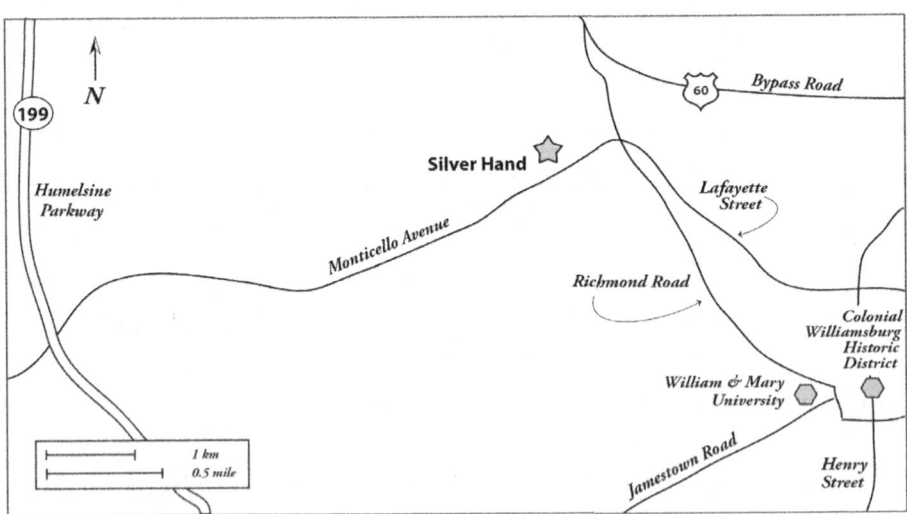

Map 8.5. Silver Hand

Silver Hand Meadery
224 Monticello Avenue, Suite C
Williamsburg VA 23185

Hours: M–W 12:00–6:00, Th–F 11:00–8:00, Sa 10:00–8:00, Su 12:00–5:00
Closed New Year's, Easter, Memorial Day, Independence Day, Labor Day, Thanksgiving, Christmas

757-378-2225
www.silverhandmeadery.com
E-mail: info@silverhandmeadery.com

Glenn and Sherri Lavender decided to start a meadery inspired in part by Glenn's interest in the historical Celtic novels of Stephen Lawhead which frequently mentioned mead. Indeed, the meadery's name comes from Lawhead's novel, *The Silver Hand*. Glenn uses honeys from Virginia and other states as well as a range of herbs and fruits in fermenting his meads, all of which have music-themed names in honor of his career as a musician in a band. Silver Hand also features honey tastings, including many of the honeys used to produce their meads. Please note, no sales by the glass are permitted except on eight Mead-Up weekends per year.

Meads: All Blues *(blueberry blossom honey, blueberries)*, Dream by the Fire *(apple cider, spices)*; Ginger Me Slowly *(ginger, avocado blossom honey)*, Heart of Gold Alfalfa, Margaritaville *(mesquite honey, lime juice, aged in tequila barrels)*, Raspberry Passion *(raspberries, passion fruit)*, Scarborough Fair *(star thistle honey, rosemary, thyme)*, Soak Up the Sun *(orange blossom honey)*, Strawberry Swing *(strawberries)*, Tangerine *(tangerines, orange blossom honey)*, Terres Brûlées *(bochet-style, cooked clover honey)*, Virginia Tonight *(aged in bourbon barrels)*.

Price Range: $20–$26

Tastings: $10 per person.

Groups: Reservations required for groups of 6 or more.

Purchasing: Online to AK, AZ, CA, CO, DC, FL, GA, HI, IA, ID, IL, IN, KS, LA, MA, MD, ME, MI, MN, MO, MT, NC, ND, NE, NH, NM, NV, NY, OH, OK, OR, PA, SC, TN, TX, VA, VT, WA, WI, WV, and WY.

Directions: From Richmond, take I-64 East to Exit 234 (Lightfoot) and turn right onto Route 199 (Humelsine Parkway). Drive for 6 miles and take the exit onto Monticello Road (VA 321 East). Continue 2 miles and turn left into the parking lot.

From Hampton Roads, take I-64 west to Exit 242A (Humelsine Parkway). Drive 1.4 miles and turn right onto U.S. Route 60 West (Pocahontas Trail). Drive 2 miles and continue straight onto Lafayette. Drive another 2 miles and cross Richmond Road. Turn right into the parking lot in 0.2 miles.

Sly Clyde Ciderworks
207 East Mellen Street
Hampton VA 23663

Hours: Tu–Th 4:00–9:00, F 2:00–11:00, Sa 12:00–11:00, Su 11:00–7:00	757-755-3130
	www.slyclyde.com
Closed New Year's, Thanksgiving, Christmas	E-mail: info@uppershirley.com

Sly Clyde was opened in 2018 by brothers Tim and Doug Smith who named their cidery after their beloved (and witty) grandfather, Clyde Smith. The tasting room is located in Hampton's historic Phoebus neighborhood in a renovated Victorian-era house that has been in the Smith family for a century. All ciders are made from Virginia apples, many from Nelson County. Sly Clyde sponsors food trucks on some weekends and has indoor and outdoor seating available for guests. The tasting line-up changes seasonally.

Ciders: Cut & Run *(ginger)*, Dry Titan, Inkjet *(blackberry)*, Jammin' *(hibiscus)*, Lime of the Ancient Mariner, Sandbar *(raspberry, lemon)*, Submersive, Surf Hopper, Swinging Compass.

Price Range: $6–$24, depending on size

Tastings: $10 per person.

Directions: From I-64 in Hampton, take Exit 268 (Fort Monroe/Phoebus) and turn onto South Mallory Street. Drive ⅓ mile to East Mellen Street and turn right. Drive two blocks to the cidery on the left.

SummerWind Vineyard
71 Eagle Nest Lane
Smithfield VA 23430

Hours: F–Sa 12:00–7:00, Su 12:00–6:00
Closed New Year's, Easter, Thanksgiving, Christmas

757-357-2173
www.swvsmithfield.com
E-mail: swvsmithfield@gmail.com

SummerWind was opened to the public in 2018 by Al and Kim Pugh after they had spent over ten years growing grapes for other wineries. The tasting room is located on the south bank of the James River with views of the river from the grounds. The Pughs work with winemaker Michael Shaps *(Michael Shaps Wineworks)* for their all-Virginia wines. SummerWind offers cheese boards, charcuterie, and light snacks for sale as well as seasonal sangrias. Live music and special events, such as yoga in the vines, are also sponsored on select weekends. Leashed dogs are welcome outside.

Sparkling Wines: Warwick Squeak *(rosé)*.

White Wines: Chardonnay, Petit Manseng, Two Rivers White.

Rosé Wines: Rosé of the Isle.

Red Wines: Cabernet Franc, Merlot, Pagan, Petit Verdot, Tormentor's Red.

Price Range: $26–$32

Tastings: $15 per person for a flight.

Directions: From the intersection of U.S. Route 258 and Route 10, head north on Main Street into Smithfield. After 0.6 mile, turn left onto North Church Street (Route 10 Business) and continue 2 miles. Turn right onto Blounts Corner Road (Route 674) and drive ½ mile. Turn right again onto Days Point Road (Route 673) and drive 1.4 miles. Turn right onto Eagle Nest Lane. The winery entrance will be 0.3 miles on the right.

Upper Shirley Vineyards
600 Shirley Plantation Road
Charles City VA 23030

Hours: W–Su 11:00–5:00
Closed New Year's, Easter, Thanksgiving, Christmas

804-829-9463
www.uppershirley.com
E-mail: info@uppershirley.com

Tayloe and Suzy Dameron opened Upper Shirley Vineyards adjacent to the historic Shirley Plantation, high on the north bank of the James River. After sampling Upper Shirley's all Virginia-grown wines, guests can linger on the shaded front porch looking out onto the vines or on the wide back veranda offering sweeping views of the James River and the Presquile National Wildlife Refuge. The winery also includes an onsite restaurant providing seated service (indoors only) for lunch and dinner and featuring locavore dishes. Winemaking is by Michael Shaps (*Michael Shaps Wineworks*). The facilities can be rented for private parties and weddings.

Sparkling Wines: Blanc de Blancs, Sparkling Rosé.

White Wines: #2 White, Chardonnay, Sauvignon Blanc, Viognier.

Rosé Wines: Rosé.

Red Wines: #1 Red, Cabernet Franc, Divertido, Petit Verdot, Tannat, Zachariah *(Bordeaux-style blend)*.

Price Range: $22–$45

Tastings: $15 per person.

Groups: Reservations requested for groups of 5 or more.

ADA accessible.

Restrictions: Bus and limo tours, reservations required.

Purchasing: Online to VA only.

Directions: From I-295 around Richmond, take Exit 22 onto John Tyler Highway (Route 5). Drive east toward Williamsburg for 10 miles and turn right onto Shirley Plantation Road. Drive 1.5 miles and turn left at the sign for Shirley Plantation. Continue to the winery's parking lot on the right.

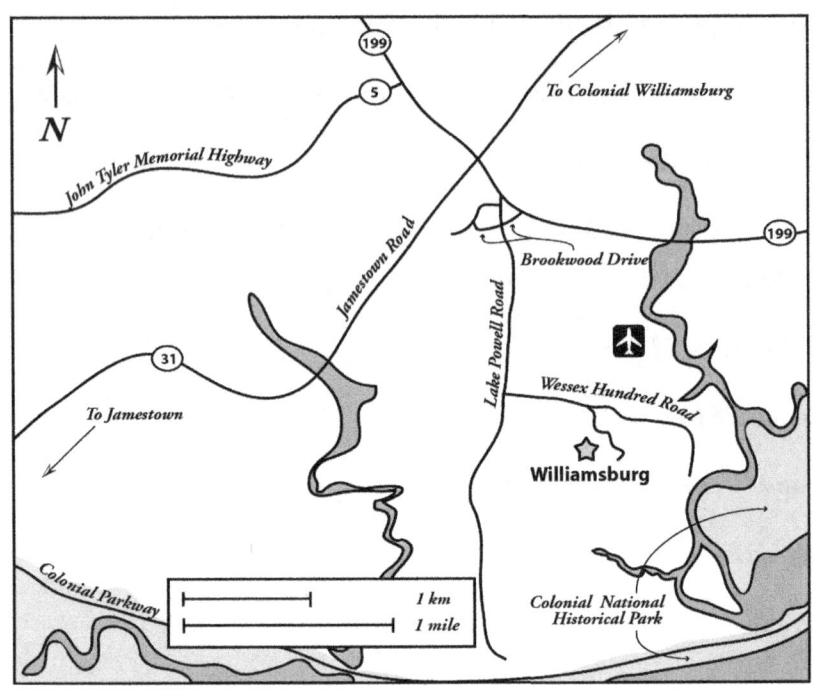

Map 8.6. Williamsburg Winery

The Williamsburg Winery
5800 Wessex Hundred
Williamsburg VA 23185

Hours: Su–Th 12:00–5:00, F 12:00–6:00, Sa 11:00–6:00 (Apr–Oct)   757-229-0999
M–Th 11:00–4:30, F–Su 11:00–5:30 (Nov–Mar)   www.williamsburgwinery.com
Closed New Year's, Thanksgiving, Christmas   E-mail: wine@wmbgwine.com

Located just minutes from Colonial Williamsburg, Williamsburg Winery is one of Virginia's largest. Founded in 1985 by the Belgian Duffeler family, Williamsburg Winery produces over 60,000 cases per year from estate-grown fruit or from other Virginia and non-Virginia vineyards. All winemaking is under the guidance of Matthew Meyer, who trained in California. The winery offers guided tours and has an onsite wine museum, as well as dining options at its Gabriel Archer Tavern and Café Provençal. The winery sponsors live music on summertime Friday nights at its covered two-story outdoor pavilion. All the facilities are available for private parties, dinners, and weddings.

Williamsburg Winery has a satellite tasting room in Williamsburg's Market Square, adjacent to the historic area.

The winery also offers overnight stays at the twenty-eight room Wedmore Place hotel on the winery grounds.

White Wines: Acte 12 Chardonnay, Arneis, Chardonnay, Governor's White, James River White, John Adlum Chardonnay, Midsummer Night's White, Petit Manseng, Sauvignon Blanc, Vidal Blanc, Viognier.

Rosé Wines: Dry Rosé, Plantation Blush.

Red Wines: Adagio, Cabernet Franc, Cabernet Sauvignon, Gabriel Archer Reserve, J. Andrewes Merlot, Mount Juliet Red, Susan Constant Red, Syrah, Trianon, Virginia Claret, Wessex Hundred Merlot, Wessex Hundred Petit Verdot.

Sweet/Dessert Wines: Licoreux de Framboise *(raspberry)*, Petite Fleur.

Seasonal Wines: Settlers' Spiced Wine.

Price Range: $12–$72

Tastings: $8 per person, $15 for reserve tasting.

Groups: Reservations required for groups of 8 or more.

ADA accessible.

Purchasing: Online purchasing for residents of AK, CA, CO, DC, FL, GA, IL, LA, ME, MD, MI, MN, MO, NH, NJ, NY, NC, OH, OR, SC, TX, VT, VA, and WI; some wines available only to VA residents.

Directions: **From I-64 Eastbound**, take Exit 234 onto Route 199 East (Lightfoot) and drive 8 miles. Turn right onto Brookwood Drive and make the first left onto Lake Powell Road (Route 617). Drive about 1 mile and turn left onto Wessex Hundred and the winery.

From I-64 Westbound, take Exit 242A onto Route 199 West (Humelsine Parkway). Drive 5 miles and turn left onto Brookwood Drive. Make the first left onto Lake Powell Road (Route 617). Drive about 1 mile and turn left onto Wessex Hundred and the winery.

WINE AROMAS

One of the most important elements of appreciating wine comes from the fragrance of the wine. Indeed, our sense of smell is so critical that we can perceive very little flavor from food or beverages without it.

Most wineries use tasting sheets to describe the aromas and tastes of the wines they present. These can be a helpful way to build our wine vocabulary, but it is important to also think about what the wine smells and tastes like to you personally. Wine aromas are generally sorted into five broad clusters: fruit, floral, vegetal and spice, animal, and roasted.

Fruit aromas include citrus (orange or grapefruit, for instance), tropical (banana or pineapple), red berry (strawberry, raspberry), black berry (blackberry, blueberry, black currant), and stone fruit (apricot, peach). Floral tones include flowers (rose, violet), trees (hawthorn, linden), and even honey.

Vegetal and spice aromas encompass green pepper, earthy smells (mushroom or truffle), spicy tones (cedar or licorice), herbs (thyme, clove), and even vanilla. A wine may have a leathery or buttery smell; these, along with musk, are in the animal group. The roasted category includes toast, roasted nuts (hazelnut or almond), coffee, chocolate, and even smoke.

One way to build an aroma vocabulary is to identify the broader category that best fits, then narrow it down to a specific aroma. For example, if a wine smells fruity, decide whether that aroma is a citrus or berry or stone fruit smell. Then choose a specific flavor, such as peach or raspberry or pineapple. Over time, you'll develop a broader set of terms to describe the wines that you are tasting.

It's also important to note that many wine terms come from plants unique to Europe and North America. In South Africa, for instance, Chardonnay may be described as having an aroma of rooibos tea. In East Asia, the aromas and flavors will be described in completely different ways. Go with what works for you.

Handy Guide to Virginia Wineries

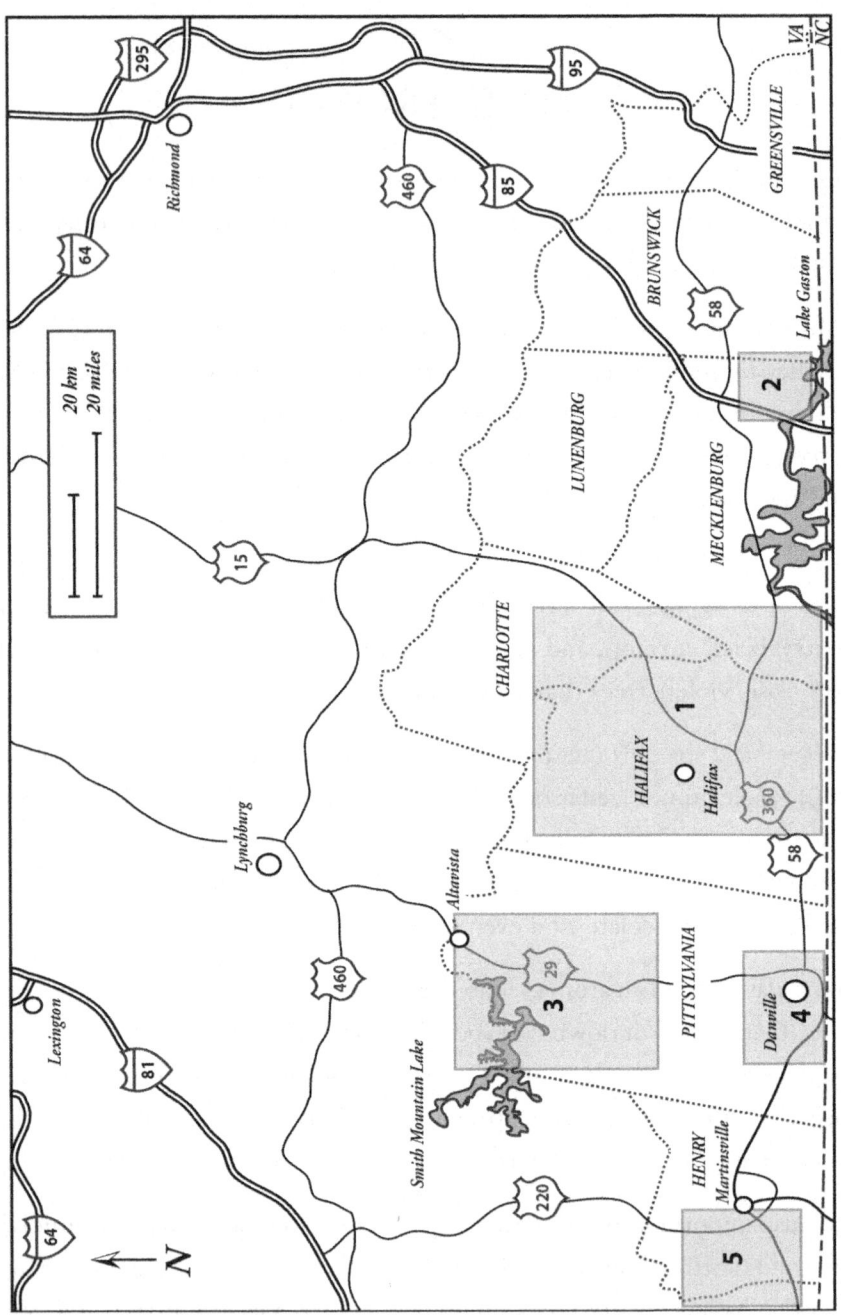

Map 9.0. South Virginia Region: (1) Halifax; (2) Rosemont; (3) Altavista; (4) Danville City; (5) Martinsville.

9. SOUTHERN VIRGINIA REGION

Centered on the Virginia-North Carolina border, the Southern Virginia region is farm country, dotted with lakes, state parks, and small towns. Sometimes called the Southside of Virginia or Southern Piedmont, the area features a rolling landscape, a long growing season, and mild winters, with 43 inches of precipitation annually, the second highest in the state. The wineries in this region are tend to be smaller, offering guests a slower pace and a chance to explore sites a little off the beaten path.

Things to see and do: Many of the region's towns offer driving and walking tours that highlight historic homes and sites. Nature lovers will appreciate the Staunton River, a popular canoeing and tubing venue, the Meherrin River's fishing options, and Lake Gaston's ample boating and sport fishing possibilities. History buffs may be interested in Red Hill, the home of Patrick Henry of "Give me liberty or give me death!" fame. Historic Noland Village near Nathalie is a restored mid-19th century village that recaptures life in rural Virginia.

The area is also home to a number of Old Order Amish families that began settling in the Nathalie area around 2005. Several have established several small businesses offering fresh-baked goods, furniture, and plants. Visitors may also encounter Amish horse-drawn buggies on roadways, so slow down and keep an eye open!

Handy Guide to Virginia Wineries

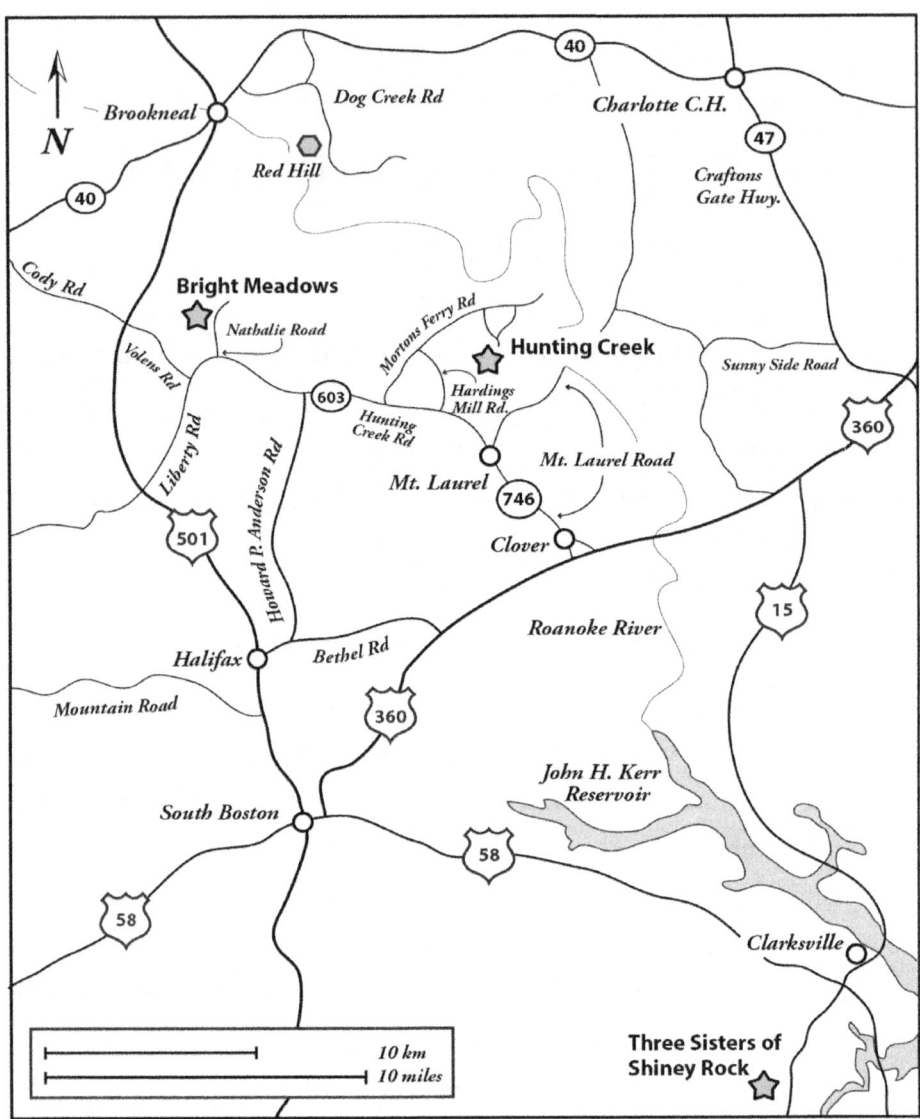

Map 9.1. Halifax

HALIFAX

Bright Meadows Farm Vineyard & Winery
1181 Nathalie Road
Nathalie VA 24577

Hours: F–Sa 11:00–6:00 (Apr–Dec)
Closed Jan–Mar, Thanksgiving, Christmas

434-349-9463
www.brightmeadowsfarm
E-mail: BrightMeadowsFarm@yahoo.com

Boyd and Shirley Archer first opened their family-operated winery to the public in 2005. Located on the grounds of a 19th-century tobacco plantation, Bright Meadows' winery production facility and tasting room are in a restored 117-year-old barn. Visitors are welcome to enjoy the walking paths and picnic areas on the property after their tastings. The facilities are available for private parties and weddings. Children and pets are welcome.

Fruit Wines: Apple, BAG *(blackberry, apple, grape)*, Blackberry.

White Wines: Bright Leaf White, Bright Meadows White *(Niagara)*.

Rosé Wines: Sunrise Surrender *(Steuben)*.

Red Wines: Bright Meadows Red *(Concord)*, Burley Red *(Chambourcin)*, Dan River Noir *(Chambourcin)*, Halifax Red *(Concord)*, Rebellion Red *(Norton)*.

Price Range: $12–$17

Purchasing: Online to AK, AL, CA, DC, FL, ID, IL, LA, MN, MO, NE, NV, NH, NM, NC, ND, OH, OR, VA, WV, and WY.

Directions: From Halifax, take U.S. Route 501 North for 7.3 miles. Turn right onto Liberty Road (Route 642) and drive another 4.6 miles. Make a slight right onto Volens Road (Route 603) and continue 1.4 miles. Bear left onto Nathalie Road (Route 644). The winery will be on the left in ¾ mile.

Hunting Creek Vineyards
2000 Addie Williams Trail
Clover VA 24534

Hours: F 4:00–9:00, Sa 11:00–6:00, Su 12:00–5:00 (mid-Apr–mid-Dec)   434-454-9219
Closed Easter, Thanksgiving, mid-Dec–mid-Apr   www.hcvwines.com
E-mail: info@huntingcreekvineyards.com

Hunting Creek Vineyards is owned by Milt and Sandy McPherson, who started a three-acre vineyard in 2002 with their son Jimmy serving as the winemaker. The tasting room is in a log cabin that offers seating both indoors, with works by local artists adorning its walls, and covered outdoor options. Hunting Creek has an annual harvest party for volunteers who help bring in the grapes. Always call ahead, especially on weekdays or the off-season to double-check that the tasting room is open. Children and leashed pets are welcome.

White Wines: Confession, Innocence, Pure Luck *(Viognier)*.

Red Wines: Decadence, Envy, Indulgence, Repentance, Temptation.

Fortified Wines: Seduction *(port-style)*.

Price Range: $18–$30

Purchasing: Online to AK, AZ, CO, DC, FL, GA, HI, IA, IL, ID, KS, LA, MA, MD, ME, MN, MO, MC, ND, NE, NH, NV, NY, OH, OR, PA, SC, TN, TX, VA, WA, WI, WV, and WY.

Directions: From U.S. Route 360 at the town of Clover, drive north on Mt. Laurel Road (Route 746). After 6.7 miles, turn left onto Hunting Creek Road (Route 603). Drive 2 miles and turn right onto Hardings Mill Road. Continue 2 miles and turn right again onto Mortons Ferry Road. Drive 3 miles and turn right onto Addie Williams Trail (portions unpaved) to the winery 1 mile on the right.

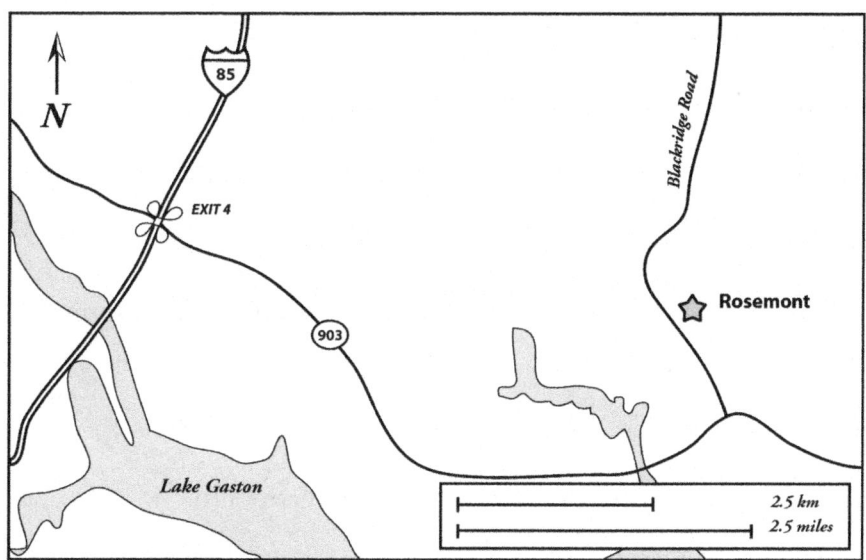

Map 9.2. Rosemont

Rosemont Vineyards & Winery
1050 Blackridge Road
LaCrosse VA 23950

Hours: M–Sa 11:00–6:00, Su 1:00–6:00   434-636-9463
Closed New Year's, Thanksgiving, Christmas   www.rosemontofvirginia.com
E-mail: sales@rosemontofvirginia.com

Rosemont Vineyards & Winery is located on the 450-acre Rosemont Estate, a working farm that has been in the Rose family since 1858. The family began planting the vineyard in 2003 and produced their first vintage five years later. All Rosemont's wines are from estate-grown fruit. The winery features special tasting menus on the weekends and also hosts an annual Harvest Festival, the Wine and Art Festival, and occasional live music and barbecues. Tours of the production area and barrel room are available. The winery may be rented for special events and weddings. Children and leashed pets are welcome.

Sparkling Wines: Extra Brut Sparkling White, Brut Rosé *(Chambourcin).*

White Wines: Block A, Lineage, Traminette, Virginia White.

Rosé Wines: Rosé.

Red Wines: 1858, Cabernet Franc, Kilravock, Merlot, Syrah, Tannat, Virginia Red.

Sweet/Dessert Wines: Blackridge Red, , Lake Country Sunset.

Fortified Wines: Milis Or, Tartan *(port-style)*, Vermouth.

Price Range: $15–$35

Tastings: $10 per person for a flight.

Groups: Reservations required for groups of 8 or more.

Purchasing: Online to CA, DC, FL, MD, MI, NC, NY, and VA.

Directions: From I-85, take Exit 4 (Bracey/Lake Gaston) onto Route 903 East. Drive about 7.5 miles and turn left onto Blackridge Road. The winery will be on the right after 1 mile.

Southern Virginia Region

Three Sisters of Shiney Rock
5484 Shiney Rock Road
Clarksville VA 23927

Hours: Sa 10:00–4:00 (Mar–Dec)   434-298-6693
Closed Christmas, Jan–Feb   www.threesistersofshineyrock.com
E-mail: threesisterswinery@gmail.com

The three sisters who launched Three Sisters of Shiney Rock in 2011 are Beth Graham, Susan Coates, and Kay Candelora, who started their winery on the former tobacco farm run by their extended Powell family. Their goal is to keep the winery as a small and very personalized operation, with grapes hand-picked and crushed in a small wooden hand press. Covered outdoor seating is available on the terrace surrounding the production facility and tasting room, with additional seating out on the grounds.

Fruit Wines: Apple, Blackberry, Perky Poma Mama.

White Wines: Scuppernong.

Red Wines: Muscadine.

Price Range: $15

Tastings: $5 per person.

Directions: From U.S. Route 15 and U.S. Route 58 at Clarksville, drive south on Shiney Rock Road (Route 723) for 5 miles to the winery entrance on the right.

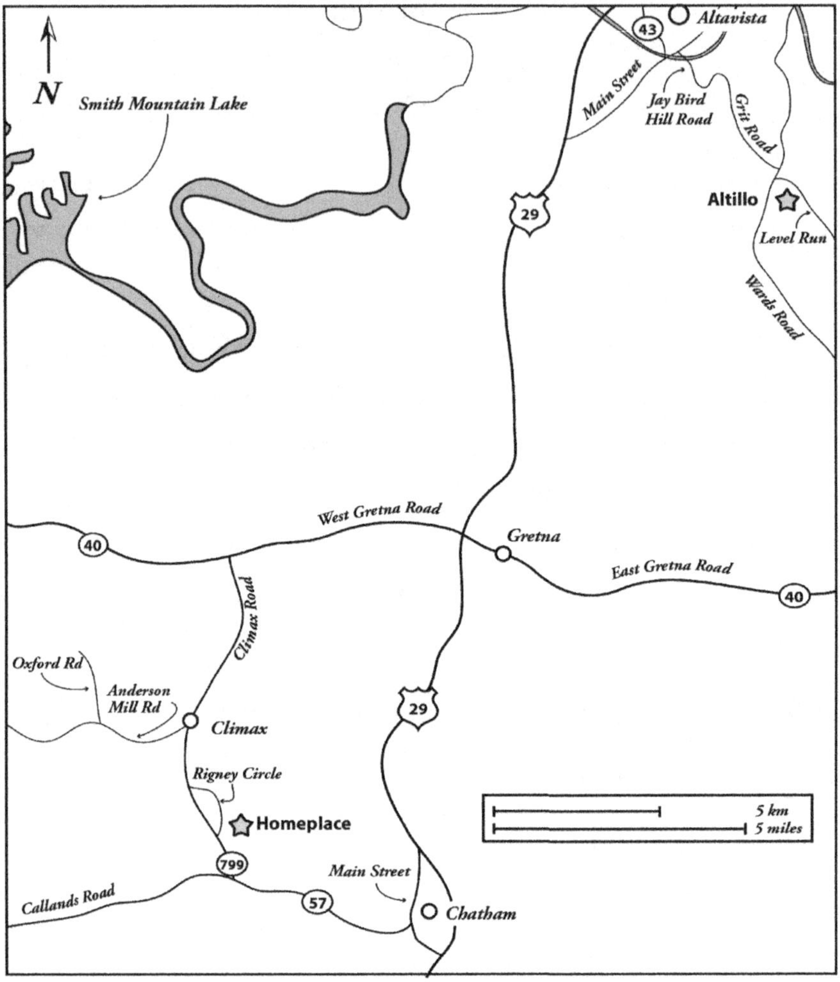

Handy Guide to Virginia Wineries

Map 9.3. Altavista

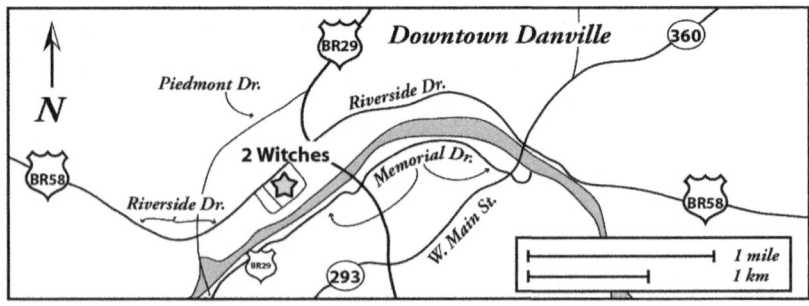

Map 9.4. Danville City

DANVILLE

2 Witches Winery & Brewing
209 Trade Street
Danville VA 24541

Hours: Th–F 5:00–9:00, Sa 2:00–9:00, Su 2:00–6:00
Closed New Year's, Thanksgiving, Christmas

434-549-2739
www.2witcheswinebrew.com
E-mail: 2witcheswinery@gmail.com

2 Witches Winery & Brewing was Virginia's first collocated winery and brew pub and was launched by Julie and Ethan Brown, who were inspired to open their endeavor after a visit to wineries and brewpubs in North Carolina. The name is from a long-ago photo of Julie and her sister wearing Halloween costumes as witches. Most of their production is currently in the form of various craft beers, with an increasing line of wines from their nearby vineyards. Seating is offered both indoors and out on the terrace surrounding the building. 2 Witches also features live music, and special events, including yoga classes, on many weekends.

Fruit Wines: Magic Apple.

White Wines: Muscat Blanc, Traminette, Viognier.

Red Wines: Cabernet Franc, Cabernet Sauvignon, Chambourcin.

Tastings: $3 per person.

Directions: From U.S. Route 29 Business South, merge onto Central Boulevard, then turn right onto Riverside Drive (U.S. 58 Business West). Turn left onto Barter Street, then right onto Trade Street. The brewpub-winery will be on the left.

Altillo Vineyards
620 Level Run Road
Hurt VA 24533

Hours: Sa 12:00–6:00
Closed New Year's, Christmas

434-324-4160
www.altillovineyards.com
E-mail: altillovineyards@yahoo.com

Altillo Winery is a small family-owned and operated vineyard that opened its doors to the public in 2010. Originally named Altavista, Altillo was launched by Bob and Eric Schenkel, who bought the property in 2000 and produced their first vintage in 2009. Altavista produces all Virginia-grown wine using both fruit from their own vineyards and from other nearby growers. The winery sponsors occasional live music and special events. Dogs are welcome.

White Wines: Chardonnay, Viognier, Vista Blanca.

Rosé Wines: Vista Rosa.

Red Wines: Cabernet Franc, Meritage, Shiraz.

Price Range: $15–$20

Tastings: $10 per person.

Directions: From the town of Altavista, take Pittsylvania Avenue (Route 668) which becomes Ricky van Shelton Drive after crossing the Roanoke River, then Jay Bird Hill Road and finally Grit Road, driving 4 miles in all. Turn left onto Level Run Road (also Route 668). Continue about ½ mile to the winery entrance on the right.

Hamlet Vineyards
405 Riverside Drive
Bassett VA 24055

Hours: Su 1:00–5:00
Closed New Year's, Easter, Christmas

276-629-2121
www.hamletvineyards.com
E-mail: va@hamletvineyards.com

Virginia and Butch Hamlet opened their winery on the grounds of Eltham Manor, their historic 300-acre farm in the foothills of the Blue Ridge. They use Virginia-grown grapes for their wines, either from their own vines or from other vineyards in the state. Winemaking is done under the guidance of Michael Shaps Wineworks. Free Wi-Fi is offered with the purchase of wine.

Sparkling Wines: VaVino *(Viognier)*.

White Wines: Bottled Blonde, Pinot Gris, Viognier.

Rosé Wines: Cardinal Rosé.

Red Wines: Cabernet Sauvignon, Eltham *(Bordeaux-style blend)*, Old Virginia Red, Petit Verdot.

Price Range: $17–$30

Purchasing: Online to VA residents only.

Directions: From Martinsville, take VA Route 57 West toward Fieldare and Stanleytown for 2 miles. Crossing the Smith River bridge and drive another 3.2 miles to the winery driveway on the left.

Homeplace Vineyard
568 Rigney Circle
Chatham VA 24531

Hours: M–Sa 11:00–5:00 (Apr–Dec)   434-432-9463
Closed Jan–Mar, Thanksgiving, Christmas   www.thehomeplacevineyard.com
E-mail: thehomeplacevineyard@yahoo.com

Joe and Brenda Williams established Homeplace Vineyard in 2005 on a farm that has been in the Williams family for four generations. After converting the tobacco fields into a vineyard, the couple began selling grapes to other wineries in the area before opening their own in 2010. The tasting room was built on the site of the original family homestead, using timbers from the old tobacco barns from the property. On many weekends, Homeplace sponsors live music, food, and sangria and wine tastings. The facility may be rented for weddings and private parties.

Fruit Wines: Cabin Sunset *(strawberry)*.

White Wines: Vidal Blanc, Viognier.

Red Wines: Cabernet Franc, Cabernet Sauvignon, Chambourcin.

Price Range: $10–$15

Tastings: $5 per person.

Directions: From Chatham, take Route 57 west for 4.5 miles. Turn right onto Climax Road (Route 799) and drive 1.4 miles. Turn right onto Rigney Circle and drive ½ mile. The winery entrance will be on the right.

Southern Virginia Region

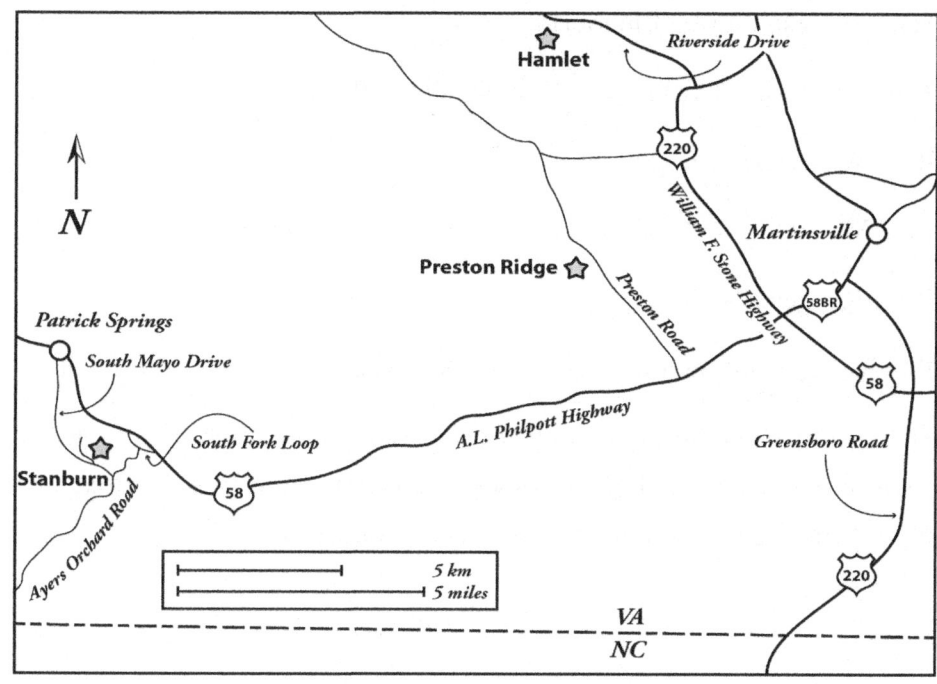

Map 9.6. Martinsville

Preston Ridge Winery
4105 Preston Road
Martinsville VA 24112

Hours: CLOSED for the 2021 season 276-957-3844
(Check website for 2022 status & hours) www.facebook.com/prestonridge.winery
E-mail: PrestonRidge@comcast.net

Preston Ridge was established by Lawrence and Lois Penn, who opened their small winery to the public in March 2010. After spending several years honing his skills as a home winemaker, Lawrence decided to open a tasting room featuring wines made from locally grown fruit. Visitors may bring a picnic lunch to enjoy on the grounds. The winery gift shop includes a range of winemaking supplies for purchase.

Fruit Wines: Apple, Blueberry.

White Wines: Chardonnay, Riesling, Vidal Blanc.

Rosé Wines: Blushing Katie.

Red Wines: Cabernet Franc, Chambourcin, Rosie Ryan.

Price Range: $14–$16

Purchasing: Online ordering to many states; contact winery for details.

Directions: From Martinsville, take the A.L. Philpott Highway (U.S. Route 58 Business) west for about 10 miles. Turn right onto Preston Road and drive 4 miles. The winery driveway will be on the left.

Stanburn Winery
158 Conner Drive
Stuart VA 24171

Hours: Open hours for 2021 posted on website
Closed mid-Dec–Mar

276-694-7074
www.stanburnwinery.com
E-mail: info@stanburnwinery.com

Nelson and Elsie Stanley got into the wine industry in 1999 when they planted a ten-acre vineyard on their 100-acre property. After selling their grapes to other wineries for over a decade, they opted to open their own winery; the name Stanburn combines Stanley with Elsie's maiden name of Burnette. The tasting room is housed in a restored old farmhouse on their Patrick County property. Son David and daughter Dawn Stanley Osborne oversee the vineyards, working with winemaker Jocelyn Kuzelka.

White Wines: Chardonnay, Highfly, Meadow Breeze, Traminette, Vidal Blanc.

Blush Wines: Bull's Blush.

Red Wines: Barbera, Big A Red, Cabernet Franc, Chambourcin, Poorhouse.

Price Range: $12–$16

Tastings: $6 per person, with souvenir glass.

Directions: From U.S. Route 58, turn south onto the South Fork loop **and** then south again onto Ayers Orchard Road. Drive 2.2 miles and turn right onto South Mayo Drive. After ¾ mile, turn right onto Conner Drive. The winery entrance will be on the right.

Handy Guide to Virginia Wineries

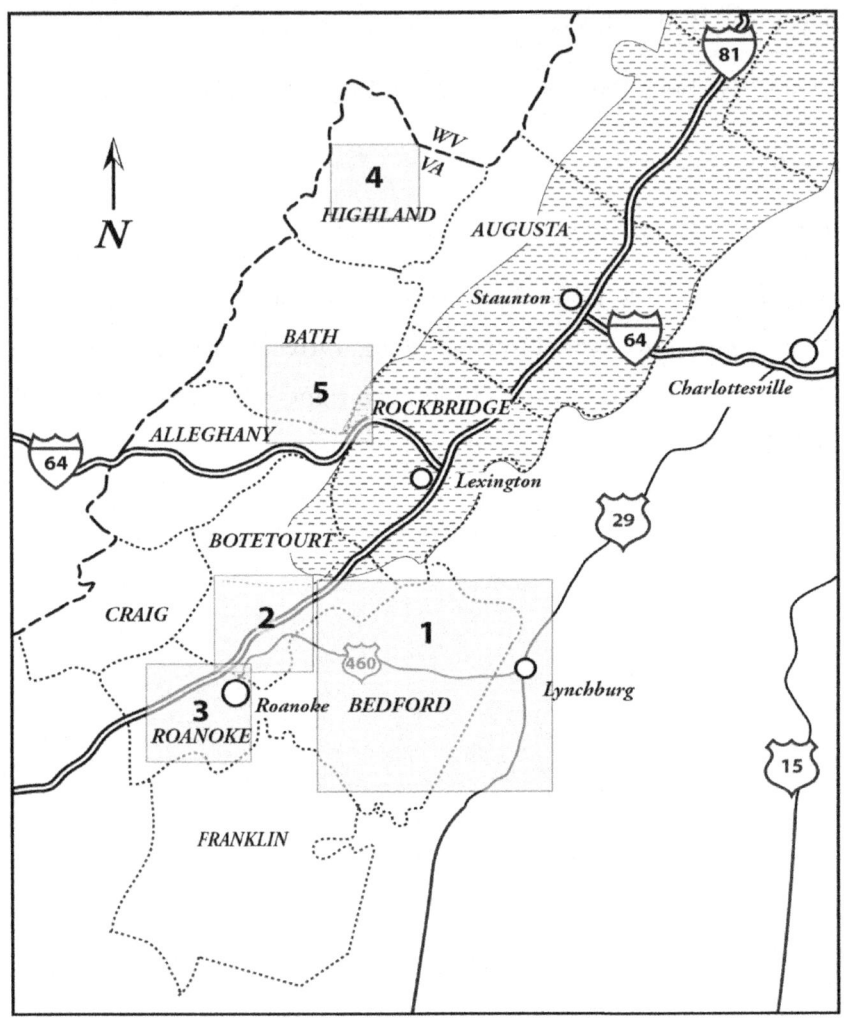

Map 10.0. Virginia Mountains Region: (1) Bedford;
(2) Roanoke (northern section); (3) Roanoke (southern section);
(4) Big Fish Cider; (5) Rock Roadhouse

10. VIRGINIA MOUNTAINS REGION

The Virginia Mountains Region is very rural and very mountainous. Craig and Alleghany Counties have but one traffic light between them, and Highland County is more alpine than southern, with the highest mean elevation of any county in the United States east of the Mississippi River. If you are looking to escape into nature, this region is a good place to go.

<u>Things to see and do</u>: The area is an outdoor enthusiast's delight, with lakes and rivers, mountains and hiking trails at every turn. Near Roanoke, visitors can hike to McAfee Knob, featured in the 2015 film, *A Walk in the Woods*, Bill Bryson's humorous memoir of his hike along the Appalachian Trail. Other attractions include Franklin County, the "Moonshine Capital of the World," where visitors can sample Twin Creeks' Sweet Mash Corn, the first legal moonshine in the county since Prohibition.

It is also an area where history abounds. The Jefferson Pools in Bath date from the early 1800s and were named after President Thomas Jefferson who "took the waters" for his health there in 1818. Jefferson's retreat, Poplar Forest, is also nearby. More modern historical markers include the National D-Day Memorial at Bedford, the American town with the highest per capita losses at that pivotal event during World War II.

<u>Winery Trails</u>: The region includes the Bedford County Wine Trail and the Wine Trail of Botetourt County. Please see Appendix I for details.

Handy Guide to Virginia Wineries

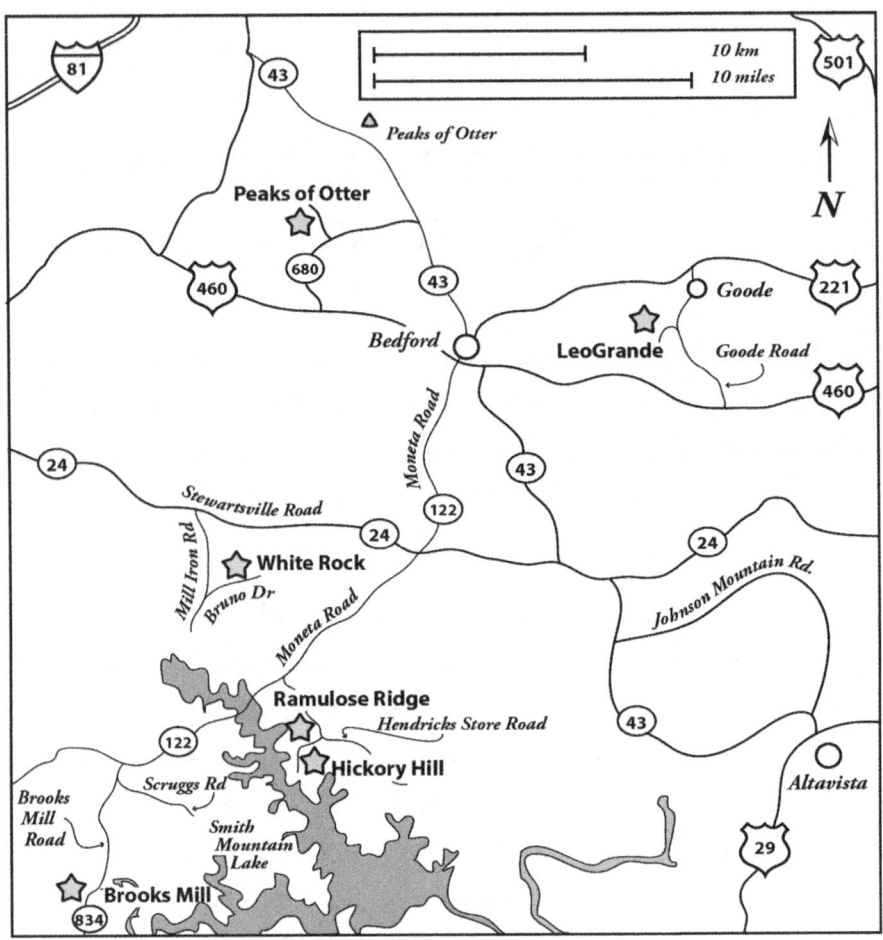

Map 10.1. Bedford

BEDFORD

Brooks Mill Winery
6221 Brooks Mill Road
Wirtz VA 24184

Hours: F–M 12:00–4:00 (Apr–Oct)
Sa–Su 12:00–4:00 (Nov–Dec)
Closed Jan–Mar, Easter

540-721-5215
www.brooksmillwine.com
E-mail: taste@brooksmillwine.com

H.T. and Rhonda Page started making fruit wine for family and friends over a dozen years before deciding to open to the public in 2008, first by appointment only and then on weekends. They offer their semi-dry to sweet wines in a tasting room housed in a converted garage on their property. With five acres of land, the Pages grow their own blackberries, blueberries, and other fruit for their production, supplementing it as needed with produce from other Virginia farmers. Children and pets are welcome.

Fruit Wines: Black & Blue, Blackberry, Blueberry, Cherry, Dry Blackberry, Dry Pear, Peach, Pear, Plum, Sweet Blackberry, Sweet Blueberry.

Price Range: $12–$14

Tastings: $5 per person

Purchasing: Online for AK, DC, FL, ID, IL, LA, MN, MO, NC, ND, NE, NH, NM, NV, OH, OR, VA, WV, and WY.

Directions: From Bedford, drive south for 20 miles on Moneta Road (VA 122), which will become Booker T. Washington Highway after crossing Smith Mountain Lake. Turn left onto Scruggs Road (VA 616) and drive 0.8 miles. Turn right onto Brooks Mill Road (VA 834). Drive another 4 miles to the winery entrance on the right.

Fables & Feathers Winery
2117 Bruno Drive
Goodview VA 24095

Hours: Th–M 11:00–6:00 (Apr–Nov)
Closed Thanksgiving

540-420-0916
www.fablesandfeatherswinery.com
E-mail: FablesandFeathersWinery@outlook.com

Pam and Tom Luedtke bought the former White Rock Winery in 2020, relaunching it in 2021 as Fables & Feathers. Their certified Virginia Green tasting room offers a covered veranda where visitors may sit and enjoy the view; outdoor seating includes a gazebo overlooking the vines. The winery also offers a farm brewery on the premises with a range of craft beers.

White Wines: Aesop's White, Chardonnay, Riesling, Sadie's White.

Red Wines: Aesop's Red, Cabernet Franc, Merlot, Pinot Noir, Sadie's Red.

Price Range: $14–$22

Tastings: $14 per person for a flight.

Directions: From Bedford, take Route 122 (Burks Hill Road, then Moneta Road) south. Continue for 7 miles. Turn right onto Stewartsville Road (Route 24) and drive 9 miles. Turn left onto Mill Iron Road (Route 653). After 2 miles, turn left on Bruno Drive. The winery is 1 mile on the left.

Hickory Hill Vineyards & Winery
1722 Hickory Cove Lane
Moneta VA 24121

Hours: W–Su 12:00–5:00 (May–Aug);
Th–Su 12:00–5:00 (Mar, Apr, Sep, Oct), F–Sa 12:00–5:00 (Nov–Feb)
Closed mid-Dec–mid-Jan

540-296-1393
www.smlwine.com
E-mail: thefurrows@smlwine.com

Hickory Hill Vineyard was founded by Roger and Judy Furrow, long-time home winemakers who opened their renovated 1923 farmhouse to the public in 2001. Hickory Hill is located on scenic Smith Mountain Lake, best known for standing in for New Hampshire's Lake Winnipesaukee in the 1991 movie, *What About Bob?* The winery does not sell food, but guests may bring their own picnics. Hickory Hill's farmhouse includes a small gift shop with crafts from local artisans and offers live music performances. Children and dogs are welcome.

White Wines: Chardonnay, Smith Mountain Lake Mist, Vidal Blanc.

Red Wines: Cabernet Franc, Cabernet Sauvignon, Merlot, Smith Mountain Lake Country Red, Sixty-Six (*Bordeaux-style blend*).

Sweet/Dessert Wines: Smith Mountain Lake Redbud, Smith Mountain Lake Sunset, Sweet Red Sail.

Price Range: $10–$20

Groups: Reservations required for groups of 10 or more.

ADA accessible.

Purchasing: Online to AK, AZ, CO, DC, FL, GA, HI, IA, ID, IL, IN, KS, LA, MA, MD, ME, MN, MO, NC, ND, NE, NH, NM, NV, NY, OH, OK, OR, PA, SC, TN, TX, VA, VT, WA, WI, WV, and WY.

Directions: From Bedford, take Route 122 south onto Burks Hill Road which will become Moneta Road. After 14.4 miles, turn left on Hendricks Store Road. Drive 2 miles and turn right on Hickory Cove Lane. The winery is 1 mile on the left.

LeoGrande Vineyards & Winery
1343 Wingfield Drive
Goode VA 24556

Hours: F–Su 11:00–6:00 (Mar–Dec), 540-586-4066
F–Su 11:00–5:00 (Jan–Mar)   www.facebook.com/leogrande-vineyard-and-winery.com
Closed Thanksgiving, Christmas, New Year's   E-mail: cmleogrande@gmail.com

Norman LeoGrande launched his boutique winery on the 400-acre working farm where he also raises Black Angus cattle and American Saddlebred horses. A renovated farmhouse serves as the tasting room; guests can also sit on the porch or the pavilion and appreciate the view of the winery's vines and surrounding mountains. The winery dogs may be on hand to greet you, or you may spot them on patrol, walking through the vines. Children and pets are welcome.

White Wines: Chardonnay, Sauvignon Blanc.

Red Wines: Barbera, Nebbiolo, Sangiovese, Syrah.

Sweet/Dessert Wines: Autumn Kiss, Roaring Rosé, Roaring White.

Price Range: $10–$25

Tastings: $5 per person.

Groups: Please call ahead for groups of 6 or more.

Directions: From Lynchburg, take U.S. Route 221 South about 9 miles. Turn left onto Goode Station Road (Route 668) into the town of Goode. Turn right onto Goode Road and drive 1.3 miles. Make another right onto Wingfield Drive. The winery will be on the right in ½ mile.

Peaks of Otter Winery & Orchards
1218 Elmos Road (GPS address)
Bedford VA 24523

Hours: Daily 12:00–5:00 (Apr–Dec),
Sa–Su 12:00–5:00 (Jan–Mar)
Closed New Year's, Thanksgiving, Christmas

540-586-3707
www.peaksofotterwinery.com
E-mail: appleseed@earthlink.net

Peaks of Otter Winery is owned and operated by Danny and Nancy Johnson, who opened the winery in 1995 on their fifth-generation apple orchard. The winery offers its own jams, jellies, relishes, and sauces, as well as two pepper wines: Chili Dawg, paired with Cheez Whiz, and Kiss The Devil, which earns an "I kissed the devil" sticker. Facebook fans receive a 5% discount on purchases. Children and dogs are welcome.

A four-bedroom guest house, Elmo's Rest, is available for weekly rental.

Fruit Wines: Blackberry Cobbler, Blackberry Jammed, Blueberry Muffin, Café Vino *(apple, coffee)*, Cinfulicious *(cinnamon)*, Chocolate Cherry Bomb, Crabapple, Cranapple Cocktail, Hunter's Raid–The Bedford Boys, Mango Tango, Peach of Otter, Pear, Plumlicious, Puff, Pure Passion, Ras Ma Tas Raspberry, Strawberry Shortcake, Strawberry Reserve, Sweet Heart, Twisted Tangerine, Vino Colada, Virginia Apple Lovers.

Grape Wines: Blue Ridge Mountain Grape, Frosty Morn, Light Grape, Sangria.

Other: Chili Dawg *(apple, chili pepper)*, Kiss The Devil *(30 chili peppers)*.

Price Range: $15–$35

ADA accessible.

Purchasing: Online to AK, AZ, CO, DC, FL, GA, IA, ID, IL, IN, KS, LA, MA, MD, ME, MN, MO, NC, ND, NE, NH, NM, NV, NY, OH, OR, PA, SC, TN, TX, VA, VT, WA, WI, WV, and WY.

Directions: From Bedford, take U.S. Route 460 West for about 1 mile. Turn right onto Route 680 (Patterson Mill Road) and drive 4.6 miles. Turn right to stay on Route 680 (Sheep Creek Road). The winery is 1 mile on the left.

Ramulose Ridge Vineyards
3061 Hendricks Store Road
Moneta VA 24121

Hours: W–Sa 1:00–5:00 (F–Sa to 8:00 in summer)
Closed New Year's, Thanksgiving, Christmas

630-485-8941
www.ramuloseridgevineyards.com
E-mail: ramuloseridge@msn.com

Longtime wine lovers Jim and Sandi Ramaker founded Ramulose Ridge on the grounds of their 100-acre property near Smith Mountain Lake, with Sandi serving as winemaker. The tasting room offers seating indoors with a fireplace for winter warmth as well as outdoors on the partially covered patio with a view of the estate's vineyards. The facilities may be rented for private events and parties. Ramulose Ridge also offers light snacks and cigars for sale (along with suggested cigar-wine pairings).

Fruit Wines: Chocolate Orange, Green Apple, Peach, Pineapple, Raspberry.

White Wines: Chardonel, Muscat, Traminette, Vidal Blanc, Viognier.

Red Wines: Cabernet Franc, Chambourcin, Malbec, Robusto, Syrah.

Sweet/Dessert Wines: Blackwater, Blush, Muscat, Tendril.

Price Range: $9–$20

Directions: From Bedford, drive south on Route 122 (Moneta Road). After 14.4 miles, turn left on Hendricks Store Road. Drive 2 miles. Turn right on Hickory Cove Lane and the winery on the right.

SERVING TEMPERATURES

A commonly held rule of thumb is that sparkling, white, and rosé wines should be served chilled, while red wines are served at room temperature. But what do "chilled" and "room temperature" really mean? And how much does temperature really matter?

To test the effect of temperature on wine for yourself, pour equal amounts of a white wine and a non-tannic red wine into glasses, cover them with plastic wrap, and refrigerate them for at least one hour. Have a friend blindfold you so that you cannot see the wine. Can you tell which is the red and which is the white?

According to wine experts, the ideal serving temperatures for white and rosé wines range from about 45 to 55 degrees Fahrenheit, and reds from 50 to 65 degrees Fahrenheit. In practice, that means whites and rosés are often served much too cold, while reds could be slightly cooler than they often are.

Colder serving temperatures tend to reduce the aroma of a wine, while warmer temperatures let it blossom. Cooler temperatures also tend to bring out the acidity and tannins in a wine, while warmer serving temperatures reduce them.

To test this, pour a glass of a tannic red, such as Cabernet Sauvignon, cover with plastic wrap, and let it chill in the refrigerator for an hour. You'll probably find that the chilled Cabernet is so astringent as to be barely drinkable. Let it warm to room temperature, however, and the tannins will soften.

Similarly, chilling a very fruity white wine will add crispness to balance out the fruit and give it better structure. Pour two glasses, cover both with plastic wrap, and put one in the refrigerator while leaving the other on the counter. After an hour, compare them. The colder wine will have a bit more acidic crispness to it.

For sparkling wines, serving temperature is also important. Colder temperatures help slow the release of the carbon dioxide bubbles in sparkling wines, helping them keep their bubbliness longer.

Handy Guide to Virginia Wineries

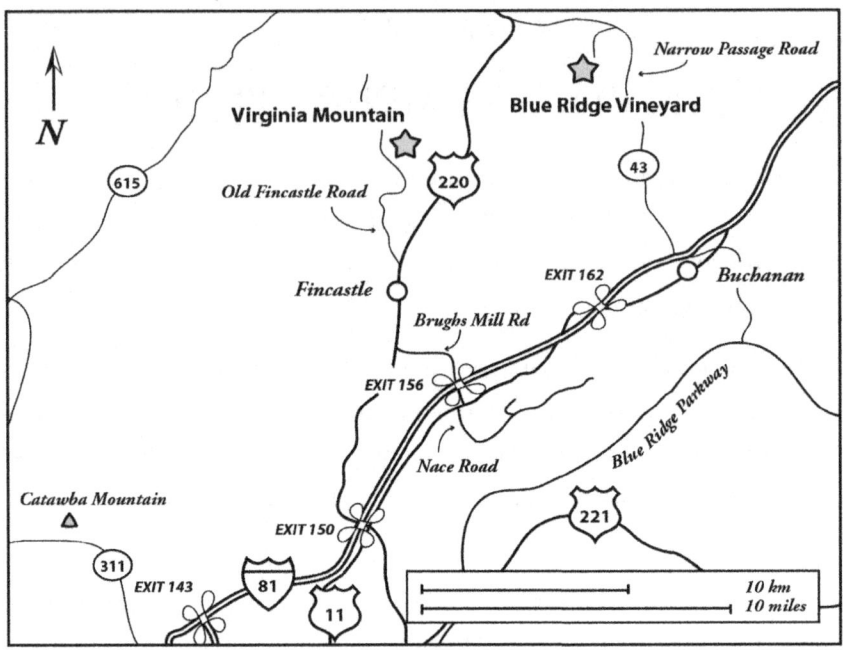

Map 10.2. Roanoke (northern section)

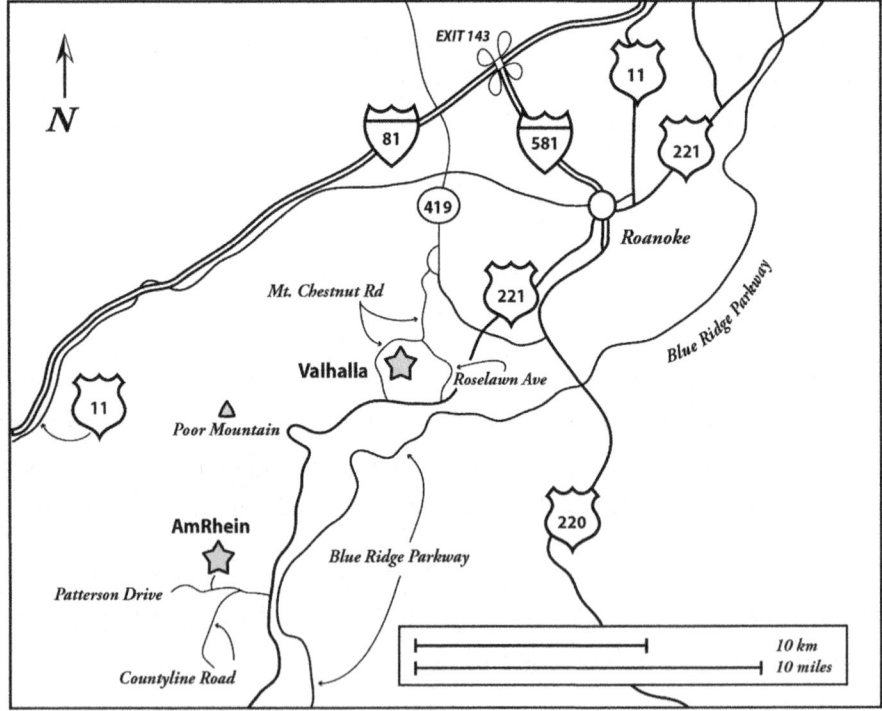

Map 10.3. Roanoke (southern section)

ROANOKE

AmRhein Wine Cellars
9243 Patterson Drive
Bent Mountain VA 24059

Hours: Th–M, 11:00–5:00 (to 7:00 on Sa) (summer);
F–Su 11:00–5:00 (Jan–Mar)
Closed New Year's, Thanksgiving, Christmas

540-929-4632
www.amrheinwine.com
E-mail: info@amrheins.com

    Russ and Paula Amrhein have owned and operated AmRhein Wine Cellars since 1995, when they purchased their 40-acre property on Bent Mountain. AmRhein's tasting room offers views of the surrounding hills and vineyards from the tables indoors and on the deck. Light fare is available for purchase, including wraps, cheese, and crackers. The winery hosts a range of special events, including live music on summer weekends, an annual Oktoberfest, and harvest soup weekends. Weather permitting, AmRhein produces a true frozen-on-the-vine ice wine from the Vidal Blanc grapes in their vineyards, which reach up to 2,500 feet in elevation. The winery is available for weddings and private events. Children are welcome.

Fruit Wines: Sangria Red, Sangria White, Vin de Pêche *(peach)*.

White Wines: Petit Manseng, Pinot Grigio, Sauvignon Blanc, Traminette, Vidal Blanc.

Rosé Wines: Rosé.

Red Wines: Aglianico, Cabernet Franc, Cabernet Sauvignon, Mélange, Petit Verdot.

Sweet/Dessert Wines: Blush, Ruby.

Price Range: $17–$27

Handy Guide to Virginia Wineries

Tastings: $5–$10 per person.

Groups: Reservations recommended for groups of 8 or more.

Directions: From Roanoke, take U.S. Route 221 South and drive 13.7 miles. Turn right onto Countyline Road and continue 1.2 miles. Bear right at the fork onto Patterson Drive. The winery will be ½ mile on the right.

Blue Ridge Vineyard
1027 Shiloh Drive
Eagle Rock VA 24085

Hours: Sa–Su, holiday M 12:00–5:00 (Mar–Dec) 540-798-7642
Closed Thanksgiving, Christmas, Jan–Feb www.blueridgevineyard.com
E-mail: blueridgevines@gmail.com

Jim Holaday and Barbara Kolb first launched Blue Ridge Vineyard in 1985 after selling their grapes to others for over 20 years. Blue Ridge's tasting room is housed in an old barn; in the summer and during special events, tasting tables are also set up outside where visitors can appreciate the outstanding views of the Blue Ridge from picnic tables or gazebo. The winery sponsors a number of events, including live music, an All-American Mutt Rescue fundraiser, and Soup 'n Sip Sundays. Children and dogs are welcome.

White Wines: Big Bear White, Equinox, Gewurztraminer, Riesling, Traminette.

Red Wines: Big Bear Red, Cabernet Franc, Pinot Noir, Solstice, Sweet Shiloh.

Price Range: $14–$25

Tastings: $5 per person.

ADA accessible.

Directions: From I-81, take Exit 162 (Buchanan) and turn onto U.S. Route 11 North. After 4.8 miles, turn left onto 1st Street (Route 43), which will become Narrow Passage Road, and drive for 11.4 miles. Turn left onto Shiloh Drive (portions unpaved). The winery will be on the left in 0.8 miles.

Valhalla Vineyards
6500 Mt. Chestnut Road
Roanoke VA 24018

Hours: F 5:00–8:00, Sa 12:00–5:00, Su 1:00–5:00 (Apr–Oct)
Sa 12:00–5:00, Su 1:00–5:00 (Mar, Nov–Dec)
Sa only 12:00–5:00, Jan–Feb
Closed New Year's, Easter, Christmas

540-725-9463
www.valhallawines.com
E-mail: valhallava@aol.com

The Vascik family established their winery in 1994 on a 2,000-foot mountain property overlooking the city of Roanoke. The opera lovers named their winery after the home of the Norse gods made famous by German composer Richard Wagner. Light snacks can be purchased in the tasting room. In cooler weather, visitors can warm up next to the floor-to-ceiling stone fireplace inside or can sit near the large outdoor fireplace on the patio. Valhalla offers winemaker dinners, wine education events, and live music in summers. The facility is available for weddings and private events. No dogs, please.

White Wines: Rheingold Chardonnay, Viognier.

Red Wines: Alicante Bouschet, Cabernet Sauvignon, Cabernet/Shiraz, Götterdämmerung, Norton, Sangiovese, Syrah, Valkyrie.

Sweet/Dessert Wines: Late Harvest Alicante Bouschet.

Price Range: $22–$30.

Purchasing: Surface mail or fax ordering for VA only.

Directions: From Roanoke, take Brambleton Road (U.S. Route 221 South). Drive 4 miles and turn right onto Roselawn Road (Route 689). Continue 2.3 miles and turn left onto Mt. Chestnut Road (Route 692). The winery will be 1 mile on the left.

Virginia Mountain Vineyards
4204 Old Fincastle Road
Fincastle VA 24090

Hours: Th–Su 12:00–6:00 (mid-Mar–mid-Dec)
Closed Thanksgiving, mid-Dec–mid-Mar

540-473-2979
www.vmvines.com
E-mail: info@vmvines.com

David and Marie Gibbs opened Virginia Mountain to the public in 2006 after several years of selling the grapes from their ten-acre vineyard. Now owned by Jacqui Sobieski and Brian Weber, the winery hosts monthly summer music evenings with local performers, "Wine, Moon, and Stars" evenings with the Roanoke Astronomy Club, and a Holiday Open House in December. The facilities may be rented for private parties or weddings. Children and pets are welcome.

Fruit Wines: Life's a Peach, Strawberry Frost.

White Wines: Acacia Gold, Chardonnay, Traminette.

Rosé Wines: Rosé.

Red Wines: Cabernet Franc, Merlot, Petit Verdot, Trinity *(Bordeaux-style blend)*.

Sweet/Dessert Wines: Virginia White, Virginia Red, Holiday Spice *(seasonal)*.

Price Range: $15–$23

Tastings: $10 per person for a flight.

Groups: Reservations required for groups of 8 or more.

ADA accessible.

Purchasing: Online to AK, AL, AZ, CA, CO, DC, FL, GA, HI, IA, ID, IL, IN, KS, LA, MA, MD, ME, MN, MO, NC, ND, NE, NE, NH, NM, NV, NY, OH, OR, SC, TN, TX, VA, WA, WI, WV, and WY.

Directions: From I-81, take Exit 150 onto U.S. Route 220 West. Drive 10.7 miles and turn left onto Old Fincastle Road (Route 655) just past the town of Fincastle. The winery will be on the right in 4.3 miles.

Handy Guide to Virginia Wineries

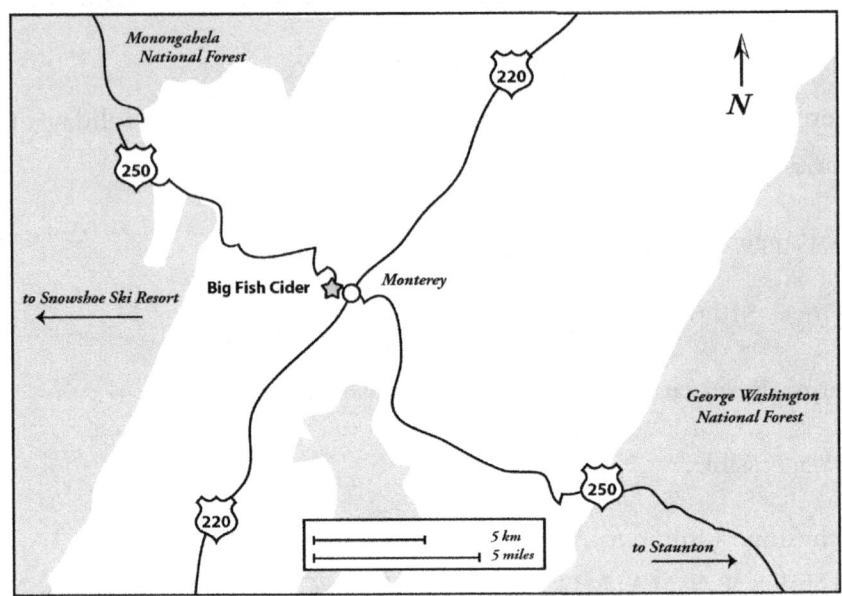

Map 10.4. Big Fish Cider

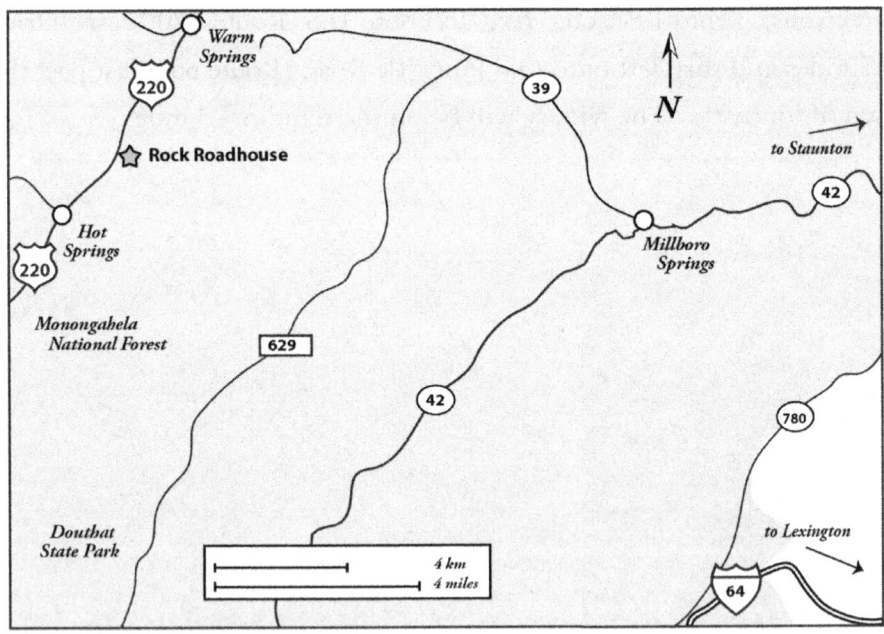

Map 10.5. Rock Roadhouse

ALLEGHANY HIGHLANDS

Big Fish Cider
59 Spruce Street
Monterey VA 24464

Hours: F 4:00–7:00, Sa 2:00-7:00   540-468-2322
Closed New Year's, Christmas   www.bigfishcider.com
                                 E-mail: info@bigfishcider.com

Big Fish Cider is located deep in the scenic Allegheny Mountains west of Staunton. Kirk Billingsley, a native of the historic town of Monterey, founded his micro-cidery in 2015, using locally grown heirloom apples to produce hard ciders that range from off-dry to semi-sweet. Indoor seating is available at the tasting room, which is housed in an old theater building with a giant rainbow trout perched on top.

Ciders: Allegheny Gold, Crabbottom Pippin, Elevation, Fireside, Highland Scrumpy, Honey Ginger, Mellifera, Monterey Maple *(aged in apple brandy barrels)*, Shady Lane Shandy *(seasonal)*, Wassail *(seasonal)*, Wild Meadow.

Price Range: $12–$18

Tastings: $5 per person.

Purchasing: Online to AK, AZ, CO, DC, FL, GA, HI, IA, ID, IN, KS, LA, MA, MD, ME, MN, MO, NC, ND, NE, NH, NM, NV, NY, OH, OR, PA, SC, TN, TX, VA, VT, WA, WI, WV, and WY.

Directions: From Staunton, take U.S. Route 250 west toward Monterey. Drive 40 miles into the town of Monterey and turn left onto Spruce Street. The cidery will be one block on the left.

Rock Roadhouse Winery
Chateau Donze Lane
Hot Springs VA 24445

Hours: F–Sa 12:00-6:00
Closed New Year's, Christmas

757-876-4009
www.rockroadhousewinery.com
E-mail: RockRoadhouseWinery@gmail.com

Bob and Rhonda Donze were inspired to start a winery after a family trip to explore the historic Allegheny region, which is home to stunning mountain views and hot springs. The two former Air Force officers have housed their winery in a rock structure built during the Great Depression by the Civilian Conservation Corps. Rock Roadhouse's vineyards first began to be planted in 2017 and are at 2,600 feet in elevation, putting them among Virginia's highest. The winery offers cheese and charcuterie platters to pair with their estate-grown wines. Leashed dogs are welcome.

Sparkling Wines: Sparkling Rosé.

White Wines: Roadhouse White, Traminette, Vidal Blanc.

Rosé Wines: Roadhouse Rosé.

Red Wines: Cabernet Franc, Corot Noir, Merlot, Roadhouse Red, Touriga.

Fortified Wines: Aviator *(port-style)*.

Price Range: $25–$45

Tastings: $20 per person for a flight.

Purchasing: Online to CA, DC, FL, MO, and VA.

Directions: From Warm Springs, turn south onto Sam Snead Highway (U.S. Route 220). Drive 3.5 miles. Turn left onto Chateau Donze Lane, just before the Summit Community Bank. The winery will be straight ahead.

TASTING TIPS

Getting the most from what a wine has to offer is a truly sensory experience that fully engages your senses of sight, smell, and taste to appreciate the complete range of characteristics of the wine in your glass. Wine tasting can be broken down into five simple steps:

1. **Look** at the color of the wine by tilting the glass slightly away from you and holding it above a white background. Notice the depth of color and, for reds, whether you can see your fingers through the wine or not. This may give a hint as to the richness or fullness of the wine.

2. **Swirl** the wine in the glass to help release the aromas.

3. **Smell** the wine, first about chin level and then by sticking your nose into the glass. Notice whether it is delicately scented or highly aromatic. Does it have a fruity or jammy aroma? Does it smell grassy or spicy? Does it have vanilla or oaky overtones? Is the aroma simple and straightforward, or is it complex, with several different flavors?

4. **Taste** the wine by getting at least a couple of tablespoons of wine in your mouth. Hold it there for at least several seconds. Notice whether the wine is light or full-bodied. Is it sweet, tannic, crisp, or fruity? As with smell, is the taste simple and straightforward, or is it more complex, with different aspects to the flavor?

5. **Reflect** on the overall taste and balance of the wine, once you have swallowed it (or spit it out into a tasting bucket, if you're tasting many different wines). How long do the flavors last in your mouth? Does one flavor stand out or is the wine balanced? Does the taste seem to evolve and change?

While wineries include their own descriptions on tasting sheets, try not to be influenced by them. Rather, think about what the wine smells and tastes like to you, and jot down your own comments on the page.

Handy Guide to Virginia Wineries

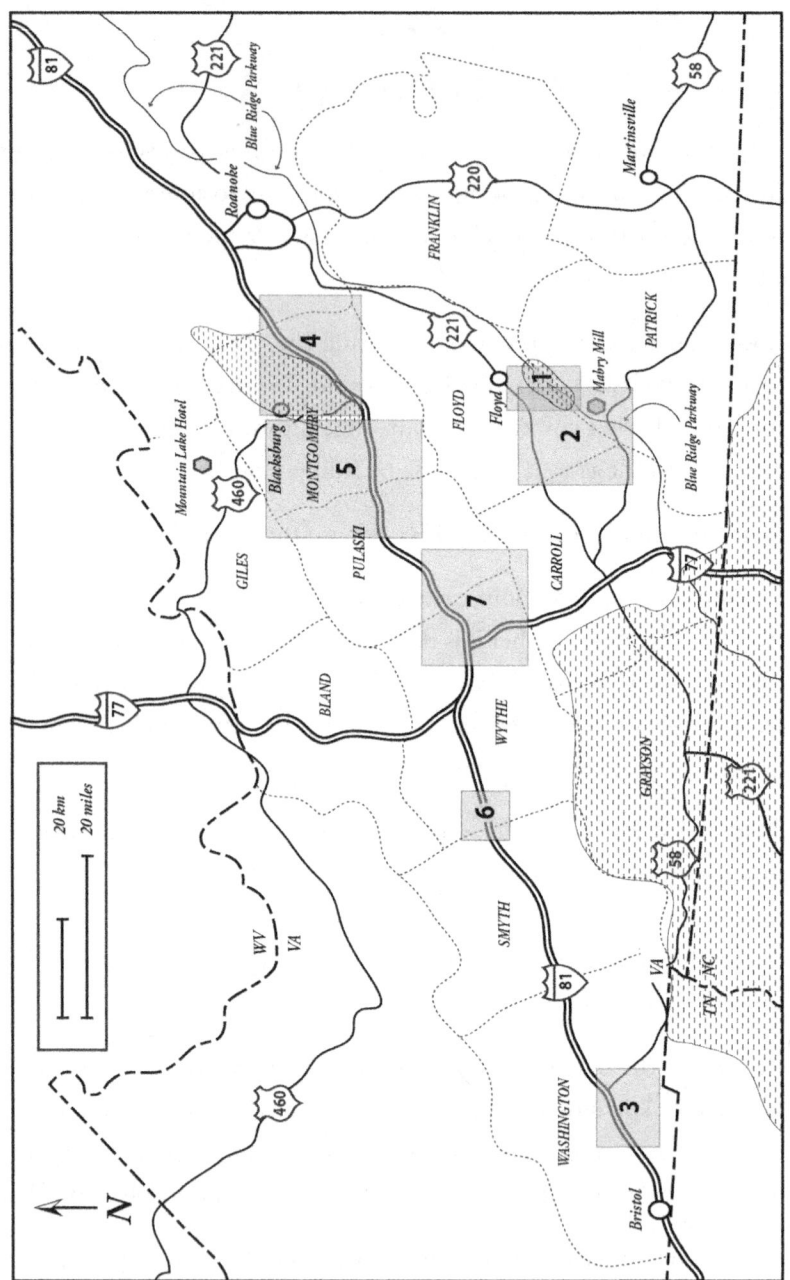

Map 11.0. Blue Ridge Region & Rocky Knob AVA: (1) Floyd; (2) Mabry Mill; (3) Abingdon; (4) Beliveau; (5) Rural Retreat; (6) Max Meadows/Pulaski; (7) Radford.

11. BLUE RIDGE & ROCKY KNOB AVA

The Blue Ridge Mountains stretch from Virginia's border with Maryland down into North Carolina. The Blue Ridge is the easternmost ridge of the Appalachian Mountain chain, and its southern portions have some of the highest elevations in the United States east of the Rocky Mountains, with some peaks in North Carolina and Tennessee reaching over 6,000 feet above sea level. As one would expect given these heights, summers in the Blue Ridge wine region are cooler than elsewhere in the state. Along with the Heart of Appalachia region, this area has the highest average precipitation in all Virginia, with just over 47 inches per year.

The Blue Ridge's wineries capture the full range of winery sizes and experiences in Virginia. From Chateau Morrisette's expansive grounds and on-site restaurant to the more intimate experience at Blacksnake Meadery, the Blue Ridge offers something for every visitor's tastes and preferences. Two of its wineries—Chateau Morrisette and Villa Appalaccia—are in the Rocky Knob AVA, the smallest AVA in Virginia, while Beliveau Estate is in the North Fork of the Roanoke AVA. (The Appalachian High Country AVA lies mostly in North Carolina and Tennessee though it does reach into Virginia as well.)

Things to see and do: Rich in natural beauty, the Blue Ridge area is perfect for nature lovers, offering multiple trails, camping sites, and fishing spots. The 469-mile Blue Ridge Parkway stretches from Waynesboro down into North Carolina (its northern extension, the Skyline Drive, meanders northward to Front Royal). It is a lovely driving tour that is popular in summer for its access to outdoor activities and in the fall for its colorful foliage displays. The Parkway's website (www.blueridgeparkway.org) lists special events and programs, fishing and hiking information, and weather closures.

Mabry Mill in Floyd County at Blue Ridge Milepost (MP) 176 is one of the most picturesque and photographed structures in the area. In addition, there are several living history sites along the Parkway in the summer, including the mid-19th century Johnson Farm and Aunt Polly's Ordinary at MP 85 in the Peaks of Otter. The Blue Ridge region is also home to one of Virginia's only two natural lakes, Mountain Lake, whose size can vary considerably due to leakage from a natural crevice in the lake bottom. The Mountain Lake Conservancy Hotel was featured in the 1987 film *Dirty Dancing* and offers special *Dirty Dancing* weekends in the summer for guests.

The Blue Ridge Region is also home to the eastern and southern portions of the Crooked Road Heritage Trail, a scenic trail that winds from Rocky Mount to Floyd, then to Stuart, where it follows U.S. Route 58 westward through Abingdon and Bristol. The trail features numerous events and places highlighting the region's deep bluegrass music history and culture. Downloadable maps and other information can be accessed at www.thecrookedroad.org.

Wine Trails: The Mountain Road Wine Experience has seven wineries in the Blue Ridge and South Virginia regions. More details are included in Appendix 1.

Handy Guide to Virginia Wineries

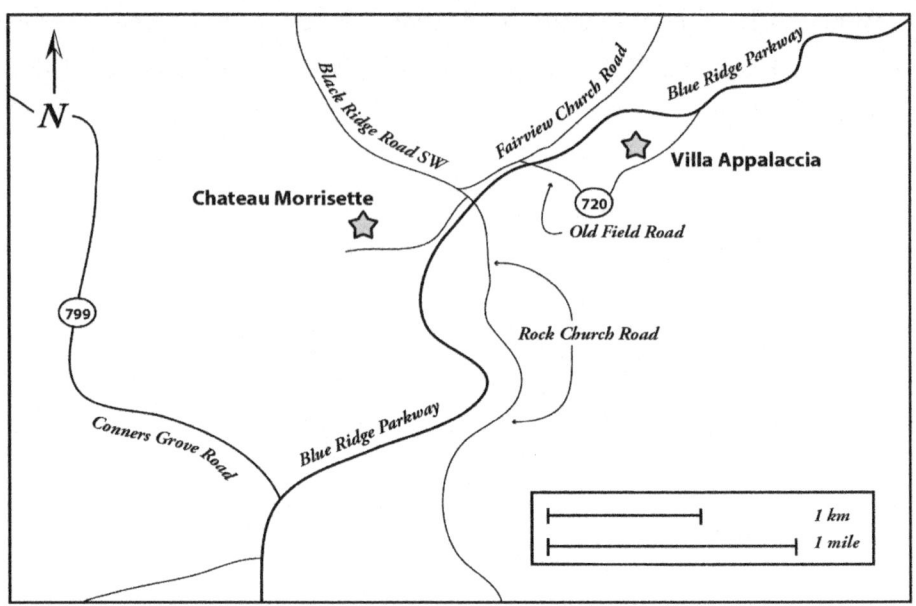

Map 11.1. Floyd

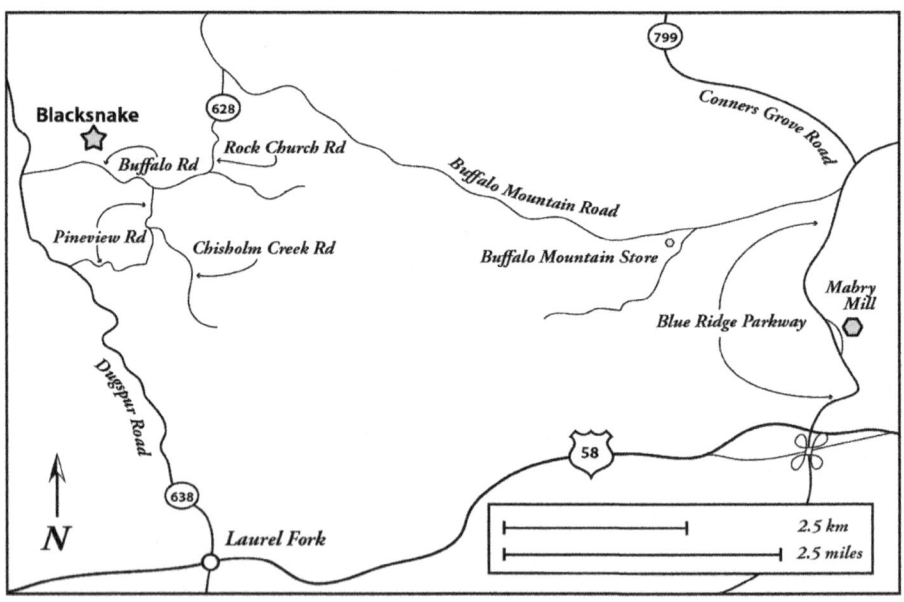

Map 11.2. Mabry Mill

BLUE RIDGE PARKWAY

Blacksnake Meadery
605 Buffalo Road
Dugspur VA 24325

Hours: Sa 11:00–5:00 (mid-Apr–Oct, but always call first) 540-834-6172
Closed Nov–mid-Apr www.blacksnakemead.com
E-mail: blacksnake@blacksnakemead.com

Teachers Steve and Joanne Villers started their meadery after several years making their own home brews. Honeybees on their Blue Ridge property now supply about half of the honey used in their production. Their meads include traditional mead as well as cyser (pressed apple cider and honey), melomel (mead with fruit), and hydromel (light mead). Blacksnake offers honey tastings and occasional holiday open houses; check the website and Facebook for details. Children are welcome.

Meads: Meloluna, Red Queen *(mead with coffee)*, Sweet Virginia, Wildflower Honey Wine.

Hydromel: Cherry Bee Brew, Ginger Bee Brew, Hoppy Bee Brew, Lime Bee Brew.

Price Range: $12–$21

Purchasing: Online to AK, AZ, CO, DC, FL, GA, IA, ID, IL, IN, KS, LA, MA, MD, ME, MN, MO, NC, ND, NE, NH, NM, NV, NY, OH, OR, PA, SC, TN, TX, VA, WA, WI, WV, and WY.

Directions: From U.S. Route 58 at the village of Laurel Fork, drive north on Dugspur Road (Route 638) for 5 miles. Turn right onto Buffalo Road (Route 628). Continue 0.6 miles and turn left into the second driveway.

Chateau Morrisette Winery
291 Winery Road SW
Floyd VA 24091

Hours: Tu–Th 11:00–5:00, F–Sa 11:00–7:00
Closed New Year's, Thanksgiving Eve & Day,
Christmas Eve & Day, New Year's Day

540-593-2865
www.thedogs.com
E-mail: info@thedogs.com

Chateau Morrisette was established in 1978 when the Morrisette family planted their first vines; it now produces over 60,000 cases of wine annually, making fifteen different wines from 150 acres of vineyards across Virginia as well as from grapes from other states. Chateau Morrisette often sponsors live music, food and wine pairing dinners, and festivals. Proceeds from several special wine label series support various charities, such as a Virginia Tech scholarship fund, medical research into canine EPI disease, and Service Dogs of Virginia and St. Francis Service Dogs. When open, the winery restaurant offers lunch and dinner. The facilities may also be rented for private parties and weddings. Children and leashed pets are welcome.

Ciders: Barrel Aged, Cherry Ginger.

Fruit Wines: Blackberry, Cherry, Farmhouse Sangria Red, Sweet Mountain Apple.

White Wines: Chardonnay, Petit Manseng, Pinot Grigio, Vidal Blanc, Viognier.

Rosé Wines: Rosé.

Red Wines: Archival, Black Dog, Cabernet Franc, Cabernet Sauvignon, Chambourcin, Merlot, Petit Verdot.

Sweet/Dessert Wines: Frosty Dog, Our Dog Blue, Red Mountain Laurel, Sweet Mountain Laurel.

Fortified Wines: Heritage *(port-style)*.

Price Range: $12–$34

Tastings: $10 per person for a flight.

Groups: Reservations required for groups of 12 or more.

ADA accessible.

Purchasing: Online for residents of VA and most other states; contact the winery for specifics.

Directions: From the Blue Ridge Parkway, turn west onto Black Ridge Road between Milepost 171 and 172. Take an immediate left onto Winery Road; the winery will be about ½ mile on right.

Villa Appalaccia Winery
752 Rock Castle Gorge
Floyd VA 24091

Hours: W–F 11:00–5:00, Sa 11:00–6:00, Su 12:00–4:30 (May–Nov)　　540-593-3100
Sa 11:00–5:00, Su 12:00–4:30 (Mar–Apr)　　www.villaappalaccia.com
Closed Dec–Mar　　E-mail: tim.block@villaappalaccia.com

Located just one mile from Chateau Morrisette, Villa Appalaccia was founded in 1995 by Stephen Haskill and Susanne Becker and is now owned by Julie and Tim Block who purchased the winery after Tim retired from a 40-year-career in the restaurant industry, spent largely in the southeastern United States and in Asia. The Blocks plan to continue Villa Appalacia's focus on Italian varietals, including Primitivo, Malvasia, Aglianico, and Corvina Veronese. In addition to indoor and covered seating on the upper terrace, visitors may relax in the music garden or play on the bocce court. Cheeses, meats, and breads are available for purchase.

White Wines: Pinot Grigio, Vidal Blanc.

Rosé Wines: Rosa.

Red Wines: Cabernet Franc, Corvina, Rustico, Sangiovese.

Sweet/Dessert Wines: Raspberry Taxi.

Price Range: $19–$24

Tastings: $7 per person for a flight.

Restrictions: No groups over 6.

Purchasing: Online to AK, AZ, CO, DC, FL, GA, HI, IA, ID, IL, IN, KS, LA, MA, MD, ME, MN, MO, NC, ND, NE, NH, NM, NV, NY, OH, OR, PA, SC, TN, TX, VA, VT, WA, WI, WV, and WY.

Directions: From the Blue Ridge Parkway, turn east onto Old Field Road (Route 720) between Milepost 170 and 172; there are two entrances to Old Field Road, one between MP 170 and 171, and another between MP 171 and 172. Follow Old Field Road (unpaved) to the winery driveway.

TASTING ROOM ETIQUETTE

Visiting wineries and trying their wines can be a pleasant and enjoyable way to spend an afternoon. The pandemic has changed some things (more wine flights, fewer guided tastings, for instance), but there are still several common elements to the experience:

1. Bring your I.D. along, especially if you are under forty. You'll need to prove you're old enough to consume alcohol.

2. By all means, ask questions about the wine, even in a self-guided tasting flight.

3. Wines are tasted in a particular order. The usual progression is sparkling to still, white to red, and dry to sweet. Dessert wines will always come last, with fortified wines (if available) closing out the tasting.

4. Even small pours add up to a lot of wine. Consider this: ten wines on a tasting list, with half-ounce pours for each, adds up to five ounces or one full glass of wine. Pace yourself. Even better, have a designated driver.

5. Remember that all Virginia wineries have the right to refuse service to guests who are visibly intoxicated. And the only alcohol allowed on the premises must have been produced by that winery itself.

6. Most important of all, enjoy yourself! Trying different wines is the best way to figure out the kinds of wines you like best.

Handy Guide to Virginia Wineries

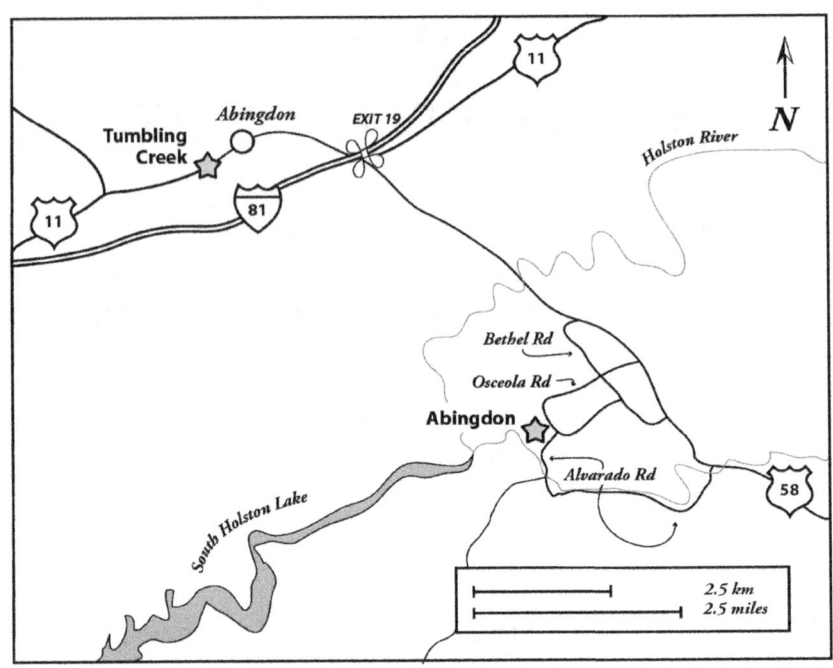

Map 11.3. Abingdon

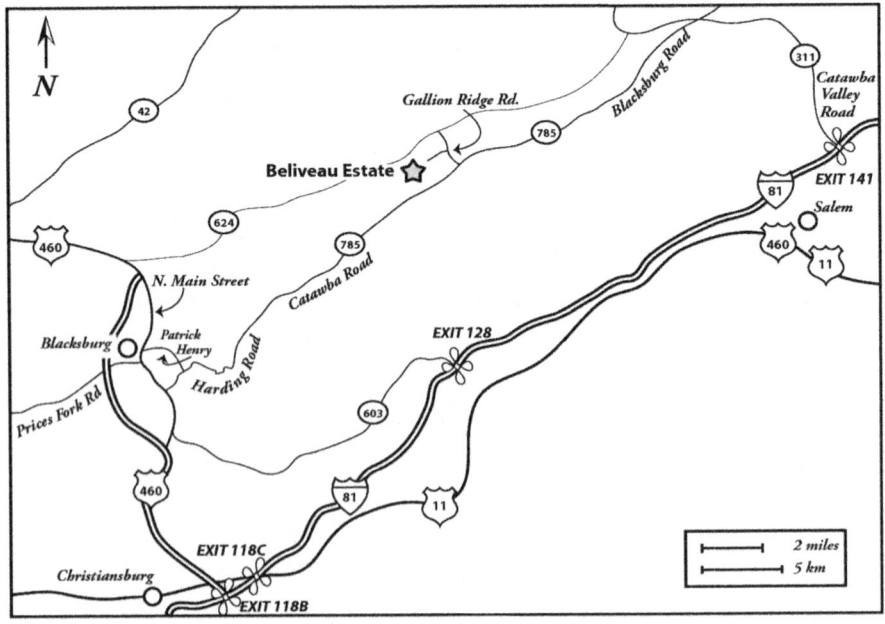

Map 11.4. Beliveau

BLUE RIDGE/I-81

Abingdon Vineyards
20530 Alvarado Road
Abingdon VA 24211

Hours: W–Su 1200–8:00 (May–Oct); 276-623-1255
W–Su 12:00–6:00 (Nov–Apr) www.abingdonvineyards.com
Closed New Year's, Easter, Thanksgiving, Christmas   E-mail: info@abingdonvineyards.com

Abingdon Winery is on the banks of the scenic South Holston River. First founded twenty years ago, the 53-acre property was purchased in 2018 by Elizabeth and Loren Gardner who decided to relocate to Virginia from northern California after helping their best friends move to the area. Guests can opt for indoor seating or outside on the grounds; a heated patio and fire pits are available in chilly weather. Abingdon is close to a number of boating, hiking, and camping sites, with the Virginia Creeper Trail a mere half-mile away and the Appalachian Trail just five miles down the road in Damascus, Virginia. Light snacks and platters are available for purchase in the tasting room.

White Wines: Steel Strings, White Oak.

Rosé Wines: Hindsight, Rainbow Rosé, Riverside Rosé.

Red Wines: Game Changer, Home Town Red, Red Hawk.

Sweet/Dessert Wines: Honeysuckle, Riesling, Sweet Siren.

Fortified Wines: Pioneer Port.

Price Range: $25–$45

Tastings: $16 per person.

Handy Guide to Virginia Wineries

Groups: Reservations requested for groups of 15 or more.

Purchasing: Online to AK, AZ, CA, CO, DC, FL, GA, HI, IA, ID, IL, IN, KS, LA, MA, MD, ME, MN, MO, NC, ND, NE, NH, NM, NV, NY, OH, OK, OR, PA, SC, TN, TX, VA, VT, WA, WI, WV, and WY.

Directions: From I-81, take Exit 19 onto U.S. Route 58 East. Turn right after 5 miles onto Osceola Road (Route 722). Drive 2.4 miles and turn right onto Alvarado Road, immediately after a sharp turn; the winery driveway will be on the right.

Beliveau Farm
3899 Eakin Farm Road
(on some GPS units: 5415 Gallion Ridge Road)
Blacksburg VA 24060

Hours: W–Su 12:00–6:00 (F to 8:00, spring–Oct)   540-961-0505
Closed New Year's, Thanksgiving, Christmas   www.beliveaufarm.com
E-mail: wine@beliveauestate.com

Joyce and Yvan Beliveau opened their winery in 2012, three years after planting their first vineyard and five years after establishing their bed & breakfast inn on a 165-acre property located twelve miles from Blacksburg. Visitors can enjoy scenic views of the hills and ponds from the tasting room's covered verandas over gourmet pizza or a cheese plate. Beliveau sponsors a Lavender Festival the last Sunday in June, as well as Tapas Nights and other special events. The facilities are available for weddings and private events. In addition to their predominately estate-grown wines, Beliveau now produces a range of gluten-free beers made from malted rice, millet, and buckwheat.

The Inn at Beliveau Estate offers five guest rooms for overnight stays; special packages are available.

White Wines: Afternoon Delight *(Chardonel, Vidal Blanc)*, Destiny *(Vidal Blanc)*, Pristine *(Chardonel)*.

Rosé Wines: Blacksburg Blush *(Chambourcin, Niagara)*.

Red Wines: Acapella *(Chambourcin, Merlot, Cabernet Franc)*, Cabernet Franc, Duchess *(Tempranillo, Pinot Noir)*, Fireside Chat *(Cabernet Franc)*, Merlot, Petit Verdot, Soul Singer *(Chambourcin)*, Sunset Sipper *(Cabernet Franc, Merlot)*, Syrah.

Sweet/Dessert Wines: Crown Jewel *(Vidal Blanc, Traminette)*, Discovery *(Niagara)*, Lovers' Quest *(Chardonel, Vidal Blanc)*, Sweet Surrender *(Concord)*, Warm Glow *(Chambourcin)*.

Fortified Wines: Transformation *(port-style Chambourcin)*.

Price Range: $15–$38

Tastings: $15–$20 per person for a flight.

Purchasing: Online to AK, AZ, CO, DC, FL, GA, HI, IA, ID, IN, KS, LA, MA, MD, ME, MN, MO, NC, ND, NE, NH, NM, NV, NY, OH, OK, OR, PA, SC, TN, TX, VA, VT, WA, WI, WV, and WY.

Directions: **If driving on I-81 from the North,** take Exit 141 (New Castle). Turn left at the exit onto North Electric Road and drive ¼ mile. Take a right onto Catawba Valley Drive (Route 311 North) and continue 7 miles. Turn left onto Blacksburg Road (Route 785) and drive another 10 miles. Take a sharp right onto Gallion Ridge Road (Route 630). The winery entrance and drive will be 1 mile on the left.

If driving on I-81 from the South, take Exit 118B toward Christiansburg/Blacksburg. Merge onto U.S. Route 460 West towards Virginia Tech. After one mile, continue onto U.S. Route 460 West and drive another 13 miles through Blacksburg. Turn right onto Coal Bank Hollow Road (Route 649). Drive about a mile and a half, and turn left onto Mt. Tabor Road (Route 624). Continue another 8 miles and turn right onto Gallion Ridge Road (Route 630). The winery entrance and drive will be 0.7 miles on the right.

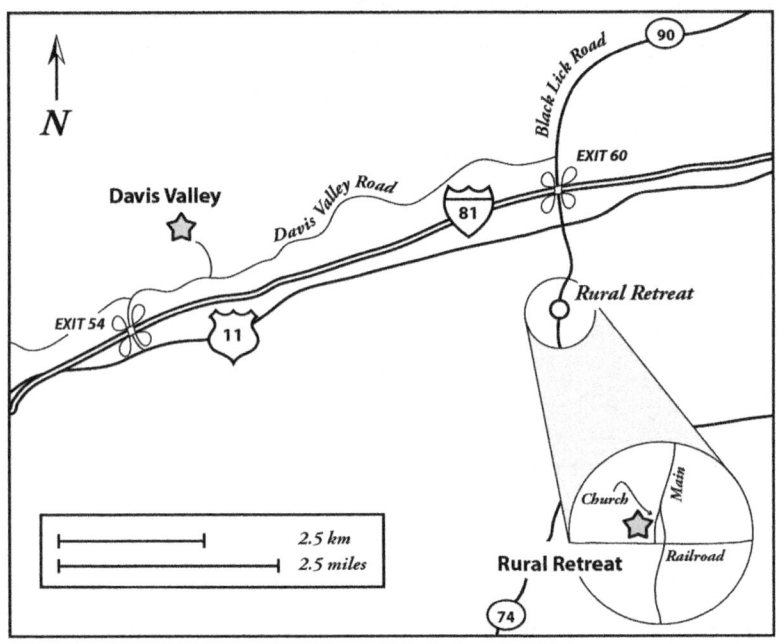

Map 11.5. Rural Retreat

Davis Valley Winery & Vineyard
1167 Davis Valley Road
Rural Retreat VA 24368

Hours: M–F, 9:30–4:30, Sa 9:00–4:00
Closed New Year's, Thanksgiving, Christmas

276-686-8855
www.davisvalleywinery.com
E-mail: info@davisvalleywinery.com

After Rusty and Ruth Rhea Cox purchased this scenic hilltop property, they converted the former dairy farm to a vineyard, with plantings that include Maréchal Foch, Norton, Corot Noir, and Steuben. Visitors can sample a flight of wines on a hundred-year-old bar in their tasting room. The winery may be rented for special events, dinners, and weddings.

Davis Valley also has a distillery on-site, producing vodka, solera-style whiskey, Owen Cox whiskies, and Appalachian Moon moonshine.

White Wines: Appalachian Breeze, Chardonnay, Davis Valley White, Virginia Breeze White.

Red Wines: Autumn Red, Cabernet Franc, Chambourcin, Davis Valley Red *(Maréchal Foch)*, Norton, Virginia Breeze Red *(Steuben)*.

Price Range: $14–$23

Tastings: $5 per person.

Directions: From I-81, take Exit 54 (Grose Close). Turn north onto Winsor Road, which will bend right and become Davis Valley Road (portions unpaved). Continue 1.4 miles to the winery on the left.

Iron Heart Winery
3742 Boone Furnace Road
Allisonia VA 24347

Hours: Sa 12:00–5:00, Su 1:00–5:00
Closed New Year's, Easter, Christmas

540-320-0203
www.iheartvirginiawine.com
E-mail: ironheartvineyard@farissfarms.com

Iron Heart was launched in 2016 by Adam Farriss and his late father, Dr. Bruce Farris, on their fourth-generation family farm, six years after starting a commercial vineyard. The winery name honors the Reed Island Iron Company that operated in Allisonia from 1881 to 1906. Both indoor and outdoor seating is available, including canopy-covered chairs overlooking Little Reed Island Creek. In addition to trying Iron Heart's wines, visitors can enjoy the ample fishing, rafting, and hiking opportunities throughout the scenic New River Valley. Iron Heart has plans to open the Salty Stash distillery on-site in late 2021.

The winery also offers several high-end restored cabins that can be rented for overnight stays or private events; see the website for details.

White Wines: Bell Ringer (white sangria), Chardonnay, Riesling, Vidal Blanc.

Rosé Wines: Chasing the Red *(Chambourcin)*, Work Water Blush.

Red Wines: Cabernet Franc, Chambourcin, Plush Run, Ting-a-Ling (red sangria).

Price Range: $15–$23

Tastings: $6–$14 per person.

Purchasing: Online to AK, AZ, CO, DC, FL, GA, HI, IA, ID, IN, KS, LA, MA, MD, ME, MN, MO, NC, ND, NE, NH, NM, NV, NY, OH, OK, OR, PA, SC, TN, TX, VA, VT, WA, WI, WV, and WY.

Directions: From I-81, take Exit 89A (Draper) onto VA Route 100 South and drive 6.7 miles. Turn left onto Gardner Road (Route 608) which will become Boone Furnace Road after 2.3 miles. Continue another 0.6 miles to Farris Farms and the winery entrance.

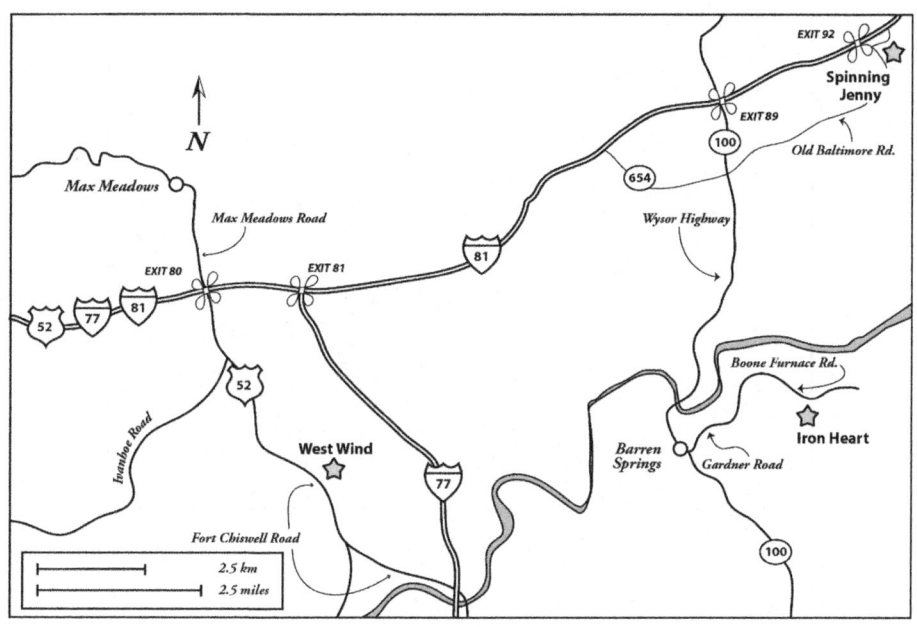

Map 11.6. Max Meadows/Pulaski

New River Vineyard & Winery
6750 Falling Branch Road
Fairlawn VA 24141

Hours: F 5:00–3:00, Sa 12:00–5:00, Su 1:00–5:00 (Apr–Dec) 540-633-0033
Sa only 12:00–5:00 (Jan–Mar) www.nrvwine.com
Closed New Year's, Easter, Christmas E-mail: newrivervineyard@gmail.com

The Wallen family first decided to enter the winery business in 2011, planting vines on their hillside property overlooking the town of Radford and the scenic New River Valley. In warmer weather, visitors can relax and enjoy the view from the patio, which offers both covered and open seating. Light snacks are available for purchase. New River also offers live music on many weekends. The tasting room can be rented for private parties.

Fruit Wines: Bearly Pear, Colonel Luze *(raspberry/tea)*, Country Apple, Sneaky Peach.

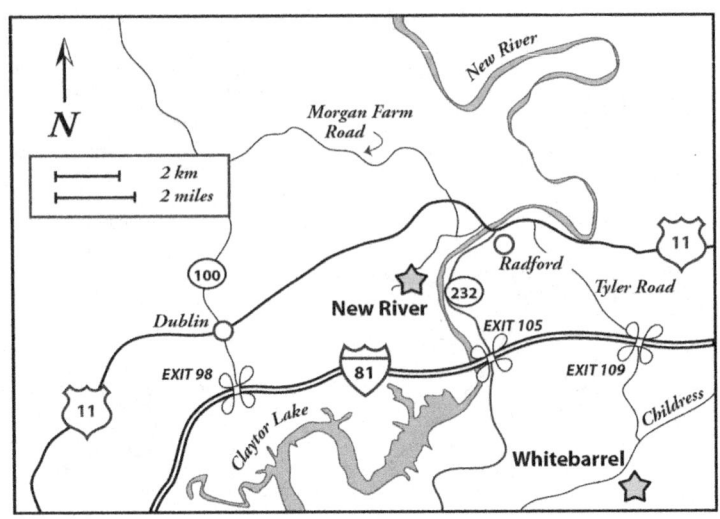

Map 11.7. Radford

White Wines: Sauvignon Blanc, Vidal Blanc, Vino Secco *(Muscadine)*, Traminette, Viognier.

Rosé Wines: Amore *(Catawba)*, Bad Wolf *(Muscadine)*.

Red Wines: Frontenac, Léon Millot, Prince of Darkness *(Merlot, cranberry)*.

Sweet/Dessert Wines: Carlos *(Muscadine)*, Depot Red *(Concord)*.

Price Range: $15–$30

Tastings: $5–$10 per person.

Groups: Reservations requested for groups of 4 or more.

Purchasing: Online to VA.

Directions: From I-81, take Exit 105 (Radford/Route 232) and turn north onto West Main Street (Route 232). Drive 4 miles and turn left onto U.S. Route 11 South. After crossing the New River Bridge, turn left onto Hazel Hollow Road (Route 626) and drive ½ mile. Turn right onto Falling Branch Road (Route 798). Drive another 1.8 miles to the winery on the right.

Rural Retreat Winery & Dye's Vineyards
201 Church Street
Rural Retreat VA 24368

Hours: Tu–Sa 11:00–5:30
Closed New Year's, Thanksgiving, Christmas

276-686-8300
www.ruralretreatwinery.com
E-mail: info@ruralretreatwinery.com

Rural Retreat is owned and operated by Scott and Linda Mecimore, who purchased Dye's Vineyards and Winery in 2007. The tasting room is located in a combination gift shop and eat-in deli, with the tasting bar toward the back. Children are welcome. The winery also offers a two-bedroom suite for overnight stays.

White Wines: Chardonnay, Riesling, Rural Retreat Blanc *(Riesling)*, Sweet Kitty White, Viognier.

Rosé Wines: Chambourcin Rosé.

Red Wines: Cabernet Franc, Cardinal Red, Chambourcin, Cripple Creek, Heart of Appalachia *(Steuben)*, Sweet Gracie Red.

Price Range: $10–$20

Tastings: $4.50 per person.

Purchasing: Online to AK, AZ, CO, DC, FL, GA, HI, IA, ID, IN, KS, LA, MA, MD, ME, MN, MO, NC, ND, NE, NH, NM, NV, NY, OH, OK, OR, PA, SC, TN, TX, VA, VT, WA, WI, WV, and WY.

Directions: From I-81 take Exit 60 onto Route 90 South toward Rural Retreat and drive 1.6 miles. Turn right onto Railroad Avenue and make an immediate right onto Church Street and the winery on the left.

Spinning Jenny Vineyard
2664 Old Route 100 Road
Draper VA 24324

Hours: F 1:00–7:00, Sa–Su 1:00–6:00 (summer)
Closed New Year's, Easter, Christmas

540-922-9829
www.spinningjennyvineyard.com
E-mail: drapergraper@gmail.com

Named for a tool that spins out wire, Spinning Jenny Vineyard was launched by Jennifer and Curtis Brown who decided to transform part of their 37-acre farm into a vineyard and winery in late 2014, officially opening to the public in 2019. Light snacks can be purchased in the tasting room. For outdoor enthusiasts, Spinning Jenny is located on the Transamerica Cycling Route 76 and near the New River Trail State Park.

White Wines: Chardonnay, Vidal Blanc, Viognier.

Red Wines: Cabernet, Chambourcin.

Price Range: $16–$20

Tastings: $7–$12 per person.

Directions: From I-81, take Exit 92 (Draper). Turn south onto Greenbrier Road (Route 658). After 0.2 miles, bear left onto Old Route 100. The winery entrance will be 0.2 miles on the right.

Tumbling Creek Cider Company
112 Court Street NE
Abingdon VA 24210

Hours: M–Tu 1:00–7:00, W–Sa 1:00–10:00, Su 12:00–7:00   276-477-7444
Closed New Year's, Easter, Christmas   www.tumblingcreekcider.com
E-mail: TC3@tumblingcreekcider.com

Partners Justen Dick, Tom McMullen, Jerry Bresowar, and Mark Finney opened Tumbling Creek in 2018, naming their cider for a creek that tumbles through the Clinch Mountain area. They use heritage apples from their own orchard and other local producers to make hand-pressed ciders at Justen's family farm. The cider hosts food trucks and live music on select weekends and has displays by local artists in the tasting room.

Ciders: Hellbender, High Trestle, Moonshot, Ridgerunner, Smoked Apple, Whitetop.

Price Range: $7–$12

Directions: From I-81, take Exit 19 (Abingdon/Damascus) onto U.S. Route 11 South toward Abingdon. Drive 2 miles into Abingdon and turn right onto Court Street NE. The cidery taproom will be on the right.

West Wind Farm Winery
180 West Wind Drive
(Alternate GPS address: 2228 Fort Chiswell Road)
Max Meadows VA 24360

Hours: M–Sa 11:00–6:00, Su 1:00–6:00   276-699-2020
Closed New Year's, Easter, Thanksgiving, Christmas   www.westwindwine.com
E-mail: info@westwindwine.com

West Wind is owned and operated by Paul and Brenda Hric on a family farm that has been in Brenda's family for four generations. The Hrics began planting their five-acre vineyard in 2003 and made their first wine in 2005. West Wind offers both indoor and outdoor seating, as well as a gift shop with candles, glassware, and pottery. The winery hosts live music at its Summer Saturdays concerts, as well as various festivals, including a fall Wine and Swine barbecue. The facilities may be rented for private events and dinners. The winery is certified Virginia Green. Children and leashed dogs are welcome

Fruit Wines: Galena Creek Blackberry, Galena Creek Peach.

White Wines: Galena Creek White, Gewurztraminer, Pinot Gris, Riesling.

Red Wines: Cabernet Sauvignon, Chambourcin, Galena Creek Red, Merlot.

Sweet/Dessert Wines: New River Red *(Concord)*, New River White *(Niagara)*.

Price Range: $13–$19

Tastings: Complimentary tasting of 3 wines, $5 for full list.

Groups: Reservations required for buses and groups of 8 or more.

Directions: From I-80/I-77, take Exit 80 at Fort Chiswell. Follow Fort Chiswell Road (U.S. Route 52) south for 4 miles to the winery entrance on the left, just past Archer Drive.

Whitebarrel Winery
4025 Childress Road
Christiansburg VA 24073

Hours: M–Th 4:00–8:00, F–Sa 12:00–8:00, Su 12:00–6:00
Closed New Year's, Thanksgiving, Christmas

540-382-7619
www.whitebarrel.com
E-mail: wine@whitebarrel.com

New Jersey native **Rik Obiso** established Whitebarrel Winery in 2007 after returning to southwestern Virginia where he had been a student at Virginia Tech some years earlier. The 16-acre vineyard was first planted that same year, with Whitebarrel's first harvest three years later. Drawing on his biotechnology experience, Rik built his knowledge of winemaking and now produces a range of wines. Light snacks and tapas are available for purchase at the tasting room, which offers both indoor and outdoor seating for visitors. The winery hosts a range of special events and live music.

Fruit Wines: Bin 101 *(apple)*, Peach, Plum.

White Wines: Bin 704, Chardonnay, Seyval Blanc, Vidal Blanc.

Rosé Wines: Bin 997.

Red Wines: Bin 214, Cabernet Franc, Cabernet Sauvignon, Chambourcin.

Fortified Wines: Bin 831 *(port-style)*.

Price Range: $20–$49

Tastings: $5 per person; $1 per taste for reserve tasting.

Groups: Reservations requested for groups of 10 or more.

Purchasing: Online to AK, AL, AZ, CA, CO, DC, FL, GA, HI, IA, ID, IN, KS, LA, MA, MD, ME, MN, MO, ND, NE, NH, NM, NV, NY, OH, OR, PA, SC, TN, TX, VA, WA, WI, WV, and WY.

Directions: From I-81, take Exit 109 (Radford) south onto Tyler Road (Route 177). Drive 3 miles and turn right onto Childress Road. The winery entrance will be 1 mile on the left.

Handy Guide to Virginia Wineries

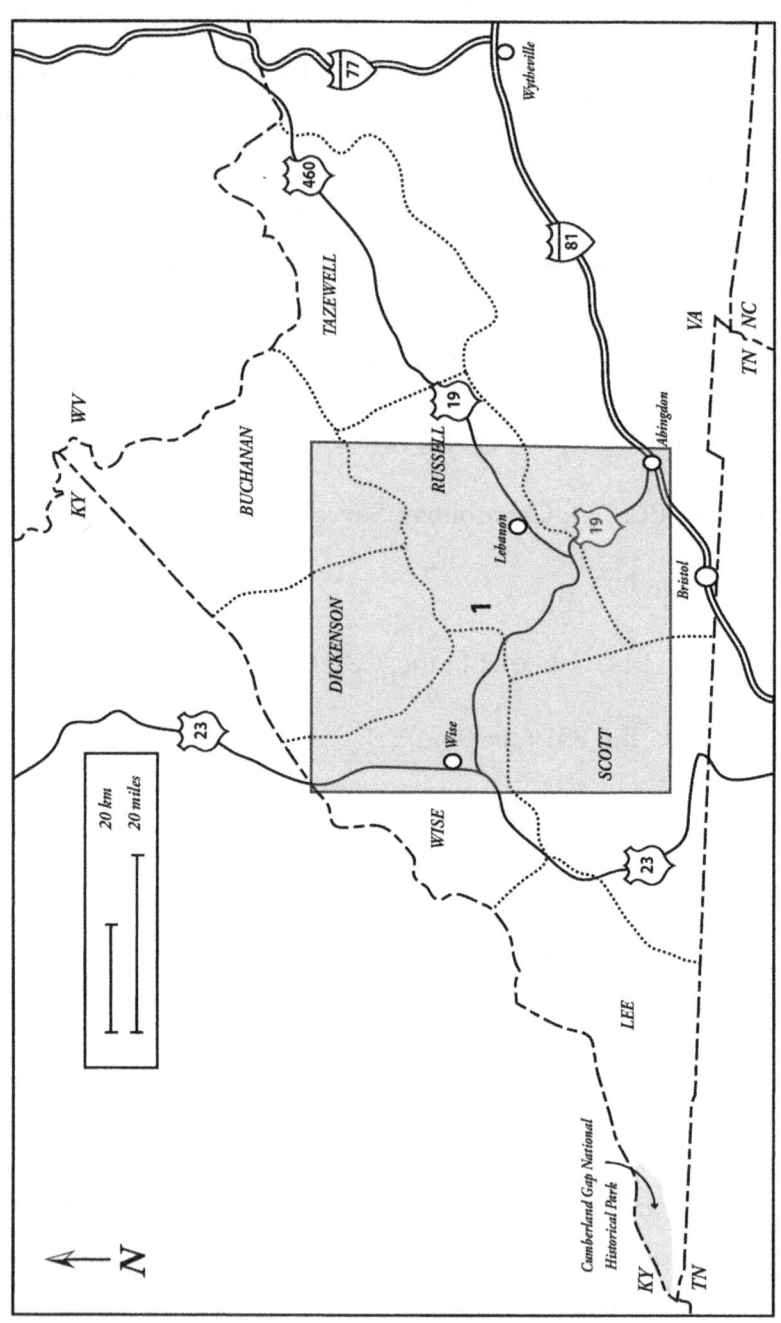

Map 12.0. Heart of Appalachia Region: (1) Heart of Appalachia

12. HEART OF APPALACHIA

The mountainous southwest corner of Virginia is an area of scenic and rugged natural beauty where river gorges cut through spectacular sandstone cliffs and rich coal seams streak through the rock formations. With its high elevations, the region has the coolest summer temperatures and highest precipitation in the state. The region's two wineries offer an intimate experience unique to the region. MountainRose honors the region's long coal-mining history in its wine names, while Vincent's Vineyard is a haven for fly-fishermen (and women).

<u>Things to see and do:</u> Multiple scenic drives allow nature lovers to enjoy the region's fall foliage. The area offers many opportunities for hiking, camping, and fishing. The region's coal mining history was depicted in John Fox's *Trail of the Lonesome Pine*, a 1913 novel adapted for film in 1936. The Heart of Appalachia Driving Tour leads visitors through various sites and towns through the region's counties; tour stages can be printed from Virginia's tourism website (www.virginia.org/heartofappalachiadrivingtour/).

The independent-minded people who settled this region brought with them a rich culture that endures in the rhythms and cadences of bluegrass and country music. This is the birthplace of country music legends June Carter Cash and the Carter Family, and Ralph Stanley. Visitors can experience the history and music of the region on the Crooked Road Heritage Trail which winds through ten counties and even more towns with local music festivals and jams; more information, including a map, is available at www.crookedroad.org.

Handy Guide to Virginia Wineries

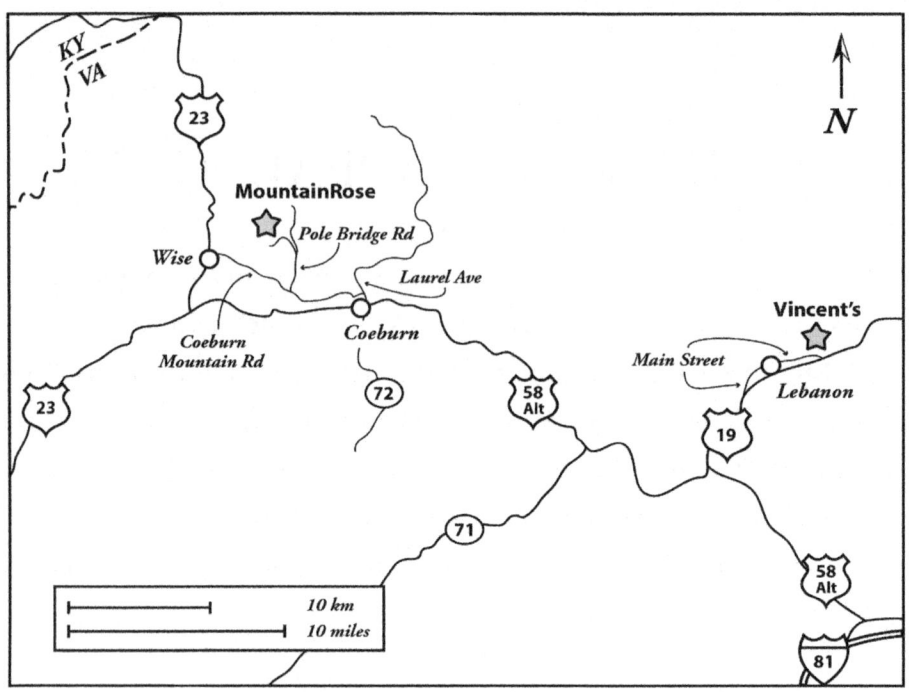

Map 12.1. Heart of Appalachia

HEART OF APPALACHIA

MountainRose Vineyards
10439 North Reservoir Road
Wise VA 24293

Hours: M–Sa 12:00–6:00, Su 1:00–5:00
Closed New Year's, Easter
Thanksgiving, Christmas

276-328-2013
www.mountainrosevineyard.com
E-mail: opie@mountainrosevineyard.com

MountainRose got its start in 1996 when David Lawson first rooted 100 grape vines from an 80-year-old Concord vine on land his family has owned since the 1850s. Fascinated by wine, David subsequently interned at the Williamsburg and Prince Michel wineries and now serves as winemaker. The estate vineyard includes plantings of Niagara, Traminette, and Vidal Blanc; the winery also has a vineyard in neighboring Russell County. In honor of the area's long coal history, the Lawsons have named their wines after old coal seams and are active advocates of reclaiming old strip-mined lands through grape and apple cultivation. MountainRose hosts a range of events at the winery, including festivals, live music, Paint-N-Sip classes, and quilt shows. The winery facilities are available for rental for private parties or weddings. Children are welcome. Please call in advance before visiting.

Sparkling Wines: Kelliokee *(Traminette)*, Persephone *(Concord)*.

White Wines: Blair White, Riesling, Splashdam White, Sweet Mountain-Rose *(Niagara)*.

Blush Wines: Darby Blush *(Chambourcin)*.

Red Wines: Concord, Dorchester Red *(Chambourcin, Tannat)*, Jawbone Red, Pardee Red *(Chambourcin, Chancellor)*.

Sweet/Dessert Wines: Autumn Gold.

Price Range: $11–$21

ADA accessible.

Purchasing: Online to AK, AL, AZ, CA, CO, DC, FL, GA, ID, IL, IA, KS, LA, ME, MD, MA, MN, MO, NE, NV, NH, NM, NY, NC, ND, OH, OR, WC, TN, TX, VA, WA, WV, and WY.

Directions: From the town of Wise, take Darden Drive east. Just past the University of Virginia campus, it will become Coeburn Mountain Road (Route 646). Continue for four miles and turn left onto Pole Bridge Road at Hard Rock Contractors. Follow Pole Bridge Road 1.8 miles and turn left onto North Reservoir Road. The winery driveway will be ½ mile on right.

Vincent's Vineyard
2313 East Main Street
Lebanon VA 24266

Hours: M–Tu, Th–Sa 11:30–5:00 (Apr–Dec) 276-889-2505
Closed Jan–Mar, 4th of July (all week), www.vincentsvineyard.com
Thanksgiving (W–Sa), Christmas (all week) E-mail: vincentsvineyard@yahoo.com

Vincent and Betsy Gilmer established this boutique winery on their sixth-generation family farm in Russell County. The winery's three-acre vineyard and tasting room are located next to Big Cedar Creek, a favorite spot for fly fishing in the foothills of Clinch Mountain. Visitors can sit and enjoy the view of the mountains and the farm's Katahdin sheep from the tasting room, which offers snacks and artisanal crafts for sale. The winery's Melody Acres Farm is available for weddings. Vincent's now has a distillery on-site, with moonshine made from a traditional family recipe. Leashed pets are welcome.

White Wines: Angler's Choice, Shepherd's White, Traminette.

Blush Wines: Make Me Blush *(Chambourcin)*.

Red Wines: Ambrosia *(Steuben)*, Cabernet Franc, Shepherd's Red.

Price Range: $11–$14

Groups: Please call ahead for group tastings.

Purchasing: Online to AK, AL, CA, DC, FL, ID, IL, LA, MN, MO, NE, NV, NH, NM, NC, ND, OH, OR, VA, WV, and WY.

Directions: From I-81, take Exit 17 (Abingdon/South Holston Dam) onto U.S. Route 19 North/U.S. Route 58 Alt. Stay on U.S. Route 19 North for 21.6 miles into Lebanon. Turn left onto East Main Street (U.S. Route 19 Business) at the first light after Walmart. Drive ½ mile to the winery entrance on right, just past Big Cedar Creek Bridge.

APPENDIX 1
VIRGINIA WINE TRAILS

Virginia has a wide range of wine trails giving visitors a nicely organized way of visiting the state's many wineries. The wine trails have a range of features, including several with passport programs that offer reduced tasting fees for visits to multiple wineries. Many also include distilleries or special features, such as cigar-wine tours.

Northern Virginia Region:

Fauquier County Wine Trail (www.visitfauquier.com/things-to-do/wineries)
 Website offers an events calendar, an interactive (and printable) map, as well as links to restaurants, dining, and, of course, wineries.

Loudoun Wine Country (www.visitloudoun.org/drink/wine-country)
 Website has a downloadable wine guide as well as links to wineries, wine tour services, local attractions, and a passport program. Also on Facebook.

Skyline Wine-Whiskey-Beer Trail (www.skylinewinetrail.com)
 Trail features wineries, breweries, distilleries, and cideries near the scenic Skyline Drive through the Shenandoah National Park. Website offers links to sites and attractions. Also on Facebook.

Handy Guide to Virginia Wineries

Shenandoah Valley Region:

Blue Ridge Whiskey Wine Loop (www.discovershenandoah.com/whiskey-wine-loop)
   Includes wineries, breweries, and a distillery from Front Royal to Luray. Website has a printable driving map and a list of attractions, including national parks and caverns. Also on Facebook.

Shenandoah County Wine Trail (www.visitshenandoahcounty.com, then select "Breweries, Wineries, Cideries, Distilleries" under **Experience** in the top toolbar)
   Website has downloadable maps of winery locations in Shenandoah County, links to local attractions, and an online Shenandoah County travel guide.

Shenandoah Spirits Trail (www.shenandoahspiritstrail.com)
   Trail includes wineries, breweries, distilleries, and cideries in the northern Shenandoah Valley area. Website offers a downloadable as well as an interactive trail map, and links to attractions. Also on Facebook.

Shenandoah Valley Wine Trail (http://shenandoahvalleywinetrail.com)
   Website includes an events calendar, links to wineries, local attractions, and a printable Google trail map from Winchester to Augusta County.

Chesapeake Bay/Northern Neck Region:

Chesapeake Bay Wine Trail (www.chesapeakebaywinetrail.com)
   Trail centers on ten wineries in the greater Northern Neck area. Website includes a printable map, dining, lodging, and local attractions, as well as passport program. Also on Facebook.

Central Virginia Region

Foothills Scenic Wine Trail (www.foothillsscenicwinetrail.com)
Website has an events calendar and downloadable maps of the two wineries near Old Rag Mountain and the Shenandoah National Park.

Heart of Virginia Wine Trail (http://hovawinetrail.com)
Passport program includes tastings at five wineries, souvenir glass, entry for prize drawing. Downloadable trail map, events calendar.

Monticello Wine Trail (www.monticellowinetrail.com)
Website has customizable and printable maps that allow visitors to create their own itineraries to over thirty wineries; also includes an events calendar, restaurants, and lodgings. Also on Facebook.

Nelson 151 (http://nelson151.com)
Website offers an events calendar, links to wineries, breweries, cideries, distilleries, restaurants, and lodgings along Route 151, as well as a printable map. Also on Facebook.

Hampton Roads Region

Colonial Virginia Wine Trail (http://ccvwt.wpengine.com)
Features five wineries along the James River, with links to the winery websites.

Williamsburg Tasting Trail (https://gowilliamsburg.com/tasting-trail)
Includes wineries, craft breweries, meaderies, and distilleries located in the greater Williamsburg area. Website offers a map, links to activities, and a newsletter.

Handy Guide to Virginia Wineries

Virginia Mountains Region:

Bedford County Wine Trail (www.thebedfordwinetrail.com)
Passport program offering a free wine glass for visiting all the county's wineries. Map with links to festivals, attractions, lodgings, and restaurants.

Wine Trail of Botetourt County (www.botetourtwinetrail.com)
Website includes a downloadable trail map, links to wineries, places to stay, and local attractions. Also on Facebook.

Heart of Appalachia Region:

Heart of Appalachia (www.heartofappalachia.com/)
Interactive map with customizable itineraries including wineries, cideries, distilleries, hiking and bike trails, scenic attractions, camping, and more.

BIBLIOGRAPHY

Frye, Keith. *Roadside Geology of Virginia*. Missoula: Mountain Press Publishing Company, 2001.
Good introduction to the geologic structure and history of Virginia; includes numerous driving trails and maps.

Halliday, James, and Hugh Johnson. *The Art and Science of Wine*. New York: Firefly Books, 2007.
An in-depth exploration of winemaking techniques for a range of noble grape varieties.

Heinemann, Ronald L., et al. *Old Dominion, New Commonwealth: A History of Virginia, 1607-2007*. Charlottesville: University of Virginia Press, 2008.
A good basic overview of the history of Virginia.

James, Victoria. *Drink Pink: A Celebration of Rosé*. New York: HarperCollins, 2017.
A quick and amusing overview of rosé wines worldwide, with multiple recipes in the second half for dishes that pair well with rosé.

Kliman, Todd. *The Wild Vine: A Forgotten Grape and the Untold Story of American Wine*. New York: Clarkson Potter, 2010.
The dual-track story of Virginia's Norton grape and of Jennifer McCloud of Chrysalis Vineyards, who is perhaps the Norton's strongest champion.

Kramer, Matt. *Making Sense of Wine*. Philadelphia: Running Press, 2003.
Elegantly written essay on wine appreciation; includes a number of good recipes and wine pairings.

Kupperman, Karen Ordahl. *The Jamestown Project.* Cambridge: Belknap Press, 2007.
Very readable study of the origins, challenges, and economic development of the Jamestown Colony.

Leahy, Richard. *Beyond Jefferson's Vines: The Evolution of Quality Wines in Virginia.* CreateSpace, 2014.
Overview of the history of modern winemaking in the state by one of Virginia's experts on wine.

Lukacs, Paul. *American Vintage: The Rise of American Wine.* Boston: Houghton Mifflin, 2000.
Excellent short history of the American wine industry, from its earliest days to the present.

McCusker, John. *The Economy of British America, 1607-1789.* Chapel Hill: University of North Carolina Press, 1991.
Scholarly examination and comparison of the economic development of the original thirteen American colonies and the Caribbean.

Pinney, Thomas. *A History of Wine in America, Volume One: From the Beginnings to Prohibition.* Berkeley: University of California Press, 1999. And *A History of Wine in America, Volume Two: From Prohibition to the Present.* Berkeley: University of California Press, 2005.
An outstanding and highly detailed two-volume history of winemaking in the United States.

Puckette, Madeline, and Justin Hammack. *Wine Folly: The Master Guide.* New York: Avery Press, 2018.
Wonderful introduction to wine and wine tasting, including a review of 100 common wine grapes and blends.

Robinson, Jancis. *The 24-Hour Wine Expert.* New York: Abrams Books, 2016.

A quck and entertaining overview of wines and wine tasting from one of the most knowledgeable and informative experts in the world.

Robinson, Jancis, and Linda Murphy. *American Wine: The Ultimate Companion to the Wines and Wineries of the United States.* Berkley, Los Angeles: University of California Press, 2012.

Excellent encyclopedia of American wine history and production, including the major wine regions and varieties.

Robinson, Jancis. *How To Taste: A Guide to Enjoying Wine.* New York: Simon & Schuster, 2008.

Very good introduction to wine tasting aimed at helping readers develop good palette pictures of the noble grape varieties.

Robinson, Jancis, ed., *The Oxford Companion to Wine.* Oxford: Oxford University Press, 2015.

A comprehensive wine encyclopedia for the true wine geek, covering wine grapes, regions, and growing methods, among other topics.

Robinson, Jancis, with Julia Harding and José Vouillamoz. *Wine Grapes.* New York: Harper-Collins, 2012.

An encyclopedia of the origins and flavors of 1,368 wine varieties.

Rowe, Walker Elliott. *A History of Virginia Wines: From Grapes to Glass.* Charleston: History Press, 2009.

A short general overview of Virginia's wine industry, including some winemaker interviews (no index).

Sanderson, Shea. *From Cabernet to Zinfandel: Flavors, Pairings, and Personalities of the World's Most Popular Wines.* Nouveau Press, 2020.
A light-hearted and highly readable look at 25 popular wine varieties.

Simonetti-Bryan, Jennifer. *The Everyday Guide to Wine* (DVD). Chantilly: The Great Courses, 2010.
An entertaining and informative video introduction to wine and wine tasting. (Be patient: Great Courses has frequent sales on this!)

Simonetti-Bryan, Jennifer. *Rosé Wine: The Guide to Drinking Pink.* New York: Sterling Epicure, 2017.
A highly readable and informative guide to the production and enjoyment of rosé wines by a wine expert who makes wine and wine appreciation approachable for everyone.

GLOSSARY OF WINE TERMS

Aglianico *(ah-lee-AH-nee-koh)*: A dark-skinned grape variety of Greek origin generally cultivated in the south of Italy, known for its dark ruby color and assertive flavor; the name is a corruption of *Ellenico*, Italian for "Greek."

Albariño *(ahl-bah-REE-nyoh)*: An aromatic white grape variety commonly grown in Spain's Galicia region as well as Portugal's Vinho Verde area.

Alcohol strength: The amount of alcohol in wine as measured in parts per one hundred; most table wines fall between 9 and 15 percent.

Alicante Bouschet *(ah-lee-cahnt boo-shay)*: A black grape from southern France; originally bred in the mid-1800s by Henri Bouschet, who crossed Petit Bouschet and Grenache grapes.

American Viticultural Area (AVA): A geographic designation usually defined by geographic and climatic boundaries, and approved by the Bureau of Alcohol, Tobacco, and Firearms; at least 85 percent of wine with an AVA designation must originate from grapes grown in that AVA.

Arandell: A red grape variety developed by Cornell University, with dense color and dark fruit aromas; suitable for organic vineyard management.

Barbera *(bar-BEAR-ah)*: A late-ripening dark-skinned grape from Italy's Lombardy region; one of that country's most commonly planted varieties.

Blaufränkisch *(blaw [rhymes with "how"] fren-kish)*: One of the most widely planted black grape varieties in Austria; known in Germany as Limberger.

Blend: Any wine made from two or more different grape varieties.

Blush wine: A very pale pink and often sweet wine, noticeably lighter than rosé, often made from black-skinned grapes (White Zinfandel, for instance).

Bordeaux-style blend: Generally used to designate a dry red wine made from a blend of two or more noble grape varieties, most often Cabernet Sauvignon, Cabernet Franc, Merlot, Petit Verdot, and Malbec.

Brut: Designation for a sparkling wine with little or no residual sugars.

Buffalo: A blue-black cold hardy American hybrid first cultivated at Cornell University and used for making juice or wine.

Cabernet Franc *(ca-behr-nay frahn)*: A French black grape with long historic roots in France, lighter in color and tannins than Cabernet Sauvignon; often used in Bordeaux blends and the most common red variety in Virginia.

Cabernet Sauvignon *(ca-behr-nay soh-vee-nyon)*: One of the most widely known red wine grapes, determined in 1997 by DNA analysis to be a cross of Cabernet Franc and Sauvignon Blanc; the primary variety used in Bordeaux, producing wines deep in color with good potential for aging.

Carmenère *(car-meh-nair)*: A dark-skinned grape producing full-bodied wines; originally from the Bordeaux region and now widely planted in Chile.

Carmine: A cross between Carignan and Cabernet Sauvignon, first produced in California.

Catawba: A pink-skinned hybrid from an unknown native American *labrusca* and European *vinifera* grape, first identified in North Carolina in 1802.

Cayuga: A white hybrid from a Seyve-Villard grape and the North American Schuyler grape, first bred in New York's Finger Lakes region in 1945.

Chambourcin *(shahm-boor-sehn)*: A French-American hybrid first developed by Joannes Seyve that produces deep red wine with an aromatic nose.

Chancellor: A red hybrid grape first bred in France where it is known as Seibel 7053; now commonly grown in the central and eastern United States.

Chardonel *(shar-doh-nel)*: A cross between Seyval Blanc and Chardonnay, first bred in New York in 1953 and commercially released in 1990.

Chardonnay *(shar-doh-nay)*: A white grape originating from the Burgundy region of France and the most widely planted white wine variety in Virginia.

Chenin Blanc *(sheh-nan-blahn)*: A white grape from France's Loire Valley; the most widely planted white grape in South Africa, where it is called Steen.

Cider: Fermented apple juice, ranging from 2 to 8.5 percent alcohol content.

Claret (CLAIR-ette): An English term from the 16th century designating red wines from France's Bordeaux region.

Concord: A highly aromatic native American *labrusca* grape widely grown in the eastern United States and named after the town of Concord, Massachusetts; most commonly used in producing grape juice and grape jelly.

Corot Noir *(koh-roh nwahr)*: A red wine hybrid between a European Seyve-Villard and American Steuben grape; first produced in New York in 1970.

Corvina Veronese *(kohr-VEE-nah veh-roh-NAY-zay)*: A red wine grape that is the predominate component of several Italian wines, including Valpolicella, Bardolino, and Amarone; also known simply as Corvina.

Cross: The result of crossing two grapes of the same species; for example, two *Vitis vinifera* grapes.

Cyser: Fermented honey and apple juice.

Dessert wine: In the United States, dessert wines are defined as wines between 14% and 24% alcohol strength; dessert wines may or may not be fortified. In Europe, often defined as sweet wines.

Dornfelder: A red grape that is a cross between the Helfensteiner and Heroldrebe varieties, first propagated in Germany in 1956 by August Herold; known for its deep color and aromatic fruit.

Dry: A wine tasting term meaning a lack of sweetness.

Eau-de-vie *(oh-duh-vee)*: A grape-based distilled spirit, such as brandy.

Fer Servadou *(fair sehr-vah-doo)*: A black grape variety from southwest France; also known simply as Fer. The Fer variety cultivated in Argentina is not related to the French variety.

Fiano: An old white variety from southern Italy and Sicily, dating from the 13th century; produces full-bodied, flavorful wines.

Filtration: A winemaking process in which sediments and particles are filtered out of the wine.

Fining: A winemaking process intended to clarify and stabilize the wine by use of a fining agent, such as bentonite or egg whites.

Finish: A wine-tasting term signifying how long the wine lingers on the palate, from short (quickly dissipates) to long (lingers for many seconds).

Fortified wine: Wine whose alcohol strength has been increased by the addition of grape spirit; port and sherry are examples of fortified wines.

Frontenac: Red, cold-hardy hybrid propagated by the University of Minnesota, made by crossing Landot Noir and a *Vitis riparia* grape.

Fruit forward: A wine tasting term indicating a noticeable fruitiness with the first taste of a given wine; also called "up-front fruit"; a characteristic of many New World wines.

Fumé Blanc *(foo-may blahn)*: Another name for Sauvignon Blanc, first coined by Robert Mondavi in the 1970s; Fumé Blanc wines often have undergone some oak aging.

Gewurztraminer *(geh-VOOHRTS-trah-mee-ner)*: A pink-skinned aromatic mutation of the Traminer grape, first reported in the Italian Tyrol region around 1000 and widely planted in Alsace and Germany; also spelled Gewürztraminer.

Golden Muscat *(moos-kah)*: A green-golden grape hybrid between Muscat Hamburg and the North American Diamond grape; first bred in New York.

Grauburgunder *(graw [rhymes with "how"]-boor-goon-der)*: The Austrian name for Pinot Gris.

Grenache *(gruh-nahsh)*: A black grape variety most commonly planted in France's southern Rhone Valley and Languedoc-Roussillon region, as well as in Spain where it is known as Garnacha.

Grüner Veltliner *(groo-ner velt-lee-ner)*: A white grape producing dry, full-bodied wines and the most widely planted variety in Austria; often called simply "Gru-Ve" *(groo-vah)* in non-German speaking areas.

Hybrid: The result of crossing two grapes of different species; for example, a *Vitis vinifera* grape with a *Vitis labrusca* grape.

Hydromel: Pure mead, often light or low-alcohol.

Ice wine: Sweet wine made from ripe grapes that are picked when frozen on the vine; also includes wines made by artificially freezing the grapes.

Kvevri: Large earthenware vessels lined with beeswax and traditionally used in the Republic of Georgia for making wine; also spelled *qvevri*.

La Crescent: A white grape variety created by the University of Minnesota; known for its cold hardiness.

Landot Noir *(lan-doh nwahr)*: A red grape hybrid of Landal Noir and Seyve Villard; most commonly grown in New York and Ontario, Canada.

Late harvest: Wine made from grapes left on the vine beyond the regular harvest time in order to concentrate the fruit and natural sugars.

Lemberger *(lem-bear-ger)*: The name given in Washington state to the Limberger grape variety, also called Blaufränkisch in Austria.

Léon Millot *(lay-ohn mee-yoh)*: A dark-skinned early-ripening hybrid first developed in Colmar, France; related to the Maréchal Foch grape.

Library Wines: Wines put aside by a winery to age, generally of higher quality than ordinary vintages; may also refer to a home collection of wine.

Madeira *(mah-DARE-uh)*: A fortified wine originally from the Portuguese island of the same name.

Malbec *(mall-beck)*: A black grape variety grown in France's Bordeaux and Loire regions; now associated with wine from Argentina and Chile.

Malolactic fermentation: A secondary fermentation that converts malic acid to the smoother tasting lactic acid in both red and white wines and producing greater flavor and smoothness in the final product.

Malvasia *(mall-vah-ZEE-ah)*: An ancient grape varietal family of Greek origin that includes mostly whites and some light-colored reds; wines are often characterized by higher residual sugars and alcohol strength.

Maréchal Foch *(mar-eh-shall fosh)*: A red grape hybrid first propagated in France, early ripening and cold hardy.

Marquette: A dark-skinned cold-hardy hybrid between Ravat, an offspring of Pinot Noir, and a hybrid combining *Vitis riparia* and *Vitis vinifera* grapes.

Mataro: A synonym for Mourvedre, often used in the United States.

Mead: A fermented drink made from honey and commonly believed to predate either beer or wine.

Melomel: Honey and fruit-based mead.

Metheglen: Mead blended with herbs or spices.

Méthode champenoise *(meh-toad sham-puh-nwahz)*: Sparkling wine made in the style of the Champagne region of France.

Meritage: A term coined in 1981 for American wines made from a Bordeaux-style blend of Cabernet Sauvignon, Cabernet Franc, Merlot, Malbec, and/or Petit Verdot; sometimes also used for white blends of Sauvignon Blanc, Semillon, and/or Muscadelle; rhymes with "heritage."

Merlot *(mehr-loh)*: A black grape variety that is the predominate red wine grape in France's Bordeaux region and widely planted in northern Italy, among other regions.

Moscato: Another name for Muscat.

Mourvedre *(moor-veh-dra)*: The second most planted black grape variety in Spain, where it probably originated near the town of Murviedro.

Muscadine: A thick-skinned grape variety native to the southeastern United States and highly resistant to phylloxera. Known for having many cultivars, including white and black varieties; often also used for juice or jams.

Muscat *(moos-kah)*: An ancient grape variety from the Mediterranean region with multiple varieties in different colors; known in Italian as Moscato.

Muscat Blanc *(moos-kah blahn)*: One of the earliest grapes grown in France, dating from ancient Roman times; also known as Muscat Canelli and White Muscat, among other names.

Muscat Canelli: Another name for Muscat Blanc.

Muscat of Alexandria: An ancient Muscat variety unrelated to Muscat Blanc and believed to have been first cultivated in Egypt.

Muscat Ottonel: A white grape variety first bred in 1852 in France from Chasselas and Muscat de Saumur.

Must: The unfermented mixture of grape juice, pulp, skins, stem fragments, and seeds produced after grapes have been crushed at the start of the winemaking process.

Nebbiolo *(neh-bee-OH-loh)*: A black grape from the Piedmont region in northwest Italy and the variety used in Italy's Barolo and Barbaresco wines.

Niagara: A green grape that is a cross between the native American Concord grape and the white Cassady hybrid.

Norton: A native American, dark-skinned grape variety bred in the 1820s by Dr. Daniel Norton on his farm near Richmond; first recognized for its winemaking potential by George Husmann of Hermann, Missouri, in the 1850s.

Orange Muscat: See Muscat Orange.

Orange Wine: Wine made from white grape varieties; it is kept in contact with the grape skins for an extended period, giving the finished product a deeper golden hue.

Petit Manseng *(puh-tee mahn-sang)*: A white grape variety from southwest France and the Pyrenees region, noted for its flavor.

Petit Verdot *(puh-tee vehr-doh)*: A black grape variety used in Bordeaux and Bordeaux-style blends, noted for its rich color.

Pinotage: A hardy red grape variety first bred in South Africa by A.I. Perold, who crossed Pinot Noir and Cinsaut, the latter also known as Hermitage.

Pinot Blanc *(pee-noh blahn)*: A relatively full-bodied white grape variety originally from Burgundy but now more commonly associated with Alsace; often grown in Germany, where it is known as Weissburgunder.

Pinot Grigio *(PEE-noh GREE-joe)*: The Italian name for Pinot Gris.

Pinot Gris *(pee-noh gree)*: A mutation of Pinot Noir with greyish blue to brownish pink berries; known in Germany as either Ruländer when sweet or Grauburgunder when dry.

Pinot Meunier *(pee-noh muh-nee-aye)*: A black grape variety often used to produce classic French champagne.

Pinot Noir *(pee-noh nwahr)*: The classic black grape variety of the Burgundy region of France, noted for lower tannins and a somewhat fruity taste.

Port: A fortified wine originally from the Douro region or Portugal, made by adding brandy to wine; may be either red or white.

Primitivo: A red grape variety grown extensively in southern Italy, mainly in Apulia, and confirmed by DNA analysis as very closely related to Zinfandel.

Reserve wines: Generally intended to designate wines of superior quality, although there are few controls on how and when the term may be used.

Residual sugar: The amount of natural grape sugar remaining in wine after fermentation, measured in percent per liter.

Retsina: A resinated wine common in Greece and Cyprus; protected by the EU as a traditional appellation.

Riesling *(reece-ling)*: The classic white wine grape of Germany, known for its aroma and flavor; also called White, Rhine, or Johannisberg Riesling.

Rkatsiteli *(ahr-kat-sah-teh-lee)*: A white grape variety first documented in the country of Georgia; widely planted in Russia and the Caucasus.

Rosé: Pink-colored wine made either by leaving dark grape skins in contact with the juice just long enough to color it, or by pressing the juice from red wine grapes in a process called "saignée."

Roussanne *(roo-sahn)*: A reddish-skinned aromatic white grape from the Rhone region in France.

Saignée *(sen-yay)*: French term meaning "bled" and designating a process for making rosé wines in which a certain amount of juice is pressed or "bled off" from dark-skinned grapes.

Sangiovese *(sahn-joh-VEH-seh)*: A red grape that is the most commonly planted variety in Italy, where it is used in producing Chianti's wines.

Saperavi: An ancient variety from the Republic of Georgia, where it is the most planted red grape.

Sauvignon Blanc *(sew-vee-nyohn blahn)*: An aromatic white grape variety, often crisp and sometimes even grassy in taste.

Sauvignon Gris *(sew-vee-nyohn gree)*: A color mutation of Sauvignon Blanc, it is increasingly used in white Bordeaux blends to add perfume and weight.

Scuppernong: A bronze-skinned grape of the Muscadine family that makes sweet, dark gold wines.

Semillon *(seh-mee-yohn)*: A golden grape variety from southwest France, frequently used in blending with other varieties; spelled Sémillon in French.

Seyval Blanc *(say-vahl blahn)*: A white grape Seyve-Villard hybrid often producing crisp wines and popular in Canada and the United States.

Sherry: A dry fortified wine from Spain, ranging in style from the pale *fino* to darker *oloroso*.

Shiraz *(shih-RAZZ)*: Name given in Australia and South Africa to the Syrah grape; Shiraz-style designates a wine that is somewhat more concentrated and fruit-driven than French Syrah.

Solera: A system of blending wines across vintage years in order to reduce the annual differences; most frequently used with Sherry.

Sparkling wine: An effervescent, fizzy wine in which carbon dioxide bubbles have been trapped in the bottle during the winemaking process; may be made from white or black grape varieties.

Steuben: A blue-black native American grape that is a cross between the Wayne and Sheridan grapes; first propagated by Cornell University.

Super-Tuscan: Term used to describe wines made by blending Cabernet Sauvignon with Sangiovese, the traditional grape variety used in Chianti.

Syrah *(see-rah)*: One of the premier black grape varieties, thought to have originated in either Sicily or ancient Persia; widely grown in France's Rhone region as well as in Australia and South Africa, where it is called Shiraz.

Tannat *(tah-nah)*: A black grape variety of Basque origin, noted for its deep color and high tannins.

Tannins: Chemical compounds from grape skins and pips (seeds) that give wine an astringent (and sometimes bitter) taste.

Tempranillo *(tem-pra-NEE-yoh)*: A red grape variety from Spain producing wines rich in color and often high in alcohol.

Teroldego *(teh-roll-DAY-go)*: An old black grape variety from northeast Italy, where it makes deeply colored and fruity wines.

Terroir *(tehr-wahr)*: A French term that describes the totality of a vineyard's environment, particularly its climate and soil.

Tinta Cão *(TEEN-tah KAWM)*: A black grape once widely planted in Portugal's Douro region and one of the five varieties traditionally used to produce port; Portuguese for "red dog."

Touriga Nacional *(too-REE-gah nah-see-oh-NAL)*: A black grape generally considered as the finest variety for port; also used to produce dry red wines.

Traminer Aromatico *(trah-mee-ner ah-roh-mah-tee-koh)*: A synonym for Gewurztraminer.

Traminette: An aromatic white grape hybrid of Gewürztraminer and a Seyve hybrid, first cultivated in 1965 at the University of Illinois.

Varietal: A wine named for the dominant grape variety from which it is made; varietals may be pure (100%) or a blend consisting of at least 75% of the grape for which the wine is named.

Verdejo *(vehr-DAY-hoe)*: An aromatic, herbaceous white grape that is the primary variety in Spain's Rueda region.

Vermentino *(ver-men-TEE-noh)*: An aromatic white grape grown in Sardinia, Corsica, and the Languedoc-Roussillon region of southern France.

Vermouth: An herb-flavored fortified wine dating from ancient Greece and Rome; vermouth is the anglicized version of Wermuth, the German word for wormwood, and was first named in the 16th century to denote a highly popular medicinal wine flavored with wormwood.

Vidal Blanc *(vee-dahl blahn)*: An aromatic white grape hybrid between Ugni Blanc and one of the parent grapes of Seyval Blanc that lends itself to sweet and late harvest wines; widely grown in Canada because of its hardiness.

Vignoles *(veen-yole)*: A French-American hybrid, originally propagated in France in 1922 and named after the French town of Vignoles; the grape is now more commonly planted in the United States.

Villard Blanc: A white grape Seyve-Villard hybrid.

Vin de Paille *(van duh pie)*: French term designating a sweet white wine, traditionally made by drying grapes on mats of straw (*paille* in French).

Vin Gris *(van gree)*: A pale pink wine made from dark-skinned grapes, characterized by little skin contact with the juice.

Vinho Verde *(VEE-nyo VER-day)*: A light, acidic Portuguese wine traditionally sold soon after fermenting; means "green wine" in English.

Viognier *(vee-oh-nyee-eh)*: An aromatic white grape variety from the Rhone region in France and increasingly planted in California and Virginia.

Virginia Century Farm: A state program recognizing farms that have been in operation and owned by the same family for at least 100 years.

Virginia Green: A program aiming to preserve and protect the environment by promoting eco-friendly practices in Virginia's tourism industry.

Viticulture: The science and practice of growing grapes.

Yeast: A single-celled agent whose key role in fermenting grape juice into wine was first described by Louis Pasteur; yeast strains may be cultivated or naturally occurring (called "wild" yeast).

White Moore's Diamond: A white native American cross between the Concord and the Iona; grown primarily in New York and Pennsylvania for juice and dry white wine.

Wine: Any fermented fruit juice, most often associated with grapes; in the United States, table wines are between 7% and 14% alcohol strength.

Zinfandel: A black grape variety widely planted in California; determined by DNA analysis to be closely related to the Italian Primitivo variety; not cultivated in Virginia.

ALPHABETICAL INDEX OF WINERIES

❧Numbers❧

12 Ridges, 167

2 Witches, 361

50 West, 75

8 Chains North, 31

868 Estate, 32

❧A❧

Abingdon, 399

Above Ground, 168

Afton Mountain, 279

Albemarle Cider Works, 293

Altillo, 362

AmRhein, 379

Ankida Ridge, 323

Arterra, 95

Ashton Creek, 217

Aspen Dale, 107

❧B❧

Backporch, 195

Barboursville, 253

Barns at Hamilton Station, 53

Barrel Oak, 96

Barren Ridge, 169

Beliveau Farm, 400

Big Fish Cider, 385

Black Heath Meadery, 218

Blacksnake Meadery, 393

Blenheim, 294

Bleu Frog, 23

Blue Bee Cider, 219

Blue Quartz, 239

Blue Ridge, 380

Blue Toad Cider, 296

Blue Valley, 97

Bluemont, 67

Bluestone, 170

Bodie, 220

Bogati Winery, 68

Bold Rock Cider, 297

Boxwood, 76

Bozzo Family, 33
Breaux, 34
Brent Manor, 298
Briedé Family, 147
Bright Meadows Farm, 355
Brix & Columns, 172
Brooks Mill, 371
Burnley, 254
Buskey Cider, 221
Byrd Cellars, 231

ஓC๛

Cana, 77
Cardinal Point, 280
Caret Cellars, 196
Carriage House, 35
Casanel, 54
Castle Glen, 222
Castle Hill Cider, 256
Cave Ridge, 149
Chapelle Charlemagne, 108
Chateau MerrillAnne, 133
Chateau Morrisette, 394
Chateau O'Brien, 109
Chatham, 189
Chester Gap, 110
Chestnut Oak, 258

Chisholm Vineyards, 259
Chrysalis, 78
Cobbler Mountain Cider, 112
Corcoran Winery & Cider, 37
Courthouse Creek Cider, 223
Coyote Hole Cider, 134
Creek's Edge, 38
CrossKeys, 173
Crushed Cellars, 39
Cunningham Creek, 299

ஓD๛

Davis Valley, 402
Delaplane, 98
Delfosse, 300
DeVault, 324
Ditchley Cider, 197
Dog & Oyster, 198
Doukénie, 40
Dry Mill, 55
DuCard, 240

ஓE๛

Eagletree Farm, 24
Early Mountain, 241
Eastwood Farm, 302
Ecco Adesso, 174
Effingham Manor, 79

Elk Island, 232

Estate at White Hall, 199

❧F❧

Fabbioli, 25

Fables & Feathers, 372

Fifty-Third, 233

Firefly Cellars, 57

Five Oaks, 260

Fleetwood Farm, 80

Flying Fox, 282

Forever Farm, 58

Fox Meadow, 99

❧G❧

Gabriele Rausse, 303

Gadino, 119

Garden Grove, 224

Gauthier, 333

General's Ridge, 201

Glass House, 261

Glen Manor, 150

Good Luck, 202

Grace Estate, 262

Granite Heights, 120

Gray Ghost, 121

Grayhaven, 235

Greenhill, 81

❧H❧

Hague, 203

Halcyon Days Cider, 176

Haley's Honey Meadery, 335

Hamlet, 363

Hammerstone, 135

Hampton Roads, 336

Hardware Hills, 304

Hark, 264

Hazy Mountain, 283

Henway Hard Cider, 69

Hickory Hill, 372

Hidden Brook, 26

Hiddencroft, 41

Hill Top Berry, 305

Hillsborough, 42

Homeplace, 364

Honah Lee, 265

Horton, 266

Hunting Creek, 356

❧I❧

Ingleside, 205

Iron Heart, 403

❧J❧

James Charles, 151

James River, 225

Jefferson, 306

Jolene Family, 337

K

Keswick, 267

Kilaurwen, 268

King Family, 284

Knight's Gambit, 269

L

Lake Anna, 136

Lazy Days, 325

LeoGrande, 374

Lexington Valley, 177

Linden, 113

Little Washington, 123

Lost Boy Cider, 21

Lost Creek, 27

Loving Cup, 308

Lovingston, 309

M

Maggie Malick, 44

Magnolia, 124

Marceline, 178

Mattaponi, 137

Mediterranean Cellars, 125

Mermaid, 338

Michael Shaps, 310

Molon Lave, 126

Monroe Bay, 206

Montifalco, 271

Morais, 128

Moss, 272

Mt. Defiance Cider, 83

Mount Ida, 313

Mountain Cove, 311

Mountain Run, 243

MountainRose, 415

Muse, 152

N

Naked Mountain, 101

Narmada, 129

New Kent, 340

New River, 405

North Mountain, 153

Notaviva, 45

O

Old Hill Cider, 155

Old House, 244

Old Trade Beer & Cider, 245

Otium Cellars, 59

Ox-Eye, 179

Alphabetical Index of Wineries

~P~

Paradise Springs, 84

Peaks of Otter, 375

Pearmund, 85

Philip Carter, 114

Pippin Hill, 314

Pollak, 286

Potomac Point, 138

Potter's Craft Cider, 315

Preston Ridge, 365

Prince Michel, 246

Purple Wolf, 180

~Q~

Quattro Goomba's, 86

Quièvremont, 130

~R~

Ramulose Ridge, 376

Rappahannock, 115

Rebec, 326

Revalation, 248

Reynard Florence, 273

Rivah Vineyards, 207

Rock Roadhouse, 386

Rockbridge, 181

Rogers Ford Farm, 139

Rosemont, 357

Rural Retreat, 407

~S~

Sassafras Shade, 226

Saudé Creek, 341

Septenary, 287

Sharp Rock, 249

Shenandoah Vineyards, 156

Silver Hand Meadery, 343

Skippers Creek, 227

Slater Run, 102

Sly Clyde Cider, 344

Spinning Jenny, 408

Spring Run, 228

Stanburn, 366

Star in the Valley, 157

Stinson, 274

Stone Mountain, 275

Stone Tower, 60

SummerWind, 345

Sunset Hills, 46

~T~

Terra Nebulo, 47

Thatch, 315

Third Hill at DeMello, 158

Three Creeks, 61

Three Fox, 103
Three Sisters of Shiney Rock, 359
Triple V, 208
Trump, 318
Tumbling Creek Cider, 409
Twin Oaks Tavern, 70
Two Twisted Posts, 48

❧U❧
Upper Shirley, 346

❧V❧
Valerie Hill, 159
Valhalla, 381
Valley Road, 288
Vault Field, 209
Veramar, 71
Veritas, 290
Villa Appalaccia, 395
Vincent's Vineyard, 416
Vint Hill Craft, 87
Virginia Mountain, 382

❧W❧
Walsh Family, 49
West Wind Farm, 409
Weston Farm, 236
White Hall, 276
Whitebarrel, 410
Wilderness Run, 141
Williams Gap, 62
Williamsburg Winery, 348
Willowcroft Farm, 63
Winchester Ciderworks, 160
Wine Reserve, 51
Winery 32, 28
Winery at Bull Run, 88
Winery at Kindred Pointe, 161
Winery at La Grange, 90
Winery at Sunshine Ridge, 91
Wisdom Oak, 319
Wisteria Farm, 162
Wolf Gap, 163

❧Z❧
Zephaniah Farm, 64

WINERIES WITH BREWERIES

❧Numbers❧
2 Witches, 361

❧B❧
Barrel Oak, 96
Beliveau Farm, 400
Blue Quartz, 239

❧C❧
Courthouse Creek, 223

❧E❧
Eagletree Farm, 24

❧F❧
Fables & Feathers, 372

❧G❧
Garden Grove, 224

❧H❧
Hazy Mountain, 283
Hillsborough, 42

❧L❧
Little Washington, 123

❧M❧
Mount Ida, 313

❧N❧
New Kent, 340
Notaviva, 45

❧O❧
Old House, 244
Old Trade, 245

❧P❧
Prince Michel, 246

❧Q❧
Quattro Goomba's, 86

❧R❧
Rockbridge, 181

T

Three Fox, 103

W

Wilderness Run, 141

Winery 32, 28

Winery at Sunshine Ridge, 91

WINERIES WITH LODGING

∼A∼
Afton Mountain, 279
Albemarle Cider Works, 293
Ankida Ridge, 323

∼B∼
Barboursville, 253
Beliveau Farm, 400
Bluemont, 67
Burnley, 254

∼C∼
Cardinal Point, 280
Chester Gap, 110
Chisholm Vineyards, 259

∼D∼
Delfosse, 300
Dog & Oyster, 198

∼E∼
Early Mountain, 241
Ecco Adesso, 174

∼F∼
Firefly Cellars, 57

∼G∼
Gauthier, 333
General's Ridge, 201
Glass House, 261

∼H∼
Hague, 203

∼I∼
Ingleside, 205
Iron Heart, 403

∼J∼
Jefferson, 306

∼K∼
Kilaurwen, 268
Knight's Gambit, 269

M

Marceline, 178

Moss, 272

P

Peaks of Otter, 375

Philip Carter, 114

Prince Michel, 246

R

Rural Retreat, 407

S

Sharp Rock, 249

Stinson, 274

T

Third Hill at DeMello, 158

Trump, 318

V

Veritas, 290

W

Williamsburg, 348

GENERAL INDEX

A

Africa, 7, 9, 321, 330
    South Africa, 235, 267, 309, 351, 429, 437
    West Africa, 145

African-American history:
    Anne Spencer home, 215
    Civil Rights in Education Trail, 215
    Frontier Culture Museum, 145
    Great Dismal Swamp, 329, 330
    Hampton University Museum, 330
    Jackson Ward, 214
    Maggie Walker home, 214
    Trail to Freedom, 18
    Virginia Civil Rights Memorial, 214

Amish community, 353

Animal charities:
    All American Mutt Rescue, 380
    Almost Home Pet Adoption, 308
    Boykin Spaniel Adoption, 58
    Rappahannock Shelter, 124
    Service dogs, 394
    SPCA fundraiser, 85, 136, 225
    Terrier rescue, 232

Apples:
    Apple labyrinth, 176
    Apple school, 155

Attractions (see also Museums):
    American Shakespeare Center, 145
    Aunt Polly's Ordinary, 390
    Chincoteague Pony Swim, 186
    Colonial Williamsburg, 329, 330
    Historic Jamestown, 329
    Johnson Farm, 390
    Mabry Mill, 390
    National D-Day Memorial, 369
    Nauticus, 331
    Virginia Air & Space Center, 330
    Virginia Aquarium, 331

B

Biking trails & tours:
    Between the Waters Tour, 186
    Southern Tip Bike & Hike, 186

Transamerica Cycling Route 76, 408
Virginia Capital Trail, 331

Books:
> *A Walk in the Woods*, 369
> *Beowulf*, 321
> *Lord of the Rings*, 235
> *Misty of Chincoteague*, 186
> *Trail of the Lonesome Pine*, 413
> *Virginia Atlas and Gazetteer*, 6
> *Virginia State Road Atlas*, 6

Breweries at wineries:
> See index on p. 447

C

Charity fundraisers:
> Cancer research, 137, 225, 327
> First responders, 333
> Literacy, 248
> Music education, 315
> Wounded Warriors, 333

Ciders, 21, 25, 37, 45, 69, 83, 89, 112, 134, 155, 160, 162, 176, 197, 206, 218, 219, 221, 223, 239, 245, 256, 272, 293, 296, 297, 315, 344, 385, 394, 409

Cigars, 185, 186, 189

Civil War sites:
> Appomattox Court House, 214, 324, 330
> Brandy Station, 19, 244
> Cedar Creek, 144
> Chancellorsville, 19
> Cold Harbor, 330
> Fort Monroe, 330
> Kernstown, 144
> Manassas, 19
> New Market, 144
> Petersburg, 214
> Sailor's Creek, 214
> Seven Days' Battles, 330
> Weyanoke, 330

D

Discounts:
> Armed Forces, 54, 89, 109, 164, 200, 228, 265, 272, 312, 333
> Firefighters & police, 89
> Teachers, 200
> Veterans, 228, 272, 312, 333

Distilleries at wineries, 83, 116, 244, 403, 404, 416

Driving Trails:
> Civil Rights in Education, 215
> Crooked Road Heritage Trail, 390
> Heart of Appalachia Driving Tour, 413
> Journey Through Hallowed Ground, 18
> Lee's Retreat, 214
> Trail to Freedom, 18

F

Fishing, 143, 185, 192, 324, 353, 390, 404, 413, 416

G

Games:
- Basketball, 324
- Bocce ball, 119, 396
- Chess, 2244
- Croquet, 270
- Disc golf, 123
- Tennis, 324

Green facilities:
- LEED, 234
- Virginia Green, 99, 114, 119, 123, 163, 372, 410

H

Hiking:
- Appalachian Trail, 19, 369, 399
- Fortune's Cove, 312
- Massanutten Storybook, 144
- Old Rag, 239, 249
- Southern Tip Bike & Hike Trail, 186
- Stony Man Mountain, 144
- Virginia Capital Trail, 331
- Virginia Creeper Trail, 399
- Westmoreland State Park, 192
- Winery walking trails, 112, 153, 301, 302

Historic homes:
- Anne Spencer home, 215
- Ash Lawn, 214, 307
- Bacon's Castle, 329
- Barbour Estate, 253
- Berkeley Plantation, 330
- George Washington Birthplace, 192
- Maggie Walker home, 214
- Mount Vernon, 18
- Monticello, 12, 214
- Red Hill, 353
- Sherwood Forest, 330
- Shirley Plantation, 330

K

Kayaking, 185, 186, 189
Kosher wine tastings, 127

M

Meads, 218, 224, 305, 335, 343, 393

Movies:
- *Dirty Dancing*, 390
- *What About Bob?*, 373

Museums:
- Casemate Museum, 330
- Frontier Culture Museum, 145
- Hampton University, 330
- Kinsale, 192

Mariner's Museum, 331
Morattico Waterfront, 192
Museum of the Civil War Soldier, 214
Steamboat Era Museum, 192
Virginia War Museum, 330
Winery (Ingleside), 205

~N~

Native Americans, 18, 137, 144, 215, 330

Natural attractions:
Assateague Island National Seashore, 185
Chincoteague NWR, 185
Eastern Shore of Virginia NWR, 185, 186
Grand Caverns, 144
Great Dismal Swamp, 329, 330
Luray Caverns, 143
Massanutten Mountain, 144
Mountain Lake, 390
Natural Bridge, 144
Old Rag Mountain, 239, 249
Presquile NWR, 346
Shenandoah Caverns, 143
Virginia Coast Reserve, 185

~P~

Polo, 284

~R~

Revolutionary War sites:
Yorktown battlefield, 329
RV overnight sites, 260, 312

~S~

Satellite tasting rooms:
Michael Shaps, 310
Morais, 128
Williamsburg Winery, 348

~V~

Vineyard tours, 88, 157, 164, 358
Virginia Century Farm, 150, 205, 207

~W~

Wi-Fi, 37, 136, 177, 179, 247, 262, 299, 363

Winery lodgings & B&Bs:
See index on p. 449

Winery restaurants:
868 Estate (Grandale), 30
Barboursville (Palladio), 253
Chateau Morrisette, 394
Upper Shirley, 346
Williamsburg (Café Provençal, Gabriel Archer Tavern), 348

ABOUT THE AUTHOR

Donna R. Gough has enjoyed learning about and appreciating wines since living in France years ago. Since then, she has visited a number of wineries in the United States, Canada, Germany, Chile, and South Africa. A geographer and analyst by profession, she lives in Northern Virginia with her family and holds a Level 2 certification from the Wine & Spirits Education Trust. She blogs about wine and visits to Virginia wineries at www.facebook.com/vawineguide.

Cover design: Kelly Brown
                kellybrowndesign.com
                kabrown.design@gmail.com

Made in United States
Orlando, FL
25 June 2024

48278455R00261